CW00971880

At the Helm

A LABORATORY NAVIGATOR

At the Helm

A LABORATORY NAVIGATOR

Kathy Barker

The Institute for Systems Biology

Seattle, Washington

kbarker@systemsbiology.org

COLD SPRING HARBOR LABORATORY PRESS

Cold Spring Harbor, New York

At the Helm: A Laboratory Navigator

©2002 by Cold Spring Harbor Laboratory Press, Cold Spring Harbor, New York
Printed in the United States of America

All rights reserved

Developmental Editor:	Jody Tresidder
Project Coordinator:	Mary Cozza
Production Editor:	Dorothy Brown
Desktop Editor:	Susan Schaefer
Book Design:	Denise Weiss
Cover Design:	Ed Atkeson

Front cover artwork was created by Jim Duffy and Maria Calisto.

Library of Congress Cataloging-in-Publication Data

Barker, Kathy, 1953–
    At the helm : a laboratory navigator / by Kathy Barker.
        p. cm.
    Includes bibliographical references.
    ISBN 0-87969-583-8 (alk. paper)
    1. Laboratories—Management. 2. Research—Management. I. Title.
Q180.57 .B37 2002
001.4—dc21

                                                            2001047486

10 9 8 7 6 5

All registered trademarks and service marks mentioned in this book are the property of the respective owners. Readers should please consult individual manufacturers and other resources for current and specific product information.

All Word Wide Web addresses are accurate to the best of our knowledge at the time of printing.

Authorization to photocopy items for internal or personal use, or the internal or personal use of specific clients, is granted by Cold Spring Harbor Laboratory Press, provided that the appropriate fee is paid directly to the Copyright Clearance Center (CCC). Write or call CCC at 222 Rosewood Drive, Danvers, MA 01923 (508-750-8400) for information about fees and regulations. Prior to photocopying items for educational classroom use, contact CCC at the above address. Additional information on CCC can be obtained at CCC Online at http://www.copyright.com/

All Cold Spring Harbor Laboratory Press publications may be ordered directly from Cold Spring Harbor Laboratory Press, 500 Sunnyside Blvd., Woodbury, N.Y. 11797-2924. Phone: 1-800-843-4388 in Continental U.S. and Canada. All other locations: (516) 422-4100. FAX: (516) 422-4097. E-mail: cshpress@cshl.edu. For a complete catalog of all Cold Spring Harbor Laboratory Press publications, visit our World Wide Web Site http://www.cshlpress.com.

Contents

Preface, vii
Acknowledgments, ix

KNOW WHAT YOU WANT, 1

The Lab Where Everyone Wants to Be   3
Start in the Right Place   7
Plan the Lab You Want   19
RESOURCES   27

YOU AS A LEADER, 29

I Was Trained to Do Everything But Run a Lab!   31
Stop Putting Out Fires!   39
Using Your Time   51
Working with a Secretary/Administrative Assistant   57
Staying Integrated   63
RESOURCES   69

CHOOSE YOUR PEOPLE, 71

Choose Your People   73
The Hiring Process   81
The Effective Interview   89
Evaluating Candidates   103
RESOURCES   113

STARTING AND KEEPING NEW LAB MEMBERS, 115

Getting Off to a Good Start   117
Training Lab Personnel   123
Mentor to All?   133
RESOURCES   141

MAKE RESEARCH THE FOUNDATION, 143

Setting the Course   145
Keeping Up   157
Writing Papers   167
RESOURCES   177

ORGANIZING THE LAB TO SUPPORT THE RESEARCH, 179

Building a Lab Culture   181
Lab Policies   187
Meetings and Seminars   201
Using Computers to Organize the Lab   213
RESOURCES   229

COMMUNICATION AS THE GLUE, 231

Communication with Your Lab   233
The Pleasures and Perils of Diversity   243
Gender Is Still an Issue   255
Learning through Conflict   259
Stress and Depression in Lab Members   263
RESOURCES   271

DEALING WITH A GROUP, 275

Lab Morale   277
Lab Romances   283
Maintaining Personnel Equilibrium   291
"I Should Have Done It Sooner!"   297
Violence in the Workplace   303
RESOURCES   309

FOR THE LONG RUN, 311

As Your Job Changes...   313
Maintaining Enthusiasm   323
Career Choices   331
Having It All   335
RESOURCES   341

INDEX, 345

Preface

As a scientist progresses through graduate school and postdoctoral training, the changes are fairly incremental and seem fairly manageable. But the move from training and bench research to principal investigator is not at all an incremental change. It is cataclysmic and catches many scientists completely unaware. All those years of training just do not seem to be preparation enough for suddenly managing people and funds and politics, in addition to managing research.

At the Helm was written to remind principal investigators (P.I.s) that they actually *are* well equipped to handle the multitude of tasks facing them. The job of running a laboratory utilizes the same skills scientists learn during their training: the processes of analysis, setting and fulfilling priorities, and communication. The vocabulary is different, but the processes are the same—It just takes lab heads a few uncomfortable years to recognize this.

The bulk of this book is based on conversations and interviews with P.I.s. They seemed to be especially concerned about dealing with people within their labs, rather than outside their labs, and *At the Helm* concentrates on these issues. Scientific survival and success also involve topics covered only lightly or not at all in *At the Helm*, such as funding and institutional politics, and whenever possible, suggested readings in topics not covered are given under Resources at the end of each section. A lot of the details of the physical side of lab management are included in my earlier book *At the Bench: A Laboratory Navigator* (Cold Spring Harbor Laboratory Press 1998) and are not described here. Many topics belong in several chapters but, for brevity, are only discussed in one.

Quotes from scientists are used to illustrate a point and to demonstrate the range of opinions over any subject. Scientists' quotes are listed anonymously, as people spoke more freely about personnel and personal matters when they could not be identified. A quote does not necessarily represent the majority opinion: It may be controversial or even provocative, but it will reflect the complexity of situations facing P.I.s.

It would be gratifying to say that I found hard and fast rules—that, for example, if you are a micromanager, it is likely that you will have fewer students who will write their own papers and therefore you should do X and all will be fine. But each person has evolved a way to deal with people in each situation. I have attempted to synthesize the particulars into general advice, with due respect to the importance of individual situations.

Yet some patterns *do* emerge. New P.I.s made many of the same mistakes. They hired early, without much thought, and often with much regret. They were too friendly with the people in the lab. They did not organize the lab right away, and then found that it was too messy and too late to change. They learned to accept—but only after a struggle—that they could not control all things and all people, and would have to work with differences, not eliminate them.

I was amazed at the variety of labs scientists have established. How tempting it was to predict to myself before an interview the kind of lab this particular person might run, and how often I was wrong! By learning to work within one's own style, each P.I. I spoke with found a highly individual approach to integrating research, communication, and personal satisfaction. Hopefully, the experiences and advice from other lab heads contained in this book will help P.I.s move from bench to helm more quickly, and with more confidence in their own talents.

Kathy Barker

Acknowledgments

The bulk of this book is based on interviews with P.I.s and others involved in laboratories. Most of the interviews took a minimum of over an hour, a huge block of time in an overbooked day, and I am very grateful for the graciousness and thoroughness of the people I spoke with. The material from these interviews was incorporated into the text of *At the Helm*. Quotes from the interviews are also used, and are listed without attribution: This anonyminity was done to maintain the privacy of the speakers and their lab members and allowed P.I.s to speak with more candor than they might otherwise have felt comfortable with.

Many ideas also came through smaller, more casual, but not necessarily less important, conversations. Not all of those names are listed, but if anyone spoke at all in front of me, it was probably internalized, and it is probably somewhere in this book, and I thank you. For interviews and conversation, I would like to thank:

Alan Aderem, Ph.D., *Institute for Systems Biology*
John Aitchison, *Institute for Systems Biology*
Matthew Albert, *The Rockefeller University*
Janis Apted, *Director of Faculty Development, M.D. Anderson Cancer Center*
Jeanne Barker, *Merck*
Laura Blinderman, *Mercer County Community College*
Gerd Blobel, *Children's Hospital of Philadelphia;*
George Bonnet, *Fred Hutchison Research Center*
Joan Brugge, *Harvard University*
Mary A. Buchanan, *Stratagene*
Livia Casiola-Rosen, *Johns Hopkins University*
Margaret Chou, *University of Pennsylvania*
Fred Cross, *The Rockefeller University*
Anindya Dutta, *Harvard Medical School*
Hongxia Fan, *Merck*
David Foster, *Hunter College of CUNY*
Irwin Gelman, *Mount Sinai School of Medicine*
Carla Grandori, *Fred Hutchison Cancer Research Center*
Michinari Hamaguchi, *Nagoya University School of Medicine*
Carrie Harwood, *University of Iowa*

Mike Jacobs, *Biolab*
Jane E. Koehler, *University of California, San Francisco*
Sally Kornbluth, *Duke University*
Sue Leschine, *University of Massachusetts*
Anne Lobeck, *Western Washington University*
Bruce Mayer, *University of Connecticut*
Julie McElrath, *Fred Hutchison Research Center*
John McKinney, *The Rockefeller University*
Peter Newburger, *University of Massachusetts Medical School*
Melissa Pope, *The Rockefeller University*
Dan Portnoy, *University of California, Los Angeles, Berkeley*
Maureen A. Powers, *Emory University School of Medicine*
Ellen Prediger, *Ambion, Inc.*
Jeffrey Ravetch, *The Rockefeller University*
James Riggs, *Rider College*
Lee Riley, *University of California, Los Angeles, Berkeley*
Jim Roberts, *Fred Hutchison Research Center*
Antony Rosen, *Johns Hopkins University*
Mark Roth, *Fred Hutchison Cancer Research Center*
Michael P. Rout, *The Rockefeller University*
David Russell, *University of Washington*
Vijayasaradhi Setaluri, *The Bowman Gray School of Medicine, Wake Forest University*
Mike Skinner, *Washington State University at Pullman*
Mark Stoeckle, *The New York Hospital–Cornell Medical Center*
Ken Stuart, *Seattle Biomedical Research Institute*
Marius Sudol, *Mt. Sinai School of Medicine*
Jane Tramontana, *Cabarrus Lung Associates*
Lu-Hai Wang, *Mt. Sinai School of Medicine*

Several people read drafts or chapters. I would like to thank Gerd Blobel, Bruce Mayer, Alan Aderem, Mike Skinner, Jeanne Barker, David Crotty, Margaret Chou, Sally Kornbluth, Lilian Gann, Jane Roskams, David Stewart, and Jan Witkowski for the very useful comments they gave after plowing through sometimes very rough drafts. And thanks to those, such as William Brock and Justin Menkes, who gave suggestions and advice to someone they had not even met.

The Cold Spring Harbor Laboratory Press team was terrific to work with, across the miles. Thanks to John Inglis, Liz Powers, Denise Weiss, Nora McInerney, Judy Cuddihy, Dorothy Brown, Mary Cozza, Jan Argentine, and Jody Tresidder. Jan and Mary were there in several capacities throughout the writing of *At the Helm*. Jody came on later, with very little time allowed for such an intense role, and I think she did fantastically. Jim Duffy captured the intended spirit of the book with his cover, showing that the helm of the laboratory is a busy but wonderful place to be.

Kathy Barker

Know What You Want

The Lab Where Everyone Wants To Be

WHAT MAKES A GOOD LAB?

For fifteen years or so, before it grew too big with success and outran its problems, the group around Delbruck and Luria formed, by all accounts—and there have been quite a number of accounts—one of the rare refuges of the twentieth century, a republic of the mind, a glimpse of Athens, a commonwealth of intellect held together by the subtlest bonds, by the excitement of understanding, the promise of the subject, the authentic freedom of the style.

JUDSON (1996, P. 45)

For years, you have probably imagined the kind of lab you would like to run as a lab head or principal investigator (P.I.). How many times have you muttered to yourself "When I have a lab, I will..."? Suddenly—after years of graduate school and post-doc'ing—you *are* the head of your own lab. You want to do the kind of research that you have always dreamed of, but instead of slotting into a well-oiled and long-functioning machine, you find you must build that machine from scratch: What worked in a well-established lab probably will not work now. You must decide what a laboratory should be, what you want *your* laboratory to be, and then figure out how to make the dream for that lab come true.

> I've tried to keep the lab an enjoyable, comfortable place to work—the sort of place I would like to be in if I were a student or technician. Perhaps I sacrifice some productivity by not making it a "pressure cooker," but I doubt I could carry that off convincingly anyway!

A happy lab is not just a luxury. It is a necessity to attract good people and maintain enthusiasm and scientific competence. You hear about wonderful labs at meetings, over coffee, in journal clubs—labs that just seem to have everything, and everyone wants to be there. Students flock to these "good" labs: The students at any institution can tell you which are the good labs, although they cannot necessarily tell you why that particular lab is a desirable place to be.

Most P.I.s base their ideas of a wonderful lab on the *happiest* lab they worked in during their training. This lab is usually the place where the love of science first struck, and it is the inspiration for the kind of science and the kind of lab they aspire to. To attract people, it must be viewed as a place that breeds good science and success.

- *Members of the lab are happy.* It is a place where people enjoy being, even when no experiments are brewing. It is a place where the lab members come for emotional support and intellectual stimulation, as well as work. For most, work is the core of their professional and private lives, and the lab is busy. Spirits are high. A happy lab is one in which the workers and P.I. enjoy working. It feels comfortable, it feels exciting, and it is stimulating. Lab workers will probably spend more time in the lab than at home. The lab is home.

- *The lab has a recognizable personality and an identifiable culture.* Although probably never spoken aloud, the members of the lab recognize that they share many of the same attitudes. It is not an erasure of individuality—in fact, often the more cohesive a lab is, the more striking the individual characters appear. But the same values are shared, and the same enthusiasms, whether for binding proteins and baseball games, or yeast and politics. There is an underlying and obvious work philosophy. Those from other labs recognize the personality of the lab as well. It has its own habits and its own culture.

- *The head of the lab is successful, or convincingly promises to be.* Especially in the beginning, the success of the lab will be measured by the P.I.s apparent success. Successful P.I.s are funded, have a number of papers in quality journals, and are invited to present their data at meetings. Perhaps their research topic is perceived as being hot, which will make them apparently even more successful. They either have just received or are expected to receive a promotion.

- *A good lab is successful.* There are a multitude of exciting projects in the lab. The people in the lab have published and are working on projects that are likely to result in publications. If the P.I. has had prior postdocs or students, they have found good jobs and postdocs. This suggests that the head of the lab not only possesses good skills, but knows how to, and is willing to, pass these skills along to the other members in the lab.

THE MAKINGS OF A SUCCESSFUL LAB

The five elements listed below are deemed to be essential to any organization's success (Brown 1985, p. 136):

- A quality or unique product.
- Proper timing.
- Adequate capital.
- People resources.
- Effective management.

Even though this is clearly recognizable as "business language," these five elements sound familiar because they are very similar to the following five basic elements needed for a good lab:

- *Good science.* If the science is good, the lab members will be motivated. If the science is good and the organization is product-oriented, you are more likely to come up with a product.

- *Political savvy.* You must have vision, know where you want to go, and when to make the move. Timing and planning are critical—for putting in grant proposals, going for tenure, switching fields, and hiring—for almost everything.

- *Funding.* Either through grants or by promoting yourself and your project, time must be spent to obtain the money you will need. Not only must you come up with the ideas, you must sell them.

- *Smart and enthusiastic people to work in the lab.* Good people are a resource, not an instantly refillable commodity. Choosing the wrong people and having not enough or too many people at the wrong time can sink the whole enterprise.

- *A Leader.* Yourself. You keep the science and the people going. You provide the inspiration and the organization and the model for doing good science.

Most P.I.s would agree that, for success of the P.I. and lab members, a lab must be built in which both good science and good character are fostered. You need good projects, you need good people, and they need you. But you do not need to publish in *Nature* to make a great lab: You can work with what you have and make a good lab, no matter what the circumstances. With 3 people or 30, you can make it the place where everyone wants to be.

Start in the Right Place

WORKING WITHIN AND WITH THE ORGANIZATION

Employees can find a job anywhere, but they commit to and want to remain with an organization whose culture they connect with. Certain cultures create and sustain strong cultural connections with their employees. In consequence, these organizations have a significant competitive advantage in finding and keeping great employees. We believe that if there is a strong connection between the core culture and the values of the people, great strides in individual and company performance occur. These organizations understand how critical it is to find and keep people who share the company's core values.

HARRIS AND BRANNICK (1999, P. XIV)

The definition of success and productivity will be defined not only by the P.I., but also by the institution in which the lab is located. Success can be anything from the production of a cancer drug to the graduation of a struggling single mother, and your idea of success should be aligned with that of the institution. Not all places support all kinds of labs. Although jobs may be hard to find, and you believe that you may not have that much of a choice, you should find the kind of institution and position in which to build your kind of lab. Otherwise, finding funds and people will be a battle and the work is going to be hard enough without starting out at cross-purposes to the mother organization.

> You have to find a job where you are expected to do good science and are treated well to do it. If you are expected to get funds, it is just like being given a hunting license, no more.

The bottom line, most P.I.s have found, is to find an institution where you can get the kind people you need to work in your lab. Go where you can do the kind of work you want to do. Do not be fooled by the delight of a job offer or the satisfaction of a good seminar and interview into thinking that you will build a good lab despite the organization. An individual lab can seldom be successful if it does not share the organizational expectations.

Before accepting any job, check out the organization! Talk to as many people as possible. Are your future colleagues happy and interested in science? Are there sufficient resources in the department to do the job? Are support staff well paid and contented? Watch out for bureaucracy. An overfed bureaucracy has a mind of its own and may exist for its own fulfillment instead of yours. Network, as someone you know will know someone at any particular organization and can give you information about the health of the organization. Always keep your goals in mind—Can you achieve these goals at this place?

No matter how well you have tried to ensure that the organization would support your views, you may not find out what is really going on until you get there. Even when you are in place, there is still time to assess the organization, for the implications of each place will profoundly affect all facets of your work, from hiring to getting grants. It may not be necessary to leave, but it is necessary to understand the goals and atmosphere of the organization in order to negotiate your needs.

INDUSTRY VS. ACADEMIA...IT IS NOT AS SIMPLE AS THAT

The differences between academic and industry labs are no longer as clear-cut as they were a generation ago, but depend on the organization to which the lab belongs. Some industry labs, particularly in small and lively biotech companies, are egalitarian and lively places, offering more personal freedoms than at a university. Other industry labs, particularly at large pharmaceutical companies, may be more rule-orientated, rigid, and hierarchical. Some labs in large companies, even within the same company, are unrecognizable from an academic lab, and the differences between a small liberal arts college lab and a large university lab can be also extensive.

Most scientists are brought up in the lab with the goal of working independently on whatever they choose to work on. It is generally assumed that this is the gold standard of research and that academia is the place in which such independence can be fulfilled. As more and more people do industrial postdocs, and find jobs outside of research as well as outside academia, the expectation of an academic-only future lessens.

Each place, each organization, has its own unique culture, but some attributes are more typically academic or industrial. Discussed below are some generalities that are often compared in science and industry and can be used as a springboard for consideration.

Intellectual freedom and inspiration

No graduate student at Yale, where the high-stakes tenure drama was played out in its unfettered ferocity and ruthlessness, could fail to understand that research was a necessary key to success. It couldn't just be any research; it had to be important, path-breaking, modern, and well-funded, published as a steady output of papers in the most prestigious scientific journals. By these measures, the molecular biologists held a decided advantage. Although they concentrated on a mere handful of model organisms—yeast, bacteria, viruses, fruit flies, and mice—their work was revealing an astonishing and deeply satisfying unity among life-forms in such matters as the genetic code, gene regulation, and biochemical pathways. They worked as teams in highly organized laboratories generously funded by grants. With money came space, power, prestige, and arrogance.

VERMEIJ (1997, P. 127)

How open is DNAX? Visitors enter unheralded and unbadged, and they have free access to the laboratories. There are no pre-employment drug screens, dress codes, or strict notebook protocols. With the labs active days, nights, and weekends, with equipment operated in crowded hallways, with daily seminars and discussion groups, and with a constant torrent of publications, the atmosphere reflects a work ethic driven by ambitious individuals rather than by an organization, academic or industrial.

KORNBERG (1995, P. 152)
ARTHUR KORNBERG, WINNER OF THE NOBEL
PRIZE FOR PHYSIOLOGY OR MEDICINE AND
COFOUNDER OF DNAX

"Working in the private sector also allows for a lot more freedom of personal expression to get the job done. If you want to get a grant, there are just so many ways to go about it," says George Boyajian, who moved from academia to industry and is now managing director for science and technology for a project finance and strategic planning venture-capital firm.

KREEGER (2000A, P. 28)

- It is true that scientists are told which projects they must work on in industry and have more intellectual freedom in academia. This independence is one of the main draws of academia and will influence the people hired, and the expectations that they and the P.I.—and the organization—will have. It is generally true, however, that projects must be choosen in areas which can be funded, and this can be as chancy as company politics. Still, in academia, it is your project and your work, and you and your lab make the decisions.

  > *A place like this, an academic health center, is very complex, with clashing values...the academic and the corporate view clash, as it must be run as a business. There are a lot of resources, but a loss of independence...*

- Academia allows not only more flexibility, but also a longer view of the project. Where a product is the desired end result, one must take a short-term view.

- Money, personnel, equipment, and support services, however, are found more readily in industry. There is also access to large-scale platform technologies.

- Projects *can* be dropped in industry, with very little notice, and at high and low ends of the totem pole. The amount of freedom you have very much depends on your position and on the policy of the particular company: It also depends on products and changes of direction issued by directors and stockholders. The effect of this on your morale, and the mood of the lab, can be catastrophic.

- In some companies, people may live for bonuses and other direct rewards for their employment. This tends to be frustrating for those there for intellectual reasons.

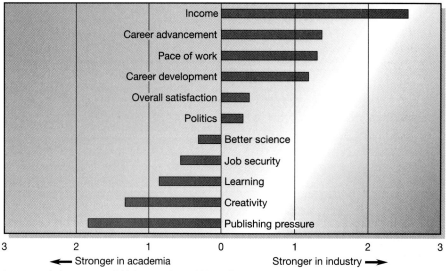

3   2   1   0   1   2   3
← Stronger in academia   Stronger in industry →

Average relative scores of 11 factors, from 162 reader responses.

FIGURE 1. Distinctions between academic and industry jobs. (Adapted, with permission, from Grimwade 2001, p. 29.)

Working conditions

- In academia, P.I.s can be burdened with teaching and the pressure of getting funds. Especially for the beginning scientist, an academic job can be much more stressful than a job in industry. In academia, a starting assistant professor has between 3 and 7 years to establish a working lab and make a professional reputation, obtain grants, teach, and perform a plethora of bureaucratic tasks.

> *Screening, screening, screening, that is what everyone is doing at my company. The immunologists are screening, the cell biologists are screening, and it gets depressing. After a while, people start to think about money and to be motivated by money and bonuses instead of science.*

- In industry, P.I.s can come in after a postdoc, at the height of their powers. They can use their research talent immediately, with people and money at their disposal to do experiments. There are fewer tasks expected as part of the job and more resources to accomplish them.

- Science in industry is often done through team-work, and even a P.I. may be part of a larger team, and must follow larger goals, preset by others. Teamwork is actually frowned upon in academia by promotion committees, although it is often essential to solving big problems.

- Secrecy is always critical on a hot project, to ensure priority for publication. But there are a multitude of reasons why projects are kept secret in industry, and this can be trying for someone used to working with a network of scientists in the same field.

- In industry, the equipment is newer, and the supplies are more readily available. Safety issues will generally be enforced more strictly.

> *It is horrible on soft money. If I don't get the grant renewed, I have to let six people go. My position would be in jeopardy. Do I want to be doing this in ten years? It's a tremendous burden.*

Coworkers

Leadership behavior is a key element in SB's (SmithKline Beecham) retention success. Managers are rewarded and promoted based upon their ability to drive the core culture. Furthermore, employees are told what they can expect from their leaders, including being involved in challenging and meaningful work, supported in their attempts to improve process, recognized and rewarded for their contributions, given honest and open feedback on their performance, and treated as a true team member through honest and fair interactions.

HARRIS AND BRANNICK (1999, P. 75)

- Teamwork is more usual in industry than in academia, and P.I.s must be able to work well with people in and outside their immediate lab. Many people are attracted to industry mainly because of the team-oriented culture. Industry also tends to foster multidisciplinary thinking significantly more than academia, in part because industry research is much more oriented to problem solving. Certain people are suited to this multidisciplinary, problem-solving, team-building atmosphere far better than the typically singularly focused approaches seen in traditional academic departments. With the current changes in science, teamwork is more and more important.

- In academia, a postdoc is considered to be in training, whereas in industry, a postdoc is more likely to be ranked as a competent scientist. The presence of trainees in academia is part of what gives fulfillment to some, but others may prefer the expectation of professionalism in industry. Randall Slemmon, assistant director of protein biochemistry at SmithKline Beecham, describes one of the differences in lab personnel in academia and in industry. "For grad students, you're teaching them and bringing them along, but the people that I now direct, sometimes they're older than I am and in certain areas have far more credentials and experience. They're professionals, so you deal with them very differently" (Kreeger 2000a, p. 28).

- A reporting line exists in industry in most places: Everyone reports to someone else, so independence feels compromised. There can be resentment about the hierarchy among lab workers, because credit is not always given to the people who have done the work.

- In industry, however, technicians can increase their status and can actually become a P.I. without a Ph.D. It is unusual, but not unheard of. In any case, often because of the money and benefits, technicians will stay at a job much longer in industry than at a university. Long-term employees bring stability, but the excitement of new and enthusiastic blood coming in every few years may be missed.

Personal issues

- Companies, especially the pharmaceutical industry, have certainly led industry in showing consideration for a work-life balance. And, in general, the smaller companies have been much more experimental about trying innovative schemes (Edwards 1999).

- Large companies can spend more on benefits, with smaller companies being more experimental in finding options for work-life issues such as adoption assistance and part-time or flextime arrangements. For example, the benefits offered in 1999 by the Immunex Corporation, a Seattle biopharmaceutical company, include a transportation subsidy, adoption assistance, a health flex spending account, and a dependent-care flexible spending account for child care and elder day care, lactation rooms, telecommuting, and job-share options (Swenson 1999).

- The individual group, however, will allow expression of the benefits in different ways: At the most liberal-on-paper company, an individual department head can effectively block any flextime arrangement. And an interested and creative supervisor can extract seemingly invisible benefits by manipulating the rules.

- Salaries are generally higher in industry (Kreeger 2000a), especially at the larger companies, than for the parallel position in academia. This is true for P.I.s, as well as for lab workers. Performance bonuses are offered at many companies, and a few companies still offer stock options.

- It is easier to have a social life in industry, and long hours are not expected as they are in academia for a new P.I. This is easier on families. In academia, although more hours of work may be required, P.I.s are generally more free to make their own hours, to work a 110-hour week, but to take a month-long vacation or to leave at 3:00 a few days a week to pick up the kids at school.

OTHER INFLUENCES ON THE ORGANIZATION

...For all the talk in business schools and in corporate America about the virtues of "flat organizations," surgeons maintain an old-fashioned sense of hierarchy. When things go wrong, the attending is expected to take full responsibility. It makes no difference whether it was the resident's hand that slipped and lacerated an aorta; it doesn't matter whether the attending was at home in bed when a nurse gave a wrong dose of medication. At the M. & M., the burden of responsibility falls on the attending.

GAWANDE (2000, P. 11)

Within academia

Academic institutions vary as much from each other as do companies. For example, medical schools and graduate schools may be completely culturally disparate. Goals are different and training is different; a nonclinical project at a medical school may not be able to recruit anyone.

A small college or university is a wonderful place for someone committed to work with students. If success and personal happiness are measured by being able to mentor and by the success and happiness of students, a small college or university could be ideal. However, the projects will have to be amenable to eager but untrained hands...will you be able to publish enough to renew grants? Most small places may not have the funds for the expensive and specialized equipment or other resources some projects need, and there may not be enough collaborators around to ever feel the excitement of the happenings in your field.

> *"People need more guidance in graduate school than in medical school. In medical school, the future is all mapped out for you, and it is easier to be a mentor."*

In addition, it is difficult to maintain a small lab in which to interact with students in a large and competitive university. The more successful you are, or the more worried that you will fail, the stronger the pull to grow will be.

The Genetics of Full Professors

Success in academia is hypothesized to require specific phenotypes. In order to understand how such unusual traits arise, we used human clones to identify the molecular events that occur during the transition from a graduate student to professor. A pool of graduate student clones were subjected to several rounds of random mutagenesis followed by selection on minimal money media in the absence of dental insurance. Students surviving this selection were further screened for the ability to work long hours with vending machine snacks as a sole carbon source; clones satisfying these requirements were dubbed "post-docs." In order to identify assistant professors from amongst the post-docs, this pool was further mutagenized, and screened for the ability to turn esoteric results into a 50 minute seminar. Finally, these assistant professors were evaluated for their potential to become full professors in two ways: first, they were screened for overproduction and surface display of stress proteins such as Hsp70. Assistant professors that displayed such proteins (so-called "stressed out" mutants) were then fused to the M13 coat protein, displayed on phages and passed over a friend and family members column, to identify those that were incapable of functional interactions. These were called full professors. Although these mutants arose independently, they shared striking phenotypes. These included the propensity to talk incessantly about their own research, the inability to accurately judge the time required to complete bench work, and the belief that all their ideas constituted good thesis projects. The linkage of all these traits suggests that these phenotypes are coordinately regulated. Preliminary experiments have identified a putative global regulator. Studies are currently being conducted to determine if overexpression of this gene product in post-docs and grad students can speed up the grad student-full professor evolutionary process.

Author unknown

Within industry

Research goals at large companies might appear to be more academic than at smaller, more product-driven companies. However, your work may not often get to a state that you think is complete in a large company, as supervisors may be more concerned with a timeline than with an answer.

Those who have worked at start-up companies are usually very enthusiastic about the workplace. The camaraderie is addictive, the pace is fast and involved, and all of the participants feel needed and caught up in the action. But a start-up company can change as a result of its own success.

Forces outside the organization

The geographical location of the institution can profoundly influence the kind of lab workers obtained and thus, the kind of science performed. One P.I., in an isolated

> *The students are more homespun, with no worldly experience. They see the game, but don't think that they are part of the game. The good stuff is being done by "someone else," and they are just observers.*

and quiet part of the country, found that he could easily attract students, but that those students were much more passive than the students at the more central and active places where he had been a student and postdoc.

A series of articles in *The Scientist* (Kreeger 2000) highlighted the impact that the location of a scientific workplace has on attracting personnel. In desirable areas, where people want to live anyway, regardless of a job, the pool of potential hires is much larger, and the competition for the good people can be tremendous.

In an area from which people are desperate to leave, ads can run for weeks before there is a response from someone qualified. No matter what area, the more universities and scientific companies in the vicinity, the more likely candidates are to be found.

ENSURE A GOOD BEGINNING

> *No one is able to teach three courses per semester, manage a $250,000/year research program, supervise seven graduate students, write four important papers per year, go to five national meetings per year, serve on six committees, and do an excellent job in every category. Nevertheless, there are institutions that expect this kind of performance. DO you want to work for one of these?*
>
> DANTZIG (1995, P. 3)

The process of looking for and applying for a job can be a fairly lengthy process: It is a good idea to start at the beginning of the last year of your postdoc. Write to people, talk, and read (references dealing with job searches and negotiations are listed at the end of the section). *Think.* Throughout the search, envision yourself in each place: Decide whether this is the best place to do your kind of work and live your kind of life. It is vital to look at each potential job in terms of achieving your aims.

You must negotiate for space and teaching responsibilities *before* accepting a job. Get the offer in writing, from someone with power enough to deliver. After the job is accepted, it may be too late. You will also need to discuss student or postdoc support. Before any meetings, be as well prepared as possible for a discussion of what you require.

Negotiate until you have conditions under which you can do the kind of science you want to do. This is the time to be very, very realistic.

To be negotiated

Negotiations for academic and industry jobs are very different. In general, only in academic jobs must the P.I. juggle teaching and administrative responsibilities as well as salary and research support. For one of the best discussions of start-up negotiations and for finding and applying for jobs, see Reis (1997).

- *Teaching.* When selecting a course, decide whether you prefer a graduate course only, or perhaps just one or two courses the first year.

- *Salary.* Check with peers at the institute and at other places. Negotiate hard, because you will not get another chance to improve your salary drastically unless you threaten to leave.

- *Lab funding.* Make sure that the funding you have calculated is sufficient until a grant or promotion kicks in.

> *Sit down and really try to come up with a budget for negotiations. Many people just take what is offered and don't try to find out what is really needed. If the standard package isn't enough, you need to know, and you need to document the proof of the cost if it is not enough. You must be able to say: Here is the proof! These are my costs for each need, projected for 1, 2, 5 years.*

- *Positions.* Find out about support for students, postdocs, technicians, secretary, etc.

- *Discretionary funding.* Many grants do not allow you to take a scientist out to lunch or buy a pack of photo printing paper for the computer. The department, however, can usually arrange to have money set aside for you to use as you please.

- *Equipment.* Be sure that all of the equipment you need is there, in good condition, and is available for use. If not, request it: This is not to come out of your funds. Find out if the department covers equipment maintenance and insurance.

> *Find out what happens to the start-up money if you do not use it. In about half the places, you use it or lose it, like a grant. The money will not used in the best way if you have to spend out by the end of a certain amount of time. Find out and negotiate this.*

- *Personal support.* Find out about mortgage help, real estate agent fees, and children's schools.

Although these items sound like apples and oranges, they can be traded. Ensuring the future of the lab must be your first priority. There are many books and articles, some included at the end of the chapter, that deal with finding a job and conducting job negotiations.

Sometimes people move within a system and are promoted from a postdoc to assistant professor in the same institution or even the same department and lab. A start-up package is usually not included in this discussion. It should be! Do not be so grateful for a promotion that you lose sight of the future. Unless there is a very good reason to do this—perhaps to solidify your qualifications for another job or to finish a project that would suffer if interrupted—carefully consider how it will fit into a 5-year plan and negotiate accordingly.

> *Make sure that you have a protected time period when you first start, protected from teaching and committees. Some places will give you a year, some will give two. This means thesis committees as well, anything that will take time from research.*

Lab renovations

...Between 1898 and 1904, the Curies had published 36 papers, won a Nobel Prize, and turned down an enticing offer for them both from the University of Geneva in Switzerland. Pierre, however, did not become a professor at a prestigious French University until 1904, when the Sorbonne, a part of the University of Paris, promised him a laboratory.... . As late as 1906, however, the university had not begun construction. When Pierre was offered a prestigious award from the Legion of Honor, he refused it, saying "I do not in the least feel the need of a decoration, but I do feel the greatest need for a laboratory." He was never to have a "real" laboratory.

McGrayne (1993, p. 27)

Lab renovations are promised as part of many job offers. Any lab renovations should be done before you arrive, as the disruption later—if promises are even kept—can be really harmful to the running of the lab. If you cannot physically check on the renovations, it helps to request an update from someone not involved in the process who will objectively assess the progress.

I should have been more careful about making sure that the lab was ready. It wasn't ready until 9 months after I got there! There were no animal facilities, and this set the lab back a year. I would have stayed longer at my postdoc. You must identify an ally in the system from whom you can get the truth, really sit the person down and ask for an absolute commitment to the date and for the truth, even negative, if something goes wrong.

You must be part of the decision-making process for the renovations. Think about the kind of work you will be doing and what each lab member will physically be doing. Visit labs. Request advice from as many people as possible, as forgetting one apparently small detail—such as having enough electrical outlets at each lab bench—can very negatively affect the lab's quality of life. P.I.s in your field who have recently been through a renovation would have the most pertinent advice. There are also companies and Web Sites that offer advice about scientific renovations. Remember generalities as well as specifics: Balance work and storage space, and, if possible, think ahead to expansion possibilities for the future. Listed below are some elements to consider:

- *Storage.* Explosion-proof refrigeration, reagent storage, biohazard and radioactive storage, and gas supply and storage.

- *Work areas.* Shared and personal. Computer and writing places, phones, hoods, and cabinets with proper exhaust.

- *Safety.* Number and location of emergency doors. Eyewashes and safety showers. Earthquake or other relevant hazards. Appropriate storage for acids and bases.

Below is a list of one researcher's lab renovation suggestions.

- Leave open wall space for freezers, centrifuges, and other equipment.

- Put enough 220-volt outlets in each room to handle all of the equipment.

- Air-condition the tissue culture room.

- Do not allow access to other equipment through the tissue culture room.

- Attach the eyewash station to the ceiling (if regulations allow) and not on the walls, to take up less space.

- Put in doors that close to convert a lab room to a dark room.

- Be sure any disabled person's counter and shelves are built to the appropriate height.

- Drawers at individual desks should be wide enough to accommodate file folders.

- Paper towel holders must be high enough to be easily torn off.

- All shelves should be adjustable with rims on the front, but not on the sides.

- Doors must be wide enough for the large −80°C freezers.

- **Changes should not be made in the renovation plans without your permission.**

Plan the Lab You Want

WHAT DO YOU NEED TO GET THERE, AND WHERE IS "THERE," ANYWAY?

What is success? And how do you know if you are successful? When asked, lab members give a variety of responses. Papers, grants, and promotions are, of course, the usual milestones of success in science. In the early days of running a lab, survival is the name of the game, and it may seem too indulgent to think further than these solid evidences of productivity.

I am not as successful as my mentors at same age, but not as unsuccessful as my own fears.

Although scientists start with grants, papers, and promotions—and the hope of contributing in a seminal way to science—the measure of success tends to become more individual with time. At the start of a career, most scientists' aspirations are similar, but they become tempered with reality and a personal life. Expectations will change—They are broadened.

A lot about being a P.I. I don't like, like the paperwork. But what is great is working with a great bunch of people, having a lab of colleagues.

P.I.s who have been running a lab for a while tend to measure success in terms of how well lab members are doing, and how productive and happy the present lab is. There is a mental switch, for that which was the means (the personnel) becomes the end. This sense of caring for the lab and its people is as fulfilling to many scientifically successful lab members as a long c.v. "There" becomes, for most, the scientific success of the members of the lab. But to arrive at whatever your view of success is, you must first get good people to do good research and write good papers.

We aren't world beaters—we do good science, but we aren't in the league of the big guys. There is a recognition of our limits, so we have to get it right and in a timely fashion.

THE MISSION STATEMENT

Most companies have a mission statement, i.e., a summary of the goals and inspirations of the group. A real business world gimmick, most scientists would assume, and it often is merely a sound bite. But writing down a few sentences to summarize the goals for your lab can help you to visualize the steps you will need to get there. You can be certain that if you do not summarize what you want your lab to be, it is going to be very, very difficult to motivate and plan. The following are a few examples of lab mission statements:

"To do good science, with friends."
"To be at the top of our field, no matter what."
"To live an integrated life at home and lab."

Each of these statements would require a different plan of attack and a different long-term plan.

THE FIVE-YEAR PLAN

A company is not a machine but a living organism, and, much like an individual, it can have a collective sense of identity and fundamental purpose. This is the organizational equivalent of self knowledge—a shared understanding of what the company stands for, where it's going, what kind of world it wants to live in, and, most importantly, how it intends to make that world a reality.

NONAKA (1991, P. 313).

As you think and plan for your present lab, it is helpful to always keep in mind your goals for the lab as your resources grow. In this way, certain decisions will be very obvious, from the apparently trivial (set up a storage system now so that in 5 years, you will not be rifling through the freezer boxes, searching container after container for a crucial piece of DNA) to the deeply philosophical (working with medical fellows has turned out to be much more rewarding than you thought, and you would like to set up a regular program of resident rotations in your laboratory).

Five years is a reasonable time to shoot for. At that time, most of your present funding will have turned over, as will have many of your present personnel. Tenure and promotion decisions will be imminent. Your personal life can undergo a lot of changes within 5 years, and might even be stable.

It may seem a bit too much introspection for you, but sitting down with a pen and paper for 10 minutes to list your 5-year goals could be the most productive 10 minutes of your career. Not only will this cement your particular vision, it will help keep you on the right pathway to get there. Consider not only your scientific life, but also both your social life and your financial situation.

Now I have a five-year plan. When I first started, by 5 years, I was expecting the Nobel prize.

Considerations for a 5-year plan

Career

- What position would you like to be in?
- How large would you like the lab to be?
- How much funding would you like to have?
- Do you see yourself at the same institution?
- Are you thinking of a shift in your career?
- How likely is it that you will succeed in your plans?

Social

- Would you like your social situation to remain the way it is?
- Do you think you would want to be spending more or less time at work?
- Are you interested in traveling, boating, or another activity that you have not been able to do because of time and money constraints?
- Do you want to start a family within the next 5 years?
- How involved do you want to be with your children, and what impact do you think this will have on your career?

Financial

- Where would you like to be living in 5 years?
- Will the expected raises or promotions enable you to live the way you would like?
- Would you welcome "extra" jobs, such as consulting?

Project

- Would you like to be working on the details of your current project?
- Would you like to remain in the same field?
- Would you prefer the pace of your research to be competitive, or would you rather do the lab work in a more leisurely fashion?

Lab culture

> *"Intense, exciting, hectic, stressful, fast-paced, focused, casual": These are some of the words that employees we know use frequently to describe their innovation-driven culture. Such a combination of diverse emotions hardly affords employees a relaxed and easygoing work environment. On the contrary, a culture of innovation is one of the most stressful work environments in existence. Yet it does offer one guarantee that is sensuously appealing: the thrill of an adventure.*
>
> HARRIS AND BRANNICK (1999, P. 51)

- Do you want a large lab or a small lab?

- What kind of relationships do you want to have with the other members of the lab?

- Do you want to work at the bench?

- Are you more comfortable with the scientific, administrative, or personal aspects of running a lab?

- Which is more important—the success of the lab or the success of the individuals?

- Do you want communication to flow freely among all members, or do you prefer to funnel research down a hierarchy?

Core values

When you decide on the values you want for your lab, you can build a culture that supports those values. Some desirable values are:

- Scientific excellence

- Social responsibility

- Scientific success

- Creativity

- Discipline

- Personal freedom

- Teamwork

- Scientific independence

- Exploring innovative science

- Learning

Once the beginnings of a lab culture take root, it becomes self-perpetuating and easier to build on. Once in operation, the lab with an identifiable culture is a self-policing force, and becomes ever more easier to run. It takes a number of years before you can sit back and realize that the lab is where you want it. There will be many starts and stops with personnel that did not work out and projects that bombed, before you have a sleek and independent lab.

GETTING OFF WITH A RUNNING START

If I could start over again, I would...

1. *Finish essential tasks in more leisurely fashion at my graduate campus, before leaving, especially the dissertation and sending it off for publication.*

2. *Start sooner, immediately after arriving on campus, to work at things like writing regularly, instead of waiting until in the mood.*

3. *Make more effort to find out about unwritten expectations for new faculty like me, early. I would start, even before leaving my graduate campus (or later, by calling*

back), to learn what to expect at my new campus by talking with the younger faculty where I was, and with people I knew who were just starting professorial careers.

4. *Read more about early experiences of new faculty.*

5. *Keep my early interactions/questions with colleagues light-hearted and nonanxious, nonobsessive.*

6. *Make more effort to know and get help from my chairperson. I'd want to learn what sorts of mistakes or oversights distinguish newcomers who are not reappointed.*

BOICE (2000, P. 221)

An enormous amount of energy surrounds the beginnings of a new lab, and the new P.I. should take advantage of the sometimes short-lived optimism and enthusiasm generated to make as many connections as possible with others in the institution.

It is important, physically and psychologically, to start out strongly with a new lab. Do allow yourself a short breather from the stress of job hunting, but do not become complacent, and forget why you are there. Start planning your research the first week and actually doing the research within 2 or 3 weeks. Busywork is not the reason you are there, so dispense with administrative tasks quickly.

To be able to start your work right away, it is helpful if most of the administrative tasks have been initiated before you arrive. Do not assume that everything will automatically be taken care of for you. Enlist an ally in the department who can check on the status of odds and ends of the lab renovations before you arrive. This is vital to getting a good start. When you are visiting your prospective institution, target someone—another member of the department, an administrative assistant, or someone in employee relations—who will be able to answer your queries and make arrangements as your proxy.

Many of the items you must arrange for at a new institution are discussed in the chapter Getting Off to a Good Start in this volume. Below is a brief list of the usual to-dos:

- Get on mailing lists
- Seminar lists
- Institutional announcements
- Grant information
- Keys to office, lab, and building
- Additional keys for lab members
- Weekend rules for entering building
- Parking weekend and weekday
- Payment, location, getting on waiting lists

Talking to other P.I.s who have started up a lab will help you to anticipate some of the problems. **One P.I. detailed some of the first year administrative problems he encountered that inhibited the efficient use of time:**

- Keys to the office did not fit.

- Phone not connected until several weeks later.

- Long and inefficient set up of e-mail/Internet access. (I waited more than 1 month.)

- Orders I placed 6 weeks before my arrival had not been processed.

- Not knowing that ordering was done through certain preferred vendors until after my purchase orders were submitted. (I had to start over with time-consuming comparison shopping. It took me a while to find out that there is the Cell Center for supply purchases.)

- No information provided about IDs/key cards for hospital and university. (I still do not have a key card.)

- No information/guidelines regarding the hiring of technicians or postdocs (including visa information for foreigners).

- No support or even guidelines regarding radiation license, recombinant DNA license, and biohazardous materials removal.

- Inefficient interaction with University accounts. (A small award I received almost 1 year ago has only now been made available to me, around the time I was asked to write a final progress report.)

- Very slow and inefficient handling of lab modifications (shelves, plumbing, and outlets, etc.)

- No support or guidelines to have my name listed in directories, students' faculty handbook, etc.

- Excessive floor cleaning every day by four people when two per floor would be more than sufficient. Saved funds could be used for secretarial support/bridging money.

Order supplies and equipment early and very carefully. Below is a checklist for ordering most of the essentials for the new lab.

General Lab Use (per person)

Aluminum foil
Autoclavable containers for microfuge tubes, etc.
Automatic pipettor
Chairs (desk *and* bench)
Forceps (flat-edged and pointed)
Gloves (disposable and nonallergenic)
Kimwipes
Magnifying glass
Paper towels
Parafilm
Pencil sharpener
Pipettors (3–4 in different capacities, bench-top holder for pipettors)

Pyrex dishes
Ruler
Safety goggles
Saran Wrap (plastic wrap)
Tape (colored and plain label and masking, biohazard, Scotch, autoclave, and tape dispensers)
Thermometers (non-mercury)
Timers
Tissues
Tupperware (plastic containers)
Vortex (holder for tubes)
Wash bottles

General Lab Use (per lab)

Autoclave bags (large and benchtop)
Balances (weighing paper and boats, spatulas, beakers, brush for cleaning)
Bottles (autoclavable, for buffers, 100, 500, 1000 ml)
Boxes, racks for freezer storage
Bunsen burner and lighters
Carboys for water and buffers
Carts (at least two)
Chairs (microscope, computer, common benches)
Column stands, holders, clamps
Desiccators and desiccant
Drying racks for glassware, detergent, plastic bins, pipette washer, glass cleaner, scrub brushes, brushes for tubes)
Duct tape
Garbage bins
Filter paper
First aid kit
Ice buckets
Eye wash station
Heating blocks
Magnetic stirplate/hotplate, magnetic stir bars
Masks
Microwave, gloves to use with microwave samples
Pipettes (glass and disposable, Pasteur, automatic and manual pipette aids)
Pipette tips and racks
pH meter (pH standards, wash bottles, pH indicator strips, electrode storage buffer, beakers, magnetic stirrer/hotplate, magnetic stir bars)
Racks (microcentrifuge, test tubes, centrifuge tubes)
Scalpels, razor blades, sharps disposal, boxes
Safety cabinets
Tape measure
Toolbox with basic tools
Tubes (disposable microfuge, 15, 50 ml, etc.)
Water baths, floating racks, thermometer, cover

Tissue Culture Room

Biohazard autoclave bags
Chemical fume hood
Freezing vials
Incubators (CO_2 tanks, straps, holders, regulators, thermometers, Fyrite)
Ice buckets
Liquid nitrogen tank, racks, tubes, cryogenic gloves, logbook
Microscope (inverted for flasks, compound for samples), extra light bulbs, cover, lens paper, immersion oil, slides, coverslips, hemocytometer and extra coverslips, Petroff-Hauser and extra coverslips, fixatives and stains
Racks for tubes
Sharps containers
Pipette aids to remain in hood
Pipettors (autoclavable) and tips
Plasticware (flasks, tubes, pipettes)
Vortex
Water bath, lead rings for bottles

Radioactivity

Autoradiographic cassettes
Autoradiographic film
Bench paper
Geiger counter
Pipettors and tips
Scintillant
Scintillation vials
Shields

Office Supplies

Cartridges for printers and photocopier
Clipboards
Envelopes 3 x 5, 8 1/2 x 11)
Folders and files
File cabinets
Graph paper
Lab notebooks
Notebooks (for equipment logs, lecture notes)

Paper pads
Pens (red, black, blue)
Paper (high quality for letters)
Printer paper
Scissors
Sharpies
Staplers and staples
White board markers

The Extras

Coffee machine
Espresso machine
Microwave for food

Radio/CD/tape player
Small refrigerator for food

Before You Order, You Should Know

Can you get office supplies from a departmental office?
Can you get ice?
Can you get distilled/deionized water?

Do you have use of or do you need: Autoclave, Dry ice, Ultracentrifuge, Scintillation machine, Spectrophotometer, Primers, Enzymes

To make a list, think in terms of the science that will be done, and what you will need for each facet of the work. List your specialized equipment, and then list the supplies needed to run and maintain it.

Borrowing a list from a colleague who has recently moved is perhaps the time-honored way of making your first order list. Other lists are available on-line and in print (e.g., the Lab Setup Checklist in the 2001 BioSupplyNet Source Book, pp. xxii–xxiii). This list details general lab supplies and equipment, as well as enzymes and reagents and chemicals that are needed for general molecular biology work.

Some P.I.s put in supply orders before they arrive, the sooner to be able to set up the lab and start experiments. Others wait until they are sure they have functional lab space complete with shelves and refrigerators, and many await the hiring of the first technician to put in the orders and put away the supplies as they arrive. But do not let an inexperienced student or technician make any decisions about even the most mundane of supplies, for deciding the style of forceps or the thickness of a beta shield requires know-how.

Many companies offer a one time start-up deal for new P.I.s. You probably can get 20% off a huge order or a percentage off if you promise to spend $5000 the first year. However, be wary of these deals, for many P.I.s have purchased in bulk only to have tubes of enzymes languish in the freezer very much past the expiration date. If you are planning a big order from a particular company, call and ask for a deal, but do not buy unnecessarily because they offer a deal.

RESOURCES

2001 BioSupplyNet Source Book, pp. xxii–xxiii. SciQuest, Farmingdale, New York.

Adler N.J. 1997. *International dimensions of organizational behavior*, 3rd edition. South-Western College Publishing, Cincinnati.

Altrock B. 1995. Science in a corporate environment. *Science's Next Wave*, Oct. 2, pp. 1–3. (http://nextwave.sciencemag.org)

Anonymous. 1996. The genetics of full professors (pers. comm.).

Azuma R.T. 1999. *A graduate school survival guide: "So long and thanks for the Ph.D.!"* (http://www.cs.unc.edu/~azuma/hitch4.html)

Beatty R.H. 1994. *Interviewing and selecting high performers*. John Wiley & Sons, New York.

Boice R. 2000. *Advice for new faculty members: Nihil Nimus*. Allyn and Bacon, Needham Heights, Massachusetts.

Boschelli F. 1999. Making the transition from academia to industry. *Am. Soc. Cell Biol. Newsletter* **22:** 12–13. (http://www.ascb.org)

Brown W.S. 1985. *13 Fatal errors managers make and how you can avoid them*. Berkley Books, New York.

Cooper R.K. and Sawaf A. 1997. *Executive E.Q. Emotional intelligence in leadership and organizations*. Grosset/Putnam, New York.

Covey S.R. 1989. *The 7 habits of highly effective people*. Simon & Schuster, New York.

Dantzig J.A. 1995. Landing an academic job: The process and pitfalls. Department of Mechanical and Industrial Engineering, University of Illinois at Urbana-Champaign, Aug. 4, pp. 1–9.

Deal T. and Kennedy A.A. 1982. *Corporate cultures*. Addison-Wesley, Reading, Massachusetts.

Edwards C.G. 1999. Get a life! New options for balancing work and home. *HMS Beagle* **54:** 1–5. (http://news.bmn.com/hmsbeagle)

Fitz-Enz J. 1997. *The 8 practices of exceptional companies. How great organizations make the most of their human assets*. AMACON Books, New York.

Gawande A. 2000. When doctors make mistakes. In *The Best American science writing 2000* (ed. J. Gleick), pp. 1–22. HarperCollins, New York.

Grimwade A. 2001. Working in academia and industry. *The Scientist* **15:** 28–29. (http://www.the-scientist.com)

Gwynne P. 1999. Corporate collaborations: Scientists can face publishing constraints. *The Scientist* **13:** 1–6. (http://www.thescientist.com)

Halim N.S. 1999. Working in industry: Researchers balance work and life. *The Scientist* **13:** 24–25. (http://www.thescientist.com)

Harris J. and Brannick J. 1999. *Finding and keeping great employees*. AMACOM Books, New York.

Jensen D. 1997. A clash of cultures: What it takes to work in industry. *Science's Next Wave*, June 13, pp. 1–3. (http://nextwave.sciencemag.org)

Joyce L. 1989. DNAX immunologists work to balance industry, Academia. *The Scientist* **3:** 1–3. (http://www.thescientist.com)

Judson H.F. 1996. *The Eighth Day of Creation: The makers of the revolution in biology*, expanded edition. Cold Spring Harbor Laboratory Press, Cold Spring Harbor, New York.

Kornberg A. 1995. *The golden helix: Inside biotech ventures*. University Science Books, Sausalito, California.

Kreeger K.Y. 1999. Search committees: The long and winding road of academic hiring. *The Scientist* **13:** 24. (http://www.thescientist.com)

Kreeger K.Y. 2000a. From classroom to boardroom. *The Scientist* **14:** 28–29. (http://www.thescientist.com)

Kreeger K.Y. 2000b. Science salaries. *The Scientist* **14:** 35. (http://www.thescientist.com)

Kreeger K.Y. 2000c. The "Where " factor, Parts I–V. *The Scientist* **14.** (http://www.thescientist.com)

Lanthes A. 1999. Some real-world observations on industrial postdocs. *Science's Next Wave*, May 7, pp. 1–4. (http://nextwave.sciencemag.org)

Levi P. 1984. *The periodic table*. Schocken Books, New York.

Lientz B.P. and K.P. Rea. 1998. *Project management for the 21st century*, 2nd edition. Academic Press, New York.

McGrayne S.B. 1993. Marie Sklodowska Curie. In *Nobel prize women in science: Their lives, struggles and momentous discoveries*, pp. 11–36. Carol Publishing Group, Secaucus, New Jersey.

Mendelson H. and Ziegler J. 1999. *Survival of the smartest: Managing information for rapid action and world-class performance*. John Wiley & Sons, New York.

Milloy S. 1995. *Science without sense: The risky business of public health research*. The Cato Institute, Washington, D.C.

Nonaka I. 1991. The knowledge-creating company. *Harvard Business Rev.* Nov.–Dec., p. 313.

Quraishi O. 1999. Similarities and differences between industrial and academic positions in the pharmaceutical industry. *Science's Next Wave*, Aug. 6, pp. 1–4. (http://nextwave.sciencemag.org)

Reis R.M. 1997. *Tomorrow's professor: Preparing for academic careers in science and engineering*. I.E.E.E. Press, New York.

Reis R.M. 1999. The right start-up package for beginning science professors. *Chronicle of Higher Education*. (http://www.chronicle.com)

Sego T. and Richards J.I. 1995. Ph.D. Interview preparation guide. (http://www.utexas.edu/coc.adv/JR/InterviewPrep.html)

Senge P.M., Kleiner A., Roberts C., Ross R.B., and Smith B.J. 1994. *The fifth discipline fieldbook: Strategies and tools for building a learning organization*. Currency/Doubleday, New York.

Sherwood N.T. 1997. Overview and comparison of family leave options in science. *Science's Next Wave* Jan. 7, pp. 1–7. (http://nextwave.sciencemag.org)

Swenson L. 1999. Awarding work/life leaders: Immunex programs garner top award. *Seattle's Child & Eastside Parent* Aug., p. 60.

Vermeij G. 1997. *Privileged hands: A scientific life*. W.H. Freeman, New York.

Wheatley M.J. 1994. *Leadership and the new science. Learning about organization from an orderly universe*. Berrett-Koehler Publishers, San Francisco.

You as a Leader

I Was Trained to Do Everything But Run a Lab!

YOUR QUALIFICATIONS FOR RUNNING A LAB

How often have P.I.s complained about having no training to run a lab. Most new P.I.s come to this conclusion within weeks of starting out: All of the training and all of the hours at the bench and buried in journals did nothing to prepare them for the actual business of running a laboratory. All too quickly, it becomes apparent that people skills and organizational skills are at least as important as the science itself and that you do not have the right ones.

> *I was trained to do everything but run a lab! Therapist, fund-raiser, educator...there is no good indicator for what will be a good P.I.*

But you are wrong. You have been trained, probably very well, to run a lab. Although you may not have been taught directly how to deal with people, you have been trained how to think and how to seek solutions and solve problems. You can define the problem and break it into solvable components. Your training gave you:

- **The ability to gather and analyze data.** To help solve any problems concerning the people in the lab, you must be able to analyze the situation. Scientifically, you have learned to identify patterns and to make sense out of seemingly random events with data, and you *will* be able to do this as well with people.

> *I'm still learning how to do this. No one ever teaches us how to do this when we first start this work, so I learned it by trial and error, and I still don't receive any feedback as to whether I'm doing this correctly. So, I don't think I was very prepared before, and I don't think I'm prepared now.*

- **Organizational ability.** You can prioritize for the short and long term. Organize your time, and your resources, to bring a project to completion.

- **The confidence to act on intuition.** Intuition is the combination of conscious and unconscious thought, the sometimes undefined but profound screen through which to make decisions.

- **Resilience.** Your feelings are going to get hurt. Although you will act with the best of intentions, people will sometimes be angry because of your decisions. Situations will go badly, and you will make mistakes. But you already know that.

- **Honesty and integrity.** You have had to be honest when dealing with your data, and with people's expectations of the data. The same honesty can help to guide others through the process of research.

- **Communication skills.** Although you sometimes struggled with projects on your own, you were able to deal successfully with people in many capacities along the way. You communicated the results of your research with your department, in a thesis, or in publications and presentations. You had at least an equilibrium relationship with benchmates and labmates.

- **Scientific know-how.** You have it. You ran projects by yourself, and successfully enough that the project was recognized as being good science by other scientists.

Twenty-two scientists were polled (Fiske 1997, pp. 1–4) at various stages of their careers and asked the following question: Of the many skills that people develop while in graduate school, which ones are the most valuable in the outside world? The top five answers were:

- Ability to work productively with difficult people.

- Ability to work in a high-stress environment.

- Persistence.

- Circumventing the rules.

- Ability and courage to start something even without knowing how.

You are well prepared to apply your training to a new but related field, that of running a lab. Perhaps you feel handicapped because you are not a "people person"—you feel uncomfortable around people and would rather not have to deal with them. Such is the stereotypic scientist, at least, the old-fashioned scientist, from another era. In this fast-moving age of collaboration and limited resources, success very much depends on how to maximize the resources of the laboratory. You *can* learn to work with the people in the lab you build.

WHAT KIND OF P.I. DO YOU WANT TO BE?

...Imaginativeness and a critical temper are both necessary at times, but neither is sufficient. The most imaginative scientists are by no means the most effective; at their worst, uncensored, they are cranks. Nor are they the most critically minded. The man notorious for his dismissive criticisms, strenuous in the pursuit of error, is often unproductive, as if he had scared himself out of his own wits—unless indeed his critical cast of mind was the consequence rather than the cause of his infertility.

MEDAWAR (1969, P. 58)

The kind of leader you are and the kind of lab you want to run are inseparable. Your style sets the tone of the lab culture. The lab will become an extension of you, so the more you know about yourself, the more you will be able to plan.

Your style makes the lab take shape. You must work the way you are comfortable.

Most P.I.'s agree that you cannot be forced to be the kind of manager that you cannot be. You can only nurture the seeds of your own personality. Some have tried to be overly friendly when they were essentially private people. Some have put distance between themselves and employees because they thought they had to and some ignored poor data because they did not want to seem overbearing. You must decide what kind of scientist and boss you want to be, and how to get there with the advantages and disadvantages of your own self.

> *Find a style that works for you and take off on your strengths.*

There are no rights or wrongs. Even the worst mistake is only a mistake in the context of the kind of lab the P.I. is trying to run and the kind of manager the P.I. wants to be.

GET YOUR STYLE DOWN...EXAMINE YOURSELF

Closely related to the role of imagination in scientific research is the question of style. No two scientists, especially effective scientists, function identically, just as no two violinists play Bach's Chaconne *in exactly the same way. I choose this example advisedly, since both violinist and scientist have limited freedom, the former being bound to the score, the latter to a factual context, but within the range of their freedom each performs with a unique personal style.*

LURIA (1984, P. 159)

Consider your likes and dislikes, as well as your strengths and weaknesses, when analyzing your style.

- *Will you be more effective at the bench or at the desk?*

  Do you like benchwork?

  Do you enjoy troubleshooting experiments for lab members?

  Have you always waited for the day when you could direct someone else's experiments?

  Would you rather talk about results or read about them?

- *Do you want to be a boss or a colleague?* Do you trust other people's interpretations of the data?

- *Why are you in science?* Are you motivated by achievement, by problem solving, by being a part of a larger group, by the lifestyle?

> *The American style of power is to be cool and collected. If you lose your temper, you show weakness and lack of control.*

- *How do you make decisions?*

  Are you impulsive or methodical?

  Do you make decisions alone, or solicit advice beforehand? Do you expect others in the lab to come to decisions with you?

- **Do you want to manage details, or just deal with the big picture?**

  Is control an issue with you?

  Do you trust the work and decisions of others?

  Do you find it difficult or delightful to delegate?

- **Do you like people?**

  Were you close to people in your student and postdoc labs?

  Would you rather not get to know the people in your lab?

  Liking people is not enough to make a good manager of people. It can help if it gives you insight.

  You may like people, but do they like you? Do you easily maintain a rapport with most people? Do you care what happens to people?

- **Do you work most effectively and comfortably with peers, bosses, or subordinates?**

BUILD ON YOUR PERSONALITY STRENGTHS

He had a temper and, while he may not have subscribed to the teutonic tradition of his own university days at Heidelberg, Germany, where one bowed obsequiously to "Herr Professor," he was still hard on his people, and he knew it.

"I won't be kind to you," he remembered telling one former associate when they started working together—he was not. That was the way he got his people "not to be stupid."

HANS KOSTERLITZ IN GOLDBERG (1988, P. 10)

Developing your leadership skills and style is a process, not a project. With each new project, with each new person, and with time, you will modify your style and come to be more and more comfortable with yourself and with your role as P.I. Finding the right balance is very, very difficult in the beginning, so do not fight yourself. Below is a list of skills and qualities that will help in being an effective P.I.:

> *I've given a lot of thought to my managing style. I know that you have to manage the lab in the framework of your own personality. I am doing it according to the only style I can follow, myself.*

- Good communicator

- Politically astute: knows how the organization works, how science works

- Problem and conflict solver: the perspective and the insight to see different sides of a story

- Good scientist: knowledge, experience, and able to see big picture

- Ambitious

- Energetic

- Optimistic

- Sense of humor

- Insightful

- Flexible

- Take risks: put other people on projects

- Well organized

- Take criticism and suggestions

- Resilient

- Mature

For example, if you are not flexible, focus on your resilience. If you are not a quick thinker, spend more time reading and writing grants. Develop new skills as needed, but work with your strengths. Keep in mind your idea of the kind of leader you want to be.

INFLUENCES ON YOUR LEADERSHIP STYLE

Here was the essential paradox again. I was supposed to be the leader and decide what was going to happen, yet everyone wanted decisions to be made democratically. It was possible, just barely possible, but still a difficult task.
BIOCHEMIST AND ANNAPURNA EXPEDITION LEADER
ARLENE BLUM (1980, P. 116)

Delbrück succeeded in creating at Cold Spring Harbor that spirit of ceaseless questioning, dialogue, and open-armed embrace of a life in science which he had learned from Niels Bohr—but with a down-to-earth American character and a good measure of his own high-minded intolerance of shoddy thinking.
JUDSON (1996, P. 48)

Power may not be something you ever wanted to think about. But now you have it—not enough, it will seem to some, and way too much, it will seem to others. Acting like a postdoc and feeling like a student should not detract from the fact that you are responsible for yourself, a project, a lab, other people, and the future.

The sooner you deal with your feelings about power, the better, as you will then be able to communicate your expectations to the lab members. Do you want power over yourself and

> *You can't be too hard-assed at a big university, you must get the reputation of being kind.*

your immediate realm only? Are you comfortable having power over the people in your lab? Why or why not? If you believe that you should have no power, that you are just another member of the team, you may actually just be uncomfortable with the power, and should know why: Do you dislike being responsible for another person's future? Do you feel scientifically incompetent to manage other people's careers?

Some of the questions of management style have to do with the source of your authority (Lientz and Rea 1998, pp. 100–101). Why do the people in the lab respect you? Why do you want them to respect you? There are two types of authority:

- **Authority derived from scientific ability.** For postdocs and students to the lab, this is your usual source of power and respect.

- **Formal authority**. You are the official boss, and thus, it is your role to make decisions and decide issues. However, this type of authority is best used infrequently to be effective, and because it does not encourage creativity.

As an extension of formal authority, your ability to reward and penalize might also be the source of your power. Again, this authority cannot be used too much to remain effective. Respect is the best way to hold power in a good lab. Partially because of your scientific ability, but more because of the mutual decision of the lab members that you are the best leader, authority granted through respect is the ideal situation.

Control: Micromanaging versus hands-off

You cannot control all aspects of the lab. This is one of the hardest lessons that a P.I. must deal with: You cannot make everything happen the way you want it to. Do you want to be involved with details, or do you think lab members should plan and figure everything out themselves? This decision depends not only on your propensity to enjoy details or not, but also on your faith in the people you work with. With inexperienced lab personnel and a limited budget, many new P.I.s find that they must watch out for every detail. Even without a micromanaging personality, letting lab members flounder until they work things out is a luxury few can afford, and new lab heads tend to set the course in detail.

> When I ask lab members to do something they don't enjoy doing, I rarely demand something if it's truly objectionable. It's always a matter of discussion and consensus.

The temptation to grant unearned independence is a seductive one! After all, this would buy you a lot of time to think and raise money. But, in the beginning, you must make sure that everything is done the way you want it. Later on, you can give in to your desire to manage details or not. However, be sure that a hands-off style does not disguise a lack of confidence to lead or to do science.

Can a boss be a friend?

...At staff meetings, Roberta generally opens discussion of issues by asking all staff members for their opinions. She invites debate about the pros and cons of proposals, but somehow, when the meeting ends, they always end up deciding—by consensus—to do what Roberta thinks best. The women on the staff are happy with Roberta as a director. They feel she listens to their points of view, and they like the rule by consensus rather than fiat. But Morton feels Roberta is manipulative. If they are going to do what she wants anyway, why does she make them waste their breath expressing opinions? He would prefer she just lay down the law, since she is the boss.

TANNEN (1991, P. 216)

The postdoc is a social time. Part of the enormous fun of being a postdoc is the camaraderie with other people in the lab, and it is hard to give up. Do you have to? Yes and no. You can act and can even truly believe that you all are equals, performing different parts in the dance of science, but it is you who ultimately has the power to fire or promote the lab worker. Your relationship with the people in your lab is not equal. You are the boss. For no matter how smoothly your lab functions as a team, you are the ultimate authority.

I think there has to be a bit of separation there...you don't want to be just one of the gang. It's one of the reasons I don't have such fun as the head of the lab. I loved it when I was a postdoc and a student and could schmooze with everyone and it was kind of a family. All of a sudden, you are alone...you have your peers, but they are also busy...I'm friendly with the people in the lab, and we have organized social things, but it isn't the same.

For some people, most of the inspiration and joy of science is in the relationships and friendships. They cannot *not* be friends with people. But many new starting assistant professors have said that trying to be friends with people in the lab was one of the biggest initial mistakes they made. Those who found that intimacy with lab workers was a mistake usually made the mistake of playing favorites. Criticism or making unpopular changes in the lab becomes more difficult, as you can be seen not as a leader, but as a traitor.

Can a boss even be a colleague?

Although it is difficult to realize that a close friendship with a lab member may bring problems, it is harder yet for new P.I.s to grasp that they might not even be able to be colleagues in the way they are used to.

New P.I.s yearn for a colleague. Science is communication and having someone to toss ideas back and forth with is not only pleasurable, but a necessity. Yet few of the members hired in the first few years in any lab will be the P.I.'s scientific equal, and treating people as if they were your scientific equal almost always backfires. You are the leader, and members of the lab are there to learn from you.

There was a familiarity that was hard to overcome. I was one of them. It was hard to take a leadership position, for they questioned me more vociferously than they do now.

In a few years, the P.I. will be able to have more equal scientific relationships with lab members. People in the lab will mature and give as much if not more to a project than the P.I. In addition, as the quality of applicants improves with the P.I.'s track record, a relationship as a scientific confidante and equal will be more grounded in reality.

What if you are not interested in people?

Perhaps you believe that your job is to think about the science, not to be a babysitter. Maybe you have no rapport with people and are not interested in developing one; perhaps you think that you have come this far without catering to anyone, and can carry on like this for the rest of your career. Maybe you are right. If you find the right pocket of research (a well-funded but noncompetitive field) and the right place (one that will continue to fund you with few results, with no requirements for you to teach or tutor) you will probably do okay.

Can you learn to connect with people, even if you never have? *Yes*. It might always be an effort for you, but you can get ever more better at it. Some people have a gift for dealing with people. Do not be discouraged by the ease with which a "natural" can handle personnel problems. You must just find the level of interaction that works for you.

Stop Putting Out Fires!

TIME IS A RESOURCE, NOT THE ENEMY

I think that a balance can be achieved by making priorities—in my (personal) experience, scientists are notorious for being unable to say "No!" and are very poor managers of their (limited) time. This leads progressively to an over-burdened, overworked, harassed and distracted individual who has no time for lab or family.

CAVEMAN (2000, P. 32 IN
"WHO IS MENTORING THE MENTORS?", PP. 32–33).

There was so much time in graduate school and in the postdoc lab, time to enough to squander—Time to redo experiments if they did not work, to work and rework the draft of a paper, and even to go out to eat and talk and drink with friends and colleagues. If the experiments did not work all week, well, there was always another week.

And there was money. Even if the lab had to be extremely careful with money, its members probably did not need to worry. All were free to fiddle and experiment and give free reign to the realm of creative science, and even if they had to count how many 50-ml conicals were used, they could sleep at night without obsessing about funds.

But there will never be enough time to do everything running a lab seems to require. This is a new ball game. New P.I.s are staggered by the demands of organizing not only their own experiments, but also those of the other lab members. Instead of having a lab of helpers, you have a lab of people who need your help. Furthermore, the time that compliance, administrative, and fund-raising duties take from their "real" jobs is seldom anticipated by new P.I.s. Below is a partial list of the P.I.'s responsibilities that is quite sobering:

- *Good science, good projects.* This is the main reason people will come to your lab. You lab works on an interesting project, and lab members learn marketable skills: Students and postdocs know that working on a project in your lab may help them get a job.

- *Motivation.* You are the heart and soul of the lab. Period. When students get depressed about their projects, you must convince them that such disillusionment is part of science and that it must be turned into a benefit. When someone is about to be scooped, you are the one that sometimes must provide the push. And you are the one who must decide when a lab member may not have the internal motivation needed to be successful.

- *Organization.* The framework for the laboratory allows research to be done as smoothly as possible. You are the architect of the functioning lab and must decide issues as diverse as the kind of research to do, as well as who should be in charge of making 20x SSC.

- *Fund-raising.* Whether in academia, where you must write a grant, or in industry, where you must justify continuance of a project, your job will be to obtain the money and resources needed to keep the lab going. Equipment, supplies, and salaries are your responsibility.

- *Publicity.* The scientific community must be kept informed of your results, which is done by writing papers and reviews and giving talks at meetings. Politics are heavily involved here, as with most aspects of your job, since societies and institutions may not be knocking at your door. You must convince the world of the importance of the research.

- *Administration.* Writing letters of recommendation, convincing the animal welfare department that you need extra mouse cages, having funds shifted from one grant to another, and dealing with Human Resources for visa and other employee-related issues are all examples of administrative tasks that are seldom considerations of the job but which can take enormous amounts of time.

- *Vision: Setting the course.* You must keep up with the field to make strategic project decisions. Researchers must know their subject, but you must provide the prospectus for each project. Reading the literature, going to talks, and networking like crazy are the main ways to learn enough to make scientific decisions for yourself and your lab.

- *Correction/criticism.* This is part of teaching, but it requires a skill different from that of imparting knowledge. You must be able to give negative advice in a beneficial way, to guide projects and behavior without inciting anger or shame.

- *Teaching.* In a new lab, you will have to teach techniques and methods to newcomers. In addition to the care of the lab, you may also have responsibilities to teach classes or lab courses. There are enormous returns for teaching, but it takes a lot of time.

- *Recruiting.* Quality people are hard to find, and you must always be on the lookout for good people. When you find them, you must do everything you can to get them.

- *Mentoring.* You will teach some or all of your lab members not only how to conduct research, but also how to navigate the personal and political mine fields that are the basis of academic and company life.

- *Departmental and institutional duties.* You were hired to run a lab, but the demands of the organization can often take up not the least of your time, but the bulk of your time. You may run a core facility, or teach several courses, or have clinical duties. You may have to entertain donors or potential investors, or organize the itinerary and visas of visiting researchers.

Managing time perhaps once seemed to be something that *managers* had to deal with, not creative bench scientists. Managing time was what you did when you were not smart enough to fly by the seat of your pants. There are those who believe time is their master and that to organize time is to give in to its demands. But if you do not control time, it will control you.

Time is not just the future, it is not something to fight against—it is a resource you must work with and manipulate to achieve your goals. Think of it as an expensive and precious reagent which you use to do more of the things you want to do, and less of the things you do not want to do. Listed below are some P.I. time complaints:

- I never have time to do the tasks I want, I always do what everyone else wants.

- I procrastinate.

- I am always interrupted.

- I work too hard and seem to go nowhere.

- I can't organize.

All of these complaints can be helped by clearly knowing your priorities and goals, organizing to achieve them, and not letting life get in the way!

SETTING PRIORITIES

Decide how you want to spend your time or it will be decided for you. You will end up doing crisis management, at the whim of anyone with a pressing need, instead of doing what is important to you. Creativity will end up at the bottom of the priority list unless you take control and make your own decisions about spending time.

Prioritize everything. Deciding what tasks are the most important is the most difficult part of managing your time. Once your priorities have been made, all other steps fall in place. Not everyone will prioritize in the same way: The way you categorize your needs and tasks is one of the hallmarks of your managing style.

> *I consider myself reasonably well-organized, but not obsessive-compulsive about it. I generally "go with the flow" most of the time, but plan my time more closely when there is a heavy workload or impending deadline, particularly for study section reviews or my own grant submissions.*

What is "important"?

It takes planning to know what is important. It also takes adjusting your priorities because what is important now will change as your lab grows and your career develops. An established 5-year plan will help you to decide what factors are important for achieving your goals.

Importance and urgency

An effective way to analyze each task is through Stephen R. Covey's Time Management Matrix (Covery 1989, p. 151). Variations on this matrix, which classifies tasks according to their urgency as well as importance, appear in many management books and are a simple and direct way to deal with both work-related and personal responsibilities and to separate your "wants" from your "needs" in the lab. The goal of this prioritization is to spend as little time as possible doing the things you do not want to do and to have as much time as possible to do the things you do want to do.

TIME MANAGEMENT MATRIX

	Urgent	Not urgent
Important	I Crises, personal or professional Pressing personal or equipment problems Deadline-driven projects	II Reading journals Relationship building Lab meetings Thinking and planning Recreation and relaxation
Not Important	III Interruptions, some calls Some mail, some reports Some meetings Many administrative tasks	IV Trivia, busywork Some mail Some phone calls Most e-mail and Web-surfing

Adapted, with permission, from Covey (1989).

Urgent and important. Some matters are inherently urgent and important and must be handled as soon as possible. A health crisis for yourself, family, or a lab member is an obvious example. Redoing the figures for a manuscript in order to get it published is urgent and important.

A grant proposal is important: A grant proposal not started until a week before the deadline is urgent and important. Most deadlines appear to be urgent and important, but few start out that way. It is procrastination as well as not recognizing the importance of a task that sends many important jobs to the urgent and important and desperate classification.

Not urgent and important. When P.I.s complain that they have no time, they usually mean that they do not have time to do the important things. These are often the tasks involved in maintenance and in avoiding problems in the future, and so are easy to put off. The key is tackling not urgent but important tasks while they are still manageable. For example, setting aside time to discuss a project with a new lab member is important. It may seem that there will be plenty of time in the future to have the discussion, but you may lose lab members or they could become mired in a sea of useless and expensive data if not done in time. Teaching a class may be important, as it might be the only way to get students interested in your institution. It might also not be important—you must decide.

The apparently least critical but most important task is to give yourself time to think. Most P.I.s complain that they never have time to think, or to talk to colleagues and lab members, or to read a journal. Unless you make the time, you will not have it.

Urgent and not important. It is not very easy to classify tasks as urgent and not important in the lab, as it is often a question of the lifelong necessity to do some things you do not want to do, and to know which ones these are and which can be dropped.

Reading someone else's research summary, although you have one due yourself in 1 week, is not immediately important to you—or it might be, if it is for a friend, or a boss. Attending a committee meeting in another department because you have missed the last six is urgent but not important.

Not urgent and not important. Busywork. Talking to someone you do not want to speak to. Attending some committees. Talking to a salesman when your lab manager would be happy to do it. These are tasks that are generally poor investments of time.

There are other ways to prioritize. You may prioritize in any number of ways: the Covey Time Management Matrix is simply one graphical interpretation. In any system, you will instinctively "nest" what you must do, i.e., breaking larger priorities into smaller priorities.

- ***You may prioritize by project.*** Give the largest amount of time to the project you have deemed to be most important, and less time to projects of lesser importance.

- ***You may prioritize by time.*** If you have many tasks of similar importance, do them in order of the date they are due.

Know when to let go of your priorities. You know your priorities and have made your lists, but an emergency or opportunity may arise and, sometimes, it just makes sense to let go of your plans. Perhaps a lab member who has never opened up to you before suddenly starts to explain plans for a project. Maybe a colleague from graduate school appears at your office door. If you know it is an opportunity and not an excuse, change your plans and do not look back. You can reprioritize tomorrow.

Keeping a log

Scientists would not write a grant or change the entire direction of their research without experimental evidence. Yet most people make decisions about the use of time based only on a "feeling" about how it is spent. Keeping a log for a day or, better still, a week, will provide the data needed to decide what changes in the organization are most important and are likely to be the most effective.

Before starting a log, estimate how much time you spend on the phone, reading, talking to lab members, or fulfilling administrative tasks. Then, for 1 week, record the task as soon as you do it. The smaller the block of time measured, the more illuminating. Record the events and tasks of the day either by time or by task. The smaller the time gap reported, the more data you will have; however, if recording so much detail will cause you to stop keeping the log, merely record your actions every hour or so. Also record your emotional response, if you can face that level of scrutiny! If you were overjoyed or depressed while engaged in a particular activity, write it down. Below is a list of questions for analyzing the log.

• What percentage of your intended jobs were actually completed?

• What jobs appear on your list, day after day, without completion?

• Is there a pattern—did you always, for example, finish tasks involving communication (meetings and phone calls) but seldom finish tasks involving writing?

• Is there a time of day when you accomplish more than at other times?

• Does place affect your performance—do you work more effectively in one place or another?

• Is there any indication that food, company, or any outside influence affects you?

A log, especially one listing tasks, will show how much time even small jobs can take. This will help you to make realistic lists.

FINDING YOUR OWN RHYTHM

Once you have prioritized what is needed to achieve your goals, you must set up your working world to maximize your time. Doing this at your favored speed is the first step. Perhaps you work in week-long bouts, staying up late to write and do experiments, and then spend a few days reading before swinging into high gear again. If you enjoy this, if it fits in with your life style, and you feel it is the most productive way for you to work, well, you are lucky, embrace it.

But with all of the new tasks you must do as a P.I., your old patterns may no longer work. Experiment with work styles and see how they work with your communication style. Try to find a working rhythm that will fit in with the lab and can be emulated; even the P.I.'s work style can end up as a source of inspiration for lab members. Below are examples of work styles:

• *Start hard, end easy.* Rather like eating your vegetables first, and rewarding yourself with dessert after, this style works on momentum and reward.

• *Start easy, end hard.* This is a way to trick yourself into getting into a project. By working first on the simpler part of a task, you gradually build up tolerance for the more difficult part.

• *Deadline fulfillment.* A single final deadline works for some; for others, staggered deadlines for each facet of a job might be preferable. Deadlines are not worth much unless they are taken seriously.

- ***Working in silence, or working with music.*** Some like to be closeted off, with no sensory input. For others, silence is too isolating and can be a distraction.

- ***Working alone, or working in collaboration.*** Isolation from people can also be a distraction to some, and an inspiration to others: For the latter, working on a table in the middle of the library is better than working in a cubicle or office.

- ***Doing one task all the way to the end, or multi-tasking.*** Completing one project at a time puts some in control, and bores others to tears.

- ***Working in bursts of time, or working in large blocks of time.*** Setting aside hours or days to work on a particular task or tasks suits those who take a long time to settle into a job, or get distracted by multi-tasking. Or work in short bursts of times. If you feel energized by a new project, or are easily bored, working on several projects at once over an extended period of time is probably best.

AVOIDING PROCRASTINATION

WUT= k exp (TL)

Or the warm-up time (WUT) necessary to return to a problem increases exponentially with the time that has lapsed (TL) since I last worked on it.

PAUL HUMKE IN REIS (1999)

Procrastination is the bane of running a lab. Since there are just too many things to do, it does sometimes seem that most details might just melt away if you wait long enough, but it does not often work out that way. If you can manage to prioritize effectively, procrastination is the next hurdle to tackle.

People do procrastinate and try occasionally to avoid doing something they do not want to do. But for many people—perhaps, for most people—procrastination is a chronic problem. There are good intentions, which repeatedly are broken. The fact that one apparently cannot keep to an agenda leads to feelings of self-doubt, which are usually suppressed by elaborate rationalization. And the cycle of delay goes on.

One psychologist (Sapadin and Maquire 1996, pp. 12–14) has outlined six styles of procrastination:

> *...I have found that I get unpleasant writing tasks done much easier if I adopt a "barf and buff" strategy: just write ANYTHING down, even if it is 50% total crap, then go back and edit it. You feel you have accomplished something in filling that terrifying blank page, and it is MUCH easier to modify something that exists (even if it needs to be drastically modified) than it is to create it out of whole cloth. And you get some idea of what you still need to do (ref, ideas, whatever) once you have something on the page.*

The Perfectionist: "...BUT I want it to be perfect!"
The Dreamer: "...BUT I hate all those bothersome details!"
The Worrier: "...BUT I'm afraid to change!"
The Defier: "...BUT why should I have to do it?"
The Crisis Maker: "...BUT I only get motivated at the last moment!"
The Overdoer: ".... BUT I have so much to do!"

There are many ways to procrastinate. Most of these are not obvious, and many masquerade as other traits in the lab. The P.I. must be able to recognize the problem for what it is—not a minor personal quirk that makes you what you are, but a debilitating pattern that can keep you from being what you could be. **Procrastination will get in the way of achievement like nothing else.** For example:

- You begin working on a grant only 2 weeks before it is due. Why? You think it is just because you did not have the time sooner, but it might be that an unfunded grant is better than the alternative: A grant worked on diligently for months, but still not funded. At least now you can say—and believe—that the grant would have been funded, had you more time to work on it.

- With grant submission time coming up, you stalk the offices of your colleagues asking for advice: Should we do more experiments? What do you think of these results? Should I submit to a different study group? Should I eliminate most of the preliminary results? Your solicitation for advice goes on for so long that there are few weeks left in which to write.

- You refuse to delegate parts of a project, not trusting anyone else to do the job correctly. Letters pile up on your desk.

- You are doubtful of your own theory on a competitive project and hesitate to put a lab member full time on the project, instead of checking and rechecking the validity of preliminary experiments.

- You have known for months that you will be presenting your latest results at an international meeting in the spring. Not a slide has been made, not a word has been written, but suddenly, 1 week before the plane leaves, the entire lab is drawn into the battle to make the figures for the slides. You leave like a conquering hero.

- You ignore the repeated requests for a letter of recommendation needed by a student in the lab. On the day before the grant is due, you write a wonderful letter, and send it to the appropriate agency by Federal Express.

- You are on three departmental committees, five thesis committees, and a study section. You also teach two courses and act as a mentor to many of the undergraduates in your classes. You have cancelled lab meetings for the past 2 months, and lament the fact, but you feel much more comfortable when everyone is asking your personal advice than in interpreting experiments.

Simply put, procrastination is the difference between your priorities and your results. Recognizing what you are doing is the first and most difficult step in solving the problem of procrastination. How to help yourself over the hurdle and keep working will be different for each reason that you procrastinate and for each particular task. The bottom line here is to *keep working*. Do not stop, do not talk, and do not complain. Start with small pieces of the project and just keep batting away. If you delay too long in finding a solution, you might become demoralized and conclude that the project was not worth doing. Other techniques for dealing with procrastination:

- *Divide a large task into smaller pieces.* Do not sit down to write a whole paper—do the "Methods" section. If that seems too big for you, divide the task into three methods to write up that evening.

- *Make an arbitrary start.* If you are so daunted that even dividing a job into smaller sections seems to be too much, just do something. Type the title page. Read one paper for a review. Chip away, and the path will quickly become clearer.

- *Set deadlines.* You are not going to be fooled by an artificial deadline, so make smaller deadlines for particular jobs.

- *Reward yourself.* Promise yourself a walk or phone call or treat.

- *Be flexible to keep interested.* Do a difficult part of the project one day; do a mindless part the next.

- *Set a deadline with another person for the completion of a task.* Promise a colleague that you will have a paper ready to be read in 1 week, and, as you should do for all such arrangements, make sure you do have it ready for reading in 1 week.

- *Work by ritual.* Follow a standard plan of action for each and all tasks. This does not allow you to fuss about getting into a project or to question your approach: A ritualized start to problem-solving provides comfort in the early, precommitment part of each task. You may, for example, always begin writing a grant, manuscript, or letter with the concluding paragraph, or you may write a one-paragraph summation of each meeting you go to.

To stamp out procrastination, long-term, develop strategies like those given above to deal with *your style* of procrastination. Avoid the tendency that most scientists have to overrationalize everything. You know when, regardless of the arguments you give yourself, you are not doing what you should be doing. If it takes checking into a hotel to write a grant, do it.

- *Making no decision is a decision.* Be sure to differentiate between dreams and goals, and carefully write down and plan projects with defined steps and finishing times. Run through the list with a friend or mentor.

- *Recognize the difference between priorities and demands.* Distinguish between what you want to do, and what others want you to do. Learn to delegate.

- *Do not create a crisis!* Enough crises will arise during your P.I. tenure that it does not make sense to generate more. Accept that you may not be interested in a particular project or plan in the beginning, and just keep plugging away.

Warning! There are times when procrastination is a hint that you really should not be doing a particular task. For example, you may be delaying the writing of a letter of recommendation for a student you do not like. Perhaps it is not because the task is distasteful, but because you just cannot write the helpful letter the student expects. In this case, you should tell the student that you are not able to write the letter. The sooner you can realize the reasons for your procrastination, the better. The burden of not doing something is much heavier that the burden of doing it.

BEING A PERFECTIONIST

Perfectionism can be a very useful trait for a scientist. Making sure a grant proposal is absolutely slick before it is handed in is an asset of perfectionism. Never forgetting the appropriate control in an experiment is another. Research success often comes down to awareness and attention to details, and the desire to get things just right fuels many projects.

But being a perfectionist can also cause many problems. Many people do not recognize that they are perfectionists, since, as for most traits, a person may be a perfectionist in some aspects of life, but not in others. Many apparently organized P.I.s, with computerized schedules and neat to-do lists, may not remember what project their postdocs are working on. Other P.I.s who run a lab like a navy submarine and can calmly and firmly fire an incalcitrant person in the lab may spend days fretting over a political situation in the department, calling dozens of people to ask for advice.

In fact, this pattern of being unable to make a decision often is part of perfectionism, as the perfectionist may feel a lack of competence in some areas and desperately scurry to compensate, not wanting to make a mistake. People are perfectionists for many reasons, and a lack of self-confidence is a major cause. The idea that perfectionism can mask a lack of confidence sounds counterintuitive, but it may not always be the case. It is easier to understand if you think about perfectionism and procrastination, when the inability to say a job is completed stops one from actually completing it.

Being a perfectionist will also influence how you deal with the people in your lab. Perfectionists often expect other members in the lab to be perfect. The productive side of this is that a perfectionist P.I. may draw the very best from the lab people, with the expectation that each person can do a tremendous job. For some people, this confidence is very motivating.

But the flip side is that the perfectionist P.I. can be terribly frustrated when others do not act as expected or live up to what the perfectionist assumes all people should do. This frustration can easily evolve into bitterness and pettiness, with the P.I. wondering why no one in the world cares about research the way I do.

A perfectionist often has trouble delegating, believing that no one will do the task appropriately—appropriately being, of course, the way the perfectionist P.I. would do it. The perfectionist simply ends up with more work than can be done merely adequately, much less perfectly. This leads to more frustration. However, if you take stock and take control of your motivation and expectations, many of the liabilities of perfectionism can be turned to assets. When you feel angry that a job is not going right, try to gain some perspective by considering:

- What are your expectations? Are they reasonable?
- Do you think other people in the lab find your expectations reasonable?
- If so, what in them is preventing them from doing the job?
- Would an outside person find these expectations reasonable?
- What would happen if you did not do the job?

A deeper analysis of perfectionism and the ways of dealing with it is covered in *Never Good Enough: Freeing Yourself from the Chains of Perfectionism*, by Monica Ramirez Basco (1999).

Time savers

Delegation

One of the hardest parts of running a lab is to learn to depend on other people as well as on yourself. This requires confidence and trust, and it is likely that little in your training prepared you for this. If anything, independence and not cooperation was stressed, and now, you must depend on people who might not even be trained.

There are several levels of delegation, the physical and the intellectual. The physical is usually the easiest to deal with. This is the delegation of tasks, usually to a technician in the beginning. Trivial tasks, of course, are the simplest to delegate: Many P.I.s are overjoyed to be able to ask someone to pour plates or clean a freezer, and people expect to receive these orders. It is expected that the P.I. will appoint someone in the lab to be in charge of lab safety and someone else to have the job of making a seminar list. But as even the physical tasks can require decision-making, delegation gets harder.

For example, for how long will you plan experiments for a lab member? For how long will you write rebuttal letters to editors for a lab member's paper? You are training scientists, after all. Every time you add an item to your "To Do" list, consider delegating the task. If you cannot delegate the whole task, delegate part of it. If you are writing a review, ask someone to find the key references and do a first draft, for a shared authorship. Whenever you have combined training with a relief from your own workload, you will considerably improve your own morale, and probably the morale of the whole lab. Do not miss the chance to lighten your load and add to the positive feelings in the lab.

Learn to read faster

Reading faster will help you work faster. Most people believe they cannot read faster, but speed-reading is more of a physical trick than a mind trick. You first learned letters and were then able to read a collection of letters as one unit: It is easy to train your eyes to see a larger unit, a group of words.

The Evelyn Wood Seven-Day Speed Reading and Learning Program, by Stanley Frank (1990), is a step-by-step guide that can double your reading speed and increase your comprehension. Through a series of hand motions, you learn to scan a page and can easily boost your reading speed in very few sessions.

Stop one-finger typing

You will probably be doing a lot of typing: Even with a secretary, there will be e-mails and some correspondence that must be personally answered. Voice recognition systems are improving. You may be dreaming of the day when you can dispense with the keyboard altogether. In the meantime, however, a few minutes a day learning to touch-type will be a great investment for the next few years.

A typing computer program can teach you the keyboard, which alone will improve your speed, even if you decide never to progress enough to be able to type without looking at the keyboard. *Mavis Beacon Teaches Typing* is an enjoyable and easy to use program.

Avoid interruptions

- *Do not answer the phone if you are working.* Listen to messages at an appointed time, or screen all calls.

- *Close your office door sometimes!* Even if you have an open door policy, set aside times when you are not to be disturbed. If you do this regularly, and make no exceptions other than emergencies, no one will be offended. The library or conference room or home can also be used for privacy, but it probably will not be as efficient as your own office, most of the time.

    At the minimum, define with whom you follow the open-door policy. You can restrict the audience to people in the lab and have other P.I.s, departmental members, salespeople, or students make appointments.

- *Stop being such a good listener about personal issues.* When someone drops by, set the time frame. After the person makes the point and gets into chitchat, get up gradually and walk to the door. Do not add to the conversation. Even nodding and saying "hummmm" can keep a conversation going. This does not mean you can no longer have casual chats or lose an easy-going and confiding intimacy with people. But, even at the risk that you will no longer be as "popular," or considered to be as "nice," you must not be at the mercy of every story that every person wants to tell you. Without being cold, you can forestall a string of stories with a simple "How about later? I have to go do something now." Just try to be sure that your antennae are always out for real need—some people may approach you casually for a conversation of the deepest importance to them.

- *Say no.* If you know you cannot do something, say no as quickly as you can. Making excuses, or saying you will get back with your answer later, just leaves you to carry an extra burden, an extra task. It makes it seem as if you are negotiating. "No" does not have to be harsh, but you do have to be firm without offending anyone. You must know your reasons for saying no, and once you do, do not let guilt change your mind. A simple "No, I cannot do that now" will usually suffice.

    Be prepared for situations that you suspect will arise. For example, if your project leader asks you to head a committee you know it will do no good to be on, what will you say? If a technician who is always late requests an extra day off, what will you say?

Using Your Time

MAKING IT EASIER TO MANAGE TIME

Motivating yourself to take control of time is the hardest task. But you will keep yourself on track by making it easy to follow your priorities. By setting up the physical environment and your daily activities, you will not have to be constantly reinventing the wheel (a common action of procrastinators).

Although it may seem unprofessional, it is usually best to keep only one to-do list and calendar for both personal and work-related tasks. Most people have their work and home lives integrated somewhat, and the use of more than one calendar means that items will be left out. However, if your schedule is coordinated with a secretary or other departmental members, a work-only calendar is called for.

The calendar and the to-do list are the heart of any time management system. You need a calendar to keep track of your appointments, and a to-do list to keep track of your priorities. Daily or weekly formats are available, but most P.I.s are too busy to get away with a weekly format. The best way is often to combine a daily calendar and a to-do list on the same page.

Choose your format for organization: Paper or computer

Although electronic devices are often presumed for time management use, they do not work for everyone. In addition, if the method of time management does not suit your personality and work style, you will very soon abandon it.

Paper

Consider a paper-based organizing system if you are visual person, often write notes to yourself, and dislike being bound to a machine. With a simple notebook, or a paper-based planner such as Filofax or Day-Timer, little time will be spent learning a system, and you will be able to record notes and make appointments as you go.

The main disadvantage of paper-based systems is that often there is only one copy of the information in the system, and the loss of that one copy can be disastrous. One solution is to carry a small book with you and then transfer the information to an office-bound book on a regular schedule. You must be completely disciplined for this to work. All systems break down with more than one version of information, so you cannot let a day go by without making sure that all information is current in both books.

Computer

If you are comfortable with computers, and with typing rather than writing information, or if your schedule is very complicated or needs to be shared or communicated to others, you will be better off with a computer-based organizing system. A computer program allows you to have multiple views of the information, e.g., a list of daily, or weekly, or monthly appointments. This is a very important tool for prioritization, as you can see the long-term picture as well as the daily and more focused one.

Computer systems are subject to failure, and you must be assured of always having the information backed-up. You must also have your own computer: If you do not have access to your calendar or to-do list whenever you need it, the organizing system will soon disintegrate.

Personal information managers (PIMs)

PIMs are computer programs that help organize information, manage contacts, and coordinate schedules. They usually have a calendar and to-do lists and a place to make notes. They hold phone numbers and can dial for you. To some extent, they can organize projects. Some can also track e-mail messages. Calendars and schedules can be sent to other people via the Internet. Hand-held organizers can exchange information with most PIMs, making it possible to carry your calendar with you and keep that information synchronized with your computer in the lab.

Coordination with hand-held computers

Good hand-held electronic organizers contain a calendar, to-do list, address and phone listings, and a place for notes and memos. They are scaled down but powerful, and either run the same PIM as your computer or can exchange information with your computer PIM. With a modem, an infrared port, or another computer port, the information on the hand-held can be synchronized with the information on the computer. This means that you not only have a way to synchronize information with your base computer or with a secretary, but also always have at least two copies of vital information.

STARTING THE DAY: THE DAILY TO-DO LIST

Every morning, as soon as you get to work, sit down and make a list of everything you want to accomplish that day. The list can be made the night before, but make sure to sit down and read it in the morning. It may help you to group your list into areas and to tackle them in that order. You might make a list of e-mails you must return, or group together the names of people you want to talk to that day. It is also important to make note of which items should be handled first.

Making the list is not enough to fix your life—you have to actually do what is on the list. To make the list functional, you must be committed to following it. And to follow it, you must make the list realistic and doable, and avoid depressingly recopying the list, day after day.

- List only about 10 items, and, if you finish all 10, you can always add other items.
- List only doable tasks. Do not put down "Write review"—you are not likely to write an entire article in a morning. Put down "Start introduction of review."
- Check or cross off each item as it is done.
- Reevaluating an undone item before putting it on the list for the next day will allow you to decide if it is still a number 1 priority or not as important as you once thought.

Make use of small pieces of time. Keep a list of tasks that can be squeezed into pieces of unscheduled time. The trick is to keep the job small—do not try to desperately squeeze 10 items into as few minutes.

10 minutes:

- Make one phone call.
- Read one paper.
- Clear the top of your desk.
- Go through one folder of "Favorites" for Web Sites; discard those not visited in 6 months.

30 minutes:

- Do a Web search on one topic.
- Clean one drawer.
- Meet a colleague for coffee.

Do not waste unexpected "free" pieces of time. Occasionally—way too occasionally!—someone will cancel an appointment or you might get to work 15 minutes earlier than usual. The first temptation is to do nothing, and to feel luxuriously for those few minutes no constraints on your time, at all. But then the time is over, and all your problems and tasks are still there anyway, and the moment of peace is gone.

On the other hand, using that time for an important but not urgent task gives you more than the 15 minutes of breathing space to take one item off that list that is always percolating in your subconscious. Listed below are examples of one productive use of just a few minutes:

- Walk with a student from the lab to discuss a paper.
- Get rid of the e-mail messages in your outbox, making sure that you have all the needed addresses.
- Clean one desk drawer.

The possibilities are endless, of course. But geting into the habit of using even small pieces of time as a gift can at least free the spectre of wasting time.

STREAMLINING CORRESPONDENCE

Letters

Letters, not read or read and unanswered, can accumulate very quickly. The trick is to deal with each quickly and to never, never deal with a letter more than once.

Answer the day's mail as part of the day's routine. If you let it pile up, to take care of when you feel like it, you will most likely have such an accumulation of paper that it will be impossible to deal with in a timely or satisfactory way. Open the mail, and deal with each letter as you open it, doing one of two of the following:

- *Throw the letter away.* Think honestly and quickly. If you are not going to attend that seminar, throw the seminar notice away. If you are not interested in updating a piece of equipment now, throw away the special offer. When you are ready, you will find out what you need to know.

- *Act on the letter.* If there is a request for a reagent, pass the letter on to the person responsible. If you are the person responsible, either get up and start the preparations for sending the letter, or put the letter aside to be acted on at a scheduled time.

Filing is a subset of acting on the letter, not an alternative to action. In the lab, you will receive little mail besides invoices that need to be filed away in a paper cemetery.

e-mail

Electronic clutter can make your life as difficult as reams of paper, and your e-mail correspondence is the prime culprit. Most people have file cabinets for letters and papers—they may not maintain the files, but there is, at least, the recognition for organization. Not so for e-mail.

- *Set up files for storage of e-mail.* For example:
    Active—incoming, unread mail arrives into the active file
    Personal
    Students
    Consulting—Company x
    Consulting—Company y
    Reference

- *Set up filters in your e-mail program to screen out advertisements.* Usually, on an institutional server, this will not be necessary.

- *Respond to incoming e-mail as soon as you receive it.* Do this by *answering the letter.* If you do not have a chance to answer appropriately, at least acknowledge receipt and say when you will be able to deal with it.

- *Remove letters from the active file.* Once action is taken, some letters can be simply deleted from the active file, but most letters will probably have to be saved. File them immediately in categorized folders.

- *Make a hard copy of critical e-mails.* File them as soon as they are printed.

- *Clear out the files.* At intervals, go through your files and dispose of anything that you do not need.

- *Clear out outgoing mail.* This does not and should not be done immediately. In fact, it is better to wait a week or so, until you are sure that the message has been received. But every 2 weeks or every month, go through the files and dispose of unneeded outgoing mail.

Back up your e-mail files regularly. Should you erase the original message when you reply? If you are responding to a particular letter, and especially if there are several points addressed, keep the original message with your reply.

Formal letters should not contain any other messages, even if the letter is in response to a particular e-mail question.

Some find letters on top of letters to be aesthetically displeasing. Unless you want to keep a record of the "conversation," or refer to a previous letter in your current one, remove the earlier letters.

Web Sites should also be organized. Set up folders to hold the main category of Web Sites, such as "Protocols," "Science Organizations," "News," and "Biotech companies."

Phone calls

Very seldom is there a good time for you to answer the phone. You will undoubtedly be on the phone longer than you might want to be. Set times for phone calls, both to make calls and to arrange for people to call you. Record the time in your calendar: Consider it to be scheduled.

- *Set up voice mail and/or answering machine.* Review your messages throughout the day.

- *Record the messages.*

- *Prioritize the messages.* List messages that require a call back on a separate list. Set aside a time each day for returning phone calls.

DEDICATE YOUR OFFICE

What is the main use of your office? The first thought is that it is the place in which to write and to deal with paper, but it is much more and should be set up to facilitate your needs. Truly consider your requirements, because even a basic item like a desk may not actually be necessary.

- *Mail and paperwork, reading, and writing.* You need a dedicated place to work, a desk for the computer and for paperwork. An alternative to a desk (or an addition to a desk) is a table. Especially if using a laptop computer, a table will give you the freedom to spread out papers, as well as a place to hold meetings.

- *Phone calls.* You need a phone and answering machine, access to your calendar and agenda, a place to take notes, and privacy.

- *Meetings.* Several chairs are all that you need. A table would be a bonus, as talking around a table rather than from across a desk tends to work much better for meetings.

- *A refuge.* Sometimes, a bit of privacy is all that you need to regain equilibrium. A chair or a couch is a great addition to any office. It is a place to read comfortably, to catnap, or even to spend an overnight during a grant deadline or a long experiment. It does, however, add an air of informality that may be inappropriate in some institutions or companies. Music can also be soothing or inspiring. Do not invest in too expensive a sound system, but equipment to play music and get the news is a good touch. Be sure you have earphones.

Maintain an organized office. Perhaps no other lab legend runs as deep as the one suggesting that a messy desk is a sign of creativity and that the owners really *can* put their finger on any piece of information on the desk at any time.

It is far, far more likely that a messy desk physically interferes with work, mentally interferes with enthusiasm, and broadcasts the fact that you are not on top of your paperwork. Yes, it can also suggest a charming irreverence for bureaucracy, but if you really were going to throw the papers away and really show them, you would have done so already.

Working with a Secretary/Administrative Assistant

IF YOU ARE SO FORTUNATE...

The administrative tasks and other paperwork needed to run a lab are usually the P.I.'s least favorite part of the job. If you are so fortunate as to have a secretary, tread happily and carefully. A secretary can relieve you of many of the administrative tasks that seem to sap your brain day after day and also be—and should be—a valued and valuable member of the laboratory. As half of a team with the P.I., secretaries will be privy to a lot of the dynamics of the lab, and their personality should also influence the lab character.

Secretarial salaries are often ridiculously low, too low to attract very competent people. In many places, secretaries will take a job as a way to get into an organization, and will then start applying for administration jobs or other secretarial positions.

What you can offer instead is (hopefully) a terrific work environment and the chance to get as much training as they can handle. This learning environment can be very motivating to people who are interactive and ambitious.

Find the right person to work with you by becoming part of the system for choosing. The hiring procedure for a secretary or administrative assistant will be done, as described in the Choose Your People section of this volume, through the Human Resources department. This is a very good idea, since there are likely to be more applicants for secretarial positions than for lab jobs. This is because secretarial applications are not as fine-tuned for each investigator as scientific hires and there are actually too few secretaries available. In addition, the process of going through many applications can be daunting.

Make yourself known at Human Resources. The better the people in that office know you, the better they will be able to match you with the right secretary. Many P.I.s do not feel comfortable judging the qualifications and training of a secretary or administrative assistant. The more applications you read, the more the relative qualifications will make sense to you. Cut down on the amount of prescreening you might do by having a very clear idea of the kinds of skills you need when you speak to Human Resources. This is a person you may be working with more closely than with anyone else in the lab, and it requires input from you to find a compatible personality.

WHAT CAN A SECRETARY DO FOR YOU?

Most P.I.s think of clerical tasks as filing, typing, and answering the phone. But carefully consider your needs and the tasks a secretary can do effectively to give you more time. Consider also the expertise of the secretary when deciding which tasks to delegate, as some jobs require more experience than others. Do not hire a highly experienced secretary to file papers. The best secretaries are highly proactive and do not like doing routine chores.

Tasks most secretaries can do:

- Typing letters, grant applications, and manuscripts.

- Filing letters, applications, course material, literature.

- Photocopying, running office errands.

- Answering the phone/answering machine, collecting information the P.I. needs to respond to the call.

> *When a secretary is doing a great job she is essentially invisible. The problem is, when she is invisible, she feels unappreciated.*

Tasks that require more experience to do:

- Prescreening mail.

- Making appointments.

- Setting up schedules for lab meetings.

> *I am trying to set things up so the secretary and technicians can do a lot of the administrative work. I don't consider myself to be a good administrator, and I don't want to invest in doing it.*

Tasks that require the most experience to do:

- Arranging your daily and out-of-town schedules.

- Screening phone calls.

- Doing searches, downloading searches into a computer reference base.

- Dealing with administrative issues, composing administrative letters.

- Tracking grant expenditures.

Tasks no secretary should be expected to do:

- Getting your coffee.

- Running personal tasks, e.g., picking up dry-cleaning or choosing personal gifts.

- Lying for you.

What do you need? If you are in the process of setting up a new lab, you need someone who can organize your office and make it more efficient for the future, someone adept at e-mail communication and word processing.

If you are in an extreme grant-writing time of your life, you require someone with skills in word processing and other programs to put together a grant. That person must have good communication skills to deal with the grants office and funding agencies.

If you are on the road a lot, you need someone to make appointments for you, arrange meetings, and keep a calendar, someone who can make decisions about priorities.

What you do not need is a bad secretary. Since you and a secretary work together as a team, your work styles must to be compatible or there could be constant tension. Although both styles do not have to be the same, they should complement each other and not clash. For example, if you are an orderly and methodical type and the secretary is a messy and spur-of-the-moment type, there will probably be trouble ahead.

Inefficiency, untrustworthiness, and lack of dependability are the signs that the secretary is not working out. A change in responsibilities may help—perhaps the secretary is underutilized or too stressed, and an adjustment is all that is needed.

EFFECTIVE DAY-TO-DAY WITH A SECRETARY

Routines

- Start your morning routine with a meeting with the secretary. Make sure that your schedules agree and that you are both clear on the day's priorities.

- Supply information of your whereabouts, and on any changes in the job or with any other information needed to do the job.

- Do not subvert the secretary's system. If it does not work for you, discuss it, but do not simply change things.

- Plan how the secretary will deal with interruptions to you. If people come by unexpectedly, who should prioritize and decide whether the visitor can see you? You or the secretary? Are there particular calls that will automatically be routed to you, no matter what is going on?

Manners

- Do not interrupt the secretary's work. Make a list of items you would like to talk about or have a prearranged time each day or week to discuss what must be done. You might even have an e-mail system set up. But phone calls and notes and casual stopping by with extra requests make it difficult for a person to stay organized and focused.

- Always say thank you.

Reporting lines

- Do everything you can to ensure that there is only one reporting line! Protect your relationship. P.I.s have found that, in administrative-heavy departments, the custom of having secretaries report to an administrator (who then deals with the P.I.) is very unsatisfactory. Negotiate to put the control back in your own hands, even if it means contributing money from your own grant instead of using departmental funds. This situation also makes it very difficult for some secretaries to become part of the lab; instead, they will feel part of the administration.

- If you do hire a work-study student to do clerical work, discuss with the secretary what that student will do. The student should then report to the secretary.

- Do not allow people in the lab to make demands of the secretary or administrative assistant. Not only does this set up an uncomfortable hierarchy within the lab, but it also can be very inefficient. If there is a special need, such as a grant deadline, the lab member should speak with you and you should then speak with the secretary. Do not give carte blanche to the needs of the lab members—define the secretary's jobs very precisely.

Privacy

- Set very strict lines to separate your public and personal life from your secretary's and vice versa. The nature of the job lends itself to intimacy and a lack of privacy, and it is essential that you develop your relationship to allow for warmth and caring, but without intruding into each other's lives.

- Leave out details. Perhaps one of you had an upsetting time at home that has affected your mood so much that you feel you must explain yourself. Do not go into details—it is enough to say that something at home disturbed you. Likewise, do not ask for details.

- Do not negatively discuss other lab members with the secretary or administrative assistant. This is harder to control than for lab members, for the relationship with the secretary is defined differently: The secretary is part of a team with you as well as a lab member. Do not put the secretary in the position of having to choose sides.

- Never ask a secretary to handle any personal information for you. It is easy to rationalize—it is tax season, I type too slow, consulting fees are part of work. But keep your private paperwork private. Some secretaries will offer assistance, truly wanting to simply help, but you may be initiating a situation that might ultimately become insulting and might compromise your privacy.

- If a secretary is keeping a schedule for you, some of your personal schedule will become known. Do not give any more details than necessary.

- A secretary is privy to very private records, such as recommendations for lab members. Before a new secretary starts, explain the absolute need to keep all information private. If a secretary does report to an administrator or other person, or also works as a secretary for others, information should not be exchanged between supervisors.

WITHOUT A FULL-TIME SECRETARY

The part-time secretary

In general, when new P.I.s are just starting out, it is likely that they only need a secretary for modest needs, and someone of little experience will be fine. The better trained a part-time secretary is, the better it will be all round. Then, instead of using that precious time for routine tasks, that person could help with more difficult organization tasks.

An alternative to a part-time secretary for clerical tasks is to hire a work-study student. Photocopying, distributing papers, and filing are jobs that can be taught with little training. Just being in a lab has turned out to be so interesting to some students that they return to take on more complex tasks.

With a part-time secretary, you should reassess every week the most productive use of that secretary's time for that week. If a grant is due, decide whether to ask the secretary to help with the grant or to pick up the slack in the wake of the grant.

Sharing a secretary

If you do not have a secretary at all, it is likely that you will share a secretary with at least one other P.I.: This is the situation with most new P.I.s. Sharing a secretary would appear to be the same as having part-time secretary, but the issue of dealing with other supervisors makes the shared secretary a situation unto itself. This situation can be a very, very difficult for all. The nature of the job is that people make

I don't know how to use a secretary. I share with a big shot, who uses her all of the time. She photocopies for me, but I write all the letters.

demands of the secretary that are not always reasonable. If more that one person is making these demands, any secretary might feel absolutely trapped. It becomes a very political situation, and some P.I.s, when given the choice between having to constantly battle another P.I. over priority and having access to a secretary, have given up the access to a secretary.

Since you will have this person's services for only a few hours a day, you must carefully prioritize what it is you need most to use these hours most effectively. This will be influenced by the way the secretary is shared and can be a very delicate negotiation.

All of the sharing partners must together designate the ground rules before deciding with the secretary how time will be parceled. What

I have a secretary for 1/6th of the time, and I sure need more time with her.

tasks will the secretary do for each person? How many hours of work a week can each lab member expect to be done? What leeway will each person grant for the crisis of another, and who will make that decision? What happens when one supervisor oversteps the bounds and makes unfair demands—to whom should the secretary go?

New P.I.s may come in on a situation of sharing and may not want to rock the boat. Although you do need to walk carefully, you must also make sure that the agreed-upon services will be available to you. This is important. The problems of a dual reporting line discussed above in the context of administrators apply here as well.

A shared secretary may be so inclined to play one supervisor against the other, and thus evade a great deal of work by claiming to be working for another at that time. But it is much more likely that the shared secretary is totally beleaguered.

MAKE THE SECRETARY PART OF THE LAB

The secretary is usually physically and mentally removed from the rest of the lab. Yet, few people in the lab are as irreplaceable. Set the tone with the other lab members that this person is a valuable member of the laboratory and must be treated with respect and courtesy.

The secretary does not necessarily have to sit on an island away from the rest of the lab. Depending on the tasks to be done, the lab might be a more reasonable place to be. For example, if one of the major jobs of the secretary is to process orders, it would work well to have the secretary accessible to the lab members, and not closeted with you.

Particularly if you are in an academic institution, it is likely that a secretary is terrifically underpaid. There are really only two main ways you can inspire, motivate, and reward a secretary: by providing the potential for new skills and advancement, and by making this individual a part of the culture and achievements of the lab.

If you can—if the secretary is not answering phones or working as a receptionist—try to be as flexible with hours as you are with the rest of the lab members. Always remember to include the secretary in lab get togethers, even for a science retreat or meeting. Even if the person declines, this acknowledgment as a member of the lab is usually greatly appreciated.

YOU AS YOUR OWN SECRETARY

Most new faculty members and company employees have no secretary and no funds for one, and, probably, no need for one. A desire, yes, but when most people think about it, they realize that they want a secretary because they want organization and structure. It seems easier to have someone else run the organizational tasks than to do them yourself.

There is a departmental secretary, who still types manuscripts for some people! But by the time I can explain something, I could have done it myself.

With good organization, a computer, and a phone answering machine or system, you will be able to get by for a few years without a secretary. Some times of the year will be frantic. Before grant deadlines, an extra pair of hands will be needed. This is when you pull in other lab members to help you write the grant, photocopy the grant, make figures, and proofread—or hire a temporary secretary.

Staying Integrated

AVOIDING ISOLATION

The early days are often exciting, but they can also be lonely and tense. Many new P.I.s start with the idea of doing groundbreaking science, but find within months that it is enough to survive and find funding and get home before midnight. During this time, P.I.s can become isolated, and lack of time is the usual cause. Most new P.I.s have moved to unfamiliar surroundings, and know few people, and the activation energy needed to create new ties becomes low priority.

It is easy to feel like an outsider

Research happens slowly when first starting a new lab, and some P.I.s think that they have nothing yet to offer to a colleague. New P.I.s in a not so active department may feel that they never have a chance to compete with the "real" people doing science elsewhere. Foreign born, female, or particular racial groups not well represented at the workplace may feel excluded. These feelings of inadequacy are common, and must be overcome. For the sake of the science, for yourself, and for the lab, it is vitally important that you stay connected to the rest of the organization and to the world outside the organization. Listed below are some ways to stay integrated:

> One mistake I made was in not asking for help or advice from a senior person or colleague because of fear of looking ignorant or of the person taking the project or the credit.

- Keep a high profile.

- Participate in departmental seminars and events.

- Meet with colleagues (try meeting with at least one colleague every week for lunch).

- Find a mentor.

Do not let lab members become isolated

Isolation is sometimes tempting but is usually poisonous. An us-against-them mentality can grow in a lab, especially when lab members are already feeling isolated by newness, inexperience, or geography. Although the P.I. and lab members may become close, the P.I. must take control to ensure that the lab does not become entrenched in isolation.

Make sure that your lab members attend classes, departmental meetings and parties, and at least some social events. Talk to them about the importance of building relationships within the organization, and lead by example. Introduce lab members to as many people as you can and include them in scientific conversations. Without communication and integration with the larger community, a lab member's career is extremely handicapped.

THE IMPORTANCE OF A MENTOR

The French biologist Andre Lwoff once wrote that "the scientist's art is first of all to find himself a good master."

PERUTZ (1998, P. 301)

Another thing that has been crucial to me has been mentors. I've been very fortunate in my career. I've always had mentors who gave me essential information that I lacked. I didn't have to seek them out. They made themselves known- little things like "if you need some help, come and see me," and they helped me to understand the organization. I once called a mentor, for example, raving about something that terribly upset me. He helped me to put the incident in perspective—to see the organization as a political entity.

THOMAS ET AL. (1992, P. 22)

Why a mentor?

You do not have to do everything alone. No matter how successful you are, mentors can help you. They can share their experience and save you from making the same mistakes. They can buoy you up when research seems more depressing than death and when you feel as incompetent as a first-year student. They provide the basis for a scientific network that you may be connected to for the rest of your life. They are role models for the kind of scientist and the kind of person you want to be.

What do you want in a mentor?

- *Success.* A mentor should be someone you admire, respect, and can learn from. In essence, when you choose a mentor, you are choosing the path you want to take. Mentors should be expert in their field. Just as the work in the lab is of primary importance in establishing the lab, so respect for a prospective mentor's research is of highest priority.

- *Connections.* The mentor should be politically savvy, aware that more than good science will be necessary for success.

- *Caring.* The mentor should be interested in mentoring and have the communication skills to work with you.

- *Integrity.* The mentor should be trustworthy and speak honestly. Your mentor should have a character you can admire, respect, and learn from. Your mentor's values should be complementary to your own; an added bonus would be similarity of or respect for your lifestyle choices.

> *I have been unable to find a mentor who can talk to me about what I need help with the most: the packaging of data. How do you put your own data together in the best way, how do you decide when to have a paper and how to present it?*

Who is a mentor?

A mentor can be anyone, peer or above, with whom you are comfortable at this stage of your life. The relationship can be a formal or informal, but you gain by having a formal mentor. It is an admission of asking for help, and you therefore need not feel embarrassed when asking for help, as you might in a friendship.

A mentor can be indistinguishable from a friend. You may have a network of friends with whom you can discuss problems and victories and never realize that you have a mentor. Do not choose someone for a mentor only because you believe this person can get you a promotion, grant, or job.

It is permissible and advisable to have more than one mentor. One person, whose position, accomplishments, goals, and personality are most compatible with yours, might be your primary mentor. You are unlikely to be the primary protégé of more than one person, at the same time. You will often have other mentors who fulfill one or two of your criteria for a mentor; one mentor might be someone who has gone through tenure in your department and guides you through that situation, another might have a home situation just like yours, and another has been in your scientific field forever.

It is very useful to have a mentor with whom you are comfortable enough to discuss some aspects of your private life, as well as with your career. There may be circumstances—race, culture, sexual orientation—that complicate your personal and scientific life and which you wish to discuss with someone who has experienced the same tensions. Discussing your private thoughts is not unprofessional if the person is the right person. Be careful of the assumption that because a person shares a particular characteristic with you, absolutely any subject will be open to discussion.

FINDING A MENTOR

Many institutions now have formal mentoring programs for new P.I.s, some more successful than others. Mentoring programs are notoriously difficult to run, with many, many more applicants than mentors available. If you have a good one at your institution, use it.

Most mentoring arrangements for P.I.s happen fairly informally and almost accidentally. You may be working with someone, and after a few months, you realize that more information than the technique you originally asked about is being passed on. A potential mentor may approach you. For example, someone in the department might notice you and offer advice about an experiment or a political situation at your organization. Accept all offers of help gratefully, and see where the interaction may lead.

> *They tried a mentoring program here, just for women, but all the women wanted it, and only 1 person volunteered to be a mentor. In the end, I got a clinician, and we didn't understand each other at all.*

With success, you will find more people who want you as a protégé. Some do this for their own agendas, wanting to promote someone within the system who furthers their own plans. Some will do it because they are more convinced that their efforts will be falling on fertile ground. Some simply do not notice you until you are successful.

- *Do not wait for someone to come to you.* If you see someone that you believe would make a good mentor, approach that person and ask for help with a particular aspect of your career. For example, you might ask for advice on the procedures for getting tenure at your university or for putting through grant applications in your institution.

- *Hire a mentor if necessary.* It is so important to have a mentor that, if you cannot find one, it is worth hiring one. You need someone who can give you objective opinions on very subjective issues and emotional issues, and hiring a management consultant—even out of your own pocket—is better than not having a mentor at all.

- *Start out small.* You cannot expect that, just by being asked, someone will be pleased to enter one of the primary, all-encompassing, master-protégé relationships that are so wonderful and helpful. This is a relationship that must evolve. Most of these relationships start out in a smaller way and then grow by tacit and mutual agreement.

- *Handling a refusal.* When you ask someone for help, be prepared for a refusal. If you are turned down, do not be bitter or cut that person off. It is much better to be refused than to be poorly mentored.

- *Informal mentoring.* A mentoring relationship does not have to be officially labeled as such. Some people are uncomfortable with a formal recognition of a mentoring relationship. They may fear the implied responsibility or may feel that the suggestion of inequality is not the kind of relationship they want.

THE MENTORING RELATIONSHIP

You should have specific goals to get the most out of the relationship and to save the time of the mentor. Both long-term and short-term goals are needed. The goals will depend on the person and the relationship: In a formal mentoring relationship, goals are discussed overtly, and in an informal one, they are more subtly suggested. Long-term goals might be political advice, personal advice, or scientific advice.

Before each get-together, no matter how informal an arrangement you have, it would help if you had a list of topics or even specific questions you would like to discuss. For example, your may want to know: How do I refuse to be on committees without offending anyone? I was refused for a grant—what should I do next? I'm having difficulty in balancing family demands and work demands.

Although you are going to a mentor for advice, go with strength. You are giving something to the mentor as well. You must value yourself. If you have the attitude that you have nothing to bring to the relationship, that you are not worth the trouble, you would be extremely lucky to find someone who would still take the time to mentor you. Mentors are not social workers or therapists.

Give back. This is a relationship, and you must always respect the needs of the mentor. Keep the mentor's goals in mind.

Reevaluate the relationship with your mentor

A good mentor may know even before you do that the situation is not ideal, but it is up to you to constantly reassess whether your expectations of the relationship are being met. Are you satisfying the needs of the mentor? Most people mentor because they want to pass on information and help, but only if it is needed and appreciated. Are you truly listening and is the advice you receive helpful? If so, are you giving your mentor the appropriate feedback? Are you satisfying the mentor's needs?

Mentoring can go bad. A mentor may actually go from being supportive to one who does more damage than good. In science, this may express itself as a mentor who takes credit for a project or experiment you have done. This may sometimes happen as your skills and capabilities approach those of the mentor, as some people are only comfortable helping someone who is clearly not an equal.

A sign that you should leave a mentoring arrangement immediately is if you find that the mentor has divulged private information. And, of course, hearing that someone you believe to be a mentor is bad-mouthing you is grounds for an immediate discussion.

More commonly, mentoring does not go bad; it just becomes less effective or rewarding for one or both parties.

Ending a relationship with a mentor

Some mentoring relationships are effective only at particular times and should be ended when they no longer work. How a mentoring relationship ends depends on the nature of the relationship: A formal relationship is best ended formally, and the informal relationship is best ended informally.

You may end a formal relationship by stating, e.g, "Thanks so much for the help with the lab, I think the problem is straightened out now. I have enjoyed our meetings, and hope you will come to me if there is anything I can do for you." Most informal relationships are ended by a gradual lessening of meetings, without acknowledgment. It is your call whether to allow the arrangement to end or to broach the topic by asking "Does this still work for you? Do you want to do something different? Shall we give it a break for a while?" Keeping avenues of communication open should always be a goal.

End all relationships with good will between you. Even if you think that the mentor's intentions were not realized, show your appreciation and stay cordial. Only deceit or sabotage merits a display of anger, and even then, you must be politically sure of your actions.

Pass on what you learn. Your interactions with your mentors, and with all those individuals you will mentor, will form the tightest link in your professional network. What you learn from your mentors becomes a part of you, and you can pass this knowledge onto other people. Personal details of the mentor, of course, should not be revealed, and respecting the privacy of the mentor should always be a priority. But the professional aspects of what you have learned are part of what will make you, in turn, a good mentor for your lab members.

RESOURCES

Albright M. and Carr C. 1997. 101 Biggest mistakes managers make: And how to avoid them. Prentice Hall Press, Englewood Cliffs, New Jersey.

Baker S. and Baker K. 1998. *Software for all projects great and small. The complete idiot's guide to project management*, pp. 295–307. Alpha Books, New York.

Barker K. 1998. *At the bench. A laboratory navigator.* Cold Spring Harbor Laboratory Press, Cold Spring Harbor, New York.

Basco M.R. 1999. *Never good enough: Freeing yourself from the chains of perfectionism.* The Free Press, New York.

Belker L.B. 1997. *The first-time manager,* 4th edition. AMACOM Books, New York.

Blum A. 1980. *Annapurna. A woman's place.* Sierra Club Books, San Francisco.

Boice R. 2000. *Advice for new faculty members: Nihil Nimus.* Allyn and Bacon, Needham Heights, Massachusetts.

Brown W.S. 1985. *13 Fatal errors managers make and how you can avoid them.* Berkley Books, New York.

Butler G. and Hope T. 1995. *Managing your mind.* Oxford University Press, New York.

Calhoun J. 1998. CET reviews the best net-ready info managers. National Mental Health Association MHIC Factsheet. (http://www.cnet.com/Content/Reviews/Compare/Netpinms)

Caveman. 2000. *Caveman.* The Company of Biologists Limited, Cambridge, England.

Cooper R.K. and Sawaf A. 1997. *Executive E.Q.: Emotional intelligence in leadership and organizations.* Grosset/Putnam, New York.

Covey S.R. 1989. *The 7 habits of highly effective people.* Simon & Schuster, New York.

Covey S.R., Merrill A.R., and Merrill R.R. 1994. *First things first.* Simon & Schuster, New York.

De Becker G. 1997. *The gift of fear.* Little, Brown and Company, New York.

Drucker P.F. 1966. *The effective executive.* Harper & Row, New York.

Duff C.S. 1999. *Learning from other women. How to benefit from the knowledge, wisdom, and experience of female mentors.* AMACOM Books, New York.

Edwards C.G. 1999. Surviving your first position. *HMS Beagle* **65:** 1–6. (http://news.bmn.com/hms-beagle)

Fiske P. 1997. The skills employers really want. *Science's Next Wave*, April 25, pp. 1–4. (http://nextwave.sciencemag.com)

Frank S.D. 1990. *The Evelyn Wood seven-day speed reading and learning program.* Barnes & Noble, New York.

Goldberg J. 1988. *Anatomy of a scientific discovery*, p. 10. Bantam Books, New York.

Goleman, D. 1995. *Emotional intelligence: Why it can matter more than I.Q.* Bantam Books, New York.

Green D.W. 2000. Managing the modern laboratory. *J. Lab. Management*, ISC Management Publications, Shelton, Connecticut.

Heller R. and Hindle T. 1998. *Essential manager's manual.* DK Publishing, New York.

Hemphill B. 1998. *Taming the paper tiger at work.* Kiplinger Books, Washington, D.C.

Hochheiser R.M. 1998. *Time management,* 2nd edition. Barron's Educational Series, Hauppauge, New York.

Hunsaker P.L. and Alessandra A.J. 1980. *The art of managing people.* Simon & Schuster, New York.

Hunsaker P.L. and Alessandra A.J. 1980. Building productive managerial relationships. In *The art of managing people*, pp. 1–16. Simon & Schuster, New York.

Judson H.F. 1996. *The eighth day of creation: The makers of the revolution in biology,* Expanded edition. Cold Spring Harbor Laboratory Press, Cold Spring Harbor, New York.

Klein G. 1998. *Sources of power: How people make decisions.* The MIT Press, Cambridge, Massachusetts.

Lientz B.P. and K.P. Rea. 1998. *Project management for the 21st century,* 2nd edition. Academic Press, New York.

Linney B.J. 1999. Characteristics of good mentors. *Physician Exec.* **25:** 70–72.

Luria S.E. 1984. *A slot machine, a broken test tube.* Harper & Row, New York.

MacFarlane J. 1998. Supervising the supervisors. *Science's Next Wave*, Aug. 28, pp. 1–3.

(http://nextwave.sciencemag.org)

Mackenzie A. and Waldo K.C. 1981. *About time!* McGraw-Hill Book Company, New York.

Marincola E. 1999. Women in cell biology: A crash course in management. *Am. Soc. Cell Biol. Newsletter* **22:** 36–37. (http://www.ascb.org)

Mavis Beacon Teaches Typing (Software). The Learning Company, Knoxville, Tennessee. (http://www.learningco.com)

Medawar P.B. 1969. *Induction and intuition in scientific thought.* The American Philosophical Society, Philadelphia, Pennsylvania.

Mendelson H. and Ziegler J. 1999. *Survival of the smartest: Managing information for rapid action and world-class performance.* John Wiley, New York.

Moody J. 1997. *Visualizing yourself as a successful college teacher, writer, and colleague: Pointers for graduate students, and college and university faculty.* University of New Haven Press, Connecticut.

Morgenstern J. 2000. *Time management from the inside out: The foolproof system for taking control of you schedule and your life.* Henry Holt, New York.

National Academy of Sciences. National Academy of Engineering, and Institute of Medicine. 1997. *Advisor, teacher, role model, friend. On being a mentor to students in science and engineering.* National Academy Press, Washington, D.C.

National Organization of Professional Organizers. (http://www.napo.net)

Perutz M. 1998. *I wish I'd made you angrier earlier: Essays on science and scientists.* Cold Spring Harbor Laboratory Press, Cold Spring Harbor, New York.

Quraishi O. 1999. Similarities and differences between industrial and academic positions in the pharmaceutical industry. *Science's Next Wave,* Aug. 6, pp. 1–4. (http://nextwave.sciencemag.org)

Reis R.M. 1999. How graduate students and faculty miscommunicate. *Tomorrow's Professor Listserve* No. 69. Stanford University Learning Library. (http://cis.stanford.edu/structure/tomprof/listserver.html)

Roe A. 1953. *The making of a scientist.* Dodd, Mead & Company, New York.

Sapadin L. and Maguire J. 1996. *It's about time! The six styles of procrastination and how to overcome them.* Viking Press, New York.

Sapienza A.M. 1995. *Managing scientists: Leadership strategies in biomedical research and development.* Wiley-Liss, New York.

Sinderman C.J. 1985. *The joy of science: Excellence and its rewards.* Plenum Press, New York.

Tannen D. 1990. *You just don't understand. Women and men in conversation.* Ballantine Books, New York.

Thomas, Jr. R.R., Gray T.I., and Woodruff M. 1992. *Differences do make a difference.* The American Institute for Managing Diversity, Atlanta, Georgia.

Tichy N.M. and Sherman S. 1993. *Control your destiny or someone else will: How Jack Welch is making General Electric the world's most competitive corporation.* Currency/Doubleday, New York.

Toth E. 1997. *Ms. Mentor's impeccable advice for women in academia.* University of Pennyslvania Press, Philadelphia.

Wacker W., Taylor J., and Means H.W. 2000. *The visionary's handbook: Nine paradoxes that will shape the future of your business.* HarperBusiness, New York.

White K. 1995. *Why good girls don't get ahead but gutsy girls do.* Warner Books, New York.

Wingerson L. 1998. Help wanted. Mentoring in biology. *HMS Beagle* **37:** 1–5. (http://news.bmn.com/hmsbeagle)

Winston S. 1983. *The organized executive. New ways to manage time, paper, and people.* Warner Books, New York.

Winston S. 1983. On secretaries: The "team of two." In *The organized executive: New ways to manage time, paper, and people.* Warner Books, New York.

Choose Your People

Choose Your People

NEW P.I. MISTAKE: HIRING BECAUSE YOU CAN

Of all choices you must make, the most important are the people who will work with you. Choosing the right people is the main way that you can influence the kind of science you will

> Choose people carefully. Don't just fill up spaces. Recruiting well is essential.

do and how pleasant and effective a workplace you will construct. Finding enough people, much less the right ones, is usually a struggle, but new P.I.s should not be any less careful in building a team. "Don't hire people just to have people" is the most often-repeated piece of advice a seasoned P.I. gives to a new P.I.

You are your best asset, and you must not weaken what has made you successful so far—your benchwork. Despite what you think, immediately hiring a technician or a student may not be advisable as soon as you start a new lab. If hiring a technician helps you work more and better in the lab, terrific, do it. But if you

> The advice that people gave me, that is incredibly true but incredibly hard to follow, is to not hire people when you first start out, just to get bodies in the lab. It is so hard not to hire people when you first start out...It is such a strong impulse, you have this empty lab, and you just want to fill it up, so it looks busy. But you often get people who are really bad. It is hard to apply the kind of criteria you should in the beginning with people.

hire someone to lessen your lab work, consider the implications very carefully. This is not the time to do less work, especially if you are more likely to spend more time in training a new lab person.

Do not hire a postdoc just because you have a slot or take on students just because they asked, and because the department will pay. But it is so tempting, most say. Finally, someone to make the buffers while you *think*. And the money for a technician might

> When I first started as an assistant professor, I didn't interview for a technician for 6 months. During that time, I worked in the lab by myself, setting up the system, free of the distraction of training someone at the same time.

not be there next year. Another reason that P.I.s hire immediately is that because of the geographical, financial, or scientific situation, there is no expectation that waiting will get a better person.

In a small lab in an undergraduate college or another place dedicated to teaching, you may feel a commitment to take on whoever wants to work with you. Even those who are determined to accept all people—some will not even check references or grades—have a bottom line of the unacceptable. Know your bottom line before your first interview. You should still wait, however, until you can do a good job with your students before you accept them in the lab.

KNOW YOUR NEEDS AND KNOW YOUR LAB'S NEEDS

Deciding on the jobs you need to fill

The kind of people you get will be dependent on your game plan. If you are well funded in an undergraduate lab, your main goal may be to nurture students, and you might be prepared to work with absolutely any personality. But there are people who can dismantle your good intentions.

When you know what bugs you, you can look for it. But you usually don't know what bugs you until after you've run the lab for a while.

If you are very ambitious, and well organized, with clear-cut research plans, you might want to hire personnel on the basis of very specific skills. This can end up being shortsighted. Skills can be quickly learned by someone who is adaptable and smart. Your research projects can swiftly change. It is far more important to hire someone who is capable of learning new techniques.

When do you need a technician/lab assistant?

When you know what science you want to do and do not have the time to do all the needed bench research, it is time to look for a technician. If the lab is already running well, and there are myriad tasks and projects that no one is getting time to finish, you may need another technician. If you are at an institution where there will unlikely be any students or postdocs, you will need technicians to fill all roles in the lab.

Ideally, I'd want a mix of students and postdocs. With students, there is a lot of down time for the first couple of years, and you can't really expect a lot out of them. In some ways, students are better than postdocs. The reality of having to get a job and making sure things are working out is a drain on the postdoc. But then, a postdoc comes in and is productive right away and leaves in three years...the student comes, and there is down time the first few years, but then they stay 5 years and drive the lab the last few years.

The role of a technician in a lab can be anything from a glorified bottle washer to an independent investigator. The technician may work on projects under guidance of the P.I., work on one project under guidance of another lab member, or may assist anyone in the lab that needs help.

When do you need a student?

Most likely, a student will need you. But when you have a lot of ideas and enthusiasm, when your research is moving well, and you have some funds and more time, there might be room

I prefer students to postdocs, as they fit my micromanagement style better. They like to be told what to do—but I do then feel very responsible for them.

for a student. Beginning students may work on small, assigned projects, or work with another lab member, until they have learned some of the ropes. In some labs, students may begin immediately working on their own projects, although those projects often will not progress without a large input of your time.

> *A lot of the reason the lab has become a fun place to work in is the students. The students are really fun to have around, even if they are totally non-productive! They are very rewarding, because they are smarter than postdocs, and you can discuss anything with them, and they come up with crazy ideas.*

When do you need a postdoc?

You need a postdoc when the lab's main project is sufficiently advanced that the development of other projects is necessary for progress. A postdoc usually comes into the lab to work on a particular project or, at least, in a particular area. You need a postdoc when you have enough projects that you can afford to turn a project over to another person. You also must be ready to give up some control. When you hire a postdoc, you must realize that postdocs are remaining longer in their postdocs as academic positions become harder to obtain (Regets 1999). And it will usually be the less competent postdocs who will stay the longest.

> *With postdocs, you have the added responsibility of getting them a job, of helping to get them a job. You have to be asking, "What's my exit strategy?" They come across the country with their families, and even when you know it is not going to work out, you might be stuck.*

When do you need a secretary?

You will probably need a secretary only when it is possible to have a secretary. Most new P.I.s must do without, and with plenty of help from technology, do fine without. In general, hire a secretary when the lab and your responsibilities have grown enough—for example, recommendations to write, reagents to send out, multiple grants to administer, postdoc applicants to meet, international meetings to attend—and you cannot accomplish the day's administrative tasks in less than an hour or so.

You may need a part-time secretary in your first years if you are applying for multiple grants or writing reports. Organizations will sometimes support a part-time secretary, but you may not get a choice about the person. Part-time needs are different from full-time needs: The needs must not be time-dependent. The chapter on Working with a Secretary/Administrative Assistant in this volume suggests ways to maximize the privilege of a secretary and how to survive without one.

When do you need a glass washer or lab aid?

You need someone to help with cleaning and prep work as soon as you are regularly doing experiments.

WHERE TO FIND THE PEOPLE YOU NEED

Was Delbrück good at picking people? "It's not so much that he's good at picking people, as that he is attracting to people. Because he is terribly intelligent. Because it is so very exciting to work with him. His ideas, the way he thinks, the order...to spend the days chewing on a problem, and writing and erasing things on the blackboard with him is terribly exciting." (Luria)

JUDSON (1996, P. 45)

Having never met him or knowing anything about Potter's work, Blobel decided on the spot to join his lab because of the force of Potter's "wonderful personality." Today, Blobel attributes his love of both biochemistry and of architecture to Potter... . "We were taught to think on our own and not to be bottle fed," Blobel recalls appreciatively.

ASCB PROFILE (1999, P. 6). GUNTER BLOBEL ON
VAN R. POTTER AT THE UNIVERSITY OF WISCONSIN

Once you are established, there will be no problem in finding competent people—they will find you. As a new P.I., however, you will have to seek out people and convince them that your lab is a good place to be. Even getting the chance to interview a good technician or secretary may be tricky. Since you are competing with more established labs for personnel, you must put out an effort to look in places that the other labs would not bother with. Never stop looking for good people, people who will fit in with your lab and add to your lab.

In general, technicians (and secretaries) are hired through the Personnel or Human Resources department at the institution. In some cases, Human Resources can be a hindrance, i.e., when bureaucratic detail takes precedence to hiring. Students and postdocs usually apply directly to the P.I., and the selection process is handled through the P.I. No matter what, you can still try to find your own applicants. Listed below are some ways to find potential applicants:

- Check with department chairmen or someone older (perhaps your own mentor) for people who have applied to them, and whom they would recommend.

- If you work in an institution without students, call a friend or a scientist at a local college, and ask for suitable applicants among the upcoming graduates for a technician job. This is a good way to get a talented person who has never had a job, who might require more training, but who might well repay you with hard work and loyalty.

- Personal friends, and friends of friends.

- People already working in the lab may have friends or acquaintances they would recommend.

- Many specialty Internet Sites post job listings.

Technicians

Fresh college graduate versus an experienced technician?

Most investigators feel that experienced technicians are worth their weight in gold. However, most also feel that such technicians are completely out of financial reach, for an experienced technician can actually get up to twice as much money as a fresh college graduate. Discussed below are two ways to find a technician.

> *Technicians are the easiest people to find when you are just starting out. A technician won't judge you and will be more willing to work for a new assistant professor.*

From within the system

Your first approach to finding a technician might well be to look at technicians who are moving horizontally through the system. This might seem to be a golden opportunity to hire a technician with experience, and you might be right. Having someone on your staff who knows the institutional written and unwritten rules can be invaluable. If the techniques of the lab are similar, you could save on training time. But it could also be a good chance to inherit a lot of ingrained problems.

> *Techs don't care that you are just starting out, that you are essentially a nobody.*

> *The most bang for the buck is these young people who want to come in and work hard for two years and move onto something else, because their motivation is so tremendous that they want to think and put in the time.*

Before you are even allowed to interview a new applicant, some institutions require that you interview all the technicians or secretaries on the lay-off list. Of course, you may be extraordinarily fortunate to find someone who was laid off for a reason not related to competence or personality (e.g., the previous P.I. might have run out of money). There might also have been a genuine personality conflict between the candidate and the P.I. or other lab members. (You can search for the real reason while checking the references.) But you will generally have candidates who did not do well in the job, and people who would also do badly in your lab.

> *I need some stability. Everyone comes for 2 years and leaves, and there is no continuity. I'm so tired and frustrated with having to invent the wheel everytime. Suddenly, no one in the lab can run polyacrylamide gels anymore, they just aren't working, and I don't have the time to go in and troubleshoot.*

Some universities and institutions will send an applicant around to all the people who need a technician. When there is a desirable applicant, P.I.s will compete for this person. In some places, the salary can be upped by the P.I., and so the well-established and well-funded labs can lure away the better candidates. Find out what, other than money, would make the job compelling for the applicant. Ambitious candidates might like to know that they may get an authorship on a paper or will be able to work independently.

> *I like fresh college graduates. Nothing we do is that technically demanding. What is needed is someone who is motivated enough to work long hours and can see himself as the author of a paper. I insist that the technician presents his or her data in lab meetings and presents papers in journal clubs, just like any other person in the lab.*

All 4 technicians I've hired in the 2 and a half years I've been here have come as referrals from friends, applying directly to me. The university only sends the applications from the candidates to the P.I.s months after the people have applied for the job. When I insisted that an ad be run in the Sunday paper, I was not allowed to see the candidates until the hiring period was over, 2 months after the advertisement: of course, by that time, the promising, proactive candidates had been taken, and I was left with substandard applicants.

From outside the system

Fresh college graduates generally do not know how to network yet and may simply go to an employment office or read the want ads when looking for a job. It is up to you to network to find the potential candidate.

If you have a technician or a student you respect, ask if any friends are looking for a job. Friends often share the same work ethic, and a friendship already under way can help grease the growth of the lab personality.

An advertisement on the Web could be used to attract ambitious candidates. A want ad in the local paper can bring in candidates, but because of the legal ramifications of this kind of advertising, this should only be done through Human Resources.

I get burned by young technicians—they leave, it is hard to talk them into staying over a year. I rely on an older technician, who makes a lot of money—and is worth it.

Secretaries/Administrative assistants

Administrative assistants, like technicians, can come from within or from outside the system and are usually found and employed through Human Resources. The same caveats as those for technicians apply here as well: someone making a horizontal move may be doing so for the wrong (for you) reasons.

High school graduates with basic office skills can do typing and filing. Office skills, typing, and word processing can be acquired from 1- to 2-year programs in office administration offered by business schools, vocational-technical institutes, and community colleges. But most skills are acquired on the job, and promotions are the usual evidence of increased skills. As secretaries gain in experience, they can earn a Certified Professional Secretary (CPS) designation by meeting certain experience requirements and passing an examination.

What often works best is to find someone who is not looking for authentication in the workplace, but works to pay the bills for the meaningful things in life. P.I.s have found a range of talented people (dancers, students, artists, opera singers) who cannot support themselves at their careers and must supplement their income elsewhere. To find these people, advertisements in various local organizations, as well as in the newspaper, are useful.

Undergraduate Students

Undergraduates drive the science in colleges and small universities and may be a large presence even in larger organizations. These students can often be found through work-study programs or through your own classes. Undergraduates can most commonly be found at their own institution. Nearby institutions without students often have an arrangement to allow students to work in their labs.

Graduate students

Graduate students can be found at a variety of locations.

- Departmental seminars and retreats, even departmental parties
- Classes and seminars
- Rotations
- Among graduating undergraduates

Physicians

Some of the places to find physicians are at:

- Meetings
- Classes and seminars
- Hospitals or clinics

Postdocs

Postdocs are found most often through your work or through word of mouth.

- A colleague may refer an applicant
- At meetings or seminars
- Over the Web
- Geographically trapped, applying locally to labs

> *Every time we published a Nature paper, I received dozens of postdoc applications.*

Industry-Academia differences

Throw a Party.
ProLaw Software

One happy hour, it struck Deborah Reese, VP of client services at this Albuquerque company: "Why couldn't job interviews be more like the revealing conversations that happen at parties?" A year later, they are. About 300 hopefuls a month fill out a detailed questionnaire. Reese invites the most promising 10 to a catered function. Her standards are high: She looks for "people who can keep their cool, are technically adept, and have incredible people skills.

The party includes games—instructing an alien how to make a peanut butter and jelly sandwich and playing the board game Mastermind. Candidates must also construct a bridge out of newspaper and masking tape that's strong enough to hold a cinder block. They build together, in silence, while staffers take notes.

A handful make it to the final round of interviews, in which Reese explains a piece of software and asks prospects to explain it back. Then she requests a five-minute presentation about a subject the applicant enjoys. It's a lot of work. But considering the quality of people who get hired, she says, "It's so worth it."

FROM BURN THIS RESUME. THREE COMPANIES TAKE A NOVEL
APPROACH TO FILLING VACANCIES. DANNHAUSER (1999, P. 26)

A uniquely personal demonstration of the SB (SmithKline Beecham) staffing process is the town hall recruiting trip. Teams of SB managers fly into medium and small-sized towns to share one-on-one about the SB culture and career opportunities. Most important, they treat the applicants as customers, sharing annual reports, giving overviews of current projects, and allowing candidates to ask any questions they like about working at SB.

HARRIS AND BRANNICK (1999 P. 73)

Many of the differences between academia and industry, described in the chapter Start in the Right Place in this volume, will impact on attracting people and hiring, although the qualities of the individual lab and institution are still the major influence. Companies do tend to recruit the people they want, whereas academic institutions depend on those who happen to apply or on local recruits. Big organizations may attract people to the company itself and then find a place for them. However, even at institutions with intense recruiting programs, obtaining one of the better candidates might well be an extremely in-house political struggle.

The Hiring Process

WORKING WITH HUMAN RESOURCES

The physical hiring process will be partially determined by the Human Resources department (HR) or equivalent at your facility; in most cases, you *will* work with HR. The HR department is a real resource and, hopefully, you will want to work with them. They generally have professionals on staff that can help with everything from hiring and firing personnel to finding apartments and visa information. Treat them as fellow professionals, and not some brand of distasteful administrator.

> I discovered, when I applied for a technician job years ago, and had a masters and all these qualifications and no one called, that the person who screened applications was a non-science person and was completely unable to match up what I could do with what was needed. When I went back to my notebook and wrote down every technique I knew on the application, I had a job within 5 days.

HR may be the primary source of candidates and may set the guidelines for salary and benefits. However, unless you know you see eye to eye with HR, do not be led by HR during hiring—you must control the entire process from start to finish, to get the candidates that *you* consider to be the best.

Developing a relationship with people in HR can be incredibly useful. It can mean the difference between being called first or last for a chance to interview a strong and promising candidate for a technician job. Allow the people at HR to get to know you so that they will be better able to identify and seek out the kind of person you want to hire.

> Scientists are not huge fans of human resources. They don't trust them...faculty have kind of a snobbish attitude.

YOUR HIRING PROTOCOL

P.I.s have their own process for determining the best candidate. For most new P.I.s, it is a completely casual process. But others, after having made dreadful mistakes in a choice of candidate, have evolved a more structured system.

A structured system objectifies the selection process. It is true that your gut reaction—your

> I never pay postdocs to come, they must have a fellowship. When I get the application, I say—look me up on Medline, and write 3 aims for prospective projects in my lab. This is a good way to screen against someone who just wants to get into the institution or the country.

first response to a person—is important if you want to choose a person you like and whom you think will fit in with the rest of the group. But to discover potential problems and incompatibilities, and to predict the likelihood of success, you need a way to create data you can analyze.

The need for a structured process grows as your lab grows. When you are just beginning, you may not have so many candidates for any position that you can compare one with another. This is when people tend to go only on gut, and structure helps you to think clearly about a particular candidate. Start early with structure. It gets you into the habit of evolving your own system and helps you avoid the early mistakes that P.I.s make. There are several steps in hiring during which you can amass data to guide in a decision:

- Screening applications

- Pre-interview phone conversation with applicants

- Checking with references

- Interviewing applicants

> *It is very hard for me to generalize about hiring. It is always a very flexible, individualized process, depending on the position, the specific people applying, and the other people, already in the lab, who will be working with the candidate.*

Your hiring process will vary with each position. Generally, the higher the level for which you are hiring, the more stringent the hiring process will be. The process you use also depends on the amount of applicants you are likely to receive for a particular job. For a technician job in a university on the west coast, for which there are many applicants, one P.I. has evolved the following procedures.

Sequence of the hiring process:
Determine your need
Solicit applicants
Read resumes: approve or reject
Call references: approve or reject
Interview candidates
Evaluate candidates
Choose candidate
Offer job
Tighten negotiations
Hire or offer job to second choice

REVIEWING RESUMES AND APPLICATION FORMS

Read resumes to understand the qualifications of the applicants. For technicians and administrative assistants, or lab aids, you will have multiple resumes to go through at once.

- Ask HR to weed out obvious nonviable candidates and go through the resumes yourself. You are best able to translate a candidate's experience and potential value in your lab.

AN EXAMPLE OF A SELECTION PROCESS

P.I. Jane Koehler started out with a very abbreviated selection process. She has settled on the following procedure for picking technicians, a seemingly very long process, but one that has resulted in qualified personnel and a happy lab (J. Koehler, pers. comm.).

1. Have HR screen candidates *loosely*.

2. Look at candidate's applications (~60 for a technician job) and sort the applications into three piles: No—Maybe—Call!

3. Call 10–12 people per position. Ask basic questions for about 20 minutes and decide which candidates to interview. Below is a list of questions to ask candidates on the phone:
   - Ask for a 2-year commitment. Do this obliquely, by asking about future plans. For example, if it is spring, and candidates are applying in the fall for graduate school the following year, they will not be here for 2 years.
   - This job requires working with animals: Would this be a problem for you?
   - Immigration status: What visa do you have? This may also suggest the limits of the work commitment possible.
   - Are you competent in sterile technique?
   - When are you available to start working?
   - Do you have other job offers? This lets you know how likely it is that the person would take your job.
   - Do you have other jobs? This would make the job hours more inflexible and may lessen commitment to your job.
   - What is your current salary?
   - How were your grades?
   - Do you have any worries about exposure to HIV or radiation (or whatever particular hazards are in your lab)?
   - What are your future plans? This tells you not only about time commitment, but also how invested the candidate is in research.
   - What are your preferred hours?: A P.I. with unusual hours should ask if these hours can be met with at least some overlap.

4. Call three or four recommenders for each of the people above. Look for evidence of completing a project and independence more than specific skills. Questions to ask recommenders about the candidate:
   - Works quickly and efficiently?
   - Understood project?
   - Asks questions?
   - Kinds of expertise?
   - Would employ again?
   - Troubleshooting ability?
   - Reliable?
   - Well organized?
   - Reason for leaving?
   - Weaknesses?
   - Passion for work?
   - Motivation?
   - Gets along with the rest of the lab?

5. Interview four or five people. Many of the questions asked are included in the list, later in the chapter, of sample interview questions.

- Look for overall structure and organization in the setup of the resume, suggesting the organizational skills of the applicant.

- Watch out for gaps and inconsistencies, particularly in periods of employment, but do not automatically reject a resume for this—this person may be a very strong candidate. What you are looking for is a masked job dismissal.

> When people contact me by email, I ask them to look me up on Medline and write three specific aims for the work they want to do and send it to me. They must do at least enough work to find out what they want to do in the lab. All the people who just look at the list of faculty here and apply to everyone are therefore selected out.

- Judge whether the work or academic qualifications are suitable.

Student and postdoc applications will more likely dribble in. The initial review may take place in an apparent vacuum, with no comparison of one applicant to another possible. A very different kind of analysis is needed, but in both cases, you must try to objectify the process. Request a resume or c.v. from students as well as postdocs. In many places, it is unusual to treat a student like an employee, but this does help you to do an initial screen. Check for an indication that the applicants are already interested in the work in your lab and that they can contribute.

> For postdocs, I look for someone who has done well. The "well" is relative, depending on where the postdoc has applied from. So, if someone has applied from China or India with one first author paper from JBC or MCB, they are pretty rare. Someone from a small college in the USA with an MCB paper, then, it will depend on what the advisor says.

INTERPRETING RECOMMENDATIONS

You will seldom receive an overtly bad recommendation. Candidates will usually request recommendations only from people who they think will give a good report. In addition, most people who would write a bad recommendation will inform the candidate.

> People are afraid of lawsuits, and don't tell the truth about a person in a recommendation. So some people don't bother checking references, since they won't get the truth.

A P.I. may write a less-than-honest recommendation to make sure the candidate finds a job, i.e., to be sure the candidate leaves the P.I.'s lab. It may be because it is time for the candidate to move on, and the P.I. truly wants the candidate to find the best available position. Sometimes the most glowing recommendations are written by P.I.s who want that person out, immediately. But usually, even the most desperate person will not be totally dishonest and will couch their problems in telltale phrases hidden among the compliments.

Rather than saying anything negative or lying by writing an outstanding recommendation, P.I.s will write an okay, but tepid report. You must comb through the recommendation to extract as much data as you can. Look for things not said. Look for the qualities you do require. An example of a tepid recommendation would be:

> I am writing in support of XX for his application to graduate school. XX was in my lab for 3 years and was a conscientious worker, always doing

---

Troubled Resident's Case Left UW with Quandary

During the year leading up to last week's fatal shootings at the University of Washington Medical Center, pathology-department officials struggled with the best way to deal with a difficult employee who ultimately turned a gun on his mentor and himself.

They had criticized his work, urged him to see a psychiatrist and fired him. Still, Dr. Jian Chen told his bosses he was "in total control." And, ultimately, he was the one who decided his life would end on the floor of an office at the University of Washington Medical Center, near the body of the man he idolized.

In a year, Chen went from a determined pathology resident to an outcast who called his bosses liars, denied he was failing and shopped for a gun as his last day of work approached... . Chen, 42, shot himself to death last Wednesday, moments after killing his mentor, Dr. Rodger Haggitt, 57, an eminent pathologist. (Reprinted, with permission, from Kelleher and Sanders 2000.)

Chen had been "recommended" for a new position at George Washington University in Washington D.C. barely a month before his murder-suicide.

---

what was suggested. Although his work resulted in only one senior author paper, he is an author on two other papers in the lab and was always willing to help the more junior lab members.

Some would interpret this as a student who worked hard, was a good team player, but had little initiative or imagination. This person would not be a good postdoctoral candidate at most academic and many industrial institutions. Some P.I.s, however, would see the capability of cooperation with others as an asset. Listed below are some pointers for interpreting a recommendation.

- *Look for strong statements:*
  Gets along with others
  Self-starter
  Staying power
  Creativity
  Asks the right questions
  Good experimentalist

- *Look for statements of weakness:*
  Moody
  Loner
  Tried hard

- *Look for a cool tone or half-statements,* as well as for certain key phrases, depending on what you want. For example, hard working versus productive is good to distinguish. Hardworking is good and is acceptable in a technician. Check to see (or ask) if hardworking is coupled with productive. Other subtle distinctions are gets along with others versus takes a leadership role and/or responsible versus independent versus does not take orders.

- *Make a list of points that must be clarified by phone.* Okay, the candidate is independent, but are suggestions accepted gratefully?

CHECKING REFERENCES *AND* THOSE WHO HAVE WRITTEN RECOMMENDATIONS

Checking references is not a formality! There exists an odd presumption that if someone has sent a recommendation, it must be okay, and there is no point in calling to check them out. Not everyone calls to check on references. Some P.I.s simply do not like to use the phone and rely on the recommendations and their own feelings to make a decision. For new P.I.s, calling to check references belongs to a level of fine-tuning that may seem, in view of the often small selection of choices, to provide more data than they can afford to deal with. If no other postdoc has applied, do you really need to know that the applicant needs constant guidance or has trouble staying motivated to write papers? Yes!

> *If I have the letter, I don't call. I just hate talking on the telephone. If I call them up, it's like saying I didn't believe the letter.*

> *I don't think they lied about her, but I don't think I was very skillful at asking questions. I didn't talk to anyone who really knew her. She came from a huge lab....and I never talked to the right person.*

> *I don't check up on them, unless there is something negative or lukewarm.*

Cut down on the amount of interviews you have to conduct by checking references before you interview, especially if you have several candidates to interview. Recommendations can be checked again after an interview, so that any questions about performance that occurred to you can be clarified. Some people check references only after the interview. What is important is to actually check the references!

Call every reference, including those overseas. If the phone number or address is wrong, or the person has moved, persist and search him out.

> *I always call now to check on recommendations, but I only learned this after hiring my first two people, two big mistakes.*

Phone conversations with references and recommendation writers

Phone calls to references and writers of recommendations will be very similar. With a letter of recommendation in hand, you will have particular questions to ask, for example: "When you say he is stubborn, what do you mean? Is there a negative side to that?" You still, however, must have a broad conversation. What do you say? Just talk. Be alert to the tone of voice used and listen to what *is not* said. If you can establish a rapport, you will be able to have an honest conversation about the candidate.

> Hello. This is xx, of xxx. I am hiring a technician, and am considering xx. I know he worked with you for xx years, and I'd like to know what you think of him as a technician.

Keep in mind the written recommendation, if there is one. Sometimes names are given as references, and these people are called directly, without a letter of recommendation.

A good start to a discussion of personality is to ask how the person got along with the other people at the job. It may be that a recommender gives a negative view of the candidate's ability to get along with others in the lab. Statements such as "He just didn't get along with anyone," or "He was disruptive" are not to be accepted. Ask for specifics, e.g., "Can you give me an example of a disagreement he had with another lab member?"

But one thing you learn pretty quickly is that advisors have a vested interest in moving the postdoc on. They are judged on their own grant applications by what their students and postdocs are doing, so it is in their own self-interest to get their people into a good lab. You have to ask questions such as "If this person applied for an NIH fellowship, would he get it?"....If you hear people hemming and hawing, you'd better stay away.

Try to get a sense of the recommender's feel for lab group dynamics. This recommender may have no feel at all for the interpersonal relations within the lab and may be relying on the opinion of a jealous or incompetent lab member. Or the problem may be a boss-employee one, attributed to a personality defect in the candidate. In addition, in a dysfunctional lab, blame is often inappropriately portioned out to a strong and intelligent and ordinarily well-liked person.

For a short period of time, I looked for people like myself until I realized that those people would be put off by me! I look for people who are thoughtful, who look for clever ways to do things. I look for nice people, and I ask the advisor if the person was nice.

A recommender may be withholding information, but will usually do this only by omission. When asked a direct question, few people lie about the candidate, but *will* give the truth. If two independent references say the same negative thing about a candidate, you probably should not choose that person, no matter what your own feeling is. Below is a list of questions to ask referees:

So you can't trust recommendations on paper, but in person, someone will usually answer questions truthfully.

What is the level of expertise?

Is she a self-starter?

How would you describe his personality?

Does she ask questions?

Is his work reproducible?

Would you hire her again?

Why is he leaving?

Is she reliable?

Is he well organized?

Did she get along with others in the lab?

How are his communication skills?

What are her weaknesses and strengths?

Is he motivated?

Does she love the work?

Does he have good sterile technique/computer skills/technical ability?

Is she productive?

How does he accept criticism?

Did she understand the project?

Does he work best on a team or independently?

Secondary references

Through one reference, you may get the name of another reference you can call, one who has not been primed by the candidate. A simple request will usually bring forth a name and a number from a reference ("Do you know someone else x worked with, someone who would also talk to me?"). You may also know or find someone in the candidate's workplace or school that you could call. Due diligence is not excessive.

Foreign applicants

Call overseas numbers as well as local or national. If there is a language problem, do as best as you can, and later find someone familiar with the language that you trust to make the call for you. There are risks in this. One P.I. spoke (or thought she was speaking) with someone abroad and had a clear and good conversation; however, when the lab worker arrived to take the job, he could actually speak no English. The Human Resources department at your institution may be willing and able to do overseas interviews in the language of the applicant.

Sometimes you can find a friend or colleague actually working or passing through the candidate's institution. This person may be persuaded to do an on-site interview for you, and this is the best way to examine a situation you cannot assess.

The inability to assess individuals or their recommendations is one of the reasons why some P.I.s are reluctant to accept foreign applicants. Another problem is that accepting some foreign applicants entails a great deal of responsibility. In some cases, you and/or the institution must sponsor the applicant for a visa. "I don't want to take the chance of finding out that the person isn't suitable, and have to send him back," said one P.I., "or keeping someone who isn't any good because I feel too bad about rejecting him."

The Effective Interview

WHAT IS AN EFFECTIVE INTERVIEW?

What do you hope to gain from an interview? A P.I. usually hopes to find out:

- If the resume and qualifications are as stated, and the applicant is technically qualified.

- If the applicant can think and solve problems.

- If the applicant will get along with you and the other lab members.

- If the applicant's goals and way of working are compatible with the lab and the organization.

> *Here's the trick for getting postdocs...don't go by the number of publications and where they have published, because much more important is what this person's expectations of this life are. You must know what environment the person came from and what they want—and what they really want, because everyone will tell you what you want to hear. But if you ask them how much they are willing to work for it, and what sacrifices they would make to achieve their goals, then you might find the truth.*

Request an interview with applicants to all jobs. Some institutions pay for travel costs for a postdoc interview. If your institution does not do this, and a candidate asks you for money for travel, it is entirely up to you and your position what to do. If you know you already very much want the candidate, it makes sense to find the money somewhere.

> *One of the mistakes I made consistently in the first few years was being blind to other people, by reading everything in a very positive light. Almost all my mistakes were in selection.*

Most new P.I.s when interviewing candidates for their first technician job—and some, for every candidate to follow—do an *undirected interview*. The interview is casual, and the P.I. tries to get the candidate to talk freely. Such an interview, if done with intelligence and empathy, can tell something about the personality of the candidate, and a lot about whether you and the applicant click. But most P.I.s agree that their first candidates hired were mistakes, and they blame their own technique in screening. In retrospect, many say, it should have been clear that trouble would come.

There are several styles of interviewing, some of which most P.I.s might find too manipulative and distasteful. For example, *stress interviewing* subjects candidates to difficult and hostile questioning to test their reaction to thinking under stress. Other techniques are more useful and can be incorporated in your interviewing protocol. *Behavioral interviewing* assumes that, if you can really find out what happened in the past, you can predict the future. Asking questions about how candidates dealt with a difficult project or with other people at a previous job can suggest how they will act in your lab, and these types of questions will probably form the basis for your interview.

Personality profiling attempts to define candidates' underlying personality by analyzing their responses to questions about real or theoretical situations. An example of this would be to ask, "Upon finding out that a close colleague had fudged data, would you approach the person or go directly to the P.I.?"

Another technique that is actually part of many postdoc interviews is the *situational interview,* when the candidate is placed in a situation that might actually be on the job. Giving a seminar, and having to field questions about one's own experiments much as are done day to day, is an example of this. Some P.I.s do give a test or request a demonstration of a technique from candidate technicians.

The only kind of interview that has had any consistent success in predicting performance in the workplace is the *structured interview,* in which all applicants are subjected to the same questions and are rated according to predetermined objective scoring (Gladwell 2000). The questions should examine past or present behavior to try to define the candidate's ability to do the job and to predict future performance in the lab.

DESIGNING YOUR INTERVIEWS

For most of us, hiring someone is essentially a romantic process, in which the job interview functions as a desexualized version of a date. We are looking for someone with whom we have a certain chemistry, even if the coupling that results ends in tears and the pursuer and the pursued turn out to have nothing in common. We want the unlimited promise of a love affair. The structured interview, by contrast, seems to offer only the dry logic and practicality of an arranged marriage.

GLADWELL (2000, P. 86)

What do you hope to gain from an interview? You must have very clear ideas about what your wants and needs are, as well as what you can get. While knowing what will *not work* for your lab or your personality, you must be flexible and accept that you may not be in a position to attract the person you want.

Purpose of the interview

- Determine the candidate's capability of performing the job.
- Evaluate the candidate's personality.
- Find out if the candidate will fit into the existing lab.
- Evaluate how you and the candidate will get along.

This information, negative and positive, is not always forthcoming. Even if the answer is nothing but positive, some people are shy, may come from a culture where you do not promote yourself, or may actually be unaware of a good trait. Negative information, i.e., information that the candidate may be unaware of or may be trying to suppress, might be trickier to find, since you will be trying to define qualities such as motivation, often across cultural barriers.

Even if you prefer a casual style of interviewing, having a set plan of questions will help you to more clearly see the merits of one candidate over another. What interviewers, even experienced ones, tend to do is to overlook the influence of context on a character trait (Gladwell 2000). If an applicant is polite to the interviewer, the interviewer may assume a range of behaviors, such as respect for authority and the ability to be considerate of fellow workers. Having set questions and a pattern to interpreting the answers can stop you from making a lot of invalid assumptions.

Make a questionnaire to suit your needs

Below is a sample all-around questionnaire as well as questionnaires to determine specific qualities, the effect of cultural differences, and the best person for each position.

A sample, all-round questionnaire

Where do you see yourself in 5 years?

Why do you want to work in this lab?

How do you think your current or last supervisor would describe you?

Your supervisor/boss is (was) _____. What was it like, working for this individual? What would you say are this person's strengths and shortcomings?

How would you describe your ideal boss? What would be this person's management style?

What would your previous supervisor say are your strengths and weaknesses?

What do you hope to be doing in 5 years?

What are the most enjoyable aspects of your current/last job/project? The least enjoyable?

To what extent do you think that luck—either fortunate or unfortunate circumstances beyond your control—has entered into your performance?

What were some of your most significant mistakes or failures?

If you could have made one suggestion to your current or past P.I., what would it be?

Can you describe a situation where a work policy called for you to do something that you did not consider to be right?

Specific questions to look for specific qualities

- **Fits in with lab culture.** If you sense that you are not fitting in with a group, what would you do? What kind of people do you like to work with?

- **Independence.** If you ran into a technical problem in the middle of an experiment, would you ask someone for help, or try to figure it out yourself. Are you a self-starter or do you prefer direction? Do you learn better from books, from other people, or from doing?

> *I try to find out the environment the person came from. It is very important to know their expectations! I ask "How much are you willing to work for this?" The number of publications isn't as important as determination.*

- **Organized.** Describe your typical workday. How do you start out, how do you decide what to work on, what ends the day?

- **Motivation.** How much are you willing to give up to do this job well?

- **Honesty/integrity.** If a friend in the lab asked you to tell the P.I.—untruthfully—that you had fed the cells over the weekend, would you?

- **Flexibility.** If the project you were hired for did not work out, would you able to work on another project?

- **Persistence.** Can you give me an example of a time when you were tempted to give up on an experiment, but managed to get it to work?

- **Collaborates/Works well with others.** When you start a new job, do you prefer to have your own project or work with someone? Do you need a project to be your own?

- **Assertiveness.** If someone started borrowing aspects of your project, what would you do?

- **Ability to learn.** How long does it take for you to get a new line of experiments going? Can you give an example?

- **Technical abilities.** Describe to me how you would do this (give an appropriate example) experiment.

Questions to determine the effect of cultural differences

How do you feel about getting in front of a committee to describe your personal accomplishments?

If an older lab colleague took credit for one of your projects, what would you do?

If friends in the lab were involved in a collaboration unknown to the P.I., would you help them?

Under what conditions would you seek another job?

If you did not understand what was being explained to you, would you persist in asking even if the P.I. got annoyed?

If your project were not working, and you thought you knew why, whom would you tell about it?

Specific questions for each position

- *Secretary*

  On occasion you may be asked to work after hours, would this be a problem for you?

- *Student*

  Why do you want to work in this lab?

  In which courses did you do best? Why?

  In which courses did you do the worst? Why?

  On occasion you may be asked to work after hours. Would this be a problem for you?

  > *I hired a summer student, and didn't ask him about his grades. In the interview he seemed okay, but he didn't understand what was happening in the lab. Afterwards, he told other people in the lab that he had barely gotten a C in organic chemistry. That would have been a clue, but I didn't think to ask.*

- *Technician*

  Is it important to work on one project?

  Would you like to have your own project?

  Would you be able to leave a project for the day, and help someone else out?

  On occasion you may be asked to work after hours, would this be a problem for you?

- *Postdoc*

  Do you prefer to work on several projects at a time or one at a time?

  > *I ask: "Describe the project you did, say what you would do better," and I ask: "What do you want to do in my lab?"*

  Where do you see the project you have outlined going? If x happens, what will you do?

  Do you want to create your own project? How would you do it?

CONDUCTING THE INTERVIEW

The P.I. must be the one to deal with the candidate. No matter how busy you are, greet the candidate as if this interview were important and valued. And *it is important.* Do not act as if you have obviously squeezed this interview in; you are probably in a position in which you should do a bit of wooing. Offer the candidate a cup of coffee or other refreshment. Outline the day or the time, as you have planned it.

> *I let them know, if you want to do the same thing everyday, and you just want to clock in and out, this is not the job for you.*

The applicant, if applying for a postdoc, should give a seminar (by prearrangement, of course). This will provide a great deal of information about the person's scientific knowledge and communication ability. Make it as early in the day as possible, as this will be a vehicle you and others can use to discuss with the candidate through the day. If your lab is small, invite others in your institution to attend the seminar. Either advertise or call those who might be scientifically curious. Also ask anyone whose opinion about the candidate you would like to consider.

- *Tour the institution,* and use the time to sell the institution and your lab.

- *Have lunch with the candidate,* with or without the rest of the lab, or ask the other lab members to do it. (You pay for the candidate's lunch!)

- *Interview the candidate.* Have questions prepared, and write down relevant answers and impressions as you go along. Try to keep on track and resist the temptation to have an enjoyable conversation. You need to obtain data.

- *Speak more of the position* and the real requirements of the job. Say what you expect. Make it clear if you expect a 50–60-hour work week, dislike people asking for help or working on other-than-assigned projects, want all lab members to write their own papers, or whatever requirements you have.

- *Have dinner with the candidate.* This might be overkill, unless the person has come a long way, or you really want to talk more.

Most P.I.s put student, secretary, and technician applicants through a more abbreviated process.

PREGNANT APPLICANTS

The unmentionable. You are a starting assistant professor, with enough money for one postdoc. The best applicant tells you that she is pregnant. Legally and morally, you cannot discriminate. But if you do not get a lot of work done in the first few years, you could lose your grants and your job. What do you do?

> One postdoc asked me how I feel about pregnant postdocs, and I said I would expect the person to give up socializing and hanging around. If you do that, there is plenty of time to get the work done. The lab isn't in a position to give a parent a less-hot project.

Particularly if you already have a child yourself, you know that few people, male or female, will put in the hours that a childless postdoc can. On the other hand, parenthood does get scientists organized: Many work fewer hours, but are so organized that they can accomplish much more in those hours.

If you have a large lab, it is easier to assume the risk of an unknown. If the new parent works so few hours that the project fails miserably, the loss can be absorbed. Make clear what you expect. But remember that the amount of work one does is not everything, that intelligence, hard work, and creativity can overcome even a lack of sleep. A pregnancy is just one of the variables you must consider.

A person does not legally have to say she is pregnant when applying for a job. But what kind of person would withhold this information? It is not necessarily your business, but most scientists would expect another scientist to give this information up front.

What can you do? Not much. If you think you cannot deal with someone pregnant, if you think you cannot adapt, your options are limited. This should be directed to all men and women. Increasingly, the partner of the person having a child, as well as adoptive parents, may ask officially for leave or to go to a lighter workload for some weeks.

Make it clear, for example, that you would always expect a 40-hour week and state the institutional maternity and paternity policy. Babies at the beginning of a job can cause problems for the worker for the next few years. Remember that you cannot predict the future for *any* person, male or female, you hire. The P.I.s that deal with maternity leave best are those who have lots of money, lots of people, and are not too hung up on control. As one P.I. said about maternity leave "If I am honest, there are months when nothing happens, anyway."

Things you cannot say during an interview

Do not ask personal questions. Avoid them, even if you feel that you have established a rapport and personal questions would be "allowed." It is improper and perhaps illegal to ask about age, disabilities, or marital status, no matter how obliquely the question is asked.

State laws vary. Some states have laws that forbid direct and indirect inquiries on topics (Yate 1994, p. 167–171; Richardson 1999) such as implied preference for a person under 40; whether the person is a U.S. citizen; about the severity or nature of a disability beyond establishing the ability of the applicant to perform the job; specific inquiries about a spouse's identity, or child care, marital status, type of discharge from military service; a request for a photograph before hiring; living situation or religion. Some topics, which may just come up innocently in casual conversation, are illegal, and ignorance of the law is usually not considered in court to be a valid excuse. It does not usually come to that, of course, but be careful. Below are examples of the way questions may and may not be asked (Richardson 1999):

- *Emergency contacts.* In case of emergency, it is lawful to ask the names of persons to be notified in case of emergency. It is not lawful to ask for the names of relatives to be notified in case of emergency.

- *Disabilities.* For applicants with an obvious disability, you may ask them to explain how they would perform the tasks with and without reasonable accommodations. It is not lawful to ask applicants if they have any disabilities, physical defects, or on-the-job injuries.

- *Marital status and family.* You can ask an applicants whether they can meet specified work schedules, and whether they have any additional responsibilities that would interfere with proper attendance. You cannot ask the marital status of an applicant, the number or ages of dependent children, any questions about pregnancy or methods of family planning, or child care arrangements.

> *I work strange hours, and I mention that. I don't require someone to work the same hours, but I mention the hours and say—do you have a problem with that, as we need some overlap. I get an idea of someone who doesn't mind being independent.*

Check with Human Resources to find the current state and federal laws concerning interview questions. Ask questions in subtle ways. Most of your applicants will be intelligent and will easily see through your questions to the expected answers.

Red flags during interviews

Always ask if someone understood the project! I had one applicant who had a lot of trouble describing what she had done, and I attributed that to nervousness, and to the fact that her English wasn't perfect. But that was a huge red flag!

Red flags are warning signs, indications that this person could be trouble.

Blaming

Not being able to take responsibility for something that has gone wrong.

Complaining about advisors and coworkers

This is tricky, because there are often valid workplace complaints. Look for the tone and for the reasons for the dissatisfaction. Specific and major complaints—"No one was given credit for ideas."—may be more credible than whines—"Everyone in the lab was unfriendly." Check through the grapevine to determine whether the candidate has come from a dysfunctional lab for if this individual does, the complaints probably have a basis.

Excessive demands

Do not be blackmailed. No matter how good or promising a candidate is, no person should demand and be given privileges not accorded everyone. Examples are visas, computers, extra salary, extra vacation time, or parking places. It cannot go well. These individuals will assume that they deserve the extra attention and/or the other people in the lab will resent you and that person. Probably, both will occur.

Lying

Should you care if someone is lying? Should you let the lies go on with the rationale that you will deal with the outcome? For most P.I.s, lying can go nowhere good. It is up to the individual P.I. to decide when bragging and stretching the truth becomes unacceptable.

Generally, there are physical clues that a person is lying (Lieberman 1998). There is discordance between words and body language, e.g., shaking of the head in a confirming gesture after a point has already been verbally made. People who are lying may try to keep physical distance between themselves and the other person, as if trying to distance themselves from the lie.

Silence is often very effective in flushing out a lie. The person, when a lie is met with silence, may continue to talk and talk in an effort to convince you of the truth. Other speech patterns may give a clue that a lie has been told. Liars will tend to use your own words to make a point. They may depersonalize an answer by offering their belief on the subject instead of answering directly. They will answer your questions, but will seldom have questions of their own for you on a topic they are lying about.

People who lie may stall for time when asked a direct question, either by delaying an answer with remarks such as "Where did you hear that?" or "I'm not sure this is the best place to discuss this" or by repeating your question back to you, "Did I get along with the supervisor in the lab? Is that what you are asking?"

Another person who lies may use humor and sarcasm to avoid answering a question ("Oh, sure, I faked data all the time"). The purpose of this is to make you feel foolish if you persist in asking the question. You should persist. Some signs of lying may appear to be signs of stress, such as fidgeting, trembling, or difficulty swallowing.

Anger

Becoming angry at a question may be a reaction to a topic the person does not want to discuss. Unless you have been rude, this is not an appropriate response to a question. Although it may not mean the person is lying, this individual certainly is not able to deal with the issue in a straightforward manner.

Interview miscellaneous

- *Lab philosophy.* Present the lab philosophy, and see how the candidate accepts it. Mention the hours, the vacations, and your attitude toward time off.

- *Time commitment.* P.I.s are sometimes advised not to request a time commitment. Yet putting months and months of training into a technician, only to have the technician leave for medical school after 1 year is a serious setback to a small and new lab. Work with Human Resources to find a legal way to ask about a 2-year commitment.

- *Invite other opinions.* Have others meet the candidate. Some P.I.s have colleagues or other lab members join in the interview, or, at least, meet with the candidate. Afterward, canvass for opinions and consider the opinions. This may be particularly important if you are going on your gut reaction. First impressions can be wrong, and even if you usually read people well, you can miss something.

SELLING THE JOB

In an interview, you must also convey the attractiveness of the work situation. Your personality will also be analyzed, and your priorities may become the data to determine whether or not a desirable candidate takes the job. If your lab is a happy one, and if you are successful, it will be easy to sell the job, as the culture of your lab is a main selling point. Of course, when the lab is new, you must try to get across to people what your plans are in building the lab. Knowing what candidates want is of prime importance: They must see your lab as a place in which to be successful and perhaps even happy.

> *By the time they come for an interview, I am pretty sure I am going to offer them a position. All the homework is done. So the interview is really for them to check out the lab. The other thing I never do is pay for anyone to come for the interview—that way, they have to be really motivated!*

What lab workers want

Technicians fill that intellectual and cultural niche that graduate students often fill at universities, says Coffman. They're young, bright, fresh-faced, open-minded, with crazy ideas and lots of questions that keep you honest.

QUOTE FROM ROBERT COFFMAN AT DNAX

JOYCE (1989, P. 2).

Lab workers include short-term and career technicians, secretaries/administrative assistants, undergraduate and graduate students, physicians, and postdocs. Listed below are the objectives of these lab members.

Career technicians:

- Money
- Status
- Learning techniques
- Papers

Short-term technicians:

- Learning techniques
- Papers
- Recommendations for school

Secretaries/Administrative assistants:

- A job
- A decent salary
- Respect
- Pleasant atmosphere
- Being part of a team
- Independence
- Chance of improvement in job position

Undergraduate students: Undergraduates come to a research lab because they like science, think they might like science, or have decided that they want to go to graduate school (the great proportion).

- Camaraderie and a sense of belonging
- Lab experience qualification
- Recommendations for graduate or medical school
- Interaction with mature scientists
- Credit for undergraduate research
- Money

Graduate students: Most graduate students come to prepare for a career in science, although not necessarily in research.

- Mentor
- Hot field
- Good project
- Fun lab
- Papers
- Recommendation for postdocs

Physician:

- If not overtly clinical, a project should be able to generate grants, probably in a clinical setting.
- Papers
- Short-term project: In general, physicians have limited time to spend in the lab.
- Organization and structure.
- Good colleagues. Medical school teaches a very us-against-them philosophy in practice. Physicians in the lab appreciate the closeness of lab members without the attached siege mentality. For most physicians, the lab is a lot of fun.
- An understanding and interested P.I. as a mentor. Whether an M.D. or Ph.D., the P.I. should understand the needs of an M.D. who wants to do research.

Postdocs: There are roughly three groups of postdoc applicants: (1) Postdocs who have had some contact with the P.I. or know a happy lab worker from that lab. The research is also of primary importance, but often, the first enthusiasm is personal. (2) Postdocs who have read papers from the lab or know of the work from meetings or word of mouth. (3) Postdocs who come for convenience or personal reasons. They want to be at a particular institution or city, or even in that country, and will go where they can get a position.

More and more postdocs, however, are discovering, either before or during their postdoc, that laboratory-based research is not for them. Along with learning the process of scientific analysis, they will also need to expand on other marketable skills that will be useful to their particular goal, such as writing, teaching, computer literacy, or interpersonal communication skills.

The postdoc is the stepping-stone to an independent career as a scientist. The major desires of a postdoc are to get "good" papers and to get a job at the end of the postdoc. In an informal survey of National Institutes of Health (NIH) postdocs, "Doing research" and "collaborations and availability of people to talk science with" tied for the second most appreciated aspect of working at the NIH in both the women's and the men's lists (Leibnitz 1999).

- Funding—no grant writing!
- Unfettered work time—no teaching, no clinical responsibilities
- Hot field
- Good project

- Interactive lab—lots of people to talk science with
- Exciting institution—lots of outside speakers—well-known place. The prestige of a famous institute on job applications can be effective. Good facilities...
- Papers. How many papers does a postdoc want? Are there ever enough? Yes and no...
- Take-away projects
- A mentor
- Marketable skills
- Recommendations
- Connections
- Some home life
- An adequate salary and living conditions

After years of graduate school, most postdoc salaries, at first, look pretty good. Postdocs do not expect to get rich, but they do expect to live a bit more comfortably than they did as students. But in some institutions, although the salary may be more than that of a student stipend, the standard of living is lower: Postdocs, unlike students, usually do not get housing or loans, may pay more taxes, and may not receive decent benefits.

In addition, it is more likely that a postdoc might have a family, and the satisfaction with the particular postdoc salary might have more to do with the postdoc's family situation than with the bottom line amount of money. One person can survive on the minimal postdoc salary, but can a spouse and two children? Spouses of foreign postdocs may be ineligible for work in a particular country. And even if they could, childcare costs are so prohibitive at some institutions that two postdoc parents cannot afford it.

Financial pressures can ruin a postdoc. There are often other family members who must be supported, or money to be sent home.

Postdoc organizations and unions are springing up at many academic institutions, and one of the goals of most organizations is facilitating just compensation for the hours and skills put in.

SELLING WHAT YOUR LAB HAS TO OFFER

Sell the job to all candidates. Even if the candidate is not your number 1 choice at the time, still work hard at selling the job. Your number 1 candidate may turn down the job, and you might have to court the other candidates anew. If you have a small lab, emphasize the one-on-one training and interaction that will be possible. Concentrate on selling yourself.

If you feel that the personality of the lab is a plus, going out all together for a meal or a drink can be a terrific way to allow the candidate to see the camaraderie in this new and wonderful job. But if the group has not clicked, and is likely to sit silently and stiffly, either invite a live wire from another lab or do a lunch alone.

Most candidates will want to speak to other members of the lab, but may find it awkward to ask you. Make the opportunity for them to do this. They may feel more comfortable asking questions of a peer.

Do not forget to discuss institutional facilities, for example, child care, schools, bonuses, and housing. The Human Resources department will, no doubt, also discuss these points, but by mentioning them yourself, you show that they are important to you.

Be honest. Stretching the truth about anything—from the anticipated victory of a project to the cost of living in the area—can be dangerous, as it is not worth the bad feelings a person who has been deceived will generate in the lab. You want the person not only to take the job, but to stay at it. Evaluate yourself and the institution fairly, although in a bright and shining light, of course! The hazards of the job should also be discussed if the person will be working with radioactivity or solvent and if there is danger of HIV exposure. You may also want to mention that overtime will sometimes be needed.

Conclude the interview by asking: What haven't we covered that you would like me to know as we evaluate you for this position? What questions do you have?

Evaluating Candidates

A GOOD FIT: SUPPORTING THE LAB CULTURE

...somewhere between 70% and 92% of all involuntary professional and managerial "performance" terminations have absolutely nothing to do with technical competence (the technical knowledge and ability to perform the work) and everything to do with cultural incompetence (the inability to fit with organizational culture).

BEATTY (1994, P. 71)

Even if you have only one applicant for a position—which is likely to be the case for student or postdoc applicants to new P.I.s—a solid evaluation will be beneficial to understanding how to choose a project or what to expect from that person. Therefore, subject all candidates for a position to a stringent evaluation. You are basically evaluating multiple factors:

- Character

- Personality

- Honesty—sense of humor—resilience

- Scientific knowledge

- Technical ability

- A good fit

> *I think I'm batting about 50% with my views of people I've hired...some people I've hired I've been ambivalent about, and have turned out to be fantastic, and other people I've thought would be great have turned out to be duds. I just find that my ability to predict what they are going to do isn't terrific.*

> *It isn't essential to like everyone, but it contributes to making the lab an enjoyable place to work. That doesn't mean I would like to be with them on a desert island, or socialize during weekends, just that we like to work with each other.*

You must also consider how the candidate will fit into the lab personality. This will be based somewhat on gut reaction, i.e., do you feel the same way about this candidate as you do about the others in your lab? But this gut reaction is based on the character and value judgments you make about people for your lab, your bottom line.

If you have included other people in the hiring process, you must listen to their opinions, even if you disagree with them. You cannot include other people and then ignore what they have to say. Defining your lab culture may not be easy for you to do. What you want to know is whether this person will:

- Fit in with the people in the lab.

- Do science the way I/we think it should be done.

- Add to the lab in a positive way, or make problems.

- Change the lab, and is that good?

Another question is, "Do I want to see this face for the next few years?" By having people in the lab meet the candidate, and by watching the interaction, you may get a better idea of how this individual will or will not fit in. But no signal is not necessarily a bad signal.

AVOIDING PREJUDICE

Evaluating People from Other Cultures

Do not let your prejudices prevent you from seeing a worthy candidate. You probably have, at least unconsciously, a list of personal attributes and behaviors that you would hope to find in every candidate. But many of these attributes are actually cultural expectations, not merely personal ones. For example, you might expect the candidate to look you in the eye and speak with you in a very straightforward manner. This might indicate to you that the person is attentive, feels confident, and would be aggressive enough to do a job well.

> *People coming out of high-flying labs assume that all people who apply to them think in the same way, and that is simply not true.*

You might also expect that candidates discuss past work experiences and expertise and to know what they want from the new position.

If a candidate comes in with eyes averted and seems unable to speak about an individual role in a previous project, you may assume that this person is not listening to you and even may not be honest. If the candidate speaks about work only obliquely, it may seem to you that perhaps the individual did not understand the work or had a much smaller role than stated in the c.v. These conclusions, based on a certain cultural background, may be completely untrue (see the chapter on The Pleasures and Perils of Diversity in this volume).

In many cultures in which there is a deep respect for authority, looking someone in the eye is considered to be a sign of disrespect. And in some places, there is no culture of positively marketing yourself; in fact, speaking only of yourself is quite impolite and impertinent.

How can you judge a person's character and not just base your decision on habits or cultural mores? Of course, can you know anyone's character in a 30-minute interview? One way might be to give the interview more time than usual, to allow the building of a rapport between you and the candidate. To find out about prior experience, you could ask about the project in general and about the other people on a project, so that the candidate can talk about personal accomplishments without seeming to brag. You could also have a multicultural team interview the candidate (Walton 1994).

Do not fall into the Ivy League trap—one that works in either direction. You cannot assume, because a particular candidate has come from a well-known place or a well-known lab, that this person is a fantastic candidate. Nor should you be negatively impressed, sure that you have a prima donna. Judge all candidates on their own achievements, character, and expertise.

Getting past the first impression

In my notes, next to that reply, I wrote "Great answer!" and I can remember at the time feeling the little thrill you experience as an interviewer when someone's behavior conforms with your expectations. Because I had decided, right off, that I liked him, what I heard in his answer was toughness and confidence. Had I decided early on that I didn't like Nolan Myers, I would have heard in that reply arrogance and bluster. The first impression becomes a self-fulfilling prophecy: we hear what we expect to hear.

GLADWELL (2000, P. 72)

An experimental psychologist compared teacher evaluations by students after a semester with the evaluations by people who had seen as little as a 2-second videotape of the teacher in action and found that the evaluations of the students and those of the videotape observers were strikingly similar. A similar but more stringent experiment performed through the University of Toledo compared the evaluations of trained job interviewers of applicants with the evaluations of people who had watched a videotape of the handshake at the beginning of each interview. Again, the observations of the job interviewers, who spent 15–20 minutes with each applicant, were highly correlated with the evaluations of strangers who had seen the applicant in an extremely brief videotape (Gladwell 2000).

> *People are so flattered that someone is applying to their lab that they are willing to suspend disbelief.*

The results of these studies may suggest the validity of the first impression. Unfortunately, the studies also point out one of the inherent weaknesses in the job interview (and, perhaps, in human nature), which is that the interviewers are only seeking to validate their first impressions.

> *I was blind about the qualities of the first people who applied to work with me. I was flattered that they selected me, and I looked at their qualities in too positive a light, not analytically.*

Watch out for the halo effect—the influence of an irrelevant trait on the interviewer's overall judgment. It is rather like reverse prejudice. For example, you may be so pleased by a candidate's love of anatomy, similar to your own when you were young, that you manage to ignore the fact that the person was obviously unable to complete any project satisfactorily.

> *I like the people I hire, and find that very important because I interact with them so much. I think that, if I didn't interact with them so much, it wouldn't be so important.*

It is not easy to separate a gut reaction from a prejudice. A "prejudice" implies a judgment based only on a categorization of the person, whereas a "gut reaction" suggests that an individual assessment has been made. Much of this distinction is semantic, but there are very gray areas. First impressions and gut reactions are important and useful tools to use when evaluating potential lab personnel. But they can be trusted best when coupled with objective data. If you really like a person, and the credentials are solid, there is much greater chance that this is a good choice than if you have a good gut reaction and three bad recommendations to go on.

> *One of the hardest things I had to adjust to when I became a P.I. was that I was going to have to work with people I didn't necessarily like.*

Do you need to like the people in your lab?

Most P.I.s do feel it is important to like the lab members they will hire. But like is a very broad word. Many people mean "approve" when they say like: Perhaps they would not want to be friends, but they respect the person. This is a fine foundation for a P.I. and lab member. Few people would accept a lab member they did not respect and could not trust.

WHAT THE VISA STATUS MIGHT MEAN TO YOU

A brief visa primer

J-1 (J-2)

The J visa is for participants in a nonimmigrant educational and cultural exchange visitors program. The program promotes the interchange of persons, knowledge, and skills in the field of education, arts, and sciences, including graduate medical education. It is probably the most common visa for postdocs. J-1 visa holders must have sufficient funds to cover all expenses, or funds must be provided by the sponsoring organization in the form of a scholarship or other stipend. They must be able to demonstrate that they intend to return to their home country.

Most J-1 visa holders, including those receiving graduate medical education, are subject to a 2-year foreign residence requirement and must return to their home country before they are eligible to apply for an immigrant or temporary worker visa. However, holders of a J-1 visa can apply for an extension of the visa or for a waiver to the 2-year residence requirement. Waivers are available for a variety of reasons, including a "No objection" statement from the home government, and the demonstration of persecution in the home country or hardship for U.S. citizens or residents relatives left behind in the U.S. In some cases, the program and visa status can be altered.

The spouse and minor children of J-visa holders may apply for a derivative J-2 visa. They must show that funds will be available to support them: Holders of a J-2 visa can get authorization from the INS to work in the U.S.

Who gets it and why: Students at all academic levels, trainees obtaining on-the-job training, professors coming to teach or do research at institutions of higher learning, research scholars, and professional trainees in the medical and allied fields. Some people frequently wish to file a waiver of the 2-year residency requirement.

H-1B (H-1)

This is a nonimmigrant, temporary worker classification, usually used in the lab for people of medical specialties. It applies to persons in a specialty occupation that requires the theoretical and practical application of a body of highly specialized knowledge requiring completion of a specific course of higher education. It is available to persons with a B.A. or B.S. and advanced degrees and includes scientists, chemists, physicians, and engineers. The employer sponsors the worker for a period of normally up to 3 years, which may be extended in 1-year increments up to a maximum of 6 years. After the 6 years, the person must spend at least 1 year outside the U.S. before applying for another visa. The employee's spouse and children are usually admitted on H-4 visas: They cannot work but can attend American schools, colleges, and universities.

An H-1B worker cannot change jobs without a visa transfer and can only work in the location specified in the visa. Be wary of someone hired through an H-1B bodyshop, a company that specializes in providing H-1B workers to other companies. The H-1B holder is therefore officially an employee of the bodyshop, and gets paid through the bodyshop, but works at another site.

Some employers will not apply for an H visa for a postdoc in the lab. Since payment of "prevailing wage" is required, even a small lab or institution might have to pay what a bustling biotech company would pay. Because of this, P.I.s sometimes look with suspicion at someone who has requested an H visa instead of a J.

H-2B

This employer-sponsored visa is available for skilled temporary workers (and seasonal agricultural workers) who do not qualify for the H-1 visa, but who can perform such services or labor that cannot be found in the U.S. This visa is a temporary and subject to the same restrictions as the H-1 visa. It is normally granted for 1 year and is not to exceed a total of 3 years.

H-3

The H-3 visa is available with the same restrictions as the H-2B, to people who come to the U.S. as trainees. The visa holder cannot engage in productive employment and must be in the U.S. for the sole purpose of training. H-3 visas are normally granted for up to 1 year, with a single extension of 6 months. The employer sponsors the trainees.

F-1

This is a nonimmigrant student visa, for academic studies. Although it can be used for high school, it is usually encountered in a college or university. Students must show that they have binding ties to a residence in their home country and that they will depart the U.S. when they have completed their studies. They must show that they have sufficient funds for the duration of their stay. Off-campus jobs may be allowed by permission after the first year. Family members may accompany the candidate if they can also meet visa requirements.

L Category

This visa is available to an alien seeking to work in the U.S. as an international "intracompany transferee." The holder of this visa must be employed continuously for at least 1 year by a company or affiliate of the U.S., working in an executive or managerial role, or be providing specialized knowledge (such as scientists). L-1 visas are generally granted for an initial period of 3 years, with either one or two extensions of 2 years, for a total of 5–7 years. An L-1 visa holder may only work for the sponsoring organization. The employer sponsors the worker.

Other visas

Candidates may hold a variety of other visas. For example, the TN visa is available only for professionals from Mexico and Canada, under the North American Free Trade Agreement.

B1 visas are used for scientists visiting for periods of less than 3 months. Other visas lab workers or physicians may hold are employment-based immigrant visas, such as the Employment First Preference (E1) visa for outstanding professors and researchers with at least 3 years of experience; the Employment Second Preference Visa (E2) visa for professionals holding an advanced degree and having "exceptional ability" or more than 5 years of experience; or Employment Third Preference (E3) visas, for skilled workers and workers with B.A. or B.S. degrees. Some visas require the guarantee of a job before they are granted.

Visa concerns

- The Human Resources department is your immediate source of information about employee and student visas. Visa requirements and time limits change frequently. Most visa business will be handled through this department. If you are personally asked to write a letter for a visa change or extension, check with Human Resources first to find out your legal obligations and whether you or the workplace is liable for that person.

- The visa can heavily influence the candidate's work and personal life. The length of the visa and the attempts at prolonging it—whether or not the spouse can work and the children go to school—may all have an effect on work. As for most personal information, the implications of holding a visa are not in the bounds of questions you can or should ask during an interview, but you should, for timing sake, know the visa statutes.

- Some P.I.s worry that individuals with a nonimmigrant visa will have to return, perhaps unwillingly, to their home countries if they do not work out. This feeling of responsibility can cause them to hesitate to hire someone whose future they hold so strongly in their hands. Most P.I.s see no problem in supporting a candidate that they definitely want in their lab, and some see supporting a postdoc for a visa as the only chance a beginning P.I. has to get a postdoc.

- Several P.I.s have helped a particular person obtain a job, only to have that individual leave for another job once the job is in hand. This is illegal, and the employer has the right to litigate and seek damages from the employee.

- As part of an employment agreement, a company will sometimes offer to negotiate a green card. This can be used to take advantage of visa holders, who may be willing to accept lower pay in the hope of receiving a card. If paychecks are not issued through you, be sure a visa holder is receiving the same pay as the others in the lab.

If Human Resources cannot answer your questions or those of your lab members, there are several Web Sites that provide forms and information, and access to a lawyer. One of these is http://www.VisaLaw.com.

WHEN YOU HAVE FEW CHOICES

The Catch-22 of starting a new lab is that you need a successful lab to attract good people, but you need good people to build a successful lab. You will probably have to scrounge and scrimp and compromise to find competent people, and you will have to learn a lot about how to get the most out of people. Especially when first starting out, you will not always be able to meet all your ideal qualifications in every—or possibly any—candidate.

Would I put up with someone who was both highly productive and objectionable? Probably; but it would be more difficult in a small lab such as mine.

At most places, a technician is your best first chance at getting a good lab member. Most technicians will not be judging your track record and might apply to you as well as to anyone else. Even with a tiny lab, you can offer benefits that might be very attractive to a technician, such as a recommendation for graduate school. Put your best effort into getting a technician in the lab, as it is the most likely investment to give you a good return at this point.

If a postdoc is a complete wash, I can't absorb that...

One personality I don't like is someone who, when you tell him how to do something, goes around to every person to find out how they do it.

Starting investigators in an academic workplace will have little chance or choice in their selection of postdoc. When a postdoc does apply, most P.I.s will immediately say yes, figuring that a bad post-doc is better than none at all. This is not true. No other position can cost you such worry if it does not work out. You must be more careful with a postdoc position than with any other hire.

If the person can't afford to be there 100%, I can't afford to take that person." So I ask if the person has another job—I don't like M.D.'s who are moonlighting.

Characteristics and qualities to avoid

Good science cannot proceed without a deep emotional investment on the part of the scientist. It is that emotional investment that provides the motivating force for the endless hours of intense, often grueling, labor.

KELLER (1983, P. 198)

Even when it is extremely difficult to find any personnel, P.I.s will have a list of people they definitely will not take, under any circumstances. (Unfortunately, many P.I.s have made their lists only in retrospect.) Below is a list of traits that P.I.s say to avoid.

- Arrogance

- Bad recommendations

- Does not appear to get along with other people

- Fought with advisor

> *I don't like aggressive, self-centered people, or those who are competitive with others in the lab.*

> *I wouldn't take someone who had a fight with his advisor, although I would call the advisor to find out the story. But generally, I wouldn't take them on.*

> *I have trouble with someone who comes and says he only wants his own project. Everyone has his "own" project, but there is overlap, and someone who can't work as a team shouldn't be there. Or someone who is difficult to get along with, I wouldn't take him, either.*

Hiring mistakes by new P.I.s

Most P.I.s have admitted to at least one serious mistake in hiring, and some of these mistakes were not just in the beginning. Most agreed that there were signs from the beginning, but that in wanting that person to work out, they ignored the indications of trouble. The range of problems with new personnel is large, encompassing everything from poor technique to not getting along with others.

> *My first technician was a mistake. I had a gut feeling against the person— I wish I had introduced him to others! I would know now. The first person is very important, because it sets the scene for how you are working. At the time, I was writing grants, setting up the lab, and didn't have enough time to spend with a technician.*

Not all mistakes attributed to bad hiring are actually bad hiring—some are due to inexperience with dealing with people in the lab afterward. But

> *I made a bad mistake in the first hire—I looked for technique in a technician, but hired someone who couldn't think."*

P.I.s also cite many examples of hiring someone for whom they had very low expectations, yet ended up with a capable employee for 5 years and a friend for life.

SAYING YES AND NO

Make sure that all candidates are called with good or bad news. If you have made a personal connection during the interview process, you may want to make some calls yourself, although Human Resources does not usually recommend this. Assurances made to candidates to make them feel better can be fodder for a grievance.

It may be uncomfortable for you, but if candidates ask why they were not the first choice, you may be able to tell them. It could be so useful for someone to know that the lack of a certain course or technique made the difference. But this can be dangerous territory, and it is one of the reasons why Human Resources may insist upon their department making the calls. For example, admitting that other lab members did not like the person might be grounds for a discrimination suit against the institution.

Do not turn down your candidates until your first choice has agreed to take the job. Let each person know as soon as possible. If something happens that your first choice, for example, accepts another job after taking yours or does not work out once on the job, you may want to call back the next candidate on the list. If you have alienated the person because you or Human Resources never called back, it may be hard to persuade the applicant to now come. You never know!

RESOURCES

ASCB Profile. 1999. Gunter Blobel. *Am. Soc. Cell Biol. Newsletter* **22**: 5–7. (http://www.ascb.org)

Beatty R.H. 1994. *Interviewing and selecting high performers.* John Wiley & Sons, New York.

Black S.D. 1999. Job interviewing strategy. *Network of Emerging Scientists.* (http://psyche.uthct.edu/nes/nes.html)

Boulakia C. 1998. The 4 management consulting interview types. *Science's Next Wave*, Feb. 6, pp. 1–3. (http://nextwave.sciencemag.org)

Brown S., McDowell L., and Race P. 1995. *500 Tips for research students.* Kogan Page, Philadelphia.

Carter N. and Schafer S. 1996. Situation of postdocs: Purpose, perseverance, vision. *Science's Next Wave*, Aug. 2, pp. 1–5. (http://nextwave.sciencemag.org)

Caveman. 2000. *Caveman.* The Company of Biologists Limited, Cambridge, England.

Dannhauser C.L. 1999. Burn this resume. Three companies take a novel approach to filling vacancies. *Working Woman*, June, p. 26.

Fiske P. 1997. The skills employers really want. *Science's Next Wave*, April 25, pp. 1–4. (http://nextwave.sciencemag.org)

Fiske P. 1997. Informational interviewing: How to be an insider at every opening. *Science's Next Wave*, March 28, pp. 1–5. (http://nextwave.sciencemag.org)

Fiske P. 1998. A postdoc bill of rights. *Science's Next Wave*, Nov. 27, pp. 1–5. (http://nextwave.sciencemag.org)

Fiske P. 1999. How to separate ideal employers from bad ones during your job search. *Science's Next Wave*, Feb. 26, pp. 1–4. (http://nextwave.sciencemag.org)

Gladwell M. 2000. The new-boy network. What do job interviews really tell us? *The New Yorker*, May 29, pp. 68–86.

Harris J. and Brannick J. 1999. *Finding and keeping great employees.* AMACOM Books, New York.

Heller R. and Hindle T. 1998. *Essential manager's manual.* DK Publishing, New York.

Jensen D. 1998a. Interviewing skills: What to do when they say "tell me about yourself." *Science's Next Wave*, July 10, pp. 1–4. (http://nextwave.sciencemag.org)

Jensen D. 1998b. Forcasting compatibility: How to select your new boss. *Science's Next Wave*, June 12, pp. 1–4. (http://nextwave.sciencemag.org)

Joyce L. 1989. DNAX immunologists work to balance industry, academia. *The Scientist* **3**: 1–3. (http://www.thescientist.com)

Judson H.F. 1996. *The eighth day of creation*, Expanded edition. Cold Spring Harbor Laboratory Press, Cold Spring Harbor, New York.

Kelleher S. and Sanders E. 2000. Troubled resident's case left UW with quandary. *The Seattle Times*, July 5, pp. 1–10.

Keller E.F. 1983. *A feeling for the organism: The life and work of Barbara McClintock.* W.H. Freeman, New York.

Leibnitz R. 1999. The NIH postdoc experience. *The Scientist* **13**: 13. (http://www.thescientist.com)

Lieberman D.J. 1998. *Never be lied to again.* St. Martin's Press, New York.

Marsh S.R. 2000. Negotiation styles in mediation. (http://adrr.com/adr1/essayb/htm)

Medley H.A. 1993. *Sweaty palms: The neglected art of being interviewed.* Ten Speed Press, Berkeley, California.

Regets M.C. 1998. What follows the postdoctoral experience? Employment Patterns of 1993 Postdocs in 1995. Division of Science Resource Studies, Nov. 27, 1999. National Science Foundation. (http://nsf.gov/sbe/srs/issuebrf/ib99307.htm)

Richardson R., ed. 1999. Lawful and unlawful interview questions. (http://courses.cs.vt.edu/~cs3604/careers/lawful.html)

Suskind, Susser, Haas, & Devine. 2001. Immigration and Nationality Law. (http://www.VisaLaw.com)

Thiederman S. 1991. *Profiting in America's multicultural marketplace.* Macmillan, New York.

United States Immigration and Naturalization Services. 2000a. Tips for U.S. visas: Employment-based visas. U.S. Department of Justice. (http://travel.state.gov//visa;employ-based.html)

United States Immigration and Naturalization Services. 2000b. Tips for U.S. visas: Temporary workers. U.S. Department of Justice. (http://travel.state.gov//visa;tempwkr.html)

United States Immigration and Naturalization Services. 2000c. TN visas: Professionals under NAFTA. U.S. Department of Justice. (http://travel.state.gov//tn_visas.html)

United States Immigration and Naturalization Services. 2000d. Visa services. U.S. Department of Justice. (http://travel.state.gov//visa_services.html)

Walton S.J. 1994. *Cultural diversity in the workplace*. Mirror Press and Irwin Professional Publishing, New York.

Winston S. 1983. *The organized executive. New ways to manage time, paper, and people*. Warner Books, New York.

Yate M. 1994. *Hiring the best*. Adams Media Corporation, Holbrook, Massuchesetts.

Starting and Keeping New Lab Members

Getting Off to a Good Start

THE FIRST DAY

When I arrived at the Rockefeller Institute, my first impression was that the atmosphere of the laboratory of Oswald T. Avery was so peaceful that I had some doubt that there was much eagerness among the workers in the laboratory. I believe it took me at least one or two months to realize the manner in which Dr. Avery conducted his department. Dr. Avery never asked anyone to do anything. In fact, he almost urged people not to do too much. Of all the persons I have known in science, he certainly was the man who most was concerned with thoughts, long thoughts and meditations, before doing experiments, instead of the usual manner of rushing in and doing as much laboratory work as possible. PIEL AND SEGERBERG (1990, P. 53)

In the summer of 1948, I applied to Dr. Joseph Aub, director of the Huntington Laboratories of the Huntington Memorial Hospital of Harvard University at the Massachusetts General Hospital), who promised me a postdoctoral position in the fall. When I reported for work, he had forgotten the agreement but assured me I could work on any number of interesting projects. To this, day, I marvel at both the casualness with which I obtained my first job and my immense good fortune in getting it.

HOAGLAND (1990, P. 37)

The first day of work will set the scene for the rest of the person's tenure. The more information imparted about the job and the people, the faster the work will start. You gain nothing by turning someone loose. This is also the day (actually, the interview and subsequent meetings might already have set the scene) that will start to establish the relationship between the two of you.

Your own first days of work should suggest to you what problems your lab workers may encounter. Did your keys to the office fit? Were all your grants and accounts ready to be billed right away? Did you know whether lab supplies should be ordered through preferred venders? Did the institution give you advice about visas? It will probably be even harder for newcomers to negotiate the institutional rules than it was for you, so do what you can to make it easier for the lab workers.

Below is a list of tips to make the first day worthwhile:

- *Arrange a specific time to meet* so that your new lab member is not sitting in the departmental library for hours, waiting for you.

- *Talk about the project.* Have papers or references ready.

- *Clarify the responsibilities* of the position, both immediate and in the coming weeks.

- *Discuss expectations.* Without trying to indoctrinate, explain the lab culture and customs, briefly. For example, talk about your open door or non-open door policy.

- *Introduce the new employee to the other members* of the lab and to the department.

- *Show the location of the lab member's work space.* Give consideration to where you place a new worker. Physical placement, if there are options, does count. If you have two available lab benches, one badly situated and one superbly fitted out, and the new recruit is given the most inconvenient bench, you are sending a message. Think ahead.

- *Show where supplies are stored.* Discuss the budget.

- *Go to lunch with the new comer,* alone or with the lab.

Depending on the kind of lab and the number of people you have, you may not be able to or want to personally guide each newcomer around all day. You should, however, have people available and primed to do the introductory tasks.

It is also helpful if you can collect as much information about the lab as possible into a lab manual, which can be updated regularly and presented to each new lab member. A list of things to do can be immensely comforting to a newcomer, and it eliminates reinventing the wheel with each new person to the lab.

Bear in mind that the most common mistake made by P.I.s is getting too close and too familiar with lab members. Excited, thrilled, and filled with the memory of the camaraderie of the postdoc community—plus a new feeling of responsibility—it is very tempting to completely befriend the new lab worker. Be welcoming and friendly, but keep a bit of distance.

Of course, if you have assessed the kind of lab you want to have and have decided that your style is to be friends with lab members, go ahead. But be sure you know what you want in the future.

PRACTICALITIES

The exact moment for your attitude talk with a new employee is a matter of personal preference. I prefer bringing the person back into the office after she has been notified she got the job. That strikes me as an ideal time to congratulate the person and give the attitude talk. It should be reinforced the first day on the job too, but in a low-key way because there are so many things on the new employee's mind that day. She's nervous; she's concerned about how she's going to like the people she is going to meet and if they will like her. But that first day is when the new employee is most receptive to what is expected.

BELKER (1997, P. 85)

Prepare ahead. Many of the details that new lab personnel must deal with can be more effectively handled by the P.I. For example, e-mail and Internet accounts, as well as phones and voice mail, may take days or weeks to be set up and should be done by the P.I. in advance of the lab member's arrival. If the person expects to work with biohazard or radioactivity immediately upon arrival, make an appointment for the necessary instruction or tests that your institution requires. It may also take months before postdoc grants, for example, are activated, and it may also take a while before your own grant begins to pay lab personnel. Below is a checklist to consider for the new employee.

- Assign lab bench and desk.

- Copy of institutional directory.

- Copy of lab manual.

- Safety issues (people to contact or phone numbers to use in emergencies).

- How to order supplies.

- How to apply for radiation or recombinant DNA licenses and any other special requirements needed for work (inoculations, etc.).

- Make sure the phone is connected, that the lab worker knows billing information (whether the lab pays for private calls, etc.), the procedure for making calls, getting messages, and being listed in the institution's directory.

- e-mail/Internet access (can take weeks to set up).

- Lab notebook (companies may assign these).

- Mail (where received and how to send it).

- Where to get stationery.

- Identification (ID/key cards). Pictures may need to be taken, and I.D. made as part of the procedure for key cards for the lab and/or hospital, animal facilities, etc.

- Keys for lab and office.

- Seminar lists (how to get onto this and other mailings, such as for the institutional newsletter).

- Health care and insurance.

- Parking.

- Personal information (banks, schools and day care, transportation).

The Human Resources department at your institution may or may not have a standard package of action for new lab workers. If not, as soon as you hire someone, begin to prepare for your new lab member's arrival.

CREATING TRAINING PARTNERSHIPS

Arranging for incoming lab members to work with an experienced lab worker is advantageous not only for the new person, but for establishing and reinforcing the sense of teamwork and collaboration. This arrangement can be limited to a series of experiments, until the newcomer has learned a series of desired techniques; it may be a semi-permanent collaboration. If defined, keep it short-term, to see how the partnership works out.

> *I always put a new person on part of a project, on a part related to the project that hadn't worked very well. That way, they have someone to whom they will naturally have to go to for advice.*

A new technician, an undergraduate student, or a beginning graduate student might be expected to perform some scud work during a training period. This should be limited and temporary and should be monitored: You do not want the new person to be taken advantage of by the enthusiastic demands of fellow lab members. But you should also monitor the toll that training takes on more experienced lab workers: You cannot expect them to sacrifice their own work indefinitely to the greater cause of the lab.

> *I put a new person on an experimental project. If it looks as if something may work, that person can experience the thrill of having discovered something.*

One arrangement that can cause trouble is the training of postdocs or M.D.s by technicians if it is done repeatedly. It simply galls some people too much to know that their salary is but a portion of that of the person being taught, and a technician who is expected to do that can easily feel resentful.

> *I put a new person on an almost-finished project, with the goal of that person being a middle author on the paper. By being responsible for "clean-up," perhaps running some of the controls for the paper, he becomes part of a team and sees how science can really work, not just the struggle.*

Even an experienced but new postdoc will benefit from the tutelage of someone from the lab. This is tricky, because some postdocs might be terribly offended if it were suggested that they work with someone. Both independence and the capacity to work with others are desirable in a lab, so the call is yours. It might work best to foster the independence, but request that the new postdoc also learn a particular technique from someone else. For a temporary arrangement, such as the demonstration of a technique to a postdoc, you do not have to worry too much about personalities. You may assume, for example, that a hard-working person might resent a lazy one, but partnerships and friendships arise in unexpected places, and this level of worry is not worth your time. Some P.I.s have found that the best way to partner workers is to match working-hour preferences.

> *I pair each new person with someone else, someone working on a project he expressed interest in. Gradually that project will differentiate into a more specific project.*

WHEN THERE IS NO ONE ELSE

When it is just you and the first person you hire, you will probably be the teacher of all phases of the work: science, practicalities, and ethics. You may be working side by side for most of the day, and the boundary between the professional and the personal will be created now. This is a very special relationship, for you and the lab member, and from day 1, you should keep in mind where you want it to go.

Should you tell about the nasty conversation you had with your partner last night? Do you want to hear about the troubles with the boyfriend/girlfriend every morning? Your relationship will be influenced not only by your own decisions, but by the personality and the caliber of that first person.

Training Lab Personnel

WHY TRAIN THE ALREADY TRAINED?

I've heard many managers sound the death knell for increased performance by saying, "We don't need to train. We employ only experienced individuals." Situations change, procedures and technology changes and yesterday's skills cannot sufficiently meet today's challenges.

BROWN (1985, P. 136)

Most of the expenses of running a lab are for salaries. Few people would spend $100,000 for a piece of equipment and leave it in a hall, manual unread, and machine unused and unserviced. Yet some P.I.s would turn the most inexperienced acolyte loose to do research, with the minimum of guidance. Even if you want to run a survival-of-the-fittest lab, and do not ever want to have an interactive lab, it makes fiscal sense to protect your investment by training new employees.

Except for the first technician hired, new lab personnel are thrown into the lab, shown a lab bench, and given a week or so to figure out the lab dynamics, the procurement of supplies and equipment, a rudimentary plus knowledge of the field, and at least a few techniques.

> One problem in coming from a crackerjack lab is that, when you are starting your own lab, it is a completely different operation. You've got a technician who has to be trained and needs daily attention and maybe a student who doesn't know anything, and a postdoc who is mediocre because no one gets great postdocs when they are first starting out. The things that worked for your advisor are not going to work for you.

While the hands-off training method is traditional in labs, it is ineffectual. Despite a lab head's deep belief that all lab workers should be completely independent, training is the best and fastest way to make lab workers competent.

Who will do the training? You will, of course, at first. This is how you will form the personality of the lab. By working at the bench, and overseeing the training of the people who come into the lab, you can be sure that the techniques and the thinking that go on are up to your standards. After a year or so, many P.I.s allow the present lab members to train incoming lab members.

WHAT SHOULD BE TAUGHT?

In my view, some advice about what should be known, about what technical education should be acquired, about the intense motivation needed to succeed, and about the carelessness and inclination toward bias that must be avoided, is far more useful than all the rules and warnings of theoretical knowledge.

RAMON Y CAJAL (1999, p. 6)

It is not carved in stone what to teach even for a technician on a particular project. You must decide what it is you want lab workers to know. There are few cases where technical training should be enough. To create and maintain an effective lab culture, all lab members should be connected to each other's projects and to the world of science overall.

- *Technical training.* How to set up, perform, and interpret an experiment.

- *Background knowledge* and the relationship of the project to the field. The relationship of the field to the rest of science, and implicitly, the relationship of science to the community.

- *Judgment skills.* Analyzing one's own experimental data, and the data of the field.

- *Communication.* Learning to listen and take directions. Expressing one's thoughts. Teaching. Getting along with other lab members. Networking. How to be in a collaboration.

- *Political skills.* The right time and place to publish. With whom to discuss one's data.

- *Organizing and giving a presentation.*

Most importantly, you must teach that it is the questions, and not the answers, that are important. For someone used to years of schooling, this concept will not be easy to teach, and yet, it might make the difference between someone who really has it and one who does not.

How different is the training of lab workers for different positions? It depends somewhat on the type of lab you want to have. In a hierarchical lab, some P.I.s give technicians and undergraduates much less background information and mentoring time than they give to graduate students and postdocs. Information is power, after all, and some people do not want a technician to ask questions, but to follow orders. The training given a technician in such a lab may be very experiment-dependent—you do this, you add this. Period.

LEARNING STYLES

No matter how alike the members of your lab seem to be, they will learn in different ways. Very often, someone may appear to be "slow" or obtuse, when in actuality this lab member simply processes information in a manner completely different from that of the P.I.

Learning styles are individual approaches to learning, the sum of each person's social, psychological, physical, and cultural background. Many paradigms, from information processing to emotional responses, have been used to understand and explain particular learning styles (Kearsley 2001), several of which have been included here. It is not reasonable to box all people into convenient categories, but even understanding that there *are* different ways to learn can help you get through to seemingly resistant learners.

Visual, auditory, and tactile/kinesthetic learners

- *Visual learners.* Learn through seeing. Best taught by chart, graphs, protocols, background reading. May learn best away from verbal disturbances. Likely to look up solutions to problems rather than ask about them. May appear to not want to interact with others because they learn better by reading and thinking than talking.

- *Auditory learners.* Learn through hearing. Likely to participate in meetings and discussions and talk about experiments with others. May appear to not be interested in background and theory of an experiment.

- *Tactile/Kinesthetic learners.* Learn through moving, touching, feeling. Best taught by doing or performing the experiment. Likely to multitask, doing several things at once with frequent study breaks. May appear to not be listening or paying attention as they move around during instruction and during work.

Motivation-defined learning styles

Below are listed the various learning styles (Kolb 1976 in Yentsch and Sinderman 1992) that are defined by motivation.

- *Dynamic*
  Seek hidden possibilities.
  Learn by trial and error; self-discovery.
  Perceive information concretely and process it actively.

- *Innovative*
  Seek meaning.
  Learn by listening and sharing ideas.
  Perceive information concretely and process it reflectively.

- *Common sense*
  Seek usability.
  Learn by testing theories in ways that seems sensible.
  Perceive information abstractly and process it actively.

- *Analytical*
  Seek facts.
  Learn by thinking through ideas.
  Perceive information abstractly and process it reflectively.

Even in the search for the Truth, there are varying approaches! Other investigators have formulated a learning style model with particular relevance for scientists (Felder and Silverman 1988). In this model, a student's learning style may be defined in part by the answers to five questions (see below) (Felder 1993; Felder and Soloman 2000).

Learning Style	Teaching Implications
• *Sensing/intuitive.* What type of information does the student preferentially perceive: *sensory*—sights, sounds, physical sensations, or *intuitive*—memories, ideas, insights?	• *Sensing learners* like learning facts and enjoy details, whereas *intuitive learners* dislike repetition and prefer innovation and working with concepts. Intuitors may work faster than sensors, but sensors are more careful.
• *Visual/verbal.* Through which modality is sensory information most effectively perceived: *visual*—pictures, diagrams, graphs, demonstrations, or *verbal*—sounds, written and spoken words and formulas?	• *Visual learners* learn best from graphs, charts, and reference books, whereas *verbal learners* may learn best by hearing a talk or lecture.
• *Inductive/deductive.* With which organization of information is the student most comfortable: *inductive*—facts and observations are given, underlying principles are inferred, or *deductive*—principles are given, consequences and applications are deduced?	• Give the steps first, and *inductive learners* can build up to the conclusion. *Deductive learners* would do better with the theory and expectations of the experiment and then understand the specifics.
• *Active/reflective.* How does the student prefer to process information: *actively*—through engagement in physical activity or discussion, or *reflectively*—through introspection?	• *Active learners* tend to like group activities more than reflective learners, who prefer working alone. Active learners are akin to the tactile/kinesthetic learner, and learn best by being active while being taught. *Reflective learners* may need time to absorb the information after it is given.
• *Sequential/global.* How does the student progress toward understanding: *sequentially*—in a logical progression of small incremental steps, or *globally*—in large jumps, holistically?	• *Sequential learners* gain understanding in linear steps, whereas *global learners* tend to learn in large jumps, appearing to suddenly understand. A global learner needs the big picture before mastering the details, whereas the sequential learners may need to work through steps before understanding the overall impact of a theory.

Adapted, with permission, from Felder (1993) and Felder and Soloman (2000).

The Learning Styles Questionnaire can be taken and evaluated on-line (http://www2.ncsu.edu/unity/lockers/users/f/felder/public/ILSdir/ilsweb.html) (Soloman and Felder 1999). This evaluation may be useful for all lab members, as well as for the P.I. Knowing how one's learning may differ from others can provide much insight when teaching the many people who come through the lab.

Why knowing about someone's learning style is useful. These learning styles are not meant to be either/or categories, but to represent areas of greater strengths and weaknesses. Appreciating the differences in motivation, drive, and retention can help you be patient when encountering some of the seemingly odd nuances you may have to struggle with. For example, you may think a visual learner or a reflective learner is avoiding you, when that person may just need time to read or absorb information before discussing it. In the lab, a global, active, or verbal learner may be considered quicker or brighter than a sequential, reflective, or verbal learner.

Knowing your own style will help you better teach others. If you are an auditory learner, giving verbal instructions in a rapid-fire way to a visual learner may lead you to believe that the person is not paying attention to you and does not seem to "get" it. Using a drawing to accompany your talk might help immensely. Or, for a tactile/kinesthetic learner, you could demonstrate a technique and simultaneously talk the person through it. Most importantly, knowing about other learning styles might stop you from judging someone to be merely lazy or distracted or noninteractive.

The culture of the lab can be influenced or even created by a predominant learning style among the personnel. There are the labs in which ideas about science and experiments are exchanged all day, verbally, quickly, and loudly, and there are labs in which ideas are exchanged mostly during thoughtful meetings, after preparation. This is part of the personality of the lab, but the P.I. must be sure that those who do not share the dominant manner of learning are not labeled negatively. Try to set the expectation that all learning styles will be supported by you and other lab members.

HOW TO TRAIN A NEW PERSON AT THE BENCH

Before the Experiment

- Plan an experiment commonly done in the lab with results that are known to the lab. This will introduce the person to the field and jargon of the lab and to commonly used reagents.

- Give the person a protocol to follow the *day before* you teach the experiment to allow the person time to look it over. Do not rely on a protocol in your head, as you are likely to leave something out or teach it in an illogical sequence.

- Provide background reading on the theoretical side of the experiment. Reading a paper involving the technique also reinforces the idea that lab experiments are real—not just an exercise.

- Have as much of the experiment set up as possible. A new person to the lab will find it difficult to differentiate the preparation from the experiment and thus be distracted with too many details.

During the Experiment

- Keep the explanations light. Say what you will do and why. If you do not know the person's learning preferences, cover your bases by talking, writing, and demonstrating.

- Be aware of the sequence of your directions. Go from simple to complex explanations, and go in the order of the steps required. Do not go back and forth between different parts of the experiment.

- Encourage note taking. Require note taking! Provide two copies of the protocol, one for the lab member to write notes on. Although it is true that some people do not learn by writing, getting used to recording details while working is an important part of bench research.

- Demonstrate the experiment. Give details of how to use the equipment. Show how to hold, manipulate, turn, and physically perform the experiment. Fear of using one machine incorrectly can overshadow the entire procedure for some people.

- Let the person hold the equipment, and do some of the experiment. But do not give so much hands-on as to cause a distraction from listening.

After the Experiment

- Show how to clean up afterward. This is the time to build in good habits and to make clear your expectations.

- Remind the person to reread the protocol—it will make so much more sense after having seen or done the experiment.

- Ask the person to repeat the experiment alone. Be around, but in the background.

For each experiment, show

- How to find and use a protocol.

- How to read through the experiment to see what might be missing.

- How to make or obtain what is needed. Include instruction about ordering.

- How to record the results.

- How to interpret the results.

- Why and how often the experiment must be repeated.

- How to troubleshoot during the experiment: What might go wrong and what should be done.

- Safety issues involved in the experiment.

- Clarify what is specific to the experiment and what is common to all experiments. You are teaching the thought process of how to do an experiment, not just the technical expertise for that particular experiment.

Be prepared to go through a failed experiment, step by step, with the lab member. If something goes wrong, you will almost always be told, "I did everything the protocol said." The person may be very resistant to going through each step, but the reason for 90% of failed experiments can be found in this way.

1. With the protocol in hand, start with the first step, and first go through the procedures. Concentrate on the inclusion of all steps, and ask questions, step by step.

2. If no omission or mistake is found, go through the protocol again, checking the actions in more detail. For example, ask, "After you centrifuged the tube, what did you do with the tube?" This is the time to ask about measurements.

3. For the next round, try to find out about the materials. "Where did you get the 1 M NaCl? How did you make it? Can I see your calculations?"

4. If no cause for the problem is found, have the person repeat the experiment. For a very junior person, you should be there to watch every step; more experienced lab members can repeat the experiment on their own.

Particular needs at the bench

Inexperienced technicians

The majority of inexperienced technicians arrive straight from college. They are likely to have majored in a science and to have met laboratory requirements. This is good and bad. They will be familiar with some of the equipment of the lab and with the general principles of experimentation and data recording. They may also be accustomed to experiments going well, as well as not having to think much in order to function in the lab.

Another good and bad side of fresh college graduates is that they are young and may not be very focused, enjoying their first "vacation" away from school. Or they may be terrifically motivated and enthusiastic. The scope of what you will teach will be influenced by personality, more than the position. P.I.s estimate it takes 6 months to 1 year to train a technician. It will not always be as labor intensive as the first weeks. Unless the person has done an independent study or other lab work, keep everything simple.

- ***Start with one small technique*** that does not require sterile work but that is a real experiment. Have the technician repeat the experiment: Learning the value of repeating experiments and getting reproducible data are important lessons to teach a college graduate just starting out.

- ***Provide a layman's description*** of the research, only. Do not bombard the person with theories and papers—keep the background information sparse. You can add information later on, but not remove the confusion that results from a mélange of information.

- ***Build slowly,*** and build everything around that first lesson and technique. Take nothing for granted.

- ***Speak slowly,*** and do not accept a nod as understanding. Ask questions to verify understanding, and make it clear that you prefer questions to mock understanding.

Undergraduates

Undergraduates should be taught very much the same way as a technician. Since they will not have done many advanced courses, they probably have less hands-on lab experience than technicians. With an undergraduate, keep background information minimal until after the experiment has been done once. Undergraduates usually are not able to process too much information or to tell the important from the nonimportant.

Graduate students

Graduate students usually come in rather untrained and leave with a huge breadth of knowledge and technical skills. The ability of a graduate student to absorb the amount of information given in the early days will vary greatly. Some should be taught like undergraduates/technicians, with emphasis on the actual experiment and not the background. Others will be ready to interpret the background and incorporate that knowledge into the experiment.

Postdocs

Most postdocs would be offended to be given training at the bench, unless it is specific training for a new technique. If you are demonstrating a new technique, provide reading material beforehand. Most postdocs will want to know as much as possible before starting an experiment.

Physicians

Clinical training consists of rotations, which are very organized. The rules in clinical training are clear, and one is strongly encouraged to follow the rules. But physicians coming to a new lab can feel very lost and out of control when told to find their own way.

The way in which information and training is conveyed can add to that sense of powerlessness. Throughout medical school, one learns a field in orderly steps, progressively gaining more complex and specialized information. But in most labs, instruction for physicians is piecemeal. A newcomer may be told to follow a certain person around in the morning, and to learn a particular technique from another person in the afternoon, without any idea how, or even if, the techniques are related to the project. In addition, the persons giving the instruction may be technicians without answers to the "why" questions, or students without the desire to have responsibility for the physician's project.

The *ideal situation* would be that one knowledgeable and experienced person would be with the physician for, say, 3 weeks. That person could explain the background, teach the techniques in an understandable progression (e.g., learning to grow cells before learning to extract DNA), help interpret results, and be there to answer questions. A young lab, however, does not always have the personnel to do this. Especially when a physician is only staying for a few months, it might be hard to rationalize adding extra work to the plate of a harried student or postdoc.

But putting the physician to work with a student or postdoc for a few weeks would be very helpful. Although technicians tend to have less prejudice against physicians (since many technicians intend to go to medical school), many do not have an understanding of the big picture. For those weeks, the student or postdoc should try to provide the technical background in a progressive and orderly way.

One way to avoid burdening lab personnel is to take over the intellectual training and as much of the technical training as possible. Knowing that the P.I. will do some of the actual training would make a lab a very desirable place to join.

Mentor to All?

MENTORING ASSUMED

I do not know a single young scientist who has ambivalent feelings about their Ph.D. adviser. There tends to be either mutual respect or mutual loathing. Some have had, and continue to have, a great personal and professional relationship with their former advisor. Others are barely on speaking terms. Yet, the strength of the advisor-advisee relationship is supposed to be one of the foundations of the Ph.D. To a great extent, that relationship not only influences the student's future direction but whether the student completes the degree at all. And still, a surprising fraction of students have difficulty with their advisor.

FISKE (1999)

Mentoring in its fullest sense is very much a master-apprentice relationship, wherein the master guides the apprentice in all aspects of science and will be the apprentice's champion long into the future. But as listed below, there are many kinds of mentoring relationships.

- Formal or casual.

- Between peers or between teacher and student.

With big labs, and the focus on money, people in labs often aren't mentored anymore.

- Passive, acting as a role model without deliberately passing on any information.

- Brief or lasting a professional lifetime.

- Completely enveloping, providing not only professional help, but personal help as well.

The organization and the kind of lab you have will suggest whether or not mentoring is part of the job. In labs at smaller colleges, the P.I. as mentor to all is usually assumed, but the level of mentoring is usually still up to you. The larger and more competitive the organization and lab, the more usual that very few will be mentored well. In the end, it is you who will decide whether to enter a mentoring relationship and to determine the limits of the relationship.

The Functions of Successful Mentors

- Demonstrating a style and methodology of doing research

- Developing an analytical approach to selection of significant questions and to choosing appropriate approaches to solving them

- Discussing the concepts in any subdiscipline, and the evolution of those concepts over time

- Exploring and evaluating the literature of the discipline and the broader body of knowledge of which it is a part

- Discussing the ethical basis for scientific research

- Considering, analyzing, and evaluating the work and conclusions of colleagues

- Transmitting, by example and discussions, the skills required for effective scientific writing

- Evaluating successful teaching techniques

- Facilitating access to the research community in the discipline (scientific societies, peer groups, international science, "in groups," etc.)

- Illustrating the methodology and significance of "networking" in science

- Developing attitudes and approaches to the many interpersonal relationships involved in being a scientist

Reprinted, with permission of Perseus Book Publishers, from Yentsch and Sinderman (1992, pp. 147–148).

QUALIFICATIONS OF AN EFFECTIVE MENTOR

Suggestions for successful mentoring

- *Success.* Having something to teach, having achieved enough success in a field to be considered competent.

- *Confidence.* It is obnoxious to be smug or patronizing, but you must believe that you are a good choice for a mentor.

- *Belief in the importance of mentoring.* A desire to pass on your secrets of success.

- *Perspective.* Able to assess what is good for the other person and not just what would have been good for oneself at that age.

- *Honesty.* You may not always be right, but you do have to say what you think.

- *Communication skills.* You must be able to listen, to hear, and to explain things in a way that each person can understand.

Suggestions that you should not be a mentor

- Believing that you got where you are without help and that everyone else should do so as well. These mentors are impatient and resentful of the assault on their time.

- Wanting to mentor to create a colleague or friend for yourself. As a P.I. mentor, a bit of self-serving is implicit in the relationship—the better the researcher, the better your lab runs—but your own interests cannot be paramount.

WHOM DO YOU MENTOR?

Outside the lab

Your main consideration for mentoring people outside your lab should be whether it will leave enough time to mentor the people inside your lab adequately as well. In the beginning, this is usually not such a problem.

Someone may ask you to be a mentor. You must first think carefully about whether or not you have the wherewithal to become a mentor. You must never take on a mentoring relationship if you cannot or do not want to fulfill the person's requirements and needs. Your expectations, and those of the person to be mentored, must be the same. When someone approaches you about being a mentor, you should discuss what the relationship is going to be before signing on the dotted line. What you should know:

> *Unless I see that the person has the components to make it, I don't go the extra mile. I only mentor people who will be successful. Mentoring is more than giving the general assistance required, it is going out of your way to bring the person to a certain level of confidence, to put them in the public eye.*

- Why the person wants you for a mentor.

- What amount of time it will require.

- What are the person's expectations? If this individual wants a friend and you want a disciple, you cannot be an effective mentor.

You can say no to a mentoring invitation. If fact, you should say no if the expected relationship is beyond the scope of what you want or can do for that particular person.

You may volunteer to be a mentor. You can do this formally or casually. People might not have the confidence to approach you, so you may have to be very explicit with your offer. You may also "have to" take charge of the relationship, at least at first. Many people, especially those from groups not used to having mentors, may actually act weak or whiny when asking someone for advice. These people may feel that they should not burden someone with their own needs and might actually work to keep information from a mentor. You can completely change somebody's life by mentoring.

A conflict of interest can be caused by taking on someone else's lab member as a protégé, and it can be fraught with political peril as well. Certainly, do not get into any such relationship secretly. Lab members should inform their own P.I. that they are speaking with you.

Within your lab

Deciding who you will mentor is critical to the creation of a laboratory spirit. Most P.I.s start out with the assumption that they will mentor all the people in the lab. But as time goes on, some grow more sure that mentoring everyone is their job, whereas others get tired of pouring time and effort into a black hole and resolve to mentor only a select few.

> *I mentor researchers, not people. I do mentor all to each's own ability at some level. Everyone gets the funding, good environment, good project, and time to do the work. I develop their careers long after they have left the lab.*

A problem develops when P.I.s assume that each person wants to be and is capable of being the kind of P.I. that they themselves are and mentor accordingly. In a competitive lab, filled with already successful postdocs and an already highly successful P.I., this works, but it is a very unlikely situation for a new P.I. to be in.

The best results come when an insightful P.I. is able to help people achieve what they want, both in the early days and in more established and successful days. In the right atmosphere, a

> *I don't mentor everyone to the same extent. I try to take them on trips and conferences with me, as it is important for the lab to see how you should behave with a group of scientists. They have to see that it doesn't matter what the results are if no one gets told. You have to talk.*

P.I. is able to guide someone to an academic career while helping someone else to get a teaching job, without charges of favoritism. But this is a very delicate situation, and it is hard to get away without a charge of favoritism being directed at you. You will decide whether you care or not.

> *I mentor all, but probably in the order: students>post-docs>technicians.*

BEING A MENTOR

> *A good mentor should have the following set of basic qualities: experience and maturity; the ability to be a good listener (i.e. the best advice may be not to rush to give advice); the ability to treat each student/postdoc as an individual and not adopt a "one size fits all" approach; and the ability not to see everyone's career through the eyes of one's own career.*
>
> CAVEMAN (2000, P. 32) IN
> "WHO IS MENTORING THE MENTORS?" (PP. 32–33)

If you are a mentor, you must believe in yourself, otherwise, you will never respect those who do believe in you. You must be critical and honest. You must be able to evaluate a person's chances constructively if you are asked "What do you think my chances of success are?"

Many new P.I.s are not sure how to wear the mantle of mentorhood. They are expected to give essential advice to people sometimes only slightly less experienced and may feel that they

> *I'm not real good at mentoring. It happens informally, as the people in the lab look at how you do things, how you handle collaborations, if you need a reagent, how you get it...you can't tell people how to do it, but they look to you to see how you did it.*

lack the age or title or honors to pull it off (even when they think they are right). Those who have been through this agree that yes, it is a problem in the beginning and yes, it will diminish as the years go by.

Flexibility is required to be a mentor. A good mentor will help individuals find their personal strengths and weaknesses, and use those qualities best, rather than

having the same agenda for every person. You must decide beforehand whether you will be a mentor for other than work situations for someone. Deciding not to be involved in the personal lives of lab members will put limits on your mentoring. For some styles, this works: You

> *I had to learn to be a mentor. Somewhere between the 3rd and 6th year of running a lab, it started to be much more fun when I realized I was more like a parent to the people in the lab.*

may not want to know intimate details of a lab worker's life. Furthermore, you may not be able to give unbiased advice. For example, if a lab member cannot work after 5 because her husband wants her to make dinner, what do you do? You may advise her that her husband is unreasonable since your own interest is promoted by her working past 5. Your advice will be self-serving. Some people can pull this off, but it is a dangerous area.

Having a mentor yourself is the best training for mentoring others.

> *I mentor, but I don't try to tell them what to do with their own careers.*

The influence of your own mentors on your mentoring style

The mentors that P.I.s have had in their training have a huge impact on the P.I.'s expectations and style in mentoring. This influence can be both positive and negative: Some P.I.s were so turned off by their supervisors that they now

> *I was influenced by the amount of time my mentors spent in the lab—they both spent much more time in the lab than their colleagues.*

mentor in reaction to the bad experience. Few people directly mimic a former mentor. Some P.I.s start off by imitation, but it soon becomes clear that the lab situation is too different from that of the mentor's to accommodate the same mentoring style. Most P.I.s pick and choose, adapting methods from one mentor for one situation and from another for a different situation.

> *It's like people looking like their dogs...it is just uncanny to see someone give a talk and realize that their mannerisms and way of speaking is just like their advisor's. It's the example you live with, just as your idea of family is your own family.*

> *I would like to be more like my graduate advisor. He had a lot of serenity, which I don't have. But his lab was bigger, so he could afford his hands-off style.*

Continuing mentors also heavily influence lab members. As P.I.s gain more experience, they will be able to acquire from veteran mentors more and more ideas that are relevant and useful.

When and how to end a mentoring relationship

Some mentoring relationships have a natural half-life. One person switches jobs, or graduates, or is involved in other topics, and the relationship gradually peters out, to the satisfaction of both.

Sometimes the mentoring relationship must be formally ended. If it is not working for one of the partners, and there is no natural end in sight, it is best to discuss a change in the relationship or terminate it altogether. Ending the relationship can be difficult if it is not working for the P.I. but it is for the lab member. Making excuses like "I won't have the time to do a proper job for you" or "I've taken on a lot of extra work, and I wonder if we can meet every month instead of every two weeks" might be fine, if you are being honest. If you really want to stop the relationship, and not merely slow it down, say so. It is immediately painful, but much better in the long run for both of you.

> *Both of my advisors found it difficult to speak directly to a person. They would ask someone else in the lab to tell a lab member that he wasn't working hard enough. I hated it, but I found myself doing it. It was a mistake, but now I know that it wasn't done out of laziness, but this indirectness helped not to hurt someone's feelings.*

If the lab member wants to "terminate" you, do not be offended. Accept it with grace, and avoid building up a resentment or sense of insecurity. It is better.

MENTORS FOR NONRESEARCH INTERESTS

Some lab members are candid about their desire to work in some aspect of science other than research, but not all P.I.s are interested in or capable of giving advice or assistance in another field.

> *If someone didn't expect to be a researcher, I would still expect him to function as one in the lab, to work hard. I would provide them with what opportunities he needs, but I don't have the contacts to help in a non-research career.*

Newer P.I.s who have largely broken free from the idea that only an academic career counts realize that there are too few research options for the amount of Ph.D.s produced. Many philosophical debates touch on the issue of how training can more closely reflect the reality of the available jobs. National Science Foundation deputy director Anne Petersen said, "The Ph.D. should be construed in our society more like the law degree. A lot of people go to law school with no plans to practice law" (Klemm 2000, p. 31–32). On the other hand, Sherrie Hans, program officer at the Pew Charitable Trusts, said in a report from the National Research

Council, "The idea of alternative careers should not be oversold to the Ph.D. students or to the scientific community as a solution to provide Ph.D.s with job opportunities. The committee found opportunities in law, journalism, and K-12 teaching to be scarce and unattractive, since they require additional training. They recommend that the Ph.D. remain a research-intensive degree" (Samiei 1998, p. 2).

There is no consensus on how to train and deal with those in the lab who are not intending to go into research. The main question is: Should expectations be the same for those who will continue in research as for those who will not? Those P.I.s who mentor all, no matter what, and whose primary interest is the individual's future, are more willing to invest time in a modified training. In larger and more competitive academic labs, as well as for training positions in industry, the lab heads demand that learning to do research well is the goal of being in the lab, no matter what that individual will do with the training.

Other mentors for your lab members. There may be particular needs on the part of your lab members to suggest the use of other mentors instead of, or along with, yourself. Peer mentors, mentors from the same field or expertise, and cultural or racial advisors might all provide added experiences. The more people your lab members can talk to, the better for everyone. If a little bit of jealousy on your part creeps in, ignore it.

Graduate students and postdocs often feel that there is no person to turn to but the P.I. Even if the P.I. is caring and effective, it does no good—personally or scientifically—for anyone for any lab member to feel disconnected from the rest of the community.

BUILDING A NETWORK

The trail of your mentor and that of people you have mentored are a network. Other networks are formed by the people you worked with during graduate school and postdoc, or from other investigators in a particular field. Your networks will overlap. As much as you can, bring the people you mentor into that network. Introduce them to outside people whenever possible, and involve them when setting up phone calls to discuss a scientific problem. Encourage your lab members to communicate as much as possible with you, with other lab members, and with scientists from other labs.

Keep in touch with former and present lab workers by collaboration or socially. This will boost camaraderie in the same, increase a sense of belonging, and help new lab members to become a part of the bigger web of science.

Mentoring can be the ultimate use of communication. In a good mentoring relationship, everyone wins, and most find a successful mentoring relationship to be one of the most satisfying experiences in running a lab. Mentoring relationships are the foundation of the networks that sustain scientists through their professional lives.

RESOURCES

Belker L.B. 1997. *The first-time manager,* 4th edition. AMACOM Books, New York.

Deal T. and Kennedy A.A. 1982. *Corporate cultures.* Addison-Wesley, Reading, Massachusetts.

Benderly B.L. 1999. Heavenly labs. How to find them. *HMS Beagle* **62**. (http://news.bmn.com/hms-beagle)

Bernstein J. 1987. *The life it brings.* Penguin Books, New York.

Brown S., McDowell L., and Race P. 1995. *500 Tips for research students.* Kogan Page, Philadelphia.

Brown W.S. 1985. Fatal error # 10. Fail to train *Your people.* In *13 Fatal errors managers make and how you can avoid them,* pp. 127–151. Berkley Books, New York.

Caveman. 2000. *Caveman.* The Company of Biologists Limited, Cambridge, England.

Dannhauser C.L. 1999. Burn this resume. Three companies take a novel approach to filling vacancies. *Working Woman,* June, p. 26.

Dantley K.A. 1999. Advisor vs. mentor: Intervention in competitive science. *Science's Next Wave,* Jan. 9, pp. 1–3. (http://nextwave.sciencemag.org)

Duff C.S. 1999. *Learning from other women. How to benefit from the knowledge, wisdom, and experience of female mentors.* AMACOM Books, New York.

Dziech B.W. and Weiner L. 1990. *The lecherous professor: Sexual harassment on campus,* 2nd edition. Illini Books, Urbana, Illinois.

Feibelman P.J. 1993. *A Ph.D. is not enough: A guide to survival in science.* Perseus Press, Reading, Massachusetts.

Felder R.M. 1993. Reaching the second tier. Learning and teaching styles in college science education. *J. College Sci. Teaching* **23**: 286–290.

Felder R.M. and Silverman L. 1988. Learning and teaching styles in engineering education. *Eng. Education* **78**: 674-681.

Felder R. M. and Soloman B. 2000. Learning styles and strategies. (http://www2.ncsu.edu/unity/lockers/users/f/felder/public/ILSdir/ilsweb.html)

Fishher B.A. and Zigmond M.J. 1999. *Attending professional meetings successfully.* Survival Skills and Ethics Program, University of Pittsburgh.

Fiske P. 1998. Dysfunctional advisee-advisor relationships: Methods for negotiating beyond conflict. *Science's Next Wave,* April 23. (http://nextwave.sciencemag.org)

Fiske P. 1999. How to separate ideal employers from bad ones during your job search. *Science's Next Wave,* Feb. 26, pp. 1–4. (http://nextwave.sciencemag.org)

Fitz-Enz J. 1997. *The 8 practices of exceptional companies. How great organizations make the most of their human assets.* AMACON Books, New York.

Gawande A. 2000. When doctors make mistakes. In *The best American science writing 2000* (ed. J. Gleick), pp. 1–22. Harper Collins, New York.

Goleman D. 1995. *Emotional intelligence: Why it can matter more than I.Q.* Bantam Books, New York.

Gould R. 1986. *Sacked! Why good people get fired and how to avoid it.* John Wiley, New York.

Harris J. and Brannick J. 1999. *Finding and keeping great employees.* AMACOM Books, New York.

Hasselmo N. 1990. Presidential statement and policy on sexual harassment. In *The lecherous professor: Sexual harassment on campus,* 2nd edition (ed. B.W. Dziech and L. Weiner). pp. 203–212. University of Illinois Press, Urbana.

Hoagland M. 1990. *Toward the habit of truth: A life in science.* W.W. Norton, New York.

Indiana State University Center for Teaching and Learning. 1999. Brief summary of select learning style models. (http://web.indstate.edu/ctl/styles/model2.html)

Kearsley G. 2001. Explorations in learning and instruction: The theory into practice database. The Theory Into Practice (TIP) database. (http://sprynet.com/~gkearsley)

Klemm W.R. 2000. Ph.D production: Global perspective. *The Scientist* **14**: 31. (http://www.thescientist.com)

Kreeger K.Y. 2000. Scientist as teacher. *The Scientist* **14**: 30–31. (http://www.thescientist.com)

Lamoureux J.A. 1998. Issues in graduate mentoring: Diverse career options and accountability in the mentor-student relationship. *Science's Next Wave,* Jan. 9. (http://nextwave.sciencemag.org)

Setting the Course

YOU PROVIDE THE FOCUS

The entire lab is built around what you have decided to focus on in research. Even when your lab is large and self-sustaining, even when it can provide motivation to all members by itself, you will always have to provide the focus. Day to day and year to year, you will set the path for the lab to travel.

PICKING PROJECTS

...It is amateurs who have one big bright beautiful idea that they can never abandon. Professionals know that they have to produce theory after theory before they are likely to hit the jackpot. The very process of abandoning one theory for another gives them a degree of critical detachment that is almost essential if they are to succeed.

CRICK (1988, P. 142)

Start with what you can do

I am suggesting to medical scientist and biologists that they might make faster progress if they would follow the lead of the astronomers and invent their own tools.

FREEMAN J. DYSON (1999, P. 44)

In today's competitive academic environment, making a sound choice of research direction is critically important. At most universities, a new faculty member has five to six years to become established before the fateful decision on granting tenure arrives. This is the interval during which one's work habits and pattern become essentially fixed. The easiest choice, and almost always the wrong one, is to follow along the path blazed toward the Ph.D. degree. There is a strong tendency to tie up loose ends, to bolster earlier conclusions with still more evidence, and to explore side issues. For a while, such a course might prove fruitful, but increasingly the work yields diminishing returns. By the time one is prepared to slay a new dragon on unfamiliar ground, so much time and effort are required to become knowledgeable enough to write a credible proposal or a meaningful paper that the tenure clock has sounded its farewell chimes.

VERMEIJ (1997 P. 129–130)

Focus early on ONE research topic and get data for ONE significant paper; write and submit the manuscript and simultaneously write and submit a grant on the subject, accept criticisms as valid, be critical in your conclusions, and never, never get an upright –70 freezer (the condenser always breaks; get the horizontal one).

The consensus among P.I.s is that one should start small, i.e., that you and your probably small lab should focus on small doable projects, and get the papers out. For some, this means conducting an area of research as close as possible to that of your postdoctoral work and that of your previous mentor. Other P.I.s say that you should focus on a new topic, but it should be a doable project for which you can simultaneously write a manuscript and submit a grant.

Ultimately, where you are and what kind of science you want to do will influence the decision of whether or not to stay in the shadow of your mentor. These are decisions better made early on—what kind of science do you want to do, and what kind of questions do you want to answer? Still, unless you are in a firmly funded position, get a few papers out if you can.

One of my main mistakes in the beginning was in not thinking creatively enough, being too conservative at first.

- **Don't let money alone dictate what you work on.** Whether you are in an industrial or academic environment, funding in some way will influence your choice of project. Unfortunately, there is a great deal of trendiness in money allocation, and clever but risky projects may not get funding. A P.I. who has achieved a solid track record as a scientist can more easily fund a project, but a new P.I. does not have that luxury and thus must make expedient choices in projects. But going only for the money leaves both motivational and functional problems. Choosing a project only because you will be paid for it may seem to be a great short-term survival tactic, but it can become a habit. As you put resources to the funded project, you invest in its success to the detriment of your other ideas. If you want to be innovative, you will sooner or later have to take a risk.

When I first started, I wanted money and wrote lots of little grants. The tendency is to go after any kind of money! But small grants are too much hassle. There is too much work with too little return.

- **Make your own reagents.** Being dependent on other labs for an important part of your work is unprofessional and risky. It is okay to request a reagent when you have something in particular, something limited, to check, but to do this for more than one experiment or collaboration is foolish.

- **Base experiments on questions.** Do not base your experiments around techniques. You should be following questions, not techniques, although you will be getting a paper or two from a technique. This can be a trap and make you feel unable to track down answers in other ways.

RFAs (request for application) are a problem. When one comes that is only peripherally connected to what the lab does, do you go after it because it is there and it will bring you money? I made the mistake of going after the money but if you get the grant, you end up getting a postdoc to work on something you are not really interested in.

- **Publish as soon as you can.** Most experienced P.I.s agree that you must make a habit, early, of publishing. This will attract people to the lab and make publishing part of the character of your lab. This will become very important on the individual level—people who drift, and do not get around to publishing, will feel that they do not fit in with the lab.

- *Try something new.* To make a major scientific contribution, you must move away from what you did as a postdoc. Many researchers feel they did not make an innovative move soon enough. The consensus is that for about a year, a year and a half, do what you are used to, and write grants, and write papers. After that, however, go for a change in topic or you will have too much to lose and might never make the break into new territory.

Hopefully, you are in a situation in which you can most easily fulfill your research plan. If not, you will have to modify your plan or move or wind up doing a lot of probably fruitless maneuvering within the institution. Be realistic about differences between your expectations and your situation. You cannot work at a small, undergraduate school and stay frustrated because your four 19-year-old lab members are not publishing regularly in *Nature*. Nor can you live in a constant state of tension because you never have the time to discuss each experiment with all 11 people in your busy institute lab. The place where you work will dictate, to some degree, the kind of P.I. you can be. You may have to change your situation, or your expectations.

MATCHING PROJECTS AND PEOPLE

She did two things: she stopped me calling her Professor Hodgkin and said, "You must call me Dorothy—we in this laboratory follow the American custom of using first names." Which I immediately found very easy to do. Then she took me round the lab "to see what I wanted to work on." I still don't understand why she did this; we had agreed that I wanted to work on insulin. She took me round all the labs to see what they were doing, when we got back to her room she said, "What do you want to do?" And I said, "I want to work on insulin," and she said "Fine." If I'd said, "B_{12}," she probably would have said, "Fine."

GUY DODSON IN FERRY (2000, P. 314)

Know your objectives

Before you can guide your lab through projects and plans, you must be one step ahead: You must know your objectives. Looking ahead to your research goals, you can begin to break your long-term science plans into smaller pieces suitable as projects for lab members. Of all the tasks of the P.I., this is the one most P.I.s feel best qualified for.

- *The lab needs:* Data for motivation and for survival.

- *The P.I. needs:* Data for grants or progress reports and publications.

- *The lab member needs:* Data for publications and continued enthusiasm; training.

> I am not as hands off as I was at first, when I was still expecting things to be as they had been with my mentor. I expected the people in the lab to figure out their own projects, but a lab that is not running well yet doesn't have projects obvious to everyone.

> I try to combine the person's particular interest(s) with the overall objectives of the lab—and the specific objectives of the grant(s). Ideally, each trainee should have one project that is almost certain to give useful, publishable results and at least one that is potentially more exciting but more of a long shot for successful completion.

Generating good data

I wasted time and effort on a trivial research question instead of a larger, more important issue—always clear in retrospect, harder to see at the time!

The most important part of any competitive or noncompetitive lab is generating good data. Each person in the lab should be part of a good, doable project that will bring in good usable data and go toward answering an important question. Projects are dispensed in a variety of ways, even within the same laboratory.

New P.I.s with few experienced people tend to assign projects or to give minimal choices. With limited resources, this probably makes

I let people choose. When people come, I outline what is going and let them choose.

I let people work on general stuff, and decide by themselves which project to do in a few weeks. People need to pick a project they are passionate about.

sense. New P.I.s may long for the day when they are not responsible for all thoughts in the lab, but it is vitally important at first that they be the source of projects. When there are many or more experienced lab workers, there will be

time for more leeway.

With time, more projects and more ideas will emerge, and thus there will be more choices to offer a new person. Then, the assignment

People choose their own project, and I try to tailor the project to their talent and interest.

At the beginning, I usually give them choices of projects to select from. This tells me if someone can get turned on by a project and take off on their own. If they don't do this, I assign a project.

of projects becomes different. Who gets the important projects? Should you give important projects to graduate students? To pregnant women? Expectant fathers? Do you put people together? Should you allow people to compete? How about risky projects?

Safety and risk

Although P.I.s want people to be independent and responsible for their own projects, they generally feel deeply responsible for the success of each project, and the implications for the future of the researcher in training. But they differ in how and why the burden of risk should be

You can take a risk with a student, because a student can have few papers and still get a postdoc. With a student, you can go for the big questions. With a postdoc, you must be more conservative, and safe.

shared. Most P.I.s would not assign anyone a risky project: The lab member must choose the risky project, with a full understanding of the risks. Most agree that a beginning student should get a small and doable project.

I wouldn't assign a risky project to a student, but I would to a postdoc. If they are willing to assume the risk, and put in the extra time, they can have a risky project—the return can be terrific! But I do make sure they have a contingency project.

While in this process of training people, P.I.s must also push the research in order to survive. Not all project bets will be successful. The line between playing it safe and taking a risk is not so clear. If you are embarking on something new:

- *Consider realistically the likelihood of success.* How easy will it be to publish? What will happen to the people actually working on the project if it does not pan out?

- *Set benchmarks* that should be met in a certain amount of time in order to keep the project viable.

- *Leave yourself an out.* Either yourself or a lab worker should continue to investigate a "safe" area of work.

> *Postdocs have to think for themselves. If you don't work independently, you don't have a future.*

> *Irresponsible people are nudged towards "meat and potatoes" projects. Responsible or ambitious people themselves pick risky projects. I don't feel terribly responsible myself for a person doing poor experiments, particularly if I've tried to nudge them toward safer ground.*

BALANCING TEAMWORK AND INDEPENDENCE

> *I learned one lesson: a director should choose good people, spread responsibility around, but keep tabs on what's going on.*
> LURIA (1984, P. 138)

Some P.I.s prefer teamwork and will gear all projects toward the sharing of intellect and resources. Others favor the academic model of independence and partition projects into smaller, autonomous pieces. Most will run the lab with a combination of teamwork and independence: A common pattern is to put new people to work with a more senior member of the lab until that person has learned enough to be more independent.

> *I am thinking ahead, while they are thinking in the present. When someone has been there for a year, I can see how the project will develop. I can outline the needed experiments, I can tell what will be the most novel point.*

But even if lab members work together as a team, most P.I.s still believe deeply in the concept of independent thought. The gold standard of training for a scientist is independence: Only a lab member who can think independently is taken seriously. No matter how increasingly common it is to have a project tackled by a team, all members of the team should bring as much independence as they can to the interaction.

Building and supporting a team

One of the finest skills a P.I. can hone is the ability to put together and maintain a group of people who can successfully work together. In many laboratories, teams will self-assemble, based on the path their individual projects take. This kind of team is basically one of peers: Each team member contributes something and answers to no other team member. The lab members involved are usually senior, and the role of the P.I. is to keep the focus of the group centered, as the various team members may campaign for individual agendas.

> *I would like people to work more independently, but I know now that not everyone can. Most postdocs do, but students don't. This was the biggest lesson for me—not everyone will be independent, and you can't make them be.*

If you are building a team yourself, you have the chance to choose people who can work together. But not many people will have the luxury of taking out the shopping list to find (1) one independent and bright team leader, (2) several bright but compliant members, and (3) one hard-working but short-sighted drone who is happy to follow the more ambitious members. It is more likely that you will patch together whomever the group project needs, and deal with the problems as they arise.

A team is a microcosm of the whole lab, but the chance of conflict is greatly increased within such a close-working group. Hostilities are intensified, rivalries are concentrated, and insecurities are magnified, and the P.I. must be always vigilant and ready to adjust the working situation.

Besides keeping the project in focus, your main job will be to maintain what you feel is the appropriate balance of power among the team members. In such a close interaction, it is inevitable that some lab member will assume control, and cause tension, for personal or scientific reasons. You cannot let that happen! Until you are ready to assign someone else to be a team leader, you *must* be the leader of the group.

To maintain equality among team members, you must communicate with each member, and not let your words just trickle down through one person. You must also constantly consider the implications of the research for each lab member when adjusting personnel and research problems: Who will get a publication? Who will be first author? Who will take away one part of the project?

Drifting...

Lab members may move to topics that are not the lab's main thrust, and the P.I. must decide how much to commit to the new field. Is it something you might want to get into? Are you interested? Or is it something that the student or postdoc *needs* to do? This may be the first sign of an independent thinker—or it may be an immature lack of focus. Give some leeway, but be prepared to refocus the person and project if too many resources will be lost during the exploration.

Secret projects

P.I.s may think they know everything that is going on in the lab. But a rite of passage for lab members is to do experiments not discussed with or assigned by the P.I. Micromanager P.I.s might take great offense at this, but others see this as a sign of independence and creativity and long to have lab members with this kind of initiative.

The role of technicians and research associates

Your best chance of getting a good person in a beginning lab is a technician. Technicians often have their own projects, and industrial and small academic labs may still run because of these technicians, guided to different extents by the P.I.

Keeping Up

WHO KNOWS MORE ABOUT THE PROJECT—YOU OR THE LAB MEMBER?

In the first year or so of a lab, P.I.s should know more than a student about a particular project. If you are fortunate enough to have an excellent postdoc, you should still be the one to know the most about the field. It might be easy to rely on someone else's energy and competence, but you are still running the lab and need to be sure it is pointed in the right direction.

> *The person doing it. If not, it wouldn't be the right person. I expect the person to know all the details and think that, if student or postdoc isn't "running the project," it won't fly.*

KEEPING UP WITH THE FIELD

Robert Kelley, of Carnegie-Mellon University, has been asking people working at a wide variety of companies the same question for many years: What percentage of the knowledge you need to do your job is stored in your own mind? In 1986, the answer was typically around 75 percent. But by 1997, the percentage had slid to between 15 and 20 percent.

GOLEMAN (1998, P. 203)

To keep up with the short-term and long-term interests of the lab, you must be able to gauge your lab's position in the field and always be nudging the lab in the right direction. The amount of information now available precludes anyone save the most persistent and enthusiastic (and probably, sleep-deprived) from knowing both the details of each project in the lab and the state of the art in your field, in

> *When I'm writing a grant or reviewing a paper, I suddenly get updated and may gain more knowledge about a topic than the students/postdocs.*

general. You need to manage information, for example, what you must know by heart, what to share with others, which information to store, which to have access to, and which to discard.

You may be the fertilizer of the lab, spending hours reading and thinking of experiments at the same time. Or you may find that you read nothing at all, relying on meetings and conversations to find out what is important. Although most P.I.s speak longingly of the first alternative, most follow more closely the second.

157

The reason P.I.s tend to do less and less reading is mainly one of time: So many things that are urgent, and not important, must be done that reading—important but not urgent—gets pushed aside. Maybe defensively, there also grows a feeling that there really is *not* anything important out there, that the only important things are happening in your own lab, and if anything happens, someone in your lab will tell you. But it is the job of the P.I. to manage the information of the lab. You need to keep up in order to put out.

WHERE TO GET INFORMATION—AND WHAT DO YOU DO WITH IT?

There is nothing but information available. At one time, the job of the P.I. might have been finding information. Now, it is more important to sort through the countless available pieces of information to discover what is useful and important for you.

Many P.I.s are still in a quandary about what to do with all of the available information and are still in the habit of making photocopies of papers or lists or protocols and filing them away. There was the fear that the piece of information might disappear forever, and it needed to be copied and kept safe. But now with the new technology, you can always again find what you need and constantly update your information effortlessly.

- *Web portals and sites.* There are many web sites that provide access to science sites of general interest, containing information about research, politics, and jobs.

  The Scientist. A good source of information of interest to most biological/clinical scientists is the newspaper *The Scientist*, available on-line (http://www.the-scientist.com/) or by free subscription. The politics of research and funding, as well as tips on supplies, equipment, and "hot topics" are covered here.

  Howard Hughes Web Site (http://www.hhmi.org/).

  The New Scientist (http://www.newscientist.com/).

  BioMedNet (http://news.bmn.com), including HMS Beagle (http://news.bmn.com/hmsbeagle/).

- *Reading.* It just is not possible to read everything any more, although you may still expect that you can. Most P.I.s manage to read *Science* and *Nature*, and perhaps two or three specialty journals: few do this routinely.

- *Lab members.* Lab members talk to other lab members, from their own labs as well as from other labs across the country. This information can sometimes be more gossipy than anything else, but it just might tell you more about what people are thinking than anything else.

- *Journal clubs.* Lab and department journal clubs can be used to update you and all of your lab members either on your own specific field or about the more generalized science knowledge base.

- *Meetings.* Whenever you go to meetings, or whenever anyone in the lab goes to meetings, a synopsis of the meeting given to the entire lab can help keep nonattendees (and sleepy attendees) on top of the most important issues. Never let a meeting go by or allow an attending lab member to let a meeting go by without looking for, remembering, and communicating the most important points.

- *Lab seminars.* Research seminars within the lab, if started with an overview of the field, help to keep newcomers connected with the field.

- *Writing papers and grants.* For many P.I.s, the only chance to sit down and read about a field is during grant time or while writing a manuscript. Some look for the opportunity to write reviews, although it is only when the review is finished that they appreciate how much they learned.

- *Networking.* Staying in touch with other friends in the field is the single best way to obtain information about your field. Make it a habit to e-mail or call acquaintances periodically, to ask a question, or to talk about one of your own experiments.

- *PubMed.* PubMed (http://www.ncbi.nlm.nih.gov/PubMed) is a Web-based, free, NIH-founded source of scientific literature and references. You can search through current and past literature to retrieve references. Hyperlinks take the user to the actual journal article. If your institution has a subscription to that journal, you can view, download, or print the article. Some investigators only use their bibliographic software to intersect with written reports, manuscripts, and grants: They use PubMed for all searches.

Try to minimize the storage of information. Instead, concentrate on efficiently and intelligently looking for and discerning what is important. The section on Using Computers to Organize the Lab in this volume contains information on looking for scientific information on the Web.

DO YOU SPEND MORE TIME WITH PEOPLE WHOSE PROJECTS ARE GOING WELL, OR GOING BADLY?

A lesson I learned was that in research one must leave people alone, especially good people. It was not an easy lesson to learn. At times, especially early in my career, I would be too eager or too impatient, interrupting a student in the midst of work or offering more suggestions than were needed. The better the students, the more important it is to leave them to themselves. Occasionally, the lazy ones need to be pushed or the neurotic ones reassured; I had some of both.

LURIA (1984, P. 135)

One of the big philosophical differences between labs is denoted by this question: Do you "reward" the people who are working hard and achieving with your time and attention? Or do you leave alone those who can achieve on their own, and nurse those in difficulty? This is an essential question for your lab and will surely impact on your science, your time

It depends more upon the individual than the success of the project. Most people like to share data frequently when a project is going well, but there's a lot of variability when the work goes badly—some come frequently with questions and problems, others hide or sulk. I try to draw out the latter, but have to overcome my own reticence to probe into failure.

management, and the spirit of the lab. It is undoubtedly more fun for P.I.s to interact with successful lab members—to talk about future experiments, papers, and prospects. But others in the lab may need you more.

> *I spend more time with people whose projects are going well. It is more fun. I like to spend time with pleasant people.*

The large, successful labs with uncaring P.I.s are legendary in science. There is the one P.I. when asked by a younger P.I. with whom one should spend more time, said firmly "You don't even say 'hello' to people whose project isn't working! You'll just encourage them! They'll stay forever!" Or the P.I. who reckoned that "one third of the people do well on their own, one third will fail, no matter what you do: Leave those alone and concentrate on the one third who will produce with your help."

> *Well, in the old days, I spent more time with people whose work was going badly, now I spend very little time with them. I will only help assess whether the project isn't going well, and I will shut the project down if it isn't working.*

A large and established lab can afford to do whatever it wants, for the most part. Some lab members can fall by the wayside, almost unnoticed, and the lab will carry on. But even if you believe that survival of the fittest is the best approach, it is unlikely that a new P.I. will attract the personnel and resources to pull it off.

> *No one's project has gone badly at the moment! But I would spend more time on the problem projects, definitely.*

Not many P.I.s would agree that they should spend any time with someone whose project is going very badly, and who is not at all motivated. But a few P.I.s would—some would be inspired to try to find a solution to the problem. The hard part for scientists to believe is that there really might be people they will not be able to help. This is not to say that certain people cannot be helped, but you may not be able to do it.

> *About the same, but the way I feel about it is different! Part of this is dictated by personality. It pays to be aggressive. If you knock on the P.I.s door to seek input, you'll get more. It pays to be aggressive in science. This is part of the selection process, this is reality—if you don't know how to ask for advice, you will fail.*

In some situations, you may have the leisure to work on developing people. Perhaps you are very well funded. Or maybe you have a commitment to education and are at a place in which your publishing track record will not make or break you. In this case, if you are skilled and careful, you might be able to help people find their own place.

> *I make each member of the lab set up milestones. I ask them to complete certain tasks by a certain time point. We set the tasks up together, both short-term and long-term milestones.*

But if your job depends on publications, you will have to triage. You may not be in the position to support those who are not supporting you. These are perhaps the most difficult issues to face, and the sooner you face them, and know what your own needs and the lab's needs are, the better.

Require written research reports from all lab members. Written research reports are an inoffensive way to learn about the status of lab projects, and a good means of helping lab members to organize their thoughts and data and to learn to write effectively. Requiring regular reports from all lab members ensures that there is no stigma attached to a written report.

Enter the information into the computer to keep track of projects and people, even using project management software or any database program that allows you to search for keywords. Written reports are not to be used instead of verbal reports, but they are especially useful if the P.I. has been away or is writing a grant.

Be sure to read and comment on the written reports. Nothing will make lab members more resentful than the feeling that they are being given busy work.

MOTIVATION

With the recognition of desire as a driving force, we begin to get a clue as to what motivates satisfied biologists: They love what they are doing. More often than they will admit, their love is for the organisms themselves. Such feelings tend to slip out around tables on Friday afternoon watering holes and in seminars presented away from home... . To a person who's never sustained a focused intellectual effort for as long as a decade, however, they reveal a critical element in the life of a biologist: the fundamental love of a chosen beast.

JANOVY (1985, P. 41)

I have respected and admired those colleagues whose scientific work seems to fill their life and pervade every minute of their wakeful time—perhaps their dreams as well. In an extreme form this concentration on science makes one expect a similar concentration in others. An anecdote is told about the great German mathematician David Hilbert, who one day seeing a young colleague in tears (his wife had left him) put his arm around the young man's shoulder and said comfortingly: "Es wird convergieren, es wird convergieren!" (It will converge.) What else could make a mathematician cry than an integral that refused to converge?

LURIA (1984, P. 121)

One of the jobs of the P.I. is to motivate people. As the leader, you provide the scientific motivation and means to keep projects focused and on target. Although P.I.s disagree over exactly how *much* incentive to give, most do realize that providing emotional motivation is also part of the job.

Why are people in the lab? Why do they want to do research? How should you treat them? The reasons for being in the lab are endlessly varied, and the background to the decision to be there will influence the motivation of each individual.

- *Self-motivators.* These people work hard to achieve goals that they prefer to set themselves. The goals may be project-driven or career-driven, but good science is behind both. They may be loners, and may not ask for help. Collaborations may be difficult unless all parties have equal contributions. Let them choose the project because they are likely to do secret experiments to find out if a pet theory is true or not.

- *Collaborators.* These lab members are motivated by the interactions with others in the lab, by working together for a common goal. Criticism may sway them from an interpretation of results, as the approval of the others in the lab matters a great deal. They work well in collaboration and on teams. They may be most compatible with a set project, with distinct goals.

- *Ambitious.* Dreaded are the lab members who use the lab time and interactions with people on the way to somewhere else. They are ambitious, but often without a love of science. They like to organize people, but many people in the lab will resent the obvious agenda of the controller, and collaboration is only possible with very few other lab members. They will cast their nets at the promising projects of others, and so need a very distinct project and careful supervision.

There are many, many other reasons why people choose to work in a lab, many more than three or twenty or a hundred. But just realizing that each person has individual motivations will help you in dealing with problems in the lab.

Most problems are motivation problems

Though according to the mythology a scientist is supposed to be eternally moved only by innate curiosity about how things work and what they can do, there is nowadays a slightly different social mechanism whereby a man is led to feel his personal inspiration and mavericity acknowledged among other men as having triumphed over ambient conservatism and caution as well as over the secrecy of nature.

PRICE (1963, P. 111)

A deficit of motivation most obviously manifests itself as a decrease in hard work, usually with a decrease in results. But it can also reveal itself as not working as cleverly or as enthusiastically as before. You may want to find out:

> I am always walking through the lab, to see what is happening. One person told me I was asking him too much about what was happening. He said "When I have something, I'll tell you. He acted rude, but I finally realized that he was doing it out of insecurity.

- *Is there a laboratory reason,* personal or scientific, that is interfering with work?

- *Is it due to the work itself?* Is it solvable? The person may not like the project, or a particular collaborator; these are problems that can be fixed. Or is it a bigger question, such as the person does not feel confident, does not like science, or feels as if nothing is going right?

- *Is the problem due to a personal crisis?* Is this crisis resolvable, i.e., is it acute or chronic? Is it a partner who resents the other working or a family member who needs immediate attention for a medical problem?

To you, as P.I., the reasons to be motivated are a clear case of cause and effect. But motivation is the sum total of a person's experience and personality, and lab members' past experiences will affect their approach to science. If you think a student or postdoc is having trouble with motivation, try to figure out the reasons for what appears to be pure self-destruction. People carry all manner of baggage with them, baggage that prevents them from believing they can achieve more than they presume (as well as baggage that may give them an entirely unrealistic and inflated picture of their abilities). In essence, part of the trick of keeping up motivation is to get past the baggage.

It is harder to handle a student whose problem is not being able to work effectively. This can usually be attributed to a lack of confidence. One may not believe that they can actually solve an important scientific problem, and may skirt around the central issue, and focus on details that are not important. A big problem in some labs is trying to get the people in the lab to realize that there is no THEY out there, that they themselves are the THEY who do science.

Reading books—biographies, memoirs, essay collections—dealing with science and real labs can help build up the lab feeling of power. Success is the best way to overcome motivation problems—success in giving a journal club, a lab meeting, writing a paper.

Even P.I.s who do not want to be involved in the personal lives of the lab members agree that motivating people during the rough times is a major part of the job. When there are no data, when experiments are just too slow, and when lab members wonder what on earth they are doing in science anyway, the P.I. can provide a sense that disappointment is normal, not a sign that all is wrong.

Motivation problems that might come with the territory

By the nature of their training or background, some people come to the lab with fairly predictable and specific needs. Considering the person's history may help prevent a negative interpretation of this individual's actions or attitudes and help understand that a motivational crisis is emerging.

Physicians

Physicians come into a lab to further a clinical specialty, to gain research credentials helpful ultimately in obtaining a job, or to gain experience to pursue research as a career. Below are listed some problems that physicians may encounter in the lab.

- *Feeling not productive.* Compared with the organized feedback of training and the fast pace of the hospital, results at the bench can be slow in coming.

  Some lab members were doubtful any physician could really be interested in basic science....

- *Feeling lost in the beginning.* This may be manifested as arrogance, as they may think they should know more than they do and are afraid to ask. Since physicians have less training and less available time than many other lab members, they would profit greatly from a mentor who takes care to help find a suitable and doable project that is likely to generate publications.

- *Not accepted in the lab.* Nonmedical departments may have a whole repertoire of M.D. jokes and stories. In many nonovertly clinical labs, there exists a strong prejudice against physicians in the lab. Students and postdocs often feel that physicians are not very interested in research (or they would have studied science instead of medicine) and that they know far less about the process of doing research than most people in the lab, but that they will be getting paid more than any of the people teaching and helping them.

But there is another side to this prejudice. Physicians in the lab are getting paid far less than what they could be making in practice. So they must *want* to be in the lab and want to learn about research. They recognize that they are lab newborns and are usually willing to learn if someone is willing to teach.

Physicians in training are accustomed to following the leader and give the boss an almost military respect. P.I.s may not be used to receiving total obedience and may take advantage. Later, if the physician has learned to become active rather than passive, the P.I. may not be able to adjust to the change.

Students

Students go into research—and so, into labs—for a great variety of reasons and with many differing goals. Some of these reasons may seem to be objectionable to a P.I., but knowing a student's goals will help you appeal to that student and to know how to treat that student.

Some students want to do research for the joy of it. They are getting an advanced degree because they want to spend their lives doing research, and they enjoy the process as well as the end result. They want an interesting project. The more savvy student will want that interesting project to be a hot one.

Others choose research because they must have a career and doing research appears to be a viable one. Some want the prestige attached to an advanced degree or just view the degree as a way to stack up options later on. And some students are just there because they are expected to be, or cannot think of anything else to do.

Postdocs

Just like students, postdocs are in a lab for many reasons. Formerly, postdocs came to the lab after receiving their degree to prepare for an academic career. Many still do. But some postdocs are bound for industry, law school, or other places, and so want to get different experiences out of the postdoc years.

Postdocs are worried about jobs and grants. Increasingly, postdocs' attention will be elsewhere, and they may ignore lab jobs and relationships and other details once considered important. This may bother those not moving on, as they may feel ignored and marginalized.

Technicians

There are two main reasons why people become technicians, and there is such a world of difference between the two that there are almost separate considerations for each.

- *Career technician.* Many people love research and science, but do not want to get a Ph.D. and or want to run a lab. Some have a particular expertise, such as embryo transplant for transgenic mice or electron microscopy of tissue samples, and are professionals in that area. In an academic lab, technicians may feel that they are not being taken seriously by other people in the lab. This is more of a problem in the academic lab, where educational credentials are weighted more heavily than experience.

- ***The temporary technician.*** Students who are ultimately headed for graduate or medical school may want to work for a year or so, not worry about academics, and make enough money to have some fun. Particularly for a technician whose job is to support the projects of others in the lab, taking orders can make one feel servile.

Secretary/Administrative assistant

An administrative assistant can be in the first step of an administrative career, or someone happy to use secretarial and organization skills long-term. It is difficult for the secretary to not be considered an important member of the lab. Even in a smaller lab, with a dedicated secretary who is physically situated near the lab, the secretary/administrative assistant can be marginalized by the other lab members. In a place where administrative assistants are shared, or whose working space is separate from the lab, they might as well be in another world, and it will be hard for them to be enthusiastic about the work in your lab.

What if an apparent lack of motivation really is a lack of ability?

Americans like to think that ability is largely a matter of attitude, but scientists do not always agree. When is a lack of being effective due not to motivation, but to ability? This is one of the critical questions that it is your responsibility to answer: You must be able to tell when a person may not be suited to independent research.

A lack of ability may be very project-dependent. Perhaps a person is not very good at troubleshooting or is oblivious to microscopical morphological changes. A change in project might find one much more suited to that person's talents and personality.

> But the work had to get done! So I would just say to her that "I know this must be incredibly frustrating for you, I know you are trying so hard! I don't know why it isn't working. But there must be other things that are less stressful for you and that you can do very well. I'll be happy to find you another job." And when people would call I would say that she does need supervision, but could be very good at doing something straightforward.

Motivate first by example

Enthusiasm is the foremost way to make sure others will follow your example. If you are depressed, or otherwise send a message that the work in the lab is not what you expected, the people in the lab will respond accordingly. If you feel a part of science, and that the work of the lab is potentially beneficial to saving human lives, the lab members are likely to follow your lead.

> I make them work hard. I come in on the weekends.

PREVENTING JOB BURNOUT AMONG PERSONNEL

The conventional wisdom is that burnout is primarily a problem of the individual. That is, people burn out because of flaws in their characters, behavior, or productivity. According to this perspective, people are the problem, and the solution is to change them or get rid of them...we believe that burnout is not a problem of the people themselves but of the social environment in which people work. The structure and functioning of the workplace shape how people interact with each other and how they carry out their jobs. When the workplace does not recognize the human side of work, then the risk of burnout grows, carrying a high price with it.

MASLACH AND LEITER (1997, P. 18)

Less dramatic but equally—if not more—costly to corporations than those employees who leave may be those who become disillusioned with the firm, but neither leave nor find creative solutions to their work-related dissatisfaction...they are talented, as evidenced by academic, job-related or outside achievements. As such, they could contribute much to their organizations. Yet none believe that they are fully appreciated by their organizations or have been given access to its "inner" group."

THOMAS ET AL. (1992, P. 47)

Lack of motivation can be attributed to feelings of powerlessness and is often called burnout. Burnout is not just something that happens to dedicated professionals after years of work: It can happen to the right person in the wrong place in a matter of months. Sometimes this can mean, or can be interpreted to mean, that the person does not have the staying power for a career which will always subject the ego to incredible ups and downs. But it can happen because of an unfortunate intersection of events: breakup of a relationship plus being scooped; a tedious project and a P.I. who is too busy to discuss it; feeling culturally disconnected from the rest of the lab; and having to deal with a sick parent. Often, maybe with help, the difficult spot can be eased, and motivation returns. Sometimes it just has to be waited out.

Keeping the doors of communication open is the best way to prevent job burnout in the lab. Preventative maintenance is much more effective than patching someone up.

Writing Papers

WHEN SHOULD A PAPER BE WRITTEN?

One aspect of research that lab members often have trouble with is deciding when there is sufficient data to write a manuscript. Should a discrete package of data be put together in a small paper for a specialty journal? Should the investigation continue until a larger story can be told? Timing and politics are at least as important as the data itself, and the P.I.'s experience will be a vital guide. It is a critical and crucial skill for you to pass on to lab members, even though you may initially feel incompletely trained yourself.

This is the crux of survival in science: All the considered hiring, late-night reading, and the endless repetition of experiments come down to the preparation and selling of the research report or manuscript. Especially in small or isolated institutions, lab members tend to see papers in the best journals as being something that other people do. Having a paper published is the best way of establishing to your lab members that they are, indeed, in the game.

Some P.I.s encourage people to start a project with the backbone of a manuscript in mind. This seems cold-blooded to some, but it is an effective and honest approach, for it forces each lab member to focus. This focus is essential for junior lab members, who tend to try multiple and interesting experiments that lead in different directions. Focus does not stifle creativity.

Certainly, once a project is under way, the figures for the manuscript should be part of the underlying rationale for the particular experiments. There are always several paths to take in a project, and the path that leads to publication in an interesting journal is the favored one in a nonrisky project. Teach the junior members to think in figures from the beginning.

Make sure that all lab members are up on their own data not only at manuscript-writing or presentation time, but all of the time. Useful—and frequent—topics of lab conversation could be to ask about not only the day's experiments, but a comparison of the day's results with other day's results, as well as for interpretations and possible clarifying experiments.

Do not let lab members move to another set of experiments until they and you understand the current set. Generating data is the easy part, and not necessarily the most important part. Very few people in your lab will have a good understanding of when and where to apply the appropriate statistical analysis. You may be lucky

WHO WILL BE ON THE PAPERS?

... I was somewhat surprised to find my name on the draft paper, since the convention in our lab was that one did not put one's name on a paper unless one had made significant contribution to it. Mere friendly advice was not enough. "Why," I asked Sydney, "have you added my name?" He grinned at me. "For persistent nagging," he said, so I let it stand.

CRICK (1988, P. 135)

Wigler also fiercely defended the interests of the people in his lab. During the preparation of the paper reporting that ras controlled adenylate cyclase activity in yeast, Mike risked his good name to ensure that Takashi Toda received top billing. In an attempt to hasten progress on the report, Wigler had earlier agreed to a collaboration with the Japanese scientists who had been studying adenylate cyclase in yeast. He'd told one of the collaborators, Isai Uno, that he would be first author on the paper, but when Wigler realized how much more work Takashi had contributed to the project, he called Japan and informed Uno's supervisors that he was very sorry but he'd changed his mind. Takashi would have to be cited first. As Wigler talked, he could hear Uno's cries of outrage in the background. Wigler felt guilty about reneging on a promise, but Takashi was his responsibility, and Takashi's needs were paramount.

ANGIER (1988, P. 297)

Aware of the time-honored enmities, the Harvard group gathered at a long table to decide the issue. Gilbert sat at one end, Efstradiadis at the other, with Villa-Komaroff and Broome in the middle. "Let's talk about authorship," Gilbert said.

"Everyone was silent," Efstratiadis recalls. "Wally raised his hand toward me as if to say, 'Speak.' I said, "I have invested more time than anybody else, but I didn't clone the gene. I think either Lydia or me should be first."

Villa-Komaroff, having contemplated beforehand what she would say, swallowed deep and said simply, "I need the paper more than you." To her great relief, Efstratiadis did not object.

On the discussion for authorship of Villa-Komaroff L, Efstratiadis A, Broome S, Lomedico P, Tizard R, Naber S, Chick WL, Gilbert W. A bacterial clone synthesizing proinsulin. (Proc. Natl. Acad. Sci. 75: 4344–4348 [1978].)

HALL (1987, P. 224–225)

Listed below are guidelines for authorship.

- Traditionally, the person who does the work is listed first. The head of the lab goes last. The second, third, etc., spots follow the first, in order of the contribution to the work.

- Collaborators are considered for authorship in the same way as the primary lab.

- The first author writes the paper, and handles all submission duties, including figure preparation, letters to the editor, and permissions.

- The corresponding author is the person who knows intellectually the most about the paper and can discuss all aspects of the paper. It may be the first author, P.I., or another author on the paper.

- If a first author leaves the lab before a paper is completely written (or does not finish within a predetermined time after leaving the lab), the second author is offered first authorship dependent on writing the paper, and acting as first author for all necessary first author duties.

- Protect your own people in authorship disputes. Do not write off a lab member to gain your own political points or to satisfy collaborators. If you have to sacrifice anyone, negotiate your own position in authorship.

- Do not put names on a paper as a courtesy or expect someone to put your own name on as a courtesy. Whether or not technicians can get authorships should be decided beforehand as a general policy and communicated to all new lab members. There are only good reasons for giving credit where credit is due, and it is very good for morale. In industry, where there is a reporting line, it is easy not to give credit to technicians.

- The Acknowledgments section is not a dump for all people who are not authors. All persons listed in the Acknowledgments should give written permission, since the presence of their names may suggest agreement with the paper.

- Unless it is absolutely and completely true, do not put yourself as the only author on a research paper (it is okay for reviews). In most cases, someone helped you with the work.

Technicians as authors

There are still P.I.s who consider technicians to be swappable units, reagents without intellectual input, and who believe that authorship is not appropriate to that station. Both in academia and in industry, authorship is still sometimes decided not by a technician's contribution, but by ranking in the hierarchy of the lab. It is usually very large labs in which this happens. In a newly established and/or small lab, technicians supply the main drive of the research and are granted more respect. As a lab fills with more senior researchers, the role of the technician is often diminished, and even technicians who have contributed heavily to a project might be left off a paper as an author.

> *Technicians do their own experiments in my lab, which will end up on a paper whose first author will most likely be someone else. The technician- as long as he or she has produced publishable data, designed experiments on his own, and has demonstrated adequate motivation—gets a second or third authorship.*

This leads to a bad spirit in the lab. Large labs can absorb or ignore this unhappiness and undervaluation of a lab member, but it still ferments a culture in which equal work does not lead to equal recognition. Fortunately, most P.I.s believe that any technician who produces data used in a manuscript should be an author or, for a smaller contribution, be cited in the Acknowledgments.

Accountability for authorships

I think it's absolutely clear that I have an immense and abiding admiration for Dr. Avery. Yet I was grieved that he came back from vacation and put his name first to the paper, whereas I considered that all the work was mine. It disturbed me very much because everybody was convinced that I had just been a pair of hands in Dr. Avery's laboratory and that everything had been Dr. Avery's work... .

It's plainly obvious to me now that in reality the most difficult part of the experiment had not been in doing things but in imagining that one could affect the pathogenesis of the pneumococcus infection by attacking a specific component of the bacterium. That idea was obviously not mine but Dr. Avery's. While I did introduce a certain originality in doing the experiment (by refusing to adopt the techniques that everybody wanted me to use), it's perfectly clear that the most original part of the work, the more difficult task of conceptualizing the problem, had been done before I came to the Rockefeller Institute.

PIEL AND SEGERBERG (1990, P. 62), RENE DUBOS,
ON THE PUBLICATION OF THE SPECIFIC ACTION OF A
BACTERIAL ENZYME ON PNEUMOCOCCI OF TYPE III
(*SCIENCE* 72: [1858] PP. 151–152, AUG. 8, 1930)

A grotesque example encountered by the Danish Committee on Scientific Dishonesty is for a company to forward a finished but authorless article concerning their own product to a recognized scientist, requesting him to appear as author of the article. The scientist correctly registered a complaint with the Committee.

RIIS (1994, P. 2)

A survey of authorships among physicists looked at the prevalence of inappropriate authorships. Four reasons for the awarding of perhaps undeserved authorships were given (Tarnow 1999):

1. The concern to sustain a relationship. For example, postdocs need a letter from a supervisor and would not then question the right of the supervisor to be on a paper.

2. Those who had made only minor contributions were given authorships, when an acknowledgment would have sufficed.

3. Scientists were included as authors based on their previous work in the field or for an expected contribution that never materialized.

4. People who had no actual part in the project but who were socially close or were in the same research group were given authorships.

Many inappropriate authorships are thus given as favors, or tokens of appreciation. This system usually works in favor of P.I.s, who are found as inappropriate authors ten times more than are postdocs (Tarnow 1999): Clearly, currying favor with a P.I. is seen as more necessary than rewarding a student, postdoc, or technician. This scientific "tipping" has come to be expected by many P.I.s and may be one of the most fraudulent practices in the lab. P.I.s find this practice difficult to deal with. The fact is that scientists are judged by their products and their papers: Promotions, grants, and tenure depend on them. If it does not hurt anyone, it is easy to rationalize, why not just routinely put your own name on all papers that come out of your lab?

Another problem is that often all the members of a team or department who work on various parts of different projects might expect to be on every paper. Indeed, many researchers are concerned with the meaning of authorships in large collaborations or teams. How will your students and postdocs achieve recognition if they are members of a team and one of ten authors?

A policy that has already been taken up by several journals is the disclosure by the authors of the contribution of each author. Authorships have become casual, with no standards clearly discernible. In general, the first author has done the bulk of the work and the last author is the head of the lab, and it is presumed that the authors in between have contributed in decreasing amounts as the name gets further from the first position (Rennie 1999), but there is no way to tell who is responsible for the work done. The following guidelines have been suggested to assure accountability (from Rennie 1999):

1. All those who have contributed to a study would decide among themselves at the end of the study what they had done.

2. The byline would contain all the individuals who contributed say, more than 5% or 10% of the work, and the names would appear in the descending order of contribution.

3. Other contributors would be listed in the acknowledgments.

4. The individual contributions would be attached to the article. For example, so-and-so did the radioimmunoasays, so-and-so made the antibody.

5. One or more of the contributors should be prepared to act as guarantor for the whole, to assure themselves that the work had been done, and to take overall responsibility.

Even if you do not formally follow these guidelines, they can be useful in the establishment of the priority of authors. Accountability is likely to be one of the ways in which researchers will be judged.

Loose Ends—Papers left unwritten

A chronic problem in laboratories is the students and postdocs who leave the lab with papers unwritten. People who leave have the best of intentions to finish papers at their new location, but they underestimate the pull that a new project and job will have on them. This can be disastrous, as you can be left with a pile of papers that need just one more experiment, an experiment that no one in the lab knows how to do.

When new people come into your lab, tell them up front what your policy is on leaving the lab with papers, especially whether or not it is permitted, and the conse-

of everyone in the lab, the less likely it is that a fraud can occur. If someone in the lab approaches you about someone else's data, or if you have suspicions about someone's data, listed below are steps that you can take.

1. Take all suspicions seriously.

2. Document the suspicion and all of the steps taken to investigate the suspicion.

3. Speak immediately to the person in question. Ask to see the raw data, look at lab notebooks, and examine whatever you need to in order to decide if there is a chance of fraud.

4. In most cases, it is likely that the fraud is a minor problem i.e., it does not involve publishing false data but is the shoddiness in the preparation of an experiment or the interpretation of data. Talk to the person you were questioning about fraud: Explain to the accuser why you feel there is no case of fraud.

5. If you are unsure whether there is fraud, speak to an intermediary at your institution, someone who can help you decide whether a formal investigation is warranted. This may be, for example, a dean or an ombudsman.

6. If you believe, after talking to an official but uninvolved and objective person, that there is a valid case of fraud, follow institutional guidelines. The first step is usually to take the case to a designated person or committee. Some institutions have a Research Integrity Officer, who can be the person approached.

Institutional guidelines when dealing with fraud

If an institution receives federal funds, they must have a policy in place for dealing with allegations of fraud. Once the fraud is reported officially, a process is started: All research records are sequestered, and the institution must investigate and determine whether there is probable fraud.

An investigation into fraud can be a long and complicated business. The Office of Research Integrity of the Office of Public Health and Science might be called in if the charges involve a health hazard or a criminal violation or if the fraud might be made public.

With all data sequestered, grants and papers cannot be written, and research can grind to a halt. P.I.s who have been in a lab being investigated describe it as a terrible experience, so draining that it may be tempting, if faced with fraud in the lab, to deal with it unofficially. The danger in this is that the P.I. would then become part of the fraud. Awareness and vigilance are the best ways to avoid the horrendous impact of fraud on the lab.

RESOURCES

Angier N. 1988. *Natural obsessions. The search for the oncogene.* Houghton Mifflin, Boston.

Applehans W., Globe A., Laugero G., and Applehan W. 1999. *Managing knowledge: A practical Web-based approach.* Addison-Wesley, Reading, Massachusetts.

Broad W. and Wade N. 1982. *Betrayers of the truth.* Simon & Schuster, New York.

Carr J.J. 1992. *The art of science. A practical guide to experiments, observations, and handling data.* HighText Publications, San Diego.

Caveman. 2000. *Caveman.* The Company of Biologists Limited, Cambridge, England.

Clifton D.O. and Nelson P. 1992. *Soar with your strengths*, pp. 43–61. Delacorte, New York.

Committee on Professional Ethics. 1999. Ethical guidelines for statistical practice. The American Statistical Association. (http://www.amstat.org/profession/ethicalstatistics.html)

Crick F. 1988. *What mad pursuit.* Basic Books, New York.

Djerassi C. 1989. *Cantor's dilemma.* Doubleday, New York.

Dyson F.J. 1999. *The sun, the genome, and the internet: Tools of scientific revolutions.* Oxford University Press, England

Ferry G. 2000. *Dorothy Hodgkin: A life.* Cold Spring Harbor Laboratory Press, Cold Spring Harbor, New York.

Feist G.J. 2000. Distinguishing "good" science from "good enough" science. *The Scientist* **14**: 31–31. (http://www.thescientist.com)

Frängsmyr T. and Lindsten J., eds. 1993a. Biography of Harold E. Varmus. In *Nobel lectures: Physiology or medicine 1981–1990*, p. 501. World Scientific, River Edge, New Jersey.

Frängsmyr T. and Lindsten J., eds. 1993b. Biography of J. Michael Bishop. In *Nobel lectures: Physiology or medicine 1981–1990*, p. 525. World Scientific, River Edge, New Jersey.

Goldberg J. 1988. *Anatomy of a scientific discovery.* Bantam Books, New York.

Goleman D. 1998. *Working with emotional intelligence.* Bantam Books, New York.

Grinnell F. 1992. *The Scientific attitude*, 2nd edition. New York: Guilford Press, New York.

Hall S.S. 1987. *Invisible frontiers.* Tempus Books, Redmond, Washington.

Hamlin S. 1988. *How to talk so people listen. The real key to job success.* Harper and Row, New York.

Hoagland M. 1990. *Toward the habit of truth: A life in science.* W.W. Norton, New York.

Hofstadter D.R. 2000. Analogy as the core of cognition. In *The best American science writing 2000* (ed. J. Gleick), pp. 116–166. HarperCollins, New York.

Huth E.J. 1999. *Writing and publishing in medicine*, 3rd edition. Williams and Wilkins, Baltimore.

International Committee of Medical Journal Editors. 2000–2001. Uniform requirements for manuscripts submitted to biomedical journals. (http://www.icmje.org)

Janovy, Jr. J. 1985. *On becoming a biologist.* Harper & Row, New York.

Kreeger K.Y. 2000. Know your legal rights. Intellectual property lawyers and tech transfer offices help researchers navigate legal issues. *The Scientist* **14**: 1–4. (http://www.thescientist.com)

Lientz B.P. and Rea K.P. 1998. *Project management for the 21st century*, 2nd edition. Academic Press, New York.

Louderback A.L. 1999. Abstract accepted: Now what? *The Scientist* **13**: 16–25. (http://www.thescientist.com)

Luria S.E. 1984. *A slot machine, a broken test tube.* Harper & Row, New York.

Martin B. 1992. Scientific fraud and the power structure of science. *Prometheus* **10**: 83–98. (http://www.uow.edu.au/arts/sts/bmartin/pubs/92prom.html)

Maslach C. and Leiter M.P. 1997. *The truth about burnout: How organizations cause personal stress and what to do about it.* Jossey-Bass Publishers, San Francisco.

Mcdawar P.B. 1964. Is the scientific paper fraudulent? *Saturday Rev.* Aug., pp. 42–43.

Medawar P.B. 1969. *Induction and intuition in scientific thought.* The American Philosophical Society, Philadelphia.

Mitchell D., Coles C., and Metz R. 1999. *The 2,000 percent solution: Free your organization from 'stalled' thinking to achieve exponential success.* AMACON Books, New York.

Motulsky H. 1995. *Intuitive biostatistics*. Oxford University Press, New York.

The New York Times. 1999. Panel casts doubt on human cloning claim. *The New York Times*, Jan. 29, p. A7.

Pacetta F. and Gittines R. 2000. *Don't fire them, fire them up: A maverick's guide to motivating yourself and your team*. New York: Simon & Schuster, Philadelphia.

Pechenik J.A. 1993. *A short guide to writing about biology*. HarperCollins College Publishers, New York.

Piel G. and Segerberg, Jr. O. 1990. *The world of Rene Dubos: A collection from his writings*. Henry Holt, New York.

Potter B. 1998. *Overcoming job burnout*, 2nd edition. Ronin Publishing, Berkeley, California.

Price D.J. 1963. *Little science, big science*. Columbia University Press, New York.

Rennie D. 1999. Lessons on authorship from high altitude: Contributors should disclose their contributions. *The Scientist* **13:** 12. (http://www.thescientist.com)

Rennie D., Yank V., and Emanuel L. 1997. When authorship fails: A proposal to make contributors accountable. *JAMA* **278:** 579–585.

Riis P. 1994. Authorship and scientific dishonesty. In *The Danish Committees on scientific dishonesty. Annual Report 1994*, Chapter 3. (http://www.forsk.dk/eng/uvvu/publ/annreport94/chap3.htm)

Schloff L. and Yudkin M. 1992. *Smart speaking*. Plume, New York.

Shilts R. 1987. *And the band played on*. Penguin Books, New York.

Stolberg S. 2001. Scientists often mum about ties to industry. *The New York Times*, April 25, p. A15.

Tarnow E. 1999. An offending survey. (http://www.salon.com/books/it/1999/06/14/scientific_authorship/print.html)

Thomas Jr., R.R., Gray T.I., and Woodruff M. 1992. *Differences do make a difference*. The American Institute for Managing Diversity, Atlanta, Georgia.

Tufte E.R. 1983. *The visual display of quantitative information*. Graphics Press, Cheshire, Connecticut.

Tufte E.R. 1990. *Envisioning information*. Graphics Press, Cheshire, Connecticut.

Tufte E.R. 1997. *Visual explanations: Images and quantities, evidence and narrative*. Graphics Press, Cheshire, Connecticut.

Vermeij G. 1997. *Privileged hands: A scientific life*. W.H. Freeman, New York.

Organizing the Lab to Support the Research

Building a Lab Culture

FOLLOW YOUR MISSION STATEMENT

A well-built, well-run team is a self-perpetuating organism. It's constantly renewing itself.

PACETTA AND GITTINES (2000, P. 103)

A mission statement, as described in the section on Plan the Lab You Want in this volume, describes the kind of research you want to do. It also implies the motivation for your research, and the kind of atmosphere in which you want to work.

When you set up a new lab, and in the tumultuous first years, there will be scores of details to arrange and manage. By keeping your mission statement in front of you always, even for the most minor of tasks, you can ensure that all the facets of the lab you build will support your goals and will not be in opposition to the lab culture you want.

If it is teamwork you want to foster, you can set up the equipment, the schedule of lab meetings, and the projects to meet that end. If independence for the lab members is your goal, the project selection will be quite different.

EXPECTATION AND CONSEQUENCES

Many young managers communicate rather well upward to their superiors, but poorly downward to their subordinates. Your subordinates will have more to say about your future than your superiors.

BELKER (1997)

P.I.s soon discover that they do not actually have a tremendous amount of immediate control over the behavior of people in the lab. What do you say when you want a certain experiment done and 6 weeks later it has not been started? The nature of research, and the implicit respect for the intelligence and capabilities of other lab workers, means that barking out orders will not necessarily get you anywhere. In addition, since many of the lab workers are temporary, or are students, there is not much you could hold over their heads: There are no obvious consequences to not doing what is expected.

You must therefore build a place in which the lab members understand your expectations and agree with those expectations and try to fulfill them. They must internalize those expectations and think of them as their own. Expectations are scientific, personal, and ethical, and all are mixed to create the particular flavor of each lab.

> In the beginning, as I was building up the group, I tended to be held hostage by particular individuals whom I felt were important to the group. So the more heavily a person contributed to the scientific outcome of the program the more I was likely to kowtow to that person's demands.

It must also be understood that there are consequences if expectations are not met. Some of the consequences are long term—if you do not perform at a certain level, there will be restrictions on the jobs you will be able to get—and some are short term—if you do not do your assigned lab job, no one will answer your telephone when you are out. Most are subtle.

You and your lab effectively are joined in a contract. You as leader are responsible for setting the expectations and consequences and running the lab in a way that supports these chosen expectations and consequences.

IMPLYING LAB ETHICS

Be a role model. The best way to communicate the ethics to your lab members is to live by those ethics. No double standards! If you expect people to be respectful and honest, you must be, as well. Listed below are ways in which you can model expected behavior:

- *Always do what you say you will do.* Be consistent. This establishes honesty and dependability as desirable traits for your lab.

- *Be respectful and considerate toward all lab members.* This applies both to subtle tactics, such as scheduling meetings when it is the most convenient time for everyone, and to the more obvious, such as not telling racist jokes.

- *Roll up your sleeves and help people in the lab.* This does not have to compromise their independence but can foster a feeling of collaboration and trust. If a postdoc is having trouble doing the front pages of a grant or a new technician cannot get a clone to grow, offer to help out.

- *Be careful.* Choose words and actions deliberately. Sloppiness of thought or action does not belong in a lab.

- *Do not ridicule the science of other labs.* Discuss the reasons you agree or disagree, but avoid sneering or bad-mouthing.

Talk about ethics with lab members. Many P.I.s find it difficult to sit down and talk about lab ethics with a new employee. Most of this information is communicated through the lab culture, and group morality keeps most behavior in check. In industrial labs, ethical issues are often covered as part of the orientation.

But especially in a multicultural research lab, not all "laws" are communicated and understood immediately: It takes several years before a lab culture becomes firm. It might be easiest to clearly spell out some of the important issues. A lab meeting over lunch would be an appropriate casual venue for such a discussion. Listed below are some topics worth discussing:

> *I sit students down to talk about basic behavior and ethics. Science is a small world, you don't know when you will meet someone who will count. You can be in a distant town, and meet someone at lunch who may review one of your grants. Also, I tell them not to say anything that you wouldn't mind getting back to the person you spoke about.*

- Conflicts of interest. Should an investigator stand to gain financially from the results of a survey funded by a company?

- What if you had a promising series of experiments, but cannot repeat the data, is it okay to report only the earlier results for a grant application?

- If an individual on sabbatical in the lab used confidential data in a manuscript, should you report this? And to whom should you report?

ESTABLISH A WORK ETHIC

A strong culture is a system of informal rules that spells out how people are to behave most of the time. A strong culture helps people feel better about what they do, so they are more likely to work harder.

DEAL AND KENNEDY (1982)

Your hours set the speed. P.I.s that work short hours will end up with personnel who work short hours, and vice versa. Your hours set the work pace of the lab. Work hard, and you not only set a good example, but can also claim the moral high ground should a dispute arise.

> *I found someone reading novels in the lab while waiting for an experiment! I am trying to get the atmosphere right, I turn the radio down, I'm trying to make it more of a work place with a good work ethic. I am trying to give a sense of urgency.*

You can request longer hours from your lab members. The argument that they have their careers ahead of them and must work for themselves is a valid one, and for truly self-motivated people, it is persuasive. But you will be working uphill to have a lab working weekends when you never show your face.

Keep everyone goal-oriented. When the lab is established and has produced at least one quality paper, it will be much easier for people to identify goals. But in the beginning, with inexperienced personnel, it will be very hard for lab members to define these goals.

You cannot expect new members to immediately work toward a *Nature* paper. P.I.s should start with smaller goals, for example, a good series of experiments, a solid departmental pre-

> *It is demoralizing for everyone in the lab to have someone who doesn't work hard, especially if that person gets a lot of attention.*

Lab Policies

SAFETY

In this place, too, nobody wasted many words teaching us how to protect ourselves from acids, caustics, fires, and explosions; it appeared that the Institute's rough and ready morality counted on the process of natural selection to pick out those among us most qualified for physical and professional survival.

LEVI (1984, P 39)

There are more national regulations governing the treatment of lab animals than exist for protecting graduate students.

SANFORD (1999, P. 3)

The way you view safety in the lab is the way your lab members will view safety issues. You are responsible for the safety of the people in your lab and cannot afford to be lackadaisical about establishing standards. Yes, it is each person's responsibility, but definite rules reduce the likelihood of unsafe events. No matter how easygoing the style of the lab, safety rules should be rigidly adhered to.

Make it clear that you will not tolerate a cavalier attitude toward safety. Do not let a macho culture of derision of safety arise! Lab members should not be allowed to decide on which safety rules they will follow and, more importantly, which they will impart to new people. If lab safety offers or demands that lab members take a course or come to a meeting, you should not scoff and try to get lab members out of the requirement. You should have very explicit rules about all safety issues. For example:

- **Radiation**
  Data sheets
  Instruction
  Background information
  Disposal
- **Pathogens, human material, and other biohazards**
- **Biohazard disposal**
- **Sharps**
- **Children in the lab**
- **Chemical storage, use, and disposal**

You should also have emergency protocols for general problems such as injury, earthquake, fire, and flood, and for specific crisis in the lab such as needle sticks, spilling of an infectious agent, or inhalation of solvents.

The Laboratory Safety Department

The Laboratory Safety Department is your source of advice and information about safety in the lab. Some labs make this department the enemy, scoffing at the rules and regulations and lists, resenting inspections and avoiding training sessions. *This is a mistake.* It is not a good department to have against you, as the potential to harass a lab for noncompliance is great.

More importantly, this department is a resource and can help in more than safety issues: Personnel training, functional lab design, and alternatives to hazardous experiments. It is all to your benefit to maintain a good working relationship with the Laboratory Safety Department.

The Laboratory Safety Officer acts as the liaison between departmental workers and the Laboratory Safety Department. But you should have your own laboratory safety officer in the lab, someone people can come to for immediate information. Institutions take safety rules very seriously, and someone must keep track of the paperwork and actual compliance with the rules in the lab.

Pregnancy and other health issues will also be dealt with by the Laboratory Safety Department. They will provide a list of guidelines for you to follow when dealing with pregnant lab personnel. Although radiation is the first concern that most women have when pregnant, there are very few labs that use enough radiation to be of harm even to not-pregnant people. Of more concern might be the use of solvents, but again, if you take precautions and obey standard safety rules, the lab will be well within the threshold for pregnant and nonpregnant personnel.

Lab personnel should inform the P.I. about a pregnancy as soon as possible. The atmosphere of the lab should encourage this. If a lab member tells you about a pregnancy, but does not wish anyone else to know, respect her request, and quietly make any alterations to lab duties that might be needed.

Not all P.I.s feel immediately sympathetic to amending the duties of a pregnant lab member. But there will be very few women who will use the pregnancy to avoid work. It can be an emotionally vulnerable time for the pregnant woman, and an appreciation and respect for these feelings might be all the P.I. needs to express to put her mind at ease.

What about "overreacters"?

Lab members may set the safety bar even higher than you do and object to doing certain lab tasks or even to other people doing those tasks. Some have a particular worry about radiation, human blood, infectious agents, solvents, or high-voltage equipment, to name the most obvious. Sometimes worry is brought out by a pregnancy. The responsibilities of the job and the work of the lab should be described before anyone signs on to the lab. But projects evolve, and not all techniques can be predicted, nor can a particular worry be predicted.

Whatever you do, do not make light of someone's fears. Do not sneer, or dismiss, or discuss the problem with others in the lab, or mention it lightly in groups. Do sit down and seriously discuss the problem. Present data and offer to set up a conversation with someone thoughtful who has done the same work.

Discuss alternatives. Is there another technique that can be done? Can the safety of the procedure be improved? Perhaps there is one part of the experiment that can be performed by someone else. Although lab members must do what they consider to be safe, the P.I. must also protect the project and the science. If a person cannot fulfill the reasonable (to you) requirements of a job or project, consider a change of project.

Emergencies and urgencies in the lab

Whether working in the lab or not, the P.I. should be informed when a critical situation, especially involving personnel safety, emerges. All lab members should have your phone number and emergency contact information: Indeed, all lab members should have everyone's phone numbers and emergency contact information. More commonly, this contact information will be used for ordinary lab urgencies; for example, a common lab scenario is that one member finds another member's cell cultures left accidentally on the lab bench, and needs to know what to do to keep those cells viable. Contact information should also be included in your lab manual.

HOURS AND VACATIONS

Hours

One of the joys of research for most people is the flexible hours. Even in large companies, which may be less flexible than academic labs, the hours worked generally follow the experiments when necessary, and therefore provide leeway for personal circumstances. This freedom is a motivator for most, but can be taken advantage of by others. In labs where hours are more rigid, and in labs where hours are more flexible, remember this: You cannot have it both ways. You should not expect a technician to be there from 8 a.m. to 5 p.m. and still come back at 10 p.m. to finish an experiment.

> *Loose hours are one of the benefits of being in research, so I won't tell anyone when to work. It is their career, and I can't dictate hours, or they will resent it. But my hours are the general guide.*

Should you enforce hours? Can you enforce hours?

Yes, you should require people to be at the lab at a time when you can interact with them. Loners and people whose research is not going well will try to avoid you: The more desperate will try to work opposite and complementary hours to yours. Try not to let this happen, as it really is a loss of control and is not good for anyone.

Be as flexible as you can be. Freedom to make your own time is one of the attractions of the job. Research does not lend itself to a 9 to 5 schedule. Especially if you have students, you will have to expect irregular hours at some times. A work-

Lab workers should be able to take a vacation when they want to. After all, they may be trying to get cheap tickets, or coordinate with a friend, or catch the best weather, and that is not your business. On the other hand, there may be certain times—just before a grant is due, for example—when it would be absolutely disastrous (or terribly inconvenient) for the administrative assistant or other lab workers to be away from the lab. Ask them to reserve the time months in advance.

If there are set vacation limits at your institution, expect lab members to abide by them. But be willing to stretch the rules to give lab members a break. University and college labs are often more lenient than industry labs about the length of vacations. Especially where many lab members are not local, and must travel long and expensive distances to go home, vacation time is sometimes not regulated at all. At such a place, you should still keep track of the number and duration of lab member's vacations. In your head, there should be a limit. And if there is a limit in your head, do let people know, so that you do not grow resentful and the lab does not grow too sloppy and loose with vacation time.

Lab members who will be unexpectedly absent from the lab should call to inform someone of this absence. You should not have to ask the reason, unless the absences are piling up or there are other work-related problems.

LAB NOTEBOOKS

Matthaei kept laboratory notes in books bound like ledgers, tall, with pale gray, thick, stiff covers and heavy pages. He wrote in ink, economically and clearly... . He had invented a complicated system whereby plans for experiments were grouped and subgrouped, lettered and numbered in logical progression in one volume, the results and calculations entered in another volume cross-indexed to the first.
JUDSON (1996, P. 459)

I have never known anybody whose notebooks, for example, were so perfect as Jim's (Watson) notebooks. He had lines and different colors, a system; at any moment he could pick out any experiment.
LURIA TO JUDSON (JUDSON 1996, P. 45)

One of your nonnegotiable rules should be that every person in the lab must keep a clear and detailed laboratory notebook. The business of the lab is results and the communication of those results, and the lab notebook is the all-important documentation of each person's research. There are dozens of reasons to keep a clear and detailed lab notebook and only one—laziness—for not. Whether the work is on an esoteric branch of clam biology or is heading toward a potentially lucrative patent, it makes sense to keep data clear and findable.

Do not rely on everyone's own sense of responsibility on this one. You are ultimately responsible for the data in the lab, and most people have never been instructed on how to keep a lab notebook. Whether you do it casually ("You know, you really shouldn't skip pages in the notebook...") or formally, make it clear that a carefully kept notebook is a requirement, and not an option.

Kind of notebook

The notebook type may be determined by the institution. Especially at large companies, there may also be policy that dictates format, daily signatures by supervisors, and lock-up at night. Everyone in the lab should use the same kind of bound lab notebook, as determined by you. Ideally, it should have numbered pages, and gridlines, and have a tough enough binding so that it does not fall apart after a few months of being folded over to fit into a bare spot on the lab bench.

Laboratory Information Management Systems (LIMS) are programs that are coupled to a database and facilitate the entry and storage of laboratory data. Generally, these systems are expensive and are designed for testing and production, rather than basic research labs. They can be very useful tools: Some will manage protocols, schedule maintenance of lab instruments, receive data from multiple instruments, or track reagents and samples (Meisenholder 1999).

Electronic lab notebook programs may be used to centralize and distribute, store, and analyze data in smaller labs, which is more practical than using LIMS programs. Some kind of computerized system is particularly useful for collaborations and large projects. However, computer files may not provide sufficient evidence of invention for patent claims, and this will prevent or restrict their use in many labs.

Maintenance of a lab notebook—with potential patents in mind

Some labs are finely attuned to the possibility of patents and are meticulous about the care of lab notebooks. Other labs can barely manage not to paste notes scrawled on paper towels in place for a record of the day's experiments. But both groups would do well to take care of the documentation of the research, as patents, fraud charges, and the writing of manuscripts require organized and clear results. The list in Do's and Don'ts for Keeping Lab Notebooks (see box) is geared toward potentially patentable research. Not all labs will find signatures and witnessing necessary, but most labs will benefit from following most of the suggestions.

Experiments are best recorded in chronological order, rather than by particular experiment. Since most people run several experiments at once, this can become confusing for any reader or even for the lab member.

A Table of Contents *should not* be considered optional. As soon as the lab notebook is received, the lab member should set aside a few pages at the beginning or end of the book and list the page numbers, leaving a blank line for the experiment recorded, as well as for listing any continuation pages for that experiment.

The P.I. should encourage lab members to write summaries of each day's work. Since some experiments are never done, one can keep putting off the summary until some never-achieved day of perfect completion. Summarizing the data of the day helps *any* reader, including the P.I., to put together the big picture. It will also help lab members to pick up where they left off, and most importantly, forces them to evaluate their data every day.

Do's and Don'ts for Keeping Lab Notebooks

A laboratory notebook is a vital record of events leading to a patentable invention. The recorded information can establish dates of conception and reduction to practice of a technology as well as the inventorship of a patent claiming the technology. Below are 14 rules you should follow when keeping lab notebooks.

#1 — Do use bound books
Inventors should use permanently bound notebooks, e.g., notebooks with spiral or glue bindings. If loose-leaf sheets are used, they should be consecutively numbered and each page should be dated, signed, and witnessed.

#2 — Do sign and date
Each notebook should be signed and dated on the inside front cover to indicate the first day the recipient started using the notebook. Each entry should be signed and dated.

An independent witness, i.e., someone who understands the technology but will not be named as a co-inventor of the invention, should sign and date each entry after the statement: "Read and understood by _____." (The witness should preferably sign the entries on a contemporaneous or fairly contemporaneous basis, but entries can also be reviewed, signed, and dated on a periodic, e.g., weekly or monthly, basis.)

#3 — Do use ink
Notebook entries should be made in ink and in chronological order. Entries should not be erased or "whited out." If an entry contains an error, a line should be drawn through the error and new text should continue in the next available space.

#4 — Don't leave blank spaces
Blank gaps between entries should be avoided. If a blank space is left on a page, a line or cross should be drawn through the blank space, and the page dated to prevent subsequent entries.

#5 — Don't modify
Prior entries should not be modified at a later date. If data were omitted, the new data can be entered under a new date and cross-referenced to the previous entry. Record experiments when they are performed.

#6 — Do use past tense
Use the past tense (e.g., "was heated") to describe the experiments that were actually performed.

#7 — Do explain abbreviations and special terms
Explain all abbreviations and terms that are nonstandard. Explain in context, in a table of abbreviations, or in a glossary.

#8 — **Do staple attachments**

Attachments such as graphs or computer printouts should be permanently affixed in the notebook (e.g., by stapling), and both the attachment and the notebook page signed and dated. If the attachment cannot be stapled, it should be placed in an envelope and the envelope stapled to the notebook page. The envelope and page should then be signed and witnessed making reference to the attachment being placed in the envelope.

#9 — **Don't remove originals**

No original pages should be removed from the notebook.

#10 — **Do outline new experiments**

When a new project or experiment is started, the objective and rationale should be briefly outlined (e.g., in a short paragraph or by providing a flowchart).

#11 — **Do record lab meeting discussions**

Relevant discussions from lab meetings should be recorded as should ideas or suggestions made by others. The names of the people making the ideas and suggestions should be carefully documented. This information may be important in establishing inventorship.

#12 — **Do provide detail**

Record test descriptions, including preferred operating conditions, control conditions, operable and preferred ranges of conditions, and alternate specific materials; test results and an explanation of the results; and photos or sketches of the results or the test device. Any conclusions should be short and supported by the factual data. Opinions or speculation about the invention should be avoided.

#13 — **Do track notebooks**

Ideally, each lab should maintain a catalogue of notebooks in which each notebook is assigned a number, and the name of the author of each notebook is recorded. Further, the date the author received the notebook as well as the date the notebook was completed and turned in should be recorded. Upon leaving the lab, the author should return all notebooks checked out by or to him.

#14 — **Do save completed notebooks**

All completed notebooks should be indexed (e.g., by number, by author, by subject area) and safely kept in a central repository, together with corresponding patent applications or patents. Lab notebooks that relate to inventions on which patents have been granted should be kept for the life of the patent plus six years.

Reprinted, with permission, from J. Peter Fasse, Esq. and Fish & Richardson P.C. (8/01).

Checking notebooks

Few P.I.s check notebooks for anyone except beginning students and technicians. This seems to be more out of a sense of not invading a person's privacy or a simple desire not to take on yet another task. Is a lab notebook private? Officially, it is not. These data are the basis of papers, funding, theories, and careers. It is tremendously important.

I don't deliberately check the notebooks, but when I am going over data, I will stress that the notebook has to be neater and cleaner.

It is not merely an individual's journal or lab dairy but the crux of everything the entire lab may depend on.

Set up an atmosphere in which it is expected that lab members will show each other, and you, their notebooks. You should demand a level of care with lab notebooks. Everything in it should be understandable not only to the owner, but to you. It would be too humiliating for most people to have the P.I. deliberately checking the notebook for neatness. But when you are looking at data, take care to mention any problems you have with neatness and format.

I sometimes check notebooks for students and technicians if someone is under performing: not to see how much work is being done but to demonstrate to the person that part of the problem may be disorganized lab records.

Do not get too far from raw data, too soon. Whether you check notebooks, or have a lab member present to you with raw data, or stop at everyone's lab bench a few times a week, you must have a feeling for the quality and results of each person's raw data. It is very easy to make assumptions on the basis of the polished data you see at a research meeting, but many a lab member has unwittingly gone astray with over- or misinterpreted data. By keeping an eye on the raw data, you can be ready to comment on the number of repetitions, alternative experiments, or the implications of a minor result.

I check raw data all the time. People in the lab know that I cannot even think straight if I do not have the gel, autorad, or counts—or at least, the graph from the counts—in front of me.

When lab members are more senior, you will be able to trust their record-keeping ability more. You should still discuss raw data, however. But as a lab advances in numbers as well as in the seniority of some members, P.I.s tend to relax their vigilance on the newest lab members at the same time as they do with the more experienced members. Whether you still go through notebooks yourself, appoint another lab member to do so, or examine data in conversations and lab meetings, you must find a way to judge the quality of the raw data of every lab member.

Ownership of the notebook

The lab notebook belongs to the lab. Lab notebooks are not personal journals, and when a lab member leaves, the notebook should be left behind, The P.I. should hold on to a lab member's notebook and other data for at least 5 years after that person has left the lab, and for the life of a patent plus 6 years if the data in the book was involved in a granted patent.

LAB JOBS

Although some P.I.s have technicians who can be dedicated to keeping the lab together, most divide the multitude of jobs and tasks among all the lab members. This helps to give everyone a shared sense of responsibility, and an understanding of the time and money needed to run a lab. Listed below are several ways that this is commonly done:

- *Each piece of equipment has a champion,* who is responsible for organizing repairs and who can be called on when something goes wrong. Choosing a person who uses that piece of equipment anyway is usually a good idea, as that person has a vested interest in the maintenance of the machine, and probably knows a lot about its foibles. But all members should make it their business to open a manual and learn about any piece of equipment, and prior usage does not have to be a mandatory requirement. In fact, some P.I.s rotate equipment care deliberately, so that no piece of equipment is a mystery to anyone.

> *Some people do their jobs, others don't. If someone isn't doing their job, the others talk about it in meetings, so public shame helps people do their jobs.*

- *A list of routine lab jobs is drawn up and divided among lab members,* usually on a rotating basis (monthly is typical). Jobs are rotated to spare individuals the tedium of unpopular jobs. If all lab members are happy with their own jobs and have no complaints, it works best to not rotate too frequently.

- *Unsafe jobs are negotiated.* Some jobs do put the attending person at more risk, and cannot be summarily assigned. Risk entitles the doer to an easier total jobs load.

- *Lab jobs and equipment jobs are mixed in assignments.* As long as everyone has approximately the same sum of time and responsibility, almost any combination will work.

Typical lab jobs

- Making commonly used buffers.
- Sterilizing tubes.
- Keeping the cold room clean.
- Updating the isotope usage records.
- Checking and filling liquid nitrogen storage.
- Keeping the library organized.
- Making and maintaining a lab meetings rotation.
- Disposing of biohazard materials.
- Maintaining hoods or other specialized working areas.
- Mailing requested reagents.

YOUR LAB MANUAL

A lab manual is perhaps the best way to inform new lab members of the ins and outs of the lab and to keep all members updated on protocols and regulations. What could be included in a lab manual? Anything you do not want to explain over and over, anything that will make the lab more functional and that can make life easier for yourself and lab members.

A lab manual must be kept fairly current if it is to be useful. You may have someone in the lab who is orderly and would be happy to update the lab manual as a lab job. Or, every year or so, you and/or other lab members could spend a day on the update. If there are many common lab protocols and recipes, put these in another book.

Try not to be too dogmatic in discussions of lab policy or customs. For example, it would be considered preachy to inform people in a lab manual that their futures are in their own hands and that they should not have more than 1 week vacation: In person or by example, you could say the same thing without the critical overtones. You could also have a copy of the lab manual on the lab's Web Site.

THE FEWER RULES, THE BETTER

Official or unspoken, the fewer and simpler the rules, the better the atmosphere. So choose your rules carefully to fit in with the philosophy of the lab and complement the cultural expectations of the group. For example:

- Follow all safety rules/follow all safety rules except you can eat at your desk.
- Lab jobs should be done by the end of each week/lab jobs must be done as soon as indicated.
- The person who finds the remainder of a reagent or supplies low should order more/the person who is in charge of supplies must check daily.
- The person who finds a piece of equipment broken shall deal with it/the person who finds a piece of broken equipment should contact the person responsible.
- If there are "private" lab benches, no one should work on anyone else's bench without permission/all areas are common use and must be cleaned up immediately after use.
- Ask permission to use other people's reagents/most reagents are for public use but each user must keep them refilled.

Contents of a Lab Manual

Phone numbers and addresses of all lab members
Contact information of lab alumni
Contact number for personal emergencies

Functional information for new lab members
    ID badges
    Getting keys
    Computer passwords and use
    Orientation course
    Radiation badge and certification
    Phone policy and voice mail password
    English as a second language course

Lab policies
    Attendance and vacations
    Time card information
    Lab jobs to be rotated
    Rules for common areas
    Lab notebooks (usage, requirements, and sample page)

Safety
    Emergency numbers and contacts
    Procedures for fire, flood, earthquake
    Radiation ordering, use, storage, disposal
    Biohazard ordering, use, storage, disposal

Supplies and Equipment
    Ordering procedures
    Storage locations for supplies

Meetings
    Schedule of meetings
    Format and expectations
    Meeting attendance policy

Common lab protocols

Common lab reagent recipes

Publications from the lab

Relevant institutional rules and policies

Sexual harassment

Meetings and Seminars

ARE MEETINGS AND SEMINARS NEEDED?

Should you have meetings? In one way, you cannot get out of it, as it only takes two people to make a meeting. In the beginning of running a lab, with only a few lab members, you may find that you are in the lab so much that you know everything that is going on and talk so frequently with the people in the lab that organized meetings do not seem to be needed. But there are good reasons to start lab meetings as soon as you start your lab.

- *It makes the lab people take the work more seriously.* In the fuss and bother of opening a lab, it may sometimes seem hard for you to believe that serious research will soon be going on. Your lab members may never have been in a lab before, and meetings will make it clear that research is not just another class project.

- *It helps you take the work seriously.* It is rather hard to believe that you really have a lab and are actually in charge.

- *It helps you organize.* With a formal or semiformal venue, you can organize thoughts, take notes, and find references. In the lab, you may have much to say, but new researchers will not always know which are the significant points in either their work or your remarks. In a formalized meeting, the priorities can be made clear.

Even if you only have one technician, you should hold regular lab meetings. During this time, you should review the data obtained since the last meeting, and plan the experiments that will be done next.

HOW TO CONDUCT MEETINGS

I was impressed by the departmental seminars, which were stamped with his personality: fifteen or twenty scientists from the lab and other hospital departments, Lipmann presiding at the head of the table, quiet, seemingly preoccupied. The speaker finishes—a long silence—one minute, two, three—awkward—I try to think of a question—then Lipmann, looking down the table or perhaps out the window, asks the incisive, perceptive, exactly right first question. The dam breaks, and a lively discussion ensues.

HOAGLAND (1990, P. 67–68)

If anything ever needs a leader, it is a meeting! Perhaps a brainstorming meeting can do without a strong leader, but other meetings need someone to move the meeting before it takes on an unproductive life of its own. Without leadership and direction, meetings can drag, avoid the point, be a stage for the egotists, and waste an awful lot of time.

- *Have an agenda.* Inform lab members of the agenda before the meeting: e-mail is perfect for this. In some cases, e-mail communication might even eliminate the reason for the meeting.

- *Make sure the room is ready.* This could be a lab job, or part of someone else's regular job. People should be physically comfortable. Lunch meetings are good for this—people feel as if they are making good use of "free" time. A coffee pot is usually a good fixture.

- *Keep the meeting to the agenda.* If someone strays from the agenda, trying to discuss individual research instead of the research of the speaker, step in. Make sure everyone moves from topic to topic.

- *Keep the ball rolling.* When conversation flags, pump it up again.

- *Encourage group participation.* Many people are very shy about contributing at meetings. If you can establish an atmosphere in which everyone talks, the meeting will be much more productive. Set up the expectation that everyone will have a say.

- *Set a time limit and stick to it.* Announce in the agenda how long the meeting will be. If there is more than one person speaking, also inform everyone how long each speaker will talk. Keep things moving.

- *Tolerate conflict but do not let it get out of hand.* Confront members who are belittling others, not telling the truth, stonewalling, or are otherwise interfering with the purpose or the vibe of the meeting.

- *Summarize frequently.* This shows that you are participating and that you care, and clarifies topics that may not be clear.

- *Keep a record of the meeting,* especially if it is about research or lab interactions.

- *Follow up.* This is a great chance to interact one-on-one with lab members. After a research meeting, for example, you could follow up with the speaker about the different points and experiments discussed at the meeting.

Your meetings are getting out of control if people show up late or not at all, are not prepared, or do not participate. If the meetings are not effective, it is time to retool. You must first show that you take the meetings seriously.

Attendance at lab meetings

Every person in your lab will probably not be able to attend every meeting. But be sure that a policy of nonattendance does not develop. Do not tolerate missing meetings. It happens sometimes, but it should not become a habit. The P.I. is not being petty by requesting that people attend meetings and be on time. However, if many lab members seem to be unhappy with the meeting, as evidenced by chronic lateness and missed meetings, ask them if there is a way to reformat the meeting to everyone's satisfaction.

Departmental seminars can be tough. They are not always relevant to everyone and, perhaps, not to your lab at all. But the other members of the department are your colleagues, and not showing up for seminars can be interpreted as a lack of consideration or respect. These meetings foster interaction with other departmental members.

Participation at lab meetings and discussions

You can require everyone to take turns presenting at journal clubs and lab meetings. You can help the lab members with their first presentations—correct language, suggest topics, and steer the discussions the way you think they should go. But you will have much less control over getting people to contribute voluntarily *during* a meeting, even a casual one.

Speaking in a crowd comes completely naturally to some and is a horror for others. People think differently, and some cannot come up with a spontaneous appropriate remark or response. Some do not want to draw attention to themselves, some are afraid to be wrong, and some are always waiting for the right time. Some just never developed the habit: It is seen as a necessity only for the very career-savvy and ambitious. But it is very important, to the individual and to the lab. Getting input from each person makes for a meeting very different from one dominated by the same one or two people.

Participation is largely a question of motivation: Unless lab members feel that they are part of the lab and can contribute, some might never take part in a discussion. People tend to stay in a particular role in the lab, but the P.I. can make oral contribution an expected part of that particular role.

During the meeting, you could go around the room and solicit opinions. This is better than singling out a particular person for comments—unless the camaraderie is such that you can, lightly, ask someone a question with humor and understanding on the part of all members.

Working up from one-on-one meetings may also help. Once someone can handle a scientific back-and-forth with the P.I., meeting with another person, perhaps one working on the same or similar project, can move this individual into feeling comfortable about exchanging ideas with other scientists. Brainstorming meetings are an excellent way to learn to speak without worrying whether one's comments are wrong or frivolous.

Teaching people to speak. Some people are motivated to contribute, but lack the public speaking skills to communicate well. P.I.s have found that a combination of giving many opportunities for each lab member to speak and finding a palatable way to criticize organization and style, does wonders.

As for most aspects of instruction and expectation in the lab, lab members must work within the context of their own personalities. Not everyone will give a charismatic and vigorous talk at departmental lab meetings; for some, their best presentations will be given in a thoughtful, step-by-step fashion. Try to accommodate each person's style and not impose yours.

- *Work on content before presentation.* If a speaker is worried about the contents of the talk, all the cosmetic adjustments to posture and voice will not help the speaker's confidence or the audience's reception. Make suggestions on organization before the talk is prepared. Suggest the appropriate time limit.

- *Make suggestions about the preparation of the slides.* This is the step most often left to chance in a busy lab, and it should not be, as the preparation of the slides is the culmination of the analysis of the data and the basis of how the data are presented. Be sure that the person knows the financial and technical aspects of slide making in your lab. Discourage last minute slide making.

- *Have the person practice the talk for you, or for the entire lab.* Record comments as you or others make them, so you can go through the comments with the person afterward: Many people will not be able to absorb the comments at the time, or may grow defensive.

- *Help the person learn to answer questions after a talk.* To avoid blank outs, teach a few pat answers to use, such as "That is a very good question. I will have to think about that and get back to you." It is usually not okay for the P.I. to answer questions, unrequested, for lab members, but the lab member should know when to defer to the P.I. to answer a question in a talk.

- *Remember that you are teaching communication,* not merely public speaking.

Helping nonnative English speakers

Giving a scientific talk in another language is a formidable task, and requires great courage. Do not force nonnative English speakers to talk too soon—but do not let too much time go by before expecting a public talk. A presentation of a former project or a journal club is a good first engagement.

- To gain confidence in speaking, nonnative English speakers (or their mentors) often write the entire talk out and then read it at the meeting. Be sure to check for correct language and grammar before the talk is presented.

- Reading a talk can make for a very flat experience for everyone. Do what you can to ensure that the sequence and presentation of data are done in as interesting a way as possible. Help the person set up slides or overheads or a computer presentation in a way that will break the monotony of long spoken paragraphs.

- Do not try to work on elimination of a monotone or accent (except, perhaps, for a few key words), as this can lead to too much stress.

- Suggest that the person make eye contact with the audience as much as possible.

- Have the person keep the talk brief.

- Never allow language problems to compromise the scientific content of the talk.

- As the nonnative English speaker gains in confidence, increase your level of criticism slowly.

RESEARCH LAB MEETINGS

Almost all P.I.s hold research lab meetings. Depending on the format, these meetings are absolutely vital because they

- Keep the P.I. informed of what is going on in the lab.

- Keep the department aware of the research (especially formal presentations).

- Bond the lab, showing how everyone's work relates to the others.

- Provide the kernel around which the lab centers.

> We have regular lab meetings, and 3 people present a week. It started with everyone speaking, but it was too much when the lab got bigger. Now more time is spent on details, but there is still room for theoretical discussion. For more formal meetings, there is an interlab meeting, so people get to practice a polished talk.

- Help presenters by forcing them to prioritize and organize the data, as well as learning communication skills.

Formal lab meetings are excellent for teaching the intricacies of a polished talk. Raw data are not usually shown in a formal lab meeting; rather, data are selected carefully and a story is constructed, much as is done in writing a manuscript. Formal meetings are not the venue for teaching lab members how to think, but they are excellent for teaching how to organize and present and sell a story. Your department may require its own formal research presentations by all students and postdocs, which should be in addition to research meetings within your own group.

Informal lab meetings are the choice of most laboratories. In these meetings, lab members show raw data, and these data, as well as the choice of the experiment, the research path followed, the interpretation of the results, and just about anything, are fair game for criticism and comment.

The P.I. sets the level of expectation and criticism. It is up to you to determine how stringent the lab meeting will be. You must know what you want to achieve in a lab meeting and then determine the best way to do this with your particular group of people. Most P.I.s try to achieve a balance between support and criticism: They moderate their remarks and the lab member's remarks to show disagreement without disapproval. In a very junior lab, this is appropriate, as young scientists can very easily have their confidence eroded by too harsh (or too honest) criticism. To achieve this balance:

- *Be honest,* or there is no point for the meetings. Criticism is an inherent part of science and is helpful and necessary.

- *Be aware of veiled ridicule.* Keep the focus on the science and be always ready to weigh in with your calm and objective scientific opinion.

- *Expect a clear and concise presentation* even in a casual format that enables all lab members to understand the theory and the specifics of the discussion.

- *Expect that the meeting be instructional for all.* Expecting participation from all members is the best way to keep everyone part of the process. Ask questions of the speaker, solicit questions from the audience, involve everyone. Ask a quiet audience member, "What would you do next?"

Other P.I.s find this restraint artificial and not useful. On the contrary, they allow free reign of criticism. Without unrestricted criticism, they believe, the lab meeting can become a rubber stamp of approval of ridiculous sidetracks in focus. "What doesn't kill you, makes you stronger," might be the motto, and this is seen most often in large and/or very competitive labs, those in which weeding out of lab members who cannot keep up is expected.

The format and the number of presenters will also help determine the climate of these meetings. If just one or two lab members speak, analysis will be in great detail, and the focus of the presentation and discussion is usually on technique and methods. If every lab member speaks at each lab meeting, there is only enough time for an overview of the project, the results of a few experiments, and a brief mention of future plans. The lab meetings in which everyone in the lab presents data are certainly easier on the presenters, as well as on the P.I. But unless the P.I. is in frequent communication with all lab members about research, this kind of meeting will not tell you enough about each project and each lab member.

Many P.I.s hold lab meetings with other labs. When your lab still has few staff, research meetings (and journal clubs) seem senseless and weak. Combining your lab meeting with another lab that has similar research interests can make the meeting seem more "real," providing critical mass and fresh perspectives for discussion. Many labs hold meetings with other labs in addition to their own meetings.

Even when the lab is bigger, the insights provided by another group of people can make for an interesting meeting. But with increased numbers of people, informal research talks become functionally difficult, unless the research interests are very closely aligned.

Topic lab meetings within the lab can be beneficial. To discuss the technical and philosophical subtleties of a project, many P.I.s have group meetings in addition to meetings for the whole lab. This kind of meeting can be held for an actively collaborating group of people or for lab members with merely a common interest. Without having to allot time to explain background or methods to those unfamiliar with the topic, these meetings can soar with details and heated discussions. But the P.I. must be aware of the delicate political situations that can arise and derail these meetings. Turf battles do need to be discussed; you must keep the meeting calm and productive and keep politics in context with the research issues.

JOURNAL CLUBS

Journal clubs are used to discuss the current and relevant literature. They are an excellent venue to teach lab members the requirements and construction of a good paper. They give junior or insecure lab members the chance to dissect a paper without anyone being offended.

Most P.I.s grew up with journal clubs in their labs, and many do not require them in their own labs. With a plethora of meetings to attend, the journal club is usually of the lowest priority. Expecially in the beginning, with possibly only one technician, a journal club seems silly, perhaps even pretentious. A few people can sit around a table in the library and talk about papers and ideas, perhaps over a beer, but a more formatted presentation will not work.

We have journal club 3x a week. Students must learn to communicate. They must learn to think. Journal clubs push the presenter—why do this? Can you think of a better experiment? It encourages them to pick only very good journals, to learn what a very good article is. After a while, they start to think hey, I can also think about these kinds of experiments. Then, I raise the bar slowly. You can't walk onto a small, isolated university and expect students to believe they will get a Nature paper. You start by going for a certain standard and then raise the standard to the next level.

Once there are four or five people in the lab, however, a journal club can be a viable addition. It does provide a way to follow the field. It can boost the lab I.Q., serving as a source of common language and background, showing the newcomers in the lab just what their extended scientific family is up to.

I hated journal clubs when I was a student and a postdoc, and I vowed never to have them when I had my own lab.

Journal clubs are an excellent way to teach critical thinking. It is often easier for people to learn critical thinking with the published literature, rather than with their own work. There is a lot of ego on the line when junior lab members present their data, and defensiveness can prevent understanding of a project's flaws. Below are some suggestions for the critical presentation and discussion of a paper:

- *Summarize the main point of the paper.* What did the authors want to do?

- *Discuss the importance of the question asked.* Place it within the context of the immediate field, and the larger field, of science.

  Journal clubs are on Friday at 5, so you can not go if you don't want. I figure if they don't know the importance of the literature, I can't make them learn it.

- *Describe the paper in detail.* Working through the figures in order is the usual way this is done.

- *Analyze the data.* Do they support the conclusions? Was each experiment necessary? Do the data seem to be reproducible? Are the methods appropriate to the experiment? Are the statistics solid?

- *Itemize the strengths and flaws of the paper.* Is it would make it better? What would you have done?

- *Compare the paper to other papers.* Is it as well done, as significant, as trustworthy as others? Did the relative stature of the authors influence your interpretation of the paper? Was this paper published in the best journal for the topic or data?

- *Is the paper well written and the data clearly presented?* Are the figures clear and easy to understand, without extraneous or distracting data? Does the introduction give you sufficient and honest background?

- *Predict the next step in the research,* and where the research might ultimately go.

Underneath the discussion might lie the thought—how does my work and my papers compare with this paper? Am I doing what I expect other authors to do?

Journal clubs can also be used to teach students and postdocs about making presentations. When discussing one's own data, there is the concern over the validity of the data, as well as worry about the presentation, and the finer points of communication may be lost. However, when lab workers can put aside worries about the data, they can concentrate on the presentation.

If you take your journal clubs seriously, be sure that each person knows what kind of presentation is expected. Be ready to help junior lab members prepare for their first journal club: This is usually left to chance and is a wasted opportunity for instruction and the building of a lab member's confidence. There are two main formats followed for journal clubs:

- *Multiple papers done briefly.* This may be the best papers of the week in a field, a review of a topic, or selected papers from one journal. This kind of journal club is good for keeping lab members up on a topic or on the general content of what is being published.

- *One or two papers discussed in depth.* These meetings are the way to give lab members an understanding of how science is approached in other labs.

The main advantage of having more than one presenter is that it keeps the program moving along and decreases monotony. Most labs have a 1-hour lab meeting, with two presenters, each of whom presents usually one or sometimes two papers.

Banning photocopies usually turns out to be an excellent idea. Insecure presenters tend to produce a flurry of photocopies, which, even cut and pasted up and kept to a single sheet, distract the speaker as well as the audience.

Chalk talks (a sentimental name used also for whiteboards) encourage a deep and simple understanding of the paper. Without any props, presenters must explain the paper as well as display their thought processes. The ability to speak without props is a valuable facility to teach lab members.

OTHER REASONS FOR MEETINGS

Then suddenly someone starts telling of a result, his or her own or one heard about at a recent meeting. Questions pop out, and soon the speaker is at the blackboard drawing, explaining, arguing, reconstructing the argument. Everyone stops eating, asks questions, suggests explanations. These impromptu sessions are truly moments of grace, when we share the human aspect of science as one would share the clear water of a cool spring.

Luria (1984, p. 122)

Lab organization and lab problem meetings

Occasionally, the lab may benefit from a meeting used to solve personnel or equipment problems in the lab. This can easily turn into a bitter gripe session, so be ready to moderate if people become more nasty than productive. All complaints should be given to contribute to a solution. As moderator, try to keep this meeting to a simple agenda, as dealing with more than a few unrelated problems gets complicated and ineffective. Some labs, instead of dedicating an entire meeting to problems, reserve 5 minutes at the end of the weekly research meeting or journal club as a gripe session.

Brainstorming meetings

Call a conference of people interested in a particular topic and let them loose, with each person presenting a variety of ideas. Someone records the discussion, but with no real evaluation of the ideas during the session. There is an informal atmosphere, people are relaxed; each person's ideas are influenced by the others and are spoken without being modulated by thoughts of feasibility or expectations.

Lab retreat meetings

Go away! Getting out of the lab to discuss research—or not discuss research—can be amazingly invigorating and effective. It can also be expensive, so you need to choose a place that gives a good return for your investment. Money usually will be had from departmental or "unspecified" funds, seldom from grants.

Booking retreats off season will be the cheaper route, with the added advantage of fewer temptations to detract from the science than in season. Wherever you go, be sure there is a meeting room large and comfortable enough for everyone and that you have sole use of that room. If meals do not come with the package, be sure that inexpensive food is available. Unused army bases, other scientific institutions, resorts, someone's cabin—almost any place can work.

If going away does not work, have a retreat at your own institution. Organize a seminar room and put aside 1 or 2 days on which no lab work is allowed, and schedule presentations. Provide food and coffee.

Most importantly, be sure to invite everyone in the lab. This is a chance for the nonscientific members to hear what is going on and to feel part of the whole-lab enterprise.

ONE-ON-ONE MEETINGS

So that, in practice, when Dr. Avery returned from vacation, hours and hours were spent for weeks doing nothing but talk. And in fact, it was chiefly Dr. Avery himself who did the talking. He would have each and every one of us in his office to review—not in the form of a systematic review, in the form of conversation—the problems he had dealt with the year before and the problems he had thought about during his vacation, which was always spent on Deer Island.

PIEL AND SEGERBERG (1990, P. 53)

Much of the value of the lab will be described in terms of how much one-on-one time you spend with lab members. At these meetings, you can better understand the results and motivation of the lab members, and they can learn, without outside pressures, how you think and act.

Scheduled meetings

Have an agenda that both of you have agreed upon before. Make it clear that you expect the person to be fully prepared, and discuss beforehand (perhaps at a prior meeting, if you meet regularly) what preparation entails. For a research meeting, a format might be:

- What was discussed or agreed upon since last meeting.
- Summary of work since last meeting.
- Were goals met—Why and why not?
- Big picture discussion—Is this research heading in the right direction?
- Other work in the field, ideas discussion.
- List of goals for next time period.
- Personal discussion—general happiness, complaints.

Both parties should takes notes at scheduled and unscheduled meetings. Topics and ideas are discussed and agreed upon, but people tend to remember only their own version.

Unscheduled meetings

An open door policy in the lab will probably mean having meetings all day. But even with a liberal open door policy you can ask someone to return in an hour, or in the afternoon, if the problem is not urgent. Sometimes P.I.s themselves will request an unscheduled meeting. Try to allow some latitude, for lab people are likely to be in the middle of experiments.

The format will depend on you and the other person. But it can be controlled, even if it is spontaneous. Deal with the problem or discussion and conclude the meeting. The informality of the arrangement sometimes makes people think that they have to chat, and it just may not be the right time for chatting.

Notes are especially important to take for unscheduled meetings, as there is no format to hang one's memories on. If there was no chance to take notes during the meeting, write down a summary of the meeting immediately after.

If you cannot have the meeting, say so. It is far better to reschedule than to make a person feel unwelcome. It may be that the requester is a whiner, and you cannot bear to listen to any moaning. Perhaps you have 1 week left for a grant, and do not want to talk to anyone. If the person must have a meeting, but you are short on time, say "I can give you 10 minutes." Then give it, totally. Do not look at the clock or indicate anxiety by body or verbal language. After 10 minutes, rise and end the meeting.

Cut back on unnecessary meetings. No doubt, you spend too much of your time in meetings that might prevent you from doing what you think your real work is—thesis committee meetings, faculty meetings, curriculum meetings, meetings with speakers, as well as meetings with applicants for positions in the department. You have no choice about attending many of the meetings. In many, you also have no choice about how that meeting is run. But if you do have or want some control, the following can help you limit the number of meetings you must attend.

- *Use the phone or e-mail.* See how many of the meeting's concerns can be handled by phone or by e-mail. A conference call could save money as well as time.

- *Combine meetings.* If the same group of people is meeting at different times, for different issues, see if it can all be handled in one meeting.

- *Limit the size of the meeting.* The more people, the more talking, the more time gone.

Lab time

As bench time drops, many P.I.'s maintain a presence in the lab by walking around and talking to everyone. This keeps them up to speed on the data and is a great way to fix experiment problems before they grow too large.

In your rounds, try to touch on everyone. It is instinctive to drift toward the lab members with the successful projects, as they are usually the most receptive to discussion. But for the person who has nothing to show, hearing a fellow lab member across the bench trill about great results is very tough, and you may be met with only monosyllabic replies from the unsuccessful. This can reinforce the common scenario in which the P.I. tends to talk to only to a select few in the lab.

> *I am always walking through the lab, asking everyone how it is going. So I probably talk to everyone every 2 or 3 days. People drop in the office to show data.*

There are several options. You can follow each person's cue, and talk or not talk. You can persist, and keep the topic to specifics ("Do you think the dosage is important in those experiments?"), to generalities ("Which approach should give the most data?"), or to banalities ("How is that power supply working out?"). Make sure, though, that what is not discussed in the walk-around time is discussed in some way, in scheduled or unscheduled meetings. The person may merely need some time and psychological space, but do not allow isolation to creep in.

THE SANCTITY OF THE OPEN DOOR

A casual visitor to the lab might gain the impression of a chaotic scene, papers piled everywhere, passionate arguments going on about something completely unrelated to research, on one occasion a baby (the Dodsons' first) suspended from a doorway in a baby bouncer. Teatime gatherings at the end of the corridor (at this point they were still in Chemical Crystallography) were an important part of the day, and if it was anyone's birthday, he or she would bring in a cake to share.

FERRY (2000, P. 316)

P.I.s cling religiously to the idea of an open door policy. After all, it typifies everything that science should be. It emphasizes the fact that access and information, data and communication are all free-flowing. For the P.I. no longer at the bench, it is the way in which to remain in contact with the lab members. Instead of your hands at the bench, what you can offer is your interest and your ear and your advice.

But you can qualify your open door time. Just as you would arrange a meeting with a lab member and would set that time aside, you can allow yourself the same consideration without denying an open door policy. Set hours for privacy, and do it without guilt.

Using Computers to Organize the Lab

WHAT CAN BE ORGANIZED?

Is the lab organized? The definition of "organized" to most P.I.s is the accessibility of information on laboratory stocks, data, and protocols. But organization is also reflected in how well information passes among the lab members: Does everyone know the latest technique? Who will be available in July to split the cells while the graduate student is on vacation? When is the next international meeting in your field? The computer can strengthen the acquisition and utilization of all information in the laboratory. And the fact that all lab members have access to the same information is a great democratizer and helps to instill a lab spirit of equality.

Organization can save you time and money, but you can surpass the limit, and don't get adequate returns for your investment.

Most P.I.s wish the labs were more organized, but it is not a huge priority, that is, until the first student leaves and no one can find a particular cell line in the freezer boxes. Resolutions are made, the crisis passes, and all goes on as before until the next person leaves. Although it is probably inevitable that there be some confusion when a long-time lab member moves on, an organized lab will not be as affected as an unorganized one.

I wish things were more organized, but there is no time. I do know where the data is, but that's about all!

It is never too late to organize. If done later in the life of a lab, some lab members will consider it to be an infringement of their rights and time and will resent these organizational efforts. It is best to establish your organizational framework early, so that organization becomes part of the laboratory personality. Then, as people come to the lab, they will assume that everything is organized and that part of this organization is their responsibility. You will not have to struggle for every bit of neatness.

Organization for organization's sake does not work. There are so many programs, so many tools and gadgets, that P.I.s so inclined may be tempted to urge the entire lab toward organizational perfection. The sensible use of the personal computer is key to the organization of the lab. The computer can, however, magnify as well as diminish problems if it is not used judiciously. Investing in ten different programs, making extensive lists of orders and procedures, and expecting full compliance will cause chaos. You can only make as many organizational rules that will work. P.I.s have found that only if the lab organizational tasks make sense, are quickly done, and will directly benefit the doer, will they themselves be done.

213

CHOOSING COMPUTER PROGRAMS

Computers are critical to dealing with the acquisition and organization of the huge fund of knowledge that any scientist must tackle, as well as with most administrative aspects of the running of the lab. Although computers are now an integral part of biology, with many labs spending more time doing science via computers than at the bench, they are underused as organizational tools.

- *Determine your computer needs.* There are many wonderful programs with lots of bells and whistles, but if you do not need the program, it will suck up your time like a vacuum. There is a particular personality that would love to tinker with a new program all day—beware if this is you! Let your needs dictate what you purchase. Although each lab has specific research as well as organizational goals, 90% of the needs are common to most labs. The best way to find the software you need is to see it in operation in another lab.

- *Simplify to be effective.* The more programs, the more crashes, as your computer tries to sort out conflicting messages among programs. Load only what you need.

- *Invest the time to learn the programs well.* Many people have programs whose capabilities they will never know because they will not read the accompanying literature or take a computer class. For each new program, spend an hour with an instruction manual, buy a user-friendly book to take on vacation, or avail yourself of any seminars or classes offered by the software company or by your own institution.

Software needs for labs

Organization

- Database for the organization of supplies in the lab.
- Searching through venders and ordering supplies.
- Managing grants.
- Utility and recovery—maintenance, diagnostics, and repair of the computer hard drive.

Communication

- e-mail to communicate with others within or outside the lab.
- Web browser to access the Internet.
- Project management.
- Personal Information Manager (PIM) to organize appointments, things to do, and phone numbers and addresses.

Fine-tuning the science

- Word processing for the writing and editing of manuscripts.

- Presentation software.

- Bibliographic software to find, store, retrieve, and integrate references into manuscripts and books.

Examples of a typical software array for a lab

Microsoft Office
Word (word processing)
Excel (spreadsheet)
Powerpoint (making slides and presentations)
Internet Explorer (WWW access)
Outlook (e-mail, things to do, appointments)
EndNote (bibliographic software)
FileMaker Pro (reagent lists, supplies for ordering)
Norton Utilities (anti-viral, fix-it and maintenance)

ORGANIZATION OF LAB RESOURCES

Cells, bacterial strains, and reagents

Keeping track of stocks and reagents is the primary definition of organization of most P.I.s. Very few P.I.s say that their labs are organized. Most ruefully wish they had started off with a system, as it seems too difficult to implement a system once research is well under way. But it is never too late to organize. It is much better to establish your framework in the beginning, but structure can be added at any time. You must keep it simple if you want people to comply with the rules.

Nothing, nothing, is computerized—there are some stocks listed in a book—and no one except me knows where anything is.

The business of the lab is to do experiments and write papers, and the reagents that you generate are vital. Results must be reproducible. Your raw material and the reagents you have generated must be stored in the appropriate place, be clearly labeled and identifiable, and be accessible to those who need them, even after the creator of the reagent has left the lab. The records for these reagents must also be clearly labeled and identifiable and be accessible to all who need them.

Lab reagents and supplies are generally kept on databases. Databases allow you to enter and organize information. Most importantly, you can search for items, effectively allowing you to reorganize and reassess the information. Some

Our ordering is computerized, the protocols are computerized—but organizing reagents doesn't work, things just don't stay in the same place. Organizing that well just isn't compatible with the lab culture. I wish it was.

P.I.s have attempted to keep lists on a word processing program, using the "search" command to look for particular words or items. This works for very simple lists, but it is more difficult to update a list. Others have tried using a spreadsheet such as Excel (http://www.microsoft. com), which allows for more manipulation of the data than does a word processing package. But a good database can do all and is more than sufficient to keep track of materials on the laboratory shelves and what needs to be ordered.

> *I've been thinking about getting a lab reagent database together—but I know I'll have a war on my hands if I try to get the lab to use it.*

An overwhelming number of labs with computerized systems use FileMakerPro (http://www.filemaker.com) for keeping lists or reagents as well as supplies. There are many other databases, such as Access (http://www.microsoft.com), but the simplicity of FileMakerPro makes it a researcher's favorite for keeping track of the flow of materials in the lab. Several companies are now making software that sits on top of a database such as FileMakerPro or Access, with more scientifically specialized commands and formats.

Below is a list of ways to get lab members to keep good records:

- *Provide computer access.* If not all lab members have their own computer, there must be one dedicated to lab business or at least, one for which lab business takes priority over other uses. One program accessed by Intranet via several computers is the best solution.

- *Keep entries simple.* Set up an outline so that each person need only type in the specific information.

- *Provide personal database files.* All lab members should have their own files within the database. Trouble starts when there is one lab file that everyone is expected to append. If one person starts to lag in entries, others feel that there is not much point in keeping information current.

At what point does a reagent become a permanent one, worthy of being recorded on the computer? In the course of experimentation, many, many tubes and plates are generated. They are saved until you know the final answer, they are saved "just-in-case," and mostly, they are saved out of great fear. The best way to deal with this

---

Information to record for lab-generated reagents

Identification of sample
Nature of substance
Origin of substance
Experiment number, passage number, or other identifier
Number of samples
Name of maker/owner
Date
Storage location

is to reserve an active spot (as opposed to a storage spot) in refrigerators, freezers, and shelves for works-in-progress. Without the clutter of dozens of extra tubes and plates in storage areas, lab members are much more inclined to take the implications of storage seriously and to keep good permanent storage records.

Distributing reagents

The sharing of reagents is an important facet of research. If you have received federal funds for your research, and/or have published your results, you are expected to send other investigators samples of antibodies, DNA, cells, animals, bacteria, and other lab-generated reagents that you have described in publications.

> *A disgruntled postdoc in the lab took all of the remaining antibody we had generated. I wrote or called everyone we had sent reagents to, to try to recover enough so we could finish our own experiments. About 90% of the people who had asked for the antibody hadn't used it yet, leaving me to wonder why they had asked for it in the first place...but we did get enough back to do the experiments.*

Keep records of all distributions

There are three ways to use the computer to streamline and maintain reagent requests.

- *Require a Request for Materials form.* Rather than haphazardly taking phone call, e-mail, and letter requests for reagents, keep a letter for the Request for Materials on the laboratory Web Site or send one by e-mail to everyone who requests a reagent. In this way, all requests can be kept in one place and in one format, simplifying your record-keeping and saving space.

Request for Materials Form

Name:
Affiliation/Organization:
Address:
Phone number:
e-mail address:
Proposed use of the requested materials:
Attached MTA, if required.

- *Send a Materials Transfer Agreement (MTA) form.* Depending on the rules of your institution and the nature of the reagent, all who request a reagent must first sign a Materials Transfer Agreement. Although there is a standardized approach suggested by NIH for transfers between academic institutions, it is more difficult to move reagents between other institutions, and thus the MTA form should be drawn up with the help of your institutional lawyers. It can be kept on your Web Site or sent by e-mail, although responses with signatures might be required to be on paper.

- *Send a standard letter along with all reagent requests you fill.* A brief letter should acknowledge that you are sending a reagent. You may have one letter for all reagents, leaving a blank to fill in the name and amount of the reagent supplied, or have a separate letter for each reagent.

The distribution of reagents should be handled centrally, i.e., all reagents should be sent through the lab, and not by each person who generated that particular reagent. A shared reagent will sometimes imply a collaboration, and the P.I. ultimately needs to make collaboration decisions for the lab. It is also easier for reagent bookkeeping if one person handles the distribution and record keeping. However, you may find youself facing a moral dilemma if a reagent took great trouble and expense to generate, and your supply is limited. There are no rules to govern this situation, and different labs handle this in different ways. Some ignore requests, some write back to say there is no more of the requested substance available, whereas others do everything they can to provide the reagent, even at inconvenience and loss to the lab.

Ordering reagents and supplies

On-line ordering is increasingly a straightforward process. There are available many options for both inquiring about products on-line and actually ordering on-line, but you probably must work within the confines of the system your organization has set up.

In some labs, a central person does the ordering and puts the entries on the computer. Some labs have one person do all the ordering, requiring a huge expenditure of time for that person. But having one person who regularly—usually, daily—combines and updates orders, and puts through the orders, can make everything run smoothly.

Some labs allow and expect lab members to put in their own order, without questioning. Even in labs with an overabundance of resources, this can lead to great redundancy and waste. The most common arrangement for ordering is one in which lab members put in their own order, but the order is funneled through one person who looks for duplications and excess. In new labs, this is usually the P.I., and in more established labs, it is a technician or lab manager.

Many computer programs are set to give a signal for items over an ordained amount, or when duplicate orders have been entered.

The interface between keeping track of supplies and ordering supplies is still hazy. Depending on the ordering system at your institution, you may not be able to completely couple your lab database system to the ordering system. Human input is still needed in most labs. However, speak to the database company to try to find a way to work this out: Some companies can suggest or include modifications to tailor the program to your exact needs.

```
┌─────────────────────────────────────────────────────────────┐
│ Information to record for purchased reagents and supplies     │
│                                                               │
│ Name of product:                                             │
│ Storage location:                                            │
│ Company of origin:                                           │
│ Catalog number:                                              │
│ Price:                                                        │
│ Size or amount:                                              │
│ Pertinent storage information (e.g., light-sensitive, expiration │
│    date):                                                    │
└─────────────────────────────────────────────────────────────┘
```

Tracking money

Larger labs may need, and small labs may want, a program dedicated to tracking expenses in the lab. Very few P.I.s track their own expenses. Most get a monthly statement of money spent from the administration of the department, and for most, this will suffice while the lab is small. But as the lab grows in resources and personnel, and if the administration cannot give you regular feedback, you might consider tracking your own expenditures.

What money-tracking programs can do for you. Money- and grant-tracking database programs allow you to search the database for order numbers, vendors, time of last purchase, and price. More importantly, for P.I.s having more than one source of funds, grant management programs can list how much has been spent on supplies, personnel, or other costs for a specific amount of time, and inform you when funds from each grant are running low.

Many labs are using grant and personnel managers (http://www.northernlights-software.com). SciPoint Data Solutions (http://www.scipoint.com) offers a package of programs based on the database Access, to deal with grants and ordering in the lab. Lab/Office Manager deals with order processing and expense analysis, GrantTrak manages and tracks multiple grants, and GrantBuilder is used in the preparation of NIH grants. GrantSlam (http://www.cayuse.com) is a database-driven software program that has the latest NIH grant proposal forms and does calculations such as indirect costs.

Protocols

Protocols evolve and must be kept on a computer, as only a computer file can cope with the constant changes. They are changed over time, and they are changed in different ways by each lab member. Either a database or word processing program is suitable for keeping track of protocols: Most labs use a word processing program.

Lab protocols versus individual protocols. Each person will modify any protocol, and these changes should be noted on the protocol. But whose protocol should be used for a new lab member? Ideally, there is a master protocol in the laboratory protocol book, and lab members keep their own version in their own files. The following information should be provided for each protocol:

- Name of the protocol
- Original source or reference
- Materials needed
- Step-by-step instructions
- Date of last modifications
- Name of user

P.I.s have even more difficulty in getting lab members to keep protocols updated than to keep stocks straight, which may be because it is harder for lab members to feel that they are benefiting from updating protocols. Some labs have a few days a year dedicated to updating protocols, a few days in which all lab members organize their own protocols.

FOSTERING COMMUNICATION

The computer allows P.I.s to stay in touch with colleagues all over the world. But even among people who may work 10 feet apart, the computer can be used as a tool to keep in touch. With your e-mail program, you can update your lab members on a meeting that you just attended. You can ask individuals you have not spoken to in a few days to update you on their projects. You can mention a paper everyone would be interested in. You can solicit suggestions for a brand for a new piece of equipment. The computer allows you a measure of frequency and intimacy that a busy schedule may not allow.

Personal Information Managers

Personal information managers (PIMs) are useful not only for personal organization, but also for the sharing of information, as many of the files can be set up to be entered by multiple users. Your PIM must work with your other computer and organizational systems and programs. If you network with other colleagues in the department, the PIM must be compatible with the communications system and with the other programs in order to exchange information about meetings and calendars. This is not the province of a computer amateur to organize, and most P.I.s should not try to set up such a system themselves.

What PIM programs can do for you. The use of PIMs for your own efficiency are described in the chapter on Using Your Time in this volume, and lab members' utilization of the calendar, addresses, and things-to-do functions can also increase personal effectiveness. If you can, provide access to a PIM for all lab members. PIMs can also be used to exchange information among you and lab members via the Intranet. Letting everyone in the lab know what your teaching and traveling schedule is—and having all lab members post their vacation schedules as well—allows coordination of lab meetings and assignments.

PIMs vary widely in strengths and weaknesses (Calhoun 1998) and should be picked for your needs and your preference for the specialized features. Some of the more popular PIMs are:

Lotus Organizer (http://www.lotus.com)
Microsoft Outlook (http://www.microsoft.com)
Symantec Act (http://www.act.com)
Netscape Calendar (http://home.netscape.com)
Sidekick (http://www.starfish.com)
Eudora Planner (http://www.sngchicago.com)

The Internet

The Internet is an indispensable tool in the laboratory. It not only is the place to find information and through which to communicate, but also provides access to data storage and organizational tools. In many cases, the resources on the Internet can be used instead of dedicated programs on your own computer.

The advantage of moving to the Internet is the reduction of costs, since you do not need to invest in as many programs or hardware for storage. The disadvantages are that a loss of Internet accessibility can paralyze your communication and analysis systems for the duration. This unlikely happening is more of a psychological barrier than a functional problem, as you can supply backup in the form of storage and alternative ways to access the Internet: For example, some P.I.s retain the potential for phone line access, even when connected to the Internet by cable. However, security issues will be more of a worry for most investigators, for as communication becomes smoother, the chances of someone obtaining illicit access to your communications becomes greater.

The following are some lab-related tasks that can be done over the Internet instead of through software programs:

- Lab books can be kept and data stored or shared with other investigators.

- Making, sending, and revising presentations.

- Data analysis.

- Ordering lab supplies and coordinating ordering with stocks.

- Finding references.

- Finding, storing, and sharing protocols.

- Journal access on line; many institutions have subscriptions to journals that individual labs can use.

The majority of labs use Microsoft Internet Explorer (http://www.microsoft.com) or Netscape Navigator (http://home.netscape.com) Web browsers. Either browser can be used with most other programs, and both are currently free and can be downloaded from the company Web Site. Many other browsers are available, such as Opera (http://www.opera.com) that strive to be simpler and faster and that offer free versions with advertising banners and paid versions with no advertising.

The laboratory Web Site is an invaluable way to communicate with your lab, as well as to communicate what your lab is all about to the rest of the world. Most of the information that can be put into a lab manual can also be posted to a laboratory Web Site, as described in the chapter on Lab Policies in this volume. The following is information that can be posted on the laboratory Web Site for people within the lab and for those outside the lab (information for lab members only can be made inaccessible to others).

For those within the lab:

- The lab manual (including protocols and lab members phone numbers)
- Lab policies
- Lab meeting and journal club schedules
- Lab job rotations
- Complaint or suggestion page
- List of lab login names and passwords for subscription sites
- Journal access
- Links to useful sites

For those outside the lab:

- Research interests. Describe different research topics separately.
- Publication lists. Keep this list updated!
- Background. Take the time to explain your field, situating your work modestly in it.
- Information on each lab member's project.
- Instructions or requirements for applying to your lab.

FINE TUNING THE SCIENCE

Data analysis and statistics programs will be geared to the particular research and are available as stand-alone or Web programs. Many pieces of equipment come with their own computers and software.

Bibliographic software

Journal clubs and your own reading and networking can keep you informed of major papers in your field, but organizing those relevant references, as well as finding lesser known but no less true publications, can be done by bibliographic software.

What bibliographic software can do for you: Bibliographic software keeps records in a way that allows them to be sorted by many criteria. You can import references from a Web searcher from other bibliographic programs. While writing a paper or grant, you can insert references in the text, and the references can be formatted automatically for any journal style.

Bibliographic software must be compatible with your word processing program, but this usually will be the case.

Personal versus laboratory bibliographic database? In the very beginning of a laboratory, one database is usually sufficient, especially when only the P.I. is writing papers and giving intellectual input. But as soon as your lab includes students or postdocs or anyone doing independent research, it works better for all lab members to have their own files within the lab program and to make their own entries.

Reference Manager, ProCIte, and EndNote are sold by the same company (http://www.isiresearchsoft.com/). Reference Manager is still an old standby in research labs, but it is being supplanted by the easier to use EndNote. Two other popular and easy to use programs are Citation (http://www.oberon-res.com) and Papyrus (http://www.rsd.com/).

Project management software

It is essential that the P.I. be aware of the status of all projects in the lab. As the lab grows larger, it becomes more difficult to know who is—or should be—doing what. Keeping track of lab meetings and conversations, and having that information readily available, will stop you from reinventing the wheel several times a week. When the lab is still small, you can jot notes in a notebook or on the word processing program. But when you want to cross-reference particular aspects of a project, it is time to move to database-based project management software.

What project management software can do for you. It can track multiple projects and keep track of tasks and resources associated with the project. Budgets can be tracked, and, for example, the costs of particular projects can be found. Calendars can show the expected time line of each project and compare all the projects in a lab.

Much of the project management software is beyond the scope of what scientists believe they need. Using it will drive many scientists absolutely crazy and remind them why they did not go into another business in the first place. It may seem to remove the importance of gut feelings. But for someone who wants to remain in touch with each project and will faithfully *use* the software, the investment in money and time will be worthwhile. Two project management programs in use are Artemis (http://www.artemispm.com/) and Microsoft Project (http://www.microsoft.com).

Word processing software

This is, most likely, the backbone of all your work in the office or lab. This is your secretary. This is where papers and grants and letters get written.

What a word processing program can do for you. Word processing programs are usually very much underused. Formatting potential is far more sophisticated than you may suspect and can provide many of the features you may associate with graphics programs. Most word processing programs provide templates for letters, can store formats (e.g., for recommendation letters), and check spelling and grammar. They are the software of choice for protocols.

Of tremendous use for P.I.s are the editing features that allow changes to be inserted in a document: Those changes are visible, as they would be on a piece of paper, but with one touch of a button, the changes can be accepted and incorporated into a finished document.

An overwhelming number of labs use either Word (http://www.microsoft.com) or Word Perfect (http://wordperfect.com). There are many other very useful programs, such as Nisus Writer (http://www.nisus.com). Many P.I.s still worry that smaller companies will fold, leaving them with unsupported and archaic programs, and tend to stick with the programs of larger companies.

Presentation software

At many international meetings, slides are no longer used. Instead, P.I.s may plug a laptop into the dedicated slide projector in the meeting room, or in a small meeting, use the laptop for a presentation. Images may be programmed to run in a sequence, manually, or can even be timed to run automatically at predetermined intervals. The benefits of this very much outweigh the inconvenience of carrying the laptop around. From 10 to 100 slides can be carried, as well as every slide you ever made. You can even change or organize your slides in the plane. In addition, if you do not want to carry your computer, you can send the information electronically, or take a Zip disk with you.

What presentation software can do for you. With presentation software, you can design your presentation, using your own material as well as material imported from the Internet or from other files.

Computer slide presentations are often referred to as "Powerpoint presentations," as this is the most commonly used slide presentation software. Microsoft PowerPoint (http://www.microsoft.com) allows you to design your presentation or import slides from other programs to present. Commonly in the lab, PowerPoint is used to prepare simple text slides, but more complicated graphics and editing of images and photographs are done with another program, often with the Adobe series of software packages.

Adobe Photoshop (http://www.adobe.com) allows one to edit images and is used to prepare figures from, for example, scannings of gels. Adobe Illustrator is used to make graphics for Web Sites and slide shows. These programs are often used together with Adobe Acrobat, which allows universal document exchange. Still, these sophisticated programs must be combined with a program such as PowerPoint to actually do the presentation.

There are also stand-alone software programs designed for slide preparation and presentation. Canvas, by Deneba (http://www.deneba.com), can be used for photo editing and to create illustrations, as well as actually doing the presentation. The ease of using one program for all facets of a slide presentation will be a priority for many P.I.s, whereas others may prefer the sophistication offered by separate, dedicated programs.

CARING FOR THE COMPUTER

There are many solutions for data storage and backup. Even with high-powered data backup options, you should have at least two independent backup systems. For example, you may store files onto a Zip drive as you are working and back up at night onto your departmental server. For smaller text files, back up onto both the hard drive and a floppy disk, Zip, or CD.

Many P.I.s assume that backup systems are inherently permanent, but nothing can be further from the truth. The storage material itself, as well as storage hardware, has a half-life, and you must routinely check that important files are truly saved and safe.

Keep at least one backup off site, in case of disaster. The reason to save information in multiple places is in case of a one-in-a-million fire or flood: It does not make much sense to keep your CD and Zip backups beside each other in a drawer. Below is a list of ways to save files:

- *Departmental or institutional servers* provide an area to store large files, such as graphics files. Some places have frequent and routine backups of all data, often onto optical discs. This is the most dependable form of long-term storage and is usually not available in individual labs.

- *Zip drives, floppy drives, and other hardware* enable you to back up while you are working in the lab. Zip discs are estimated to have a dependable lifetime of only 1 year, making them most suitable for temporary storage of information. CD disc half-life is much longer, with years rather than months. They are also very inexpensive, making them the choice of many individual labs.

- *Internet backup or file hosting sites* can store very large amounts of information. For free or for a fee, you can send data manually or at a programmed time to a Web Site, and then access it from any other Internet-enables device.

Some storage sites, such as My Docs Online (http://www.mydocsonline.com/), allow selected files to be sent to other people via the Internet, so you need not tie up someone's computer during transfer time. This site can also be used to move files from one of your computers to another. The strength of @backup (http://www.back-up.com/) is the easy restoration of previously stored data.

MAINTENANCE AND REPAIR

The expense of contracting with a computer consultant is often so prohibitive that many P.I.s tend to patch things together until a crash requires a reformatted hard drive or a new computer. Even with a departmental computer guru, getting a computer fixed seldom happens quickly or effectively enough for any busy lab. To help prevent problems:

- *Severely restrict downloads.* Not only can viruses be introduced via downloads, but the introduction of new programs can also slow down or crash the computer.

- *Restrict computer usage to the appropriate people.* This is generally understood in labs, but a computer in a central place might be used more freely.

- *Remove programs only by using the uninstall feature.* Do not merely delete the program.

- *Do not load the computer with programs.* There may be plenty of space on the drive, but the chance of program incompatibilities is increased with each new program.

- *Make sure lab members do not download programs* or even load purchased or "borrowed" programs without discussing it with you first. This is true even for computers that are dedicated to lab member usage, as you are the one who ultimately must handle any computer troubles. The exception is if you have a knowledgeable person in the lab that is in charge of the computers.

- *Have a reboot disk on hand for every computer.* P.I.s generally do the reboot, sometimes under instructions by a computer program installed on the computer, or with the help of a utility program. The reboot disk allows you to start a computer that has crashed so completely that you cannot turn it on.

You can handle most computer problems yourself with one or more of the following:

- *Built-in diagnostic tools.* Many computer manufacturers install diagnostic programs on the computer. These might diagnose the problem or diagnose *and* fix the problem, or facilitate on-line help from a company technician.

- *Web-based support sites.* The major computer companies have their own Web Sites, where you can look up the symptoms of the problem and receive instructions on fixing it, or e-mail the problem to a technician. There are also independent Web Sites that offer or sell help for computer problems. The following independent support portals provide help, usually for a fee, for computer hardware and software problems: All.com, Attenza.com, Pcsupport.com, and PCPitstop.com.

- *Customer support by phone.* Computer companies have help lines, and these were once a major selling point for companies. But as companies have gotten bigger, and the wait for a technician has gotten longer, most people prefer to use the Web-based customer support sites.

Utility and recovery programs for maintenance, diagnostic, and repair are a very good investment for computers in the lab, especially if you do not have a resident computer guru. This software is priceless in an emergency, enabling you to recover "lost" data, and to stop crashes and freezes midstream. It is also good for maintenance and for detecting and ridding your system of viruses.

Two popular utility programs are Norton Systemworks (http://www.symantec.com) and McAfee's Nuts & Bolts (http://www.mcafee.com/) that contain anti-virus capabilities.

Installing a utility program will not take care of all of the problems: In fact, the installation of such a program can cause software incompatibility problems. But the benefits outweigh the disadvantages if you do not always have an expert at your service. Disk and system repair and performance optimization are also available as part of computer operating systems, but they do not provide the range of service or ease of use as a stand-alone utility program.

RESOURCES

A.S.C.B. 1998. Designing productive lab meetings. *Am. Soc. Cell Biol.* **21:** 7–8. (http://www.ascb.org)

Amber D. 2000. Scientists, publishers, societies—And turf. *The Scientist* **14:** 1–15. (http://www.the-scientist.com)

American Productivity Quality Center. 1999. Applying benchmarking skills in your organization. (http://www.apqc.org/training)

The American Society for Cell Biology. 1998. Designing productive lab meetings. *Am. Soc. Cell Biol. Newsletter* **21:** 7–8. (http://www.ascb.org)

Anholt R.R.H. 1994. *Dazzle 'em with style: The art of oral scientific presentation.* W.H. Freeman. New York.

Baker S. and Baker K. 1998. *Software for all projects great and small. The complete idiot's guide to project management,* pp. 295–307. Alpha Books, New York.

Baker S. and Baker K. 1998. *The complete idiot's guide to project management.* Alpha Books, New York.

Belker L.B. 1997. *The first-time manager,* 4th edition. AMACOM Books, New York.

Beveridge W.I.B. 1950. *The art of scientific investigation.* Vintage Books, New York.

Blanchard F.A., Lilly T., and Vaughn L.A. 1991. Reducing the expression of racial prejudice. *Psychol. Sci.* **2:** 101–105.

Booth W.C., Colomb G.G., and Williams J.M. 1995. *The craft of research: A researcher's companion.* University of Chicago Press, Illinois.

Briscoe M.H. 1990. *A researcher's guide to scientific and medical illustrations.* Springer-Verlag, New York.

Briscoe M.H. 1995. *Preparing scientific illustrations: A guide to better posters, presentations, and publications.* Springer-Verlag, New York.

Calhoun J. 1998. CET reviews the best net-ready info managers. National Mental Health Association MHIC Factsheet. (http://www.nmha.org)

Caprette D.R. 2000. Guidelines for keeping a laboratory record. (http://www.rice.edu/~biolabs/tools/notebook/notebook.html)

Christensen J. 2000. On the Web, as elsewhere, scientists prove a demanding lot. *The New York Times,* June 7, p. 20.

Covey S.R., Merrill A.R., and Merrill R.R. 1994. *First things first.* Simon & Schuster. New York.

Deal T. and Kennedy A.A. 1982. *Corporate cultures.* Addison-Wesley, Reading, Massachusetts.

Fasse J.P. 2000. Do's and don'ts for keeping lab notebooks. Fish & Richardson P.C. (http://www.fr.com/practice/pdf/LABBOOKS.pdf)

Francis A.L. 2000. The search is on(line). *The Scientist* **14:** 24. (http://www.thescientist.com)

Goleman D. 1995. Managing with heart. In *Emotional intelligence: Why it can matter more than I.Q.,* pp. 148–163. Bantam Books, New York.

Gopen G.D. and Swan J.A. 1990. The science of scientific writing. *Am. Scientist* **78:** 550–558.

Green D.W. 2000. Managing the modern laboratory. *J. Lab. Management,* ISC Management Publications, Shelton, Connecticut.

Guernsey L. 1999. What employers can view at work. *The New York Times,* Dec. 16. Ref ID: 207

Gwynne P. 1999. Corporate collaborations: Scientists can face publishing constraints. *The Scientist* **13:** 1–6. (http://www.thescientist.com)

Hall S.S. 1997. *A commotion in the blood. Life, death, and the immune system.* Henry Holt and Company, New York.

Heiner K. and Lahti D. 2000. Hazard awareness & management manual (HAMM). Fred Hutchinson Cancer Research Center, Seattle. (www.fhcrc.org)

Hemphill B. 1998. *Taming the paper tiger at work.* Kiplinger Books, Washington, D.C.

Hoagland M. 1990. *Toward the habit of truth: A life in science.* W.W. Norton, New York.

Hochheiser R.M. 1998. *Time management,* 2nd edition: Barron's Educational Series, Hauppauge, New York.

Judson H.F. 1996. *The eighth day of creation: The makers of the revolution in biology,* Expanded edition. Cold Spring Harbor Laboratory Press, Cold Spring Harbor, New York.

Klein R.C. 2000. Protecting frozen samples. *Am. Lab.* **32:** 42–44.

Knapp L. 2001. A sick computer? Web-based support sites and built-in diagnostic tools make fixes easier than ever. *The New York Times*, Jan. 28, pp. D1–D8.

Kreeger K.Y. 2000. Scientist as teacher. *The Scientist* **14:** 30–31. (http://www.thescientist.com)

Levi P. 1984. *The periodic table.* Schocken Books, New York:.

Luria S.E. 1984. *A slot machine, a broken test tube.* Harper & Row, New York.

Lynch F. 1995. *Draw the line: A sexual harassment-free workplace.* The Oasis Press, Grants Pass, Oregon.

Medawar P.B. 1969. *Induction and intuition in scientific thought.* The American Philosophical Society Philadelphia.

Meisenholder G. 1999. The paperless lab: Database systems for the life sciences. *The Scientist* **13:** 19. (http://www.thescientist.com)

Millman H. 2001. How to keep vendors from quietly violating your privacy. *The New York Times*, Jan. 18, p. D9.

Morgenstern J. 2000. *Time management from the inside out: The foolproof system for taking control of you schedule and your life.* New York: Henry Holt, Philadelphia.

National Technology Transfer Center. 2001. How to use your laboratory notebook. (http://www. nttc.edu/training/guide/sece05.html)

Pacetta F. and Gittines R.. 2000. *Don't fire them, fire them up: A maverick's guide to motivating yourself and your team.* Simon & Schuster, New York.

Perkel J.M. 2001. The essential software toolbox. *The Scientist* **15:** 19. (http://www.thescientist.com)

Piel G. and Segerberg, Jr. O. 1990. *The World of Rene Dubos: A collection from his writings.* Henry Holt, New York.

Sanford S. 1999. The grad school survey. *HMS Beagle* **68:** 1–6. (http://news.bmn.com/hmsbeagle)

Schloff L. and Yudkin M. 1992. *Smart speaking.* Plume, New York.

Schneider I. and Hand L. 1999. E-commerce offers life scientists purchasing options. *The Scientist* **13:** 4. (http://www.thescientist.com)

Smaglik P. 1999. Fee vs. free in online research. *The Scientist* **13:** 11. (http://www.thescientist.com)

Teich A.H. and Frankel M.S. 1992. *Good science and responsible scientists: Meeting the challenge of fraud and misconduct in science.* American Association for the Advancement of Science, Washington, D.C.

Tufte E.R. 1990. *Envisioning information.* Graphics Press, Cheshire, Connecticut.

University of California, Berkeley 2000a Recommended search strategy: Search with peripheral vision, pp. 1–5. Library of the University of California, Berkeley, 1–5. (http://www.lib.berkeley.edu/TeachingLib/Guides/Internet/Strategies.html)

University of California, Berkeley. 2000b. Search the Internet: A graduated approach in 5 steps, pp. 1–2. Library of the University of California, Berkeley. (http://www.lib.berkeley.edu/Help/search.html)

Winston S. 1983. *The organized executive. New ways to manage time, paper, and people.* Warner Books, New York.

Communication as the Glue

Communication with Your Lab

UNDERSTAND TO BE UNDERSTOOD

Scientists are communicators par excellence; the process is their life's blood. They freely circulate written accounts of their investigation among their colleagues, both before and after publication; they run up astronomical phone bills in discussing their work; they peruse one another's grant applications; they incessantly visit one another's laboratories, giving lectures, talking, and doing experiments using one another's equipment. They attend innumerable scientific meetings, and worry to varying degrees that their colleagues might steal their ideas or do their experiments before they can. On the whole, the habit of candor and the knowledge that science thrives on it keep the system open.

HOAGLAND (1990, P. 79)

Randy Schenck, training and development associate at Burroughs Wellcome, says his company's project teams may be composed of as many as 12 people. Because these team members report to 12 different project managers, each of whom may be making competing requests, 150% of somebody's time is being asked for. Project team members have to make decisions about whose instructions to follow, Schenck says, on the basis of influence, not authority. "Learning how to communicate an idea helps ensure that one's own project will take priority over a competing assignment that a team member may be given."

SPECTOR (1989, P. 3)

If you cannot communicate, you are not likely to be successful. Forget the image of the scientist working alone, struggling against the forces of the universe. Communication is about getting your results out to people, convincing people to come work with you, and explaining the importance of your work to grant and project reviewers. In the lab, communication is what will bring and keep the lab together. But communication is not just about what you want. Unless you communicate not only to be understood yourself, but also to understand what others are trying to say, you are wasting your time and your people.

> *As a lab head, you forget that your words carry more weight than other people's words. You cannot talk as candidly about others as you did as a postdoc, you aren't one of the gang.*

How obvious this seems. But many new P.I.s believe that their job is to point out the right thing to do, that it is not their responsibility to figure out *why* someone is not doing the right thing. If you do not understand why an individual is doing something, you will not be able to deal with it. Try, try, try to understand what lab members want and the reason behind what they are doing.

- *What to communicate.* Everything—Results, papers, funding decisions, project status. What *you* think about someone else's results, new papers, etc. Your code of ethics. What makes you angry or happy in the lab. And, depending on the kind of lab you want, how you feel about politics, music, teaching, traveling.

- *How to communicate.* Use all forms of communication available! Lab meetings, notice boards, e-mail, notes, as well as one-on-one talks. Be aware of cultural differences in communication; remember that something may not be understood in the way you may assume it is. Extend communication lines to everyone! Nothing polarizes a lab faster than one in which the P.I. communicates with some lab members but not others.

- *When to communicate.* Always. Whether it is in a lab meeting or a chance meeting in an elevator, use the chance to make or strengthen the bond between you. Do not be a mystery to your lab; do not make your thoughts obscure.

- *What not to communicate.* Feelings and emotions about other lab members. Disparaging and biased remarks about other labs.

LEARNING TO LISTEN

Listening is one of the most valuable traits that a new manager can demonstrate, for two important reasons: First, if you do a great deal of listening, you will not be thought of as a know-it-all, which is how most people perceive someone who talks too much. Second, by doing a lot of listening and little talking, you'll learn what is going on. You'll learn none of it by talking.
BELKER (1997, P. 20) CHAPTER 4,
LEARNING TO LISTEN, PP. 20–25

Listening is the single most important way to communicate well. Often, while "listening," people are composing their own comments and are waiting for an opening to speak and thus miss a lot of what the speaker is trying to communicate. Even worse, many people are actually thinking of totally unrelated topics while trying to catch a keyword every now and then and look as if they are listening.

Listening is not the same as hearing. Hearing is a passive endeavor, whereas listening is active. What you must avoid is that late-afternoon-seminar type of extremely passive listening, where knowing the key phrases and terms lends you a façade of understanding. Whether you are trying to help a lab member settle a personal problem in the lab or are discussing the ramifications of a piece of exciting data, you must concentrate and focus on understanding what is being said. Look as if you are listening.

- Look at the person who is talking to you.

- Nod your head affirmatively to indicate agreement, frown to show commiseration, smile to show that you are enjoying the conversation.

- Comment occasionally on what the speaker is saying, without actually taking over the conversation.

- You cannot listen when you are talking!

- Do not communicate boredom or lack of interest by fiddling with pencils, opening drawers, doodling. Do not answer the phone when having a meeting with someone: Have someone else answer the phone, use an answering machine/voice mail, or just do not answer.

- Keep your mind on the conversation. If you are having trouble concentrating, at least think about the speaker's problems, rather than your own.

- Even when you are on the phone, do not check your e-mail or open letters. You might miss something, and your lack of attention will be palpable to all but the most dedicated egotist.

Variations in listening

Inadvertent interruptions—and the impression of domination—came about because the friends had different conversational styles. I call these styles "high considerateness" and "high involvement," because the former gave priority to being considerate to others by not imposing, and the latter gave priority to showing enthusiastic involvement. Some apparent interruptions occurred because high-considerateness speakers expected longer pauses between speaking turns. While they were waiting for the proper pause, the high involvement speakers got the impression they had nothing to say and filled in to avoid an uncomfortable silence.

TANNEN (1990, P. 196)

Listening styles will be influenced by geography, even within the United States. Differences in listening may be even more exaggerated when dealing with different genders or among people from different countries, and of different ages. Below is a list of examples of listening styles.

> *Even my listening was misinterpreted! I would interrupt someone, you know, help her with the story—but then, the whole room would stop talking, and I would be handed the conversational ball!*

- ***Nodding or making murmurs of apparent assent*** at regular intervals. In some places, this may be misinterpreted as agreement.

- ***Repeating words of a statement or story*** may be done to show empathy, but non-native speakers may repeat familiar or key words to improve their own understanding.

- *Interrupting before the end of a story* to continue the story. This is interpreted as facilitated listening on the east coast and interrupting on the west coast.

- *Maintaining body stillness* can show attention. Others might consider it correct to bring the body closer to the speaker.

SPEAKING EFFECTIVELY

- *Say what you mean.* Whether from fear of making even a microdecision, or worry about offending someone, or just not wanting to think at the moment, many P.I.s routinely give ambiguous answers to questions. Ambiguous answers will always come back to haunt you. People will interpret your words in their own way and not what you want them to mean. Rather than seeming fair, you will appear weak. If an answer cannot be supplied immediately, specify a time when a straightforward answer will be given.

- *Avoid sarcasm.* Not only is sarcasm unlikely to be understood by many nonnative English speakers, it is often offensive to all. As a way of giving feedback, it is especially negative and ineffective.

- *Eliminate statements that constitute a total rejection* of the other person's personality, outlook, or work. Some examples are "Your problem is that you *always*...," "You *never*...," and "I *really* dislike it when you... ."

- *Ask questions only when you are willing to listen to the answer.* Rhetorical questions do not really work. Asking questions when you know the answer—or think you do—is insulting to many and a clear signal that you are telling, not asking. Asking questions and listening carefully to the answers is effective communication, but asking and not listening will be ineffective.

Giving constructive criticism

Give compliments and encouragement, but be firm when needed. Praise in public, criticize in private. Being criticized in public is humiliating and will very seldom be effective. Time your criticism. Right after something has gone wrong, a lab member may not be able to listen constructively.

Orders and requests

When is your request really an order? You have to know, yourself, when a request is an order. Only then can you communicate it properly. The following list shows increasing amounts of order over request. Each may be typical of a P.I., and each will be more effective in some situations than in others.

- "Good. So, you'll do the control we spoke about?"

- "I'd do that other control as soon as possible."

- "When you have the results of that control, please let me know."

- "Run that other control this week..."

- "Run that other control before you do anything else."

If something is very important or urgent, tell rather than ask. Asking makes it sound unimportant. Make it seem critical if it is and do not leave understanding to chance.

How to stop conversations

There is one problem with becoming a good listener—people will want to talk to you about science, and perhaps about everything else. This is often a problem for new P.I.s, and particularly for female P.I.s: People in the lab, and from outside the lab, flock to a good listener. You are the one who must set the limits when it is time for the talking to stop.

You can be subtle. "Well, I'll think about that and get back to you," or "Let's discuss that at the meeting" can end a work discussion that has gone on too long. Subtle (and not-so-subtle) nonverbal communication can work as well, such as changing your posture, putting one hand on the phone or computer keyboard, or glancing at a clock.

It is harder to be subtle if someone is discussing something personal or trivial. Then, it might be best to be direct. "Look, we can go on and on about this. How about talking over lunch later?" is one approach, good only if you really want the conversation to continue at another point. If you really want to end the conversation, preventative medicine is the best answer, in the end. You cannot be everything to everyone. Learning to stop—or prevent—conversations is one of the most important time-management techniques you can learn (this is also covered in the chapter Stop Putting Out Fires in this volume).

NONVERBAL COMMUNICATION

Yes, even those rational creatures, the scientists, use nonverbal communication. Emotions and nuances are expressed as much through nonverbal communication as through verbal. Researchers in the area of nonverbal communications claim that as much as 90% of the meaning transmitted between two people in face-to-face communications can come via nonverbal channels (Hunsaker and Alessandra 1999a, p. 65). Learning to read those signs is not new age nonsense—it provides data. When dealing with lab members, keep an eye out for:

- Posture—Upright, hunched and withdrawn.

- Eye contact—Strong, erratic, absent.

- Voice—Loudness and expressiveness—Timidity, aggressiveness.

- Hand motions—Exuberant and extended, or hesitant and close to the body.

Do not go too overboard to derive meaning from every movement. Be aware of differences in each individual's behavior, rather than just assuming "Whoa, no eye contact! Being evasive!" Does that person usually have eye contact? Is there any pattern to when the person does and does not make eye contact? Does this instance break the pattern?

In a multicultural setting, it is not as easy to interpret changes in a pattern of use of a particular gesture as it is in a very homogeneous crowd. Some few inborn gestures are the same all over the world, but acquired gestures differ. Examples of behaviors often used to show sincerity and respect are eye contact and how close a person stands to someone when speaking, yet the meaning of these behaviors differs widely from place to place.

Nonverbal communication can also work in opposing directions even in the same cultural background. The various interpretations of a smile are an example. A smile can put a person at ease, but it can also cause someone to take you less seriously. Some P.I.s, especially women, have found that just reducing the number and intensity of smiles throughout the day is sufficient to get lab members to take them more seriously.

A P.I. must also allow for emotional stresses, which can influence how a person communicates nonverbally. You may interpret a turned back as being a rejection of you, when an individual may merely be trying to gain emotional control.

BUILDING RAPPORT

> When others form first impressions of you, their experience tells them they are probably correct, which means you have the burden to persuade them that they are wrong. This would be an uphill battle even if others were truly open to the possibility that they misjudged you. But, in reality, others tend to resist even persuasive evidence if it contradicts their first impressions.
>
> DIMITRIUS AND MAZZARELLA (2000, P. 78)

You can create rapport by finding common ground. It does not come naturally to all, but everyone can learn the basics. You may be a "dot-the-i" kind of scientist who painstakingly repeats experiments again and again and has trouble adjusting to a new theory. Your first postdoc may work best in creative snatches of weeks, coming in at 2 p.m. and working wildly through the night. You will never see an issue in the same way. Neither of you will want to change your approach to science. You may find each other inflexible. The postdoc may not have the skills to do something that, to you, should obviously be a priority. Without an understanding of why each of you reacts oppositionally, conflict can continue to build.

I had to start to enjoy the differences between individual lab members, to see them as strengths, just as I did with my own kids.

But you do have things in common. You both may love science desperately; you both may believe in a particular theory or have suffered through the same series of boring lectures. Find your common ground. Ask what the person thinks about a particular paper. Talk about an experiment. If direct scientific questions seem threatening (and they might to someone who views you as an untouchable authority figure), ask what the person likes about science. Topics other than science may be easier to start with. You can relate to someone personally and still remain professional.

Small talk is not so small! It is invaluable for showing people that you are interested in them enough to try to start a conversation. Small talk can relax you and others before a possible confrontation and let everyone know that what will follow is not meant to be as drastic as it might sound. It is an icebreaker with new people. As the P.I., the onus of directing the tone of conversation is upon you, and the better you are at the initial conversations, the easier further conversations will be. The problem is to not ask anything very personal, and if you sense that the other person is becoming uncomfortable, steer the conversation in another direction. The following are a few examples: How was the move?, How is your children's school?, How do you find the weather?, Have you found the bus system useful?

To make small talk, you must be interested in the person. See it as an experiment, and try to figure out the clues to the personality that will open the doors of conversation.

Small talk may be especially useful with the spouses and partners of lab members. Many people have a difficult time in talking to the nonscientific family of a lab member or with the nontechnical and administrative staff. Some scientists are so uncomfortable talking to nonscientists that they lapse into a patronizing mode, something that you should avoid. Generally, just being interested gets you over the first hurdle. Three tips for establishing and building rapport in a conversation (Lieberman 1998, p. 76):

- *Match posture and movements.* Respond nonverbally to help build rapport. If a person has a hand in a pocket, put your hand in your pocket. If a person makes a certain gesture with the hand, after a moment, you casually make the same gesture. If a student is sitting down at lunch, you sit down.

- *Match speech.* Try to match the person's rate of speech. If the person is speaking in a slow, relaxed tone, do the same. If speaking quickly, then you speak quickly.

- *Match key words.* If the person is prone to using certain words or phrases, employ them as you speak. For instance, if an individual says, "The offer is designed for incredible gain for both parties," later in the conversation you might say, "I like that the offer is designed to offer incredible gain..." Make sure not to mimic the person. Obvious copying of another's movements is unproductive. A simple reflection of aspects of the person's behavior or speech is enough to make that individual feel comfortable.

FOR THOSE WHO WILL NOT SPEAK

It is very difficult to communicate with an individual who does not respond to you. There are several ways in which lab members can be unresponsive. They may not engage, or give answers, or give monosyllabic answers to your questions. This may result from shyness, or an inability to make small talk, or fear of making a mistake in front of the boss.

> *I can't get them to talk to me—it's the major communication issue. I always think it's my fault.*

Reticence can result from such respect for an authority figure that one cannot have a conversation as between equals. This is likely the case if you see that the person is relaxed in conversation with peers. The choices to deal with this will depend on your style and your interpretation of what would work.

You could stick to the strictly scientific, which would narrowly box in the kind of responses the person would have to make. Or you could try to make the person feel more comfortable with you by engaging in a personal conversation.

There are those who respond verbally, but who are not really dealing with the intent of your conversation. They nod, they smile, they seem to understand why you want a particular experiment done, and then, it is as if the conversation had never taken place. The person who will not speak and probably is not listening is a particular bane of P.I.s. Keep written records of the conversations. It might even be effective to request that the person respond to you in writing.

> *The worst thing is when someone is not interested in what I or other members of the lab have to say about his project. The student or postdoc can do his project and move on—usually to an unsuccessful science career—without much success in my lab, but the absence of definite progress towards some common goals hurts the lab in terms of funding or publication success.*

WORKING WITH EMOTIONS

> *Power in organizations is the capacity generated by relationships. ...how a workplace organizes its relationships; not its tasks, functions, and hierarchies, but the patterns of relationship and the capacities available to form them.*
>
> WHEATLEY (1994, p. 38–39)

Science is a very emotional occupation. It is not the protocols or the philosophy that keep scientists fueled, it is the emotions. The thrill of discovery, the misery of being scooped, the satisfaction of giving a good talk, the pride in a postdoc's triumphs—these are some of the emotions that make up the fabric of a scientific life. This is what it is really all about.

> *I lost 2 years in the lab because of one incident where I lost my temper publicly. A student, not from the lab, told all the other students about the incident, and not one person even did a rotation with me for another couple of years.*

How much emotion to express will depend on your personal style as a P.I. But emotions are not on a separate list from, say, intellectual responses: It is not that emotions should be expressed only if you are a buddy P.I. and should not be expressed if you wish to have a more remote role. It is which emotions, and how and when to express them, that are the real decisions.

Emotions do belong in the lab. They are a resource, not just along for the ride. So for you, as leader, they should be under control at all times, or most times. The effect of a brief negative storm on your part might clear the air for you, but it could linger for months among the other members of the lab, causing anger or depression or anxiety.

Recognize and articulate your emotions and instincts. It is those half-formed realizations that make one feel uncomfortable. Once you can organize your feelings, you can deal with the problems creating the emotion.

Dealing with your anger

Frustration is thwarted anger. But it is better to be frustrated than to turn your temper loose in the lab.

- *You should not rage about someone* in the lab to another lab member. Tell a colleague, a spouse, a neighbor, but do not purge to one of your subordinates. You should try to appear to be objective.

- *Anger at a situation can be expressed,* but anger at a person in the lab should be only rarely expressed.

- *Do not give in to personal attacks,* even if you have a close relationship with a lab member. During the actual conversation, the recipient of such an attack will usually just close down and, afterward, will not listen to anything you have to say, anyway. Furthermore, statements that attack a person's character or personality lead to resentment that can smolder for years. Often, when a lab worker and P.I. finally sit down to work out a difficult relationship, it turns out that the lab worker has been bothered by a remark or argument that occurred months or even years ago.

- *Do not speak in anger.* One outburst, and you may suffer the repercussions for years, especially if your outburst has been overheard. In institutions where people have a lot of choice about the lab they choose, this single eruption of temper could put you at the bottom of the list.

- *Eliminate passive-aggressive remarks.* Unexpressed anger is often channeled into passive-aggressive behavior (getting back at people without telling them why, rather than confronting them head on). Criticizing someone constantly, making cynical comments, and stubbornly obstructing an action are some of the manifestations of unexpressed anger. It is true that you should not have an outburst, but neither should you avoid an outburst, and instead take verbal swipes at someone in the lab. Define the issue that is bothering you, and if you decide that you must discuss it, do it calmly and honestly.

- *Choose your battles.* Prioritize what will make you angry! There are times when it is appropriate to be furious at someone and to let that person know immediately, and there are times when you should take a walk to calm down and figure out how to act. If the new graduate student from across the hall has once again not cleaned up the balance after using it, it usually would make sense to calm down before you "request" that the individual learn to clean up. You want this person to understand why one does not leave a balance dirty, not tell the whole department about your apoplectic response. But if you find that radioactivity has been spilled all over a room and that the person should not even been using it, anger is very appropriate. This is a safety issue that might be worth alienating someone over.

Although anger may cause the most overt problems personally and in the lab, other emotions also deeply affect everyone. Disappointment can lead to irritated behavior and depression—not clinical depression necessarily, but a surface misery that can affect everyone. Being obviously disappointed in a lab member's performance can lead to avoidance and shame on the part of a this person, feelings that may not be overcome.

Try not to let your mood swings influence the lab

As a manager, Nusslein-Volhard gave herself mixed grades. "I'm moody. Sometimes I have depressed moods, and then I'm very enthusiastic again... . It's sometimes difficult for people who worked with me...I would exaggerate in both directions. I'd get very excited about things, and then also very negative about things, and neither would be totally justified.

CHRISTIANE NUSSLEIN-VOLHARD,
NOBEL PRIZE IN PHYSIOLOGY OR MEDICINE 1995
MCGRAYNE (1998, P. 401)

Whatever you do is likely to be amplified in the minds of the people in the lab, so try to be more careful than you would have as a postdoc or student. You are also serving as a role model for behavior as well as science, so demonstrate the effective use of emotions in the lab.

Predictability is part of building trust. Although lab members may immediately like you, belief in your honesty and reliability needs time and experience to flourish. Trust is only acquired after lab members can identify predictable behavior in you and make inferences about your character, based on your behavior. If your behavior and moods are erratic, it will take much longer for lab members to gain confidence in you.

The Pleasures and Perils of Diversity

RECOGNIZING CULTURAL DIFFERENCES

Professional cultures offer common ground globally, since their values and behaviors are often similar across the larger boundaries of nationalities and ethnic groups... . The extraordinary strength of professional cultures means that they often have more meaning for people than a corporate culture. And why not? A professional culture is a lifelong choice—whereas a person can move in and out of a corporate culture on a daily basis, literally leaving it at the office.

O'HARA-DEVERAUX AND JOHANSEN (1994, P. 44)

that ways of speaking do not in and of themselves communicate psychological states like authority, security, or confidence. We perceive them to connote those states because we associate certain ways of speaking with people we assume feel those emotions. Because Japanese adults learn to be indirect, they associate indirectness with maturity and power. Because middle-class European-American women are more likely to give orders and make requests in an indirect way, we associate indirectness with powerlessness and insecurity—emotions that women in our society are expected to have. And the situation is reinforced by the negative response people are likely to get if they do not speak in expected ways.

TANNEN (1994A, P. 99)

As if the human mind were not hard enough to fathom, on top of that, all individuals, with their cultural and religious or class ways of looking at things, will also interpret lab events, and science itself, differently.

Most P.I.s do recognize that there are cultural differences among lab members. They may be tempted to ignore the differences and to recognize only the culture of the lab. The complexity is overwhelming, and given that it might not even be possible to truly understand another culture, acting as if everyone were just the same may seem to be the most sensible way to handle these differences.

But it is vital to remember that one's culture cannot be shed or ignored: It is not just a few habits and recipes that can be discarded. Culture provides the framework for how each individual perceives right and wrong, beauty, honesty, and relationships—and how this person will report data. Even when immersed in the overlaying culture of the lab, background culture continues to influence a person's thoughts and behavior. This culture is not necessarily one from a foreign land, but it may be formed by race, gender, age, or economic background.

Communication across cultural and other gaps can sometimes be perilous, but the benefits of a diverse lab can add a rare and delightful depth to the lab's interpersonal relationships as well as to the science itself. What many scientists most fondly remember of labs are those times when people came together to share their own culture, across all boundaries.

Recognizing differences is not the same as stereotyping! Stereotyping (a printing term, referring to the metal plates used to make an exact copy) is an inflexible characterization of a group of people, resulting in an inability to recognize individual personalities. Positive—as well as negative—stereotyping has repercussions. For example, there is often a presumption in the lab that people of a particular culture will be more hardworking than others. If an individual works as hard as the Americans in the lab but is not as hardworking as the P.I. believes this lab member "should" be, there is already a cloud over the head of that worker.

The black box between the cultures was highlighted for me recently by one of my advisor's students, who wanted to come visit me while he was in the US. I told him that would be fine, but when he wrote again to set up a time, I forgot to answer his e-mail right away. However, he never wrote again and just never came (he went to other places in the area, I think). When I finally remembered to write and ask when he was coming, he said he had already been to the US and gone home; apparently it was against Japanese culture to write again and "pester"—he figured if I hadn't answered right away, I really didn't want him to come. I explained to him that some Americans, including me, expect to be pestered, especially since we don't always remember to answer all of our e-mails right away. He was pretty funny and said that's probably the reason Japanese men don't do well trying to date American women—when they are rejected, they won't try again...

Before you can think of the effects of other cultures on the lab, it is helpful to consider the effects of your own cultural background. Most people feel that they are not prejudiced, not realizing how much of the culture they have internalized. This is particularly true for Americans, who have grown up in a culture that elevates individuality and gives many Americans the feeling that they do not belong to a particular culture at all.

Pretending that your native culture does not exist indeed would be a disservice to all lab members, for whom learning to navigate the subtleties of this system might make the difference between success and failure. Lab members depend on the P.I. and their interactions with the P.I. as a model for dealing with the politics of science. Be understanding of cultural backgrounds, but you must be true to your own self and culture—only then, can the expectations of you and your culture be clear.

Understanding cultural differences is integral to understanding the people in the lab. Without an understanding of cultural differences, the P.I. may make unfair assumptions about a person's character. You may conclude that a person is shifty, because of no eye contact, or that another person is untrustworthy, because not all details of a family situation were told to you at the interview, when these individuals may have been acting, from their point of view, completely respectfully and appropriately. You cannot necessarily predict someone's behavior, based on nationality, race, religion, or gender, but you can better understand this person's actions and responses. The following are five useful variables to consider when dealing with differences across cultures.

- *Language:* The structure, vocabulary, and meanings of written or oral communication. This can be a standard language, or specialized jargon. People express themselves best in their native language, and the use of another language, and its restriction on expression, can make one feel trapped and misunderstood.

- *Context:* The elements that surround and give meaning to a communication event. The fact that the P.I. walked by and did not acknowledge the new student can be construed as rudeness or pre-coffee exhaustion, depending on the particular student and particular P.I.

- *Time:* The way the past, present, and future are related varies. Time can be a resource to some, and a state of being, a law of nature, to another. Some will structure the events of the day around a meeting at a certain time; others will make the meeting only by chance.

- *Equality/power:* The types of relationships between individuals or groups, dependent on status and authority. The relationships between males and females are an example of power relationships that are culture-dependent.

- *Information flow:* How messages flow between people and levels in the lab. For example, one P.I. might tell students that they are not doing well, while another might find it more appropriate to suggest that a senior postdoc talk to the student. Or a student from one culture may find it impossible to directly question a conclusion of the P.I. (O'Hara-Deveraux and Johansen 1994, p. 50).

Good intentions are not sufficient to promote understanding between cultures, nor are a few words in another language or an all-lab trip to Chinatown. It takes a true shaking-up of your comfort zone to really *get* the differences between cultures. At first, when dealing with persons from another culture, the similarities will strike you. Later, the differences will be glaringly or subtly obvious and only later, after awareness and your own analysis of the differences, can those differences be appreciated.

Cultural–Diversity Quiz: How's Your "Cultural I.Q."?

The following quiz will give you an idea of how much you already know about cultural diversity. In some cases, there is more than one correct response to each question

1. On average, how long do native-born Americans maintain eye contact?
   a. 1 second
   b. 15 seconds
   c. 30 seconds
2. *True or false:* One of the few universal ways to motivate workers, regardless of cultural background, is through the prospect of a promotion.
3. Learning to speak a few words of the language of immigrant clients, customers, and workers is:
   a. Generally a good idea as the effort communicates respect for the other person.
   b. Generally not a good idea because they might feel patronized.
   c. Generally not a good idea because they might feel offended if a mistake is made in vocabulary or pronunciation.
4. *True or false:* American culture has no unique characteristics; it is composed only of individual features brought here from other countries.
5. When communicating across language barriers, using the written word:
   a. Should be avoided; it can insult the immigrant or international visitor's intelligence.
   b. Can be helpful; it is usually easier to read English than to hear it.
   c. Can be confusing; it is usually easier to hear English than to read it.
6. *True or false:* Behaving formally around immigrant colleagues, clients, and workers—that is, using last names, observing strict rules of etiquette—is generally not a good idea as it gives the impression of coldness and superiority.
7. In times of crisis, the immigrant's ability to speak English:
   a. Diminishes because of stress.
   b. Stays the same.
   c. Improves because of the necessity of coping with the crisis.
   d. Completely disappears.
8. The number of languages spoken in the U.S. today is:
   a. 0–10
   b. 10–50
   c. 50–100
   d. 100+
9. *True or false:* Immigrant families in the United States largely make decisions as individuals and have generally abandoned the practice of making decision as a group.
10. When you have difficulty understanding someone with a foreign accent:
    a. It probably means that he or she cannot understand you either.
    b. It probably means that he or she is recently arrived in this country.
    c. It is helpful if you listen to all that he or she has to say before interrupting, the meaning might become clear in the context of the conversation.
    d. It is helpful for you to try to guess what the speaker is saying and to speak for him or her so as to minimize the risk of embarrassment.

11. When an Asian client begins to give you vague answers before closing a deal, saying things like "It will take time to decide, or "We'll see," the best thing to do is:

    a. Back off a bit, he or she may be trying to say "no" without offending you.

    b. Supply more information and data about your service or product, especially in writing.

    c. Push for a "close," his or her vagueness is probably a manipulative tactic.

    d. State clearly and strongly that you are dissatisfied with his or her reaction so as to avoid any misunderstanding.

12. Apparent rudeness and abruptness in immigrants is often due to:

    a. Lack of English-language facility.

    b. A difference in cultural style.

    c. Differing tone of voice.

13. *True or false:* Many immigrant and ethnic cultures place greater importance on how something is said (body language and tone of voice) than on the words themselves.

14. The avoidance of public embarrassment (loss of face) is of central concern to which of the following cultures?

    a. Hispanic

    b. Mainstream American

    c. Asian

    d. Middle Eastern

15. *True or false:* One of the few universals in etiquette is that everyone likes to be complimented in front of others.

16. In a customer-service situation, when communicating to a decision maker through a child who is functioning as interpreter, it is best to:

    a. Look at the child as you speak so that he or she will be certain to understand you.

    b. Look at the decision maker.

    c. Look back and forth between the two.

17. Which of the following statements is (are) true?

    a. Most Asian workers like it when the boss rolls up his or her sleeves to work beside employees.

    b. Taking independent initiative on tasks is valued in most workplaces throughout the world.

    c. Many immigrant workers are reluctant to complain to the boss as they feel it is a sign of disrespect.

    d. Asians are quick to praise superiors to their face in an attempt to show respect.

18. *True or false:* The "V" for victory sign is a universal gesture of good will and triumph.

19. Which of the following statements is (are) true?

    a. It is inappropriate to touch Asians on the hand.

    b. Middle Easterner men stand very close as a means of dominating the conversation.

    c. Mexican men will hold another man's lapel during conversation as a sign of good communication.

20. Building relationships slowly when doing business with Hispanics is

    a. A bad idea; if you don't move things along, they will go elsewhere.

    b. A bad idea; they expect native-born professionals to move quickly so will be disoriented if you do not.

    c. A good idea; it may take longer, but the trust you build will be well worth the effort.

BETWEEN P.I. AND LAB MEMBERS

Before coming to King's she had spent a happy and fruitful few years working in Paris. But the contrast in her new job was a shock. First, she found that Wilkins thought she would work under his direction, when she expected to be working independently on DNA. Second, there was a mutual incomprehension that made it impossible to resolve their differences. Among French colleagues, Franklin's direct and combative personal style aroused no comment—vigorous and heated debate was a normal feature of scientific discourse, and no one took offence. At King's, only her assistant Raymond Gosling gave as good as he got, and they became friends. Wilkins responded to attack with immediate withdrawal. Their styles were so incompatible that they barely spoke in the two years she was there.

FERRY (1998, p. 274) DESCRIBING THE RELATIONSHIP
BETWEEN MAURICE WILKINS AND ROSALIND FRANKLIN

The P.I.s style of communication with lab members will set the stage for all other interactions. But even if you have carefully considered the kind of P.I. you want to be, with the implicit communication style that goes with that kind of P.I., there are other influences on the way you communicate with individuals. There are day-to-day assumptions you may make. For example, you may assume that:

There is a mythology of the white person. Those of us who come from abroad don't understand how pluralistic America is and don't understand that someone can look not exactly like the expected and still have a seat at the table.

- When you explain your ideas or interpretation of a project, people will enter into a lively discussion about your ideas and their own.

Answers

1. a	6. False	11. a	16. b
2. False	7. a	12. a, b, and c	17. c
3. a	8. d	13. True	18. False
4. False	9. False	14. a, c, and d	19. c
5. b	10. c	15. False	20. c

Determining Your Cultural I.Q.

Number Correct	Evaluation
16–20	Congratulations! You are a "cultural-diversity genius" and are no doubt doing very well in the multicultural business world.
11–15	You are culturally aware and are probably very receptive to learning more about cultural differences.
6–10	Oops! You have a ways to go, but are obviously interested in the subject and see the need to learn more. That's an important first step.
0–5	Do not be discouraged. The knowledge reflected in this quiz is new to most professionals in the United States.

Reprinted, with permission, from Thiederman (1991a, pp. xix–xxiii. What This Book Can Do for You).

- Complimenting people in front of the lab will be appreciated.

- People will be eager to be given part of a hot, exciting project.

> *Cultural differences are a big part of the lab. The main problem in the lab with this is mis-communication in minor ways. For example, "Yes, it didn't work" is very confusing to some people. But I don't expect anything! I try to treat everyone within his or her own context. I don't think you can expect people to overcome their cultural differences, it puts too much stress on them.*

The cultural background of lab members will profoundly influence how each deals with authority. And your background will also influence how you feel about others, and how you treat them. No matter how objective you feel you are being, your behavior is a product of your own background. Discussed below are some of the common issues between P.I. and lab members of different cultures.

Dealing with authority

The Chinese believe that one should not question authority, and in order not to allow a boss to lose face, may not inform the P.I. of problems or make suggestions for change. The Japanese also tend not to argue with authority figures. To the Chinese, maturity is important, and a younger boss would command less respect than an older one. Some non-American P.I.s have reported that lab members, especially those who are also not American, have trouble accepting P.I.s perceived as not being a member of the American "club" as worthwhile authority figures.

Lab members of other cultures who dispute a P.I.'s authority may not do it verbally or publicly or at all obviously. A lab member may follow orders or suggestions very easily, suggesting acceptance of the P.I. as an authority, but still put down the P.I. in private or make plans to move labs without informing the P.I.

You cannot force someone to see you as an authority figure. So why *would* people come to the lab if not prepared to accept you as boss? One reason is that they may not know that they have any prejudices until forced to deal with a situation with you day after day. Some know they will have a problem, but figure that the advantages outweigh the disadvantages. For example, individuals who might have trouble getting into a chosen lab may take a lab with an authority figure that they cannot truly respect, out of desperation. Having someone in the lab that does not respect you can be a huge problem. If you both believe that this situation will not change, it is best to soon ease this person out of the lab, no matter how productive.

Directness vs. indirectness

Americans pride themselves on directness. To Americans, directness implies honesty and trust and is a very desirable characteristic to display. This is not true of all cultures, and sometimes undecipherable differences in the preferred level of directness among people are the single biggest impediment to communication in the lab.

For example, the Chinese believe that truth is relative to circumstances and human obligations. Telling another what they believe that person wants to hear instead of the absolute truth is part of hospitality (Kenna and Lacy 1994, p. 15). This can be a real problem in the lab, as they may try harder to get a result that they believe the P.I. "needs," rather than to face up to the fact that the particular line of experimentation is not working.

Expressing emotion

Each culture has a list of emotions that might be permissible to express and that are expected to be repressed. Even showing happiness, considered to be fine in America, can be in bad taste in other cultures.

Admitting mistakes

Many Asian cultures will not admit to not understanding your instructions because they regard that as an insult to one's teaching ability: To ensure that someone has understood what you said, you must ask questions.

Nonverbal communication

The Chinese will nod—not in agreement with a point, but to show that they are listening to you. This is an example of the communication problems that may occur in a diverse lab; not only are the cues different, but the intent sometimes is as well, and figuring out the difference is not always easy.

There are very few assumptions that you can make about nonverbal communication across cultures. Some people are extraordinarily gifted at connecting with people, seeming to transcend all cultural issues, but for others, deciphering nonverbal communication is an impossibility. But with each person, certain patterns will begin to be recognizable, and verbal discussions will help cover the gaps that may exist in communication.

Language differences

Often native speakers of a language have a hard time realizing that two notions labeled identically in their language are seen as highly distinct concepts by speakers of other languages. Thus, native speakers of English feel the verb "to know" as a monolithic concept, and are sometimes surprised to find out that in other languages, one verb is used for knowing facts, a different verb for knowing people, and there may even be a third verb for knowing how to do things.

HOFSTADTER (2000, P. 126)

It is hard to imagine the alienating effect of coming to a new lab without fluency in the host language. Not only must they try to decipher the cultural code, they must do it without the benefit of shared language, and might never be sure whether they has made the correct interpretation. Scientific instructions might be very intimidating if they are not understood. Comprehension of a foreign language is usually achieved in advance of the

> It doesn't help people to not have to learn English, otherwise, they are more like slave labor.

ability to speak it. Listed below are some ways to make it easier for someone to understand you.

- *Speak slowly and clearly.* Many people learn a language through books and recorded conversation and will find your speech easier to understand if each word is distinct and recognizable.

- *Avoid slang.* This is more difficult than it sounds!

- *Avoid expressions such as "Takes one to know one,"* or "A rolling stone gathers no moss," phrases which seem ripe with meaning to one of your own culture, but will confuse nonnative speakers.

- *Use body language to back up what you are saying.* Use it carefully, but sparingly.

- *Back up oral descriptions with written descriptions.* This should actually be done when giving instruction to native as well as nonnative speakers to accommodate different learning styles (see chapter on Training Lab Personnel in this volume), but it is vital in getting a meaning across a language barrier.

- *Require the use of English only in the lab.* But if you hear several people speaking their language together, do not jump to conclusions about laziness or arrogance: Try to imagine the loneliness of not hearing one's own language and allow this solace. Sometimes it may be the only way someone can get an important or technical point across.

- *Help non-English speakers in giving presentations.* It may be excruciating for the presenters (and for the audience!) the first few times, but you are not doing any big favors by not letting them speak and practice English and presentation skills.

Situational differences

There are cultural differences, which may result in very specific situations for you to deal with as described below.

Money

Some institutions will have very narrow limits on what you can pay the people in your lab. Sometimes this is a real hindrance but generally, these regulations will protect you from those who demand more.

Citizens of some countries, because of federal laws, do not need to pay taxes. Effectively, people from these countries may be paid as much as 20–39% more than other lab members. Should you try to even up the salaries? Sometimes. Should you try to augment the rent for a larger apartment for families with children? Sometimes. When people receive different salaries for the same work, there will always be disgruntlement. You will need to make value judgments and decide whether to keep such information secret, or to communicate the reason for the discrepancy.

Negotiations for salary

Scientists often find money negotiations to be distasteful, especially at the level of postdoc. For some, it is a matter of ego. To work in their lab, they think, is such a privilege that any money is an amazing extra. For some, it is the suggestion that if you are thinking about money, you are not thinking about science.

Among American scientists, overt discussions of money and acquisitions are considered distasteful. Japan, Austria, and Italy emphasize assertiveness, competitiveness, and the acquisition of money and material things as desirable. In the Netherlands and Sweden, nurturing and the quality of life are considered to be more important (Umiker 1996, p. 178–179), and a scientist from these countries might be less likely to try to negotiate for a higher salary.

Family responsibilities

A member of the lab from another country may have a spouse that cannot work. This may cause some financial pressure, to which the response might be to work harder to move ahead faster. Some lab members might be supporting parents or even siblings, and have extended family duties, duties that may seem optional to you, but are not to that person.

One situation many P.I.s have encountered is the decision to hire a family member of someone in the lab. Do you hire the spouse, as requested, as a technician? You may be bound by institutional laws, but it is probably your decision. It usually works out well for all parties: The major complaint of lab members is that the family members interact in a way deemed offensive by the majority in the lab. As P.I., you must feel comfortable to protect the rights of all lab members, even if it means stepping into a family dispute.

Cultural differences among lab members

There are, of course, fraternities, cliques, parochialism, and disdain for the outsider. Within these loose enclaves, formal lines of communication and grapevines work well. Between them, they may work poorly. My lecture, and the following brief discussion, proceeded in an atmosphere of imperious disdain from the podium, as though I had entered the Ritz dining room without a tie.

HOAGLAND (1990, PP. 81–82)

Cultural differences contribute to the overall flavor of the lab. Below are listed some differences among cultures that affect the lab:

- *Secrecy about lab results.* Disseminating information, intellectual property.
- *Treatment of "nonequals."* Some people would not consider any support persons as being members of the lab.
- *Collaboration.*
- *Socializing.*

- *Family.* Different cultures have different ideas about the status of individual family members. Scientists tend to expect people to be equal, and the treatment of a spouse as an unequal can be a cause of prejudice.

Americans overemphasize identification with their jobs. They have a hard life, with nothing and no one to fall back on if something goes wrong. This is scary to other people, the fact that the American culture doesn't help you. So people from other cultures tend to stick together.

Lab prejudices and subcultures. Many of the same issues that plague the relationship of the P.I. and lab members are also in play in the interactions among the members of the lab. These issues are not only racial or gender-dependent, but also arise from seemingly innocent sources, such as educational background. The following minicultures—and prejudices—can arise in the lab.

- *Age.* Young and enthusiastic versus older, more experienced, and perhaps, cynical.

- *Scientific background.* Ivy league versus state school, M.D. versus Ph.D., famous lab versus obscure lab.

- *Single versus married.* Disparaging remarks such as "He's never here at nights..." from those without families.

- *Sexual orientation and lifestyle.*

- *Male or female majority.*

The lab culture may actually be based on one of these minicultures. One of the problems with having a definite lab culture is that it suggests an us-against-them mentality, which can go bad. It is the job of the P.I. to encourage the best of cultural identification, which is the sense of identity, without allowing the lab to become exclusive.

THE BALANCE BETWEEN ACCOMMODATION AND FAIRNESS

Culturally different people appreciate respect, understanding, and compromise. They do not, however, expect Americans to adopt the specific features of their culture or to use the nineteenth-century phrase, "go native." To do things like look away just because the Asian is more comfortable with indirect eye contact or stand very close to the Middle Eastern male because that is the way it is done in the Middle East can be taken as patronizing and insincere.
                                            THIEDERMAN (1991B, P. 31)

At the same time that you are trying to be respectful and understanding of cultural differences, you will be trying to treat everyone fairly. Does "fairly" mean that everyone is treated the same? Do you give concessions to some members and not to others? Do you have a blanket policy, or make individual exceptions? What can a P.I. do...

- *Set a standard for how you treat everyone,* and how you expect all members to treat each other. Make the lab culture the dominant culture. Generally, people in labs want to be seen first as scientists, and most will not want to be singled out as females or foreigners.

You can't expect someone to go against their own culture. It sets up too much stress.

- *Be vigilant about your own behavior* and about the behavior of lab members. Often lab personnel—or you—will not want to discuss these differences for fear that talking about these issues publicly will make the differences more obvious and more exaggerated. You may need to be the one who takes the lead and deals with problems.

- *Intervene with lab members who have a problem with cultural issues.* When the problem is persistent on the part of an individual, mentoring may help ease that person through personal, gender, and cultural differences. You, however, may not be the right person to mentor that particular individual, and if so, you may want to pair the person with someone who will best understand the background and approach of the lab member.

- *Bring all lab members into the lab culture.* In a multicultural lab, it is vitally important for the lab to have its own culture, one that everyone shares. But it is all too easy for subcultures to form in a group, and a solid lab culture with strong values can prevent one subculture prevailing to the exclusion of others. Without the feeling that they share a community, working toward the same goals, one person's success is another's failure, and most interactions by nature will be adversarial.

- *Avoid favoritism.* Bending too far for one or several lab members' problems can cause great resentment among other lab members and will have the same result as overt prejudice. There is a fine line between accommodation and favoritism, and there is no way to predict what will or will not work: It so depends on the individuals involved.

- *Show interest in and respect for other's background.* Treat family members respectfully—greet children and spouses. As when visiting another country, learning at least some words of greeting in a lab member's native language is a great sign of your recognition of the culture, and your respect for this. But be sure to do the same for all lab members.

- *Do not allow anyone to be marginalized.* In a mostly homogeneous lab, the problems are different. Here individuals who are different may feel isolated and can easily feel marginalized. They can actually *be* marginalized. This is something you can work to prevent and solve.

- *Treat each person and each situation as a unique one.* You will not always understand or be able to satisfy everyone. Sometimes you will set a standard of behavior, and expect everyone to conform, and sometimes you will allow for differences and accept a wide range of behaviors. For example, a male member may not be able to treat the women in the lab without being patronizing, and you will have to explain the expectation in your lab to him. On the other hand, putting a woman in charge of such a person might be more than he can adapt to at the time, and it might be better if he learns to handle a woman collaborator first. Each crisis and problem will need a tailored solution.

Gender Is Still an Issue

GENDER AND COMMUNICATION

Surveys have identified these workplace communication problems:
Men are too authoritarian.
Men don't take women seriously.
Women are too emotional.
Men don't accept women as co-workers or bosses.
Women often don't speak up.

Tingley (1994, p. 12)

In most places, and for most scientists, overt differences in the way men and women are treated seem minimal. But they exist. An example of the still-present effects of gender is that many P.I.s feel constraints on how close they can become with an member of the opposite sex. While a male P.I. might share a room with a male post-doc at a conference, it would not go unnoticed if the postdoc were a woman. A well-intentioned query about a weekend can sound intensely personal across gender lines. Gender issues can also get you and your lab into a lot of trouble if they stray into the area of sexual harassment (see the chapter on Lab Romances in this volume).

As with cultural differences, it is difficult to discuss gender differences without falling into stereotypes: Generalizations are useful only as a framework. But even preschool males and females have learned to interact with each other in very different and predictable ways (Coates 1993), and these patterns are reinforced with age. Many Americans do not want to recognize that a large part of how they communicate is shaped by culture rather than personality. As a P.I., it is very important to recognize that your words may be taken in different ways, depending on whether you are a man or a woman, and that lab member's intentions, actions, and communication will be colored by their gender.

It is tempting to extend knowledge of patterns of communication between genders to deeper differences, say, in motivation. This is tricky, and dangerous, and is likely to be wrong. Try to understand differences, not create more.

IMPLICATIONS AND INTERPRETATIONS OF SPEECH

. *...Each takes one side of the argument and tries to muster all the arguments he can think of for that side, while trying his damnedest to undercut and attack the arguments for the other side. This is done regardless of his personal convictions, and regardless of his ability to see the other's point of view, just as lawyers are supposed to make the best argument they can for their client and try to undercut the opponent's case by whatever means they can. From such ritual opposition is supposed to come truth or, in the case of the legal system, justice.*

TANNEN (1994B, P. 57)

Male speech patterns are taken as the norm for how a P.I. should speak to lab members. Directness and firmness are suggested by shorter sentences, made without qualifiers: This is taken as confidence and authority. Woman's speech tends to be more indirect than males. They use more hedges at the end of each sentence, often to take the sting out of a negative or strong statement ("I think there might be a better way to approach that problem..."), to establish rapport ("you know"), or confidence ("I'm sure"), leading listeners to feel that the speaker is unassertive.

Unlike men, women tend to look for agreement. They soften orders with a questioning voice. Instead of saying "Please" when asking someone to do something, they may apologize ("I'm sorry to ask you this at such a busy time, but could you have your comments on the grant ready by tomorrow?"). The following are the differences between female and male speech patterns (Tannen 1994a,b).

Patterns of female speech:

- Hesitation in words, as if searching for the word, not knowing the correct answer.

- Rising intonations at the end of the sentence, suggesting that she is questioning her own words.

- Mitigating statements with qualifiers. "It is the right way to do it, *I think.*"

- Talking about herself and her life, relating the subject of discussion to herself to establish rapport.

Patterns of male speech:

- Complex sentences.

- Use of slang. This implies an intimate and superior knowledge of the subject.

- Resisting interruptions.

- Talking to the group as a whole.

Women are accused of being too serious, men are accused of being insulting. This is a common lab scenario: A woman complains that the man at the next bench is offensive; he says he is just trying to lighten up the always tense working atmosphere.

A big difference also exists in male and female approaches to humor. Women tend to tell stories and anecdotes instead of jokes and to base their humor on self put downs. Men are more likely to put down others, and to do this in jokes, one-liners, and quips (Tingley 1994, p. 165).

Sexual jokes are much more likely to be told by men than women, and women are more likely to be offended. Especially in the present climate of worry about sexual discrimination, sexual jokes exacerbate the male-female differences.

HOW GENDER-ASSOCIATED SPEECH PATTERNS AFFECT THE LAB

The management literature points out that male supervisors/managers tend to greet confrontation situations abruptly and curtly, and the source of dissatisfaction is identified early. Women, on the other hand, state that they are more likely to internalize conflicts and may not take advantage of appropriate early response in the form of comment or constructive criticism... . Fearing to be misunderstood by either the staff member or the first-line supervisor, a woman manager may prefer writing warnings and exchanges of memos instead of direct person-to-person resolution of conflict. This can be considered diplomatic or political, but much time and energy of talented people may be absorbed in the process.

YENTSCH AND SINDERMAN (1992, P. 129)

...Many men feel women don't tell them directly if they are doing something wrong, and many women feel that men don't tell them directly enough if they are doing well.

TANNEN (1994A, P. 68)

Women tend to downplay their authority, and try to make people feel comfortable. In speech, they may sound tentative. Males wield their authority with less apparent ambivalence. Men tend to give direct orders, women to say "Let's get that done."

Women often try to save the pride of their subordinates, and verbally put lab workers at ease if they make mistakes. But they expect everyone to realize that although they are friendly and kind, they are still the boss. This only works, however, with people who understand this style of communication. To those with other expectations of a P.I.'s behavior, some woman P.I.'s styles reduce their feelings of respect for a boss.

Women tend to say sorry habitually, apparently accepting blame, when at most commiseration is implied ("I'm sorry the experiment will go past five o'clock, but those time points are really important").

> *As a student, I much preferred going to the males than the females in the lab for advice about experiments. The women qualified everything they said, and gave suggestions and options for a course of action. The men would say, "Add salt". And if the advice was wrong—well, I'd much rather get a solid command even if it resulted in a botched experiment, than to have to think about what I should do.*

Some males from within the same apparent culture also have trouble with a female boss. Often, the trouble is not overt—most lab people know how they are supposed to act and can put up a good façade. One of the major problems woman P.I.s have encountered is that males from some cultures may not want to collaborate or take orders from them.

- *Behavior at meetings.* Although women are perceived as being more talkative than men, men generally do more talking at meetings. It is not uncommon that all the comments made after a talk are made by men.

- *Giving instruction.* Men give instructions with authority—or may be seen as giving advice with authority. It is why some people find it easier to "follow" a male. Others would rather take advice or instruction from people who are presenting themselves as equals, male or female, making the instructions seem more doable and achievable.

- *Scientific discussions.* Even when discussing a seemingly innocuous piece of data, men and women can favor completely different modes: Men tend to fight for their "side" with great conviction, whereas women tend to consider both points of view simultaneously.

- *Taking credit for achievements: Bragging versus modesty.* Men from many cultures, and women from a few, may consider boasting and displaying accomplishments to be requirements. They may take another person's modesty and dislike of personal advertisement to be false modesty and evidence of insecurity. Women tend to not want to offend someone or earn their dislike by "flaunting" their good points and deeds.

It would seem that an easy fix would be to recommend women to display their accomplishments more. The problem is that women are often judged by the standard of what a woman should be, and what is acceptable and assumed from a man would be looked at with distaste from a woman. In other words, although women may be judged poorly for not acting like men, they are judged even more poorly when they do. This is also true for males who have a personality profile closer to what is thought to be female. However, there is only so much you can worry about!

Personalities are so varied in the lab that the male-female differences may hardly be noticeable. A majority of either males or females can, however, change the tenor of the lab. Some P.I.s seem to attract mostly males or mostly females, or to hire mostly males or females: Most noticeable are the female P.I.s with a predominantly female lab population. The similarities of communication style can make males or females more comfortable with a P.I. of the same gender.

Even if you have worked carefully and successfully at eliminating apparently very male or very female characteristics from your interactions, other people still have their own baggage and will respond to you as to how they perceive you, and not as you perceive yourself. So, although it is helpful to consider the influence of your gender on your role as boss, it is usually useless to pander to other's thoughts.

Learning through Conflict

NEGOTIATION

...When two people, A and B, meet for a discussion, there are actually six different personality roles involved. For A has three separate personalities present: A1, the person that A actually is; A2, the person A believes to be his or her self-image; and finally A3, the person that A appears to be. The same threefold personalities of course apply to B, making six altogether.
NIERENBERG (1986, P. 51)

Common interests must be sought—in a good negotiation, everybody wins something. Always be on the alert to convert divergent interests into channels of common desires.
NIERENBERG (1986, P. 35)

Negotiation is the art of coming to an agreement and depends completely on communication. It is part of every aspect of your day: Whether you are arranging a date for a meeting, buying a microscope, hiring a technician, or deciding the authorship of a paper, you must be fluent in the give and take of negotiation. P.I.s who are able to create a supportive relationship with all the relevant people they deal with have an important negotiating talent. As head of the lab, you must remember: Negotiation is not just about convincing someone of your point of view, it also involves listening to the other person's point of view.

> *I talk to each person, every day. One person was feeling too much pressure from that and was thinking of leaving and I said fine, let's restructure things...let's leave it that you'll call me when you feel you have something to say, and I won't ask. It's working.*

The phrase, WIN WIN, has entered into common language. It suggests that, in a negotiation between two parties, both sides get what each wants. This is the situation that you will most often find in the lab—that you, the negotiator, will be negotiating positively both for yourself and for the other person. An example of this is trying to convince postdocs to do a particular series of experiments that they are not enthusiastic about. You try to convince them that doing the experiments would be useful to their project and future (hopefully, this and the other points you may be debating are true), whereas they are attempting to convince you that the experiments do not make sense.

259

But sometimes you may be working against one lab member's needs, or even against both your own and the lab member's apparent needs, for the sake of the future or for another lab member. Settling authorships and working out overlapping projects are times when this kind of tricky negotiation must be done. Through all the day-to-day dealings, the overall benefit of the entire lab must always be considered, as well as the benefit of each individual. These are the trickiest negotiations, for you must believe and demonstrate that each person will benefit in some other way, or at another point in time, with each decision or series of decisions. Below is a list of helpful hints to use in any negotiation:

- *Have as much information at hand as possible* before the negotiation.

- *Know what you want.*

- *Know what you are prepared to give up to get it.* And in a negotiation, you do have to give something up.

- *Try to understand your opponent's motivation and needs.* Carefully remember the other perspective. You may be remembering that the person was late every day for a week, and this individual remembers spending repeated weekends at the lab.

- *Listen and empathize.*

- *Negotiate problems, not demands.* If someone does make a demand, this is a warning sign that all is not well, and further negotiations based on the demand can only end badly. Many P.I.s have been held hostage by someone in the lab on whom they depend, and most have found that the first demand will be followed by more. Do not be blackmailed.

- *Avoid having extraneous people in a negotiation.* Do not have someone there whose opinion you are not really going to consider. Everyone has an agenda or a cause, so try to keep each negotiation as simple as possible.

EMOTIONS UNDERLIE RESPONSES

Emotion is perhaps the most important component of negotiations, even when the discussion is conducted in cool intellectual language. Considering only the intellect of the person you are negotiating with will be very ineffectual, for each person's reactions will depend on complicated and usually subliminal instincts. You must try to see the emotions behind actions, and reinterpret those actions—trying to understand your own emotional responses at the same time.

People have a great resistance to truly reexamine any issue. The following are some of the convolutions we go through to keep ourselves from hearing what we do not want to hear (Nierenberg 1986, p. 49):

- *Projection.* Attributing one's own motives to someone else, usually unconsciously.

- *Displacement.* Scapegoating, taking out aggression on a person who is not the source of the difficulty.

- *Repression.* The exclusion from conscious thought of feelings and wishes that are repugnant or painful to the individual.

- *Reaction formation.* After repressing a feeling, acting or thinking in completely the opposite way.

Putting yourself in the other person's position can help you see through the emotions involved. Insight into another person will usually not come to you immediately: Piece by piece, you gather the data and build an understanding of that person's responses. Furthermore, people firmly and deeply believe that they are motivated by good, honorable, and moral intentions and that they are seeing the problem in a perfectly rational way. People have a great capacity to rationalize any position as the "right" one. Each of us has an image of ourselves that is good, and this self-image may seem to have little to do with the image seen by the rest of the world. In any negotiation, try to see past the action of individuals to their motivations, as this will explain why they are doing what they are doing and saying what they are saying.

CONFRONTATION AND CONFLICT RESOLUTION

No matter how mild mannered you are and how nonconfrontational you want to be, you will have to deal with people and issues head-on at times. Most people dread conflicts, and particularly dislike being in the middle of someone else's conflict. However, there are few situations in the lab that will give you more data, so try to use each conflict as a rapid way to better understand the people involved.

> Almost all advice giving in science is confrontational. You are telling people, yes, your conclusions are interesting but they are probably not my conclusions or yes, you put in a lot of effort but you didn't do the right controls. In situations like that, some people ignore things because they don't want to give advice like that or say anything unpleasant. But if you don't, you aren't training.

Adjust your confrontation style for each interaction. Confrontation styles will be different when they involve people of different cultures, of different ages, and/or with different goals. There can be so much variation in confrontation styles that the mildest of reproaches can be taken as being intensely personal and offensive. So, even if you like your cards on the table and are not at all worried about confrontation, it may help the effectiveness of your interactions to think about the implications of your style, and alter it to suit the circumstances. Below are some techniques for disagreeing (Hamlin 1989, p. 239).

- *Respect each other's ideas.* Differ with the ideas, not the person. Differing with the person can incite resentment.

- *Listen and support first.* Hear out the whole idea and positively commend some aspect of it.

- *Ask questions.* Get more facts before you disagree. The answers may further support your thoughts—or they may demonstrate that you are wrong.

- *Be specific and constructive.* Sometimes you and the other person disagree about different topics. Before you get into a completely negative frame of mind about the disagreement, check on the specific question.

- *Disagree nonjudgmentally.* Do not be arrogant. Criticize impersonally. This is easiest to do by disagreeing with an idea or experiment, not with the person.

- *Offer another solution.* Say why you disagree, and how you think the issue might be settled. Or ask the person to come up with another solution.

Do not mistake attack for confrontation. With a confrontation, you approach an individual with a problem you have with this person's behavior, or someone approaches you. This is done with the hope of resolving the problem.

With an attack, the fight is no longer simply about an issue, but is about the person, and the emotions stirred up by that person. Do not be drawn into an attack about yourself or another person. Say clearly that you think all parties involved should speak only of the specific facts of the problem and not to speculate until all facts are in.

Be careful of disguised and subtle attacks. You are dealing with people who probably have the finesse not to say "He stole my ideas!" but could lead you quietly to that conclusion under the guise of presenting data in a rational manner.

BACKING OFF

An important part of resolving a conflict is to know when to halt the interaction. Sometimes you realize you do not have all the facts and must get more information before you proceed. Sometimes someone has become too emotional, and needs to calm down. And an incubation period, even if everything is going fine, may just help to clarify the situation for everyone. You will know that a cooling off period is needed when communication stalls or when confrontation turns to attack. Sum up any successes the discussion has engendered so far, and say what it is that must still be resolved. Set a meeting for the near future, within a week, and try again.

Getting help. There may well be times when you are too close to a situation, either personally or officially, to be able to resolve a conflict with a clear head. There should be a known chain of command that both the lab head and the lab worker know they can go through in case there is a tough conflict.

Stress and Depression in Lab Members

REACTIVE RESPONSES

In the lab—where many scientists spend ten to twelve hours each day, six to seven days a week—everything is tightly controlled. Tedious tasks demand absolute concentration, because a single error can wreck months of work. During our lab's weekly meeting, every detail of every experiment is intensely scrutinized and challenged as we search for those hidden, threatening mistakes. Is this the natural habitat of the obsessive-compulsive?

GROOPMAN (2000, P. 53)

Stress is part and parcel of lab work: Papers must be handed in on time, grants are rejected, work gets scooped, and experiments stop working. Some people, the so-called type-A personalities, seem to thrive on stress, generating crises to keep themselves sharp and busy. Others react badly to it, becoming jittery and snappish. Some work harder, some will weep. Still others have a shutdown of feeling, and appear depressed.

How a person feels and responds to acute and chronic stress is very personal and individual. You cannot tell people when to feel stressed or how to behave when tense, unless they are taking the stress out on someone else in the lab. But you must be able to judge when someone's behavior is not just a reaction to a lab situation, but has taken on a life of its own and is no longer controllable.

DEALING WITH STRESS

Act as a role model in dealing with stress. How you act in a stressful situation will influence how those in your lab respond. If you do not act as if the end of the world had come when a paper is rejected, the lab people are more likely to be calm. If you are not nasty-tempered in the week before a grant is due, your people are less likely to be—now, and for the rest of their lives. Show that all stress does not have to be internalized, but can be dealt with before it becomes a problem.

Be proactive about teaching lab members how to handle stressful situations. For example, when a paper is rejected, do not just let the student stew about negative

263

reviews. Sit down, and guide the student through the steps to take when responding to a negative review. Make a plan, and be encouraging. Are the criticisms valid? Will you submit the paper to another journal? Will you fight the review? Help the student turn the disappointment into action. Help your lab members to remain in control.

Control is the issue. It is when people feel not in charge of their lives that stress can have such a deleterious effect. Competition, when a lab member working on a hot project knows that another lab is very close to the same answer, can cause stress, but that stress, while exhausting, can feel exhilarating. Being scooped, with its implications for the future of the project, is very stressful, but the stress can be dealt with positively, as described above.

But if, for example, a lab member was scooped because someone used information supplied in a confidential grant application from your lab, the stress can become anger and frustration. This sense of having no control is one reason people cite for leaving science.

As P.I., it is important to put control back in the hands of the lab member. Teach lab members what actions they can take in situations, and do everything you can yourself to rectify a situation that treats a lab member poorly. By doing nothing yourself, you add to the person's sense of being powerless and trapped.

Some things that happen in labs—in life—cannot be fixed, and sometimes one has to breathe deeply and move on. While you do the best you can to demonstrate ways to deal with situations, it is ultimately the character of the lab members that will determine whether they will be able to conquer stress.

The way in which lab members work can cause great stress between lab members and the P.I. Some lab members might get on the P.I.'s nerves because of the way in which they set up experiments, think through problems, and arrive at decisions. If you find yourself chronically tense or angry at lab members, consider whether it is their personality or actions that trouble you.

Stress can be diminished or intensified by the laboratory atmosphere. In a supportive atmosphere, individuals will be buoyed by other lab members during bad times. A happy lab is a buffer, and a tremendous stress reducer. In fact, stress can actually bring people together beneficially, in an us-against-them reaction—as long as the lab interactions dissipate the stress and provide perspective and humor. A lab in which everyone becomes bitter is not what you want.

Stressed lab members might put a lot of strain on the other members of the lab, by irritability, by obsessively talking about a disturbing situation, or by treating people differently from the way they normally would. For the most part, lab members can work this out themselves. But be ready to step in and talk to the person who acts badly and is obviously putting strain on the others. Refusing to cooperate with other lab members or treating them rudely is not to be tolerated, no matter what has happened.

DEPRESSION AND OTHER ILLNESSES

While the severely depressed do distort life to the negative, the mildly depressed are quite possibly the most accurate observers of life in our midst. They perceive with crystal clarity the truth that, when the glass is half-full, it is also half empty.

RATEY AND JOHNSON (1997, P. 68)

Perhaps because labs tend to be so tolerant of a range of behaviors, depression can be taken to be almost an interesting if dark reaction to the ups and downs of research. As with all personality differences, there may even be a benefit to mild depression. People with milder forms of depression, the "shadow" forms, generally are not anxious, whereas people with severe depression almost always are (Ratey and Johnson 1997). And people with mild forms of depression add qualities of insight and humor that add greatly to a lab dynamic. At any rate, it is not always possible to dissect a person cleanly into pathology and personality.

Some people, after a major disappointment, are deflated and seemingly depressed for a while. They may act flat while they mentally deal with the problem. This is a common response to stress. But if it goes on too long, or occurs even in the absence of a reason, you may suspect clinical depression. This is a devastating illness that often renders a person unable to communicate, work, or function. Below is a list of the symptoms of depression (National Mental Health Association 1998).

- Depressed mood most of the day, nearly every day.
- Reduced interest or pleasure in all or almost all activities.
- Significant weight loss or weight gain, or a significant decrease or increase in appetite.
- Trouble sleeping or sleeping too much.
- Psychomotor agitation or retardation.
- Fatigue or loss of energy.
- Feeling worthless or guilty in an excessive or inappropriate manner.
- Problems in thinking, concentrating, or making decisions.
- Recurrent thoughts of death, a specific suicidal plan, or a suicide attempt.

    Note: Symptoms of depression may vary according to an individual's age and culture (e.g., complaints of weakness, tiredness, or "imbalance," instead of sadness or guilt, in Asian cultures; or irritability and social withdrawal in children).

Other mental disorders may affect lab members. Stress can have a powerful effect on all people, but to those with schizophrenia, bipolar disorder, obsessive-compulsive disorder, and anxiety disorders such as panic attacks, stress can act as a triggering agent. This is not to say that people with these disorders necessarily handle stress any less well than anyone else or that lab work is more stressful than other jobs: Everything depends on the person, the situation, and the timing.

PROTECTING AND WORKING WITH LAB MEMBERS
WITH MENTAL DISORDERS

The Americans with Disabilities Act (ADA) protects people with a physical or mental impairment that substantially limits one or more major life activities, but individuals are only protected under this law if they already have a record of the disability and have disclosed the disability.

According to the ADA, an employer is required to make a reasonable accommodation to provide an equal employment opportunity for an employee with a disability. Accommodation for a psychiatric disability might include time off for scheduled meetings or support groups, extending additional leave to allow a lab member to keep a job after a hospitalization, and a schedule that includes flextime. Each person may be helped by a different accommodation.

Mental disorders are not considered in the same light as more obviously physical diseases or problems. There is still a stigma to mental illness, and this stigma is more exaggerated in some cultures than others. For some people, it is a sign of weakness to admit to or "give in to" mental illness.

Mental disorders are not as visible as a physical problem to the afflicted person or to others. People are far less likely to go to a doctor promptly for a mental health problem, which means that problems go without treatment for a longer time and are more likely to be pushed to a crisis point at work. Even if a person has gone for medical help, mental disorders are not always easy to diagnose. Many people have seen multiple doctors over a period of years before diagnosis and treatment, and treatment itself may require time for adjustment.

Asking a person about a mental problem seems personal and invasive. Coworkers, who might easily say, "You are looking a bit pale," would hesitate to say, "You are very snappish lately," or "Is everything okay? You seem very sad."

The attitudes of the P.I. and lab members are critical in creating an atmosphere in which a handicap will be accepted, and in which any problems that arise might be solved. Knowing that someone has a problem is not grounds for prejudice or suspicion. With counseling and/or medication, mental illness can be controlled, and these diseases should be considered in the same light as all others: All people may be struck with an illness or trauma or domestic crisis at any time, and the P.I. should offer as much support as possible.

Mental illnesses clearly have a greater effect on the lab than a person's more obviously physical malady. A change in a person's personality can completely alter how the lab members communicate with each other. Some people in the lab might have an aversion to mental illness. Tolerance and acceptance of diversity hold for mental illness, and you should not tolerate any harassment of any kind for those who suffer from it.

Privacy is very important for many people. The P.I. may have privileged information about a lab member that should be respected. Yet, the issue of disclosure on the part of someone with a mental disability is indeed a difficult one. Disclosure may bring help and accommodation, but it may also reap prejudice and a lack of privacy. It may bring the expectation of trouble, and put the lab worker in the position of being constantly scrutinized for signs of a breakdown.

You do not need to be watching out for atypical behavior. You do not need to be always on edge, anticipating a mental crisis on the part of anyone in the lab. But in a lab in which there is communication, where lab members are considered in light of their strengths and abilities, a P.I. should take note when an individual is acting unusual.

If you believe that someone may having any kind of trouble, observe and talk with the person. This is not the time for sarcasm or timidity in dealing with the problem. If you suspect someone is depressed, or if lab members come to you with suspicions, speak with the person immediately.

Ask if anything is wrong. Ask if there is anything you can do, or if the person has had thoughts of suicide. Explain that you have noticed a change in behavior and that you are worried. Do not simply believe a denial, which is the most likely answer you will hear. People will be afraid that if they do have a problem, they may lose the job or that something will go on their record, so they do not want to admit to the boss that there is a problem.

If you believe that there is a problem, ask the person to speak to a trained professional. You cannot force individuals to see a counselor or physician or threaten loss of the job if they do not.

If someone has an acute or severe mental health problem, to whom should you turn for help? Over a period of days, weeks, or hours, a lab member may suffer from a crisis. Increasingly, depending on the problem, the person may become obsessional, delusional, erratic, and show other signs of having lost control. You may have been unsure of a problem before, but the situation is now clearly a serious health problem.

- *Do not leave the person alone.* While you are checking out your options, have a few people stay with the person.

- *Stay calm.* Do not lecture. Let the person talk as much as needed.

- *Speak to Human Resources to check on procedures,* but be prepared to cope with the situation yourself. Check around to see if there is an M.D. in the department or institution who can talk with the person and can help smooth the hospital admission: Do anything you can to avoid having the person sit in a waiting room for 4 hours before being seen by a harried stranger.

- *Find family or friends important to the lab member* to keep in touch with the person and the medical people. Many people would not want to have a boss hanging around a hospital, but be prepared to step in.

- *Be ready to intervene* to ensure that the person gets full consideration by the insurance company for the institution. The person is probably not able to be concerned with finances at the time of a crisis.

SUICIDE

Suicide is an infrequent but very real happening in laboratories. By the time they have been in science long enough to be running a lab, most P.I.s have known someone in their lab or institution who has committed suicide.

Especially if you do not have a close personal relationship with the lab members, the signs may not be easy to detect. You will not always be able to tell if a person is suicidal, except in retrospect. One investigator recalled a postdoc who stayed in the lab until late in the evening, setting up the next day's experiment with a coworker, before going home to overdose on prescription medicine. He had been joking with other lab members, and no one had any indication that he was upset or depressed. Another investigator knew of a student who came in on the weekend to feed the department's rabbits, and then drove away, wrote a note, and killed himself that evening.

If someone in the lab comes to you with worries about someone else in the lab, listen very, very carefully. Most people assume that they are mistaken about the possibility of someone committing suicide. You may be brushed off by that individual, but if you feel there are problems, persist in asking questions. Below are some suicide warning signs (National Mental Health Asociation 1996).

- *Verbal threats* such as "You'd be better off without me," or "Maybe I won't be around anymore."

- *Expressions of hopelessness and/or helplessness.*

- *Previous suicide attempts.*

- *Daring and risk-taking behavior.*

- *Personality changes* (i.e., withdrawal, aggression, moodiness).

- *Depression.*

- *Giving away prize possessions.*

- *Lack of interest in the future.*

The impact on other lab members who are dealing with the aftermath of suicide in the lab will be great. Most likely, the other lab members were close to the person who died and are stunned and regretful. Suicide is a violent act and devastating to friends and family. Lab members might feel sadness, guilt, loss, and insecurity in the surviving relationships in the lab. Some people may grow depressed and lose motivation, and some will throw themselves into working around the clock. Each person will deal with the loss and shock on a very individual level, and by a very individual timetable. It would be a mistake to be judgmental about anyone's way of coping.

This is the time to keep your door open. You have your own grief to deal with in your own way, but if you can, keep the talking going. Encourage discussion and encourage lab members to see a counselor if they feel the need.

It is not your fault. Perhaps you tried unsuccessfully to intervene and to help with someone who showed signs of suicide. Or perhaps you did not even know there was a problem. While a majority of people who commit suicide have a mental or emotional disorder (National Mental Health Association 1996), many would be considered to be low risk for suicide and it probably could not have been anticipated. In any case, do not be haunted by what could have been.

What you do not want to be is the lab head who noticed a problem and did nothing, thinking that it was none of your business and that you did not want it to be your business. Even if you did ignore obvious signs, another person's suicide is still not your fault, but few people would want to be in that position. As one P.I. said of the possibility of a lab member committing suicide while in the lab, "Not on my watch..."

RESOURCES

Albright M. and Carr C. 1997. *101 Biggest mistakes managers make: And how to avoid them.* Prentice Hall Trade, Englewood Cliffs, New Jersey.

Angier N. 1991. Women swell ranks of science, but remain invisible at the top. *The New York Times* May 12, pp. C1, C12.

Barker K. 1998. *At the bench. A laboratory navigator.* Cold Spring Harbor Laboratory Press, Cold Spring Harbor, New York.

Belker L.B. 1997. *The first-time manager*, 4th edition. AMACOM Books, New York.

Blanchard F. 1991. Reducing the expression of racial prejudice. *Psychological Sci.* **2:** 158.

Boschelli F. 1999. Making the transition from academia to industry. *Am. Soc. Cell Biol. Newsletter* **22:** 12–13. (http://www.ascb.org)

Brown J. 1999. Lifting as they climb: Can graduate student mentors aid the cause of affirmative action? *University of Massachusetts Magazine,* Spring, pp. 26–31.

Brown W.S. 1985. *13 Fatal errors managers make and how you can avoid them.* Berkley Books, New York.

Calhoun J. 1998. CET Reviews the Best Net-Ready Info Managers. National Mental Health Association MHIC Factsheet. (http://www.cnet.com/Content/Reviews/Compare/Netpinms)

Case J. 1995. *Open book management. The coming business revolution.* Harper/Collins Publishers, New York.

Christensen J. 2000. On the Web, as elsewhere, scientists prove a demanding lot. *The New York Times*, June 7, p. 20.

Coates J. 1993. *Women, men and language*, 2nd edition. Longman Publishing, New York.

Cooper R.K. and Sawaf A. 1997. *Executive E.Q.: Emotional intelligence in leadership and organizations.* Grosset/Putnam, New York,

Covey S.R. 1989. *The 7 habits of highly effective people.* Simon & Schuster, New York.

Dimitrius J.E. and Mazzarella M. 2000. *Put your best foot forward.* Scribner, New York.

Dube J. 2001. Office Wars. *ABC News* July 29. (http://www.abcNEWS.com)

Fast J. 1991. *Body language in the workplace.* Penguin Books, New York.

Goleman D. 1995. *Emotional intelligence: Why it can matter more than I.Q.* Bantam Books, New York.

Gornick V. 1990. *Women in science.* Touchstone, New York.

Groopman J. 2000. The doubting disease. When is obsession a sickness? *The New Yorker* April 4, pp. 52–57.

Hamlin S. 1988. *What's the problem? Why we don't communicate well in the workplace. How to talk so people listen. The real key to job success*, pp. 1–20. Harper and Row, New York.

Hamlin S. 1989. *How to talk so people listen. The real key to job success.* Harper & Row, New York.

Hoagland M. 1990. *Toward the habit of truth: A life in science.* W.W. Norton, New York.

Hofstadter D.R. 2000. Analogy as the core of cognition. In *The best American science writing 2000* (ed. J. Gleick), pp. 116–144. HarperCollins, New York.

Hunsaker P.L. and Alessandra A.J. 1999a. *The art of managing people.* Simon & Schuster, New York.

Hunsaker P.L. and Alessandra A.J. 1999b. Using body language effectively. In *The art of managing people*, pp. 163–177. Prentice-Hall, Englewood Cliffs, New Jersey.

Jamieson D. and O'Mara J. 1991. *Managing workforce 2000: Gaining the diversity advantage.* John Wiley and Sons, New York.

Jensen D. 1998. Forecasting compatibility: How to select your new boss. *Science's Next Wave* June 12, pp. 1–4. (http://nextwave.sciencemag.org)

Kanare H.M. 1985. *Writing the laboratory notebook.* American Chemical Society, Salem, Massachusetts.

Kelleher S. and Sanders E. 2000. Troubled resident's case left UW with quandry. *The Seattle Times* July 5, pp. 1, 10.

Kenna P. and Lacy S. 1994. *Business China. A practical guide to understanding Chinese business culture.* PassPort Books, Chicago, Illinois.

Kevles D.J. 1998. *The Baltimore case: A trial of politics, science, and character*. W.W. Norton, New York.

Latour B. and Woolgar S. 1986. *Laboratory life*. Princeton University Press, Princeton, New Jersey.

Lieberman D.J. 1998. *Never be lied to again*. St. Martin's Press, New York.

Marincola E. 1999. Women in cell biology: A crash course in management. *Am. Soc. Cell Biol. Newsletter* **22:** 36–37. (http://www.ascb.org)

Marsh S.R. 2000. Negotiation styles in mediation. (http://adrr.com/adr1/essayb.htm)

Martinet J. 1992. *The art of mingling: Easy, fun, and proven techniques for mastering any room*. St. Martin's Press, New York.

McGrayne S.H. 1998. Christiane Nüsslein-Volhard. In *Nobel prize women in science: Their lives, struggles and momentous discoveries*, pp. 380–408. Carol Publishing Group, Secaucus, New Jersey.

Mendelson H. and Ziegler J. 1999. *Survival of the smartest: Managing information for rapid action and world-class performance*. John Wiley & Sons, New York.

National Mental Health Association. 1996. Suicide—General Information. MHIC Factsheet. (http://www.nmha.org/infoctr/factsheets/81.cfm)

National Mental Health Association. 1999. Stress: Coping with everyday problems. MHIC Factsheet, pp. 1–3. (http://www.nmha.org/infoctr/factsheets/41.cfm)

The New York Times. 1994. When mood affects safety: Communications in a cockpit means a lot a few miles up. *The New York Times* June 26.

Nierenberg G.I. 1986. *The complete negotiator*. Nierenberg & Zeif Publishers, New York.

Nierenberg J. and Ross I.S. 1985. *Women and the art of negotiating*. Barnes and Noble Books, New York.

O'Hara-Deveraux M. and Johansen R. 1994. *Globalwork: Bridging distance, culture, and time*. Jossey-Bass Publishers, San Francisco.

O'Hara-Deveraux M. and Johansen R. 1994. A multicultural perspective: Transcending the barriers of behavior and language. In *Globalwork: Bridging distance, culture, and time*, pp. 35–73. Jossey-Bass Publishers, San Francisco.

Ratey J.J. and Johnson C. 1997. *Shadow syndromes*. Bantam Books, New York.

Reid T.R. 1999. *Confucius lives next door. What living in the East teaches us about living in the West*. Random House, New York.

Reis R.M. 1999. How graduate students and faculty miscommunicate. *Tomorrow's professor listserve* No. 69. Stanford University Learning Library. (http://cis.stanford.edu/structure/tomprof/listserver.html)

Sanders E. 2000. UW couldn't stop troubled doctor from buying gun. *The Seattle Times* June 30, pp. 1, 20.

Sanders E. and Kelleher S. 2000. E-mail told of troubled UW doctor. *The Seattle Times* Oct. 18, pp. B1–B5.

SIEC ALERT. 1998. Suicide Information and Education Center (SIEC) (http://www.siec.ca)

Spector B. 1989. Courses teach scientists to sell their ideas, manage others. *The Scientist* **3:** 1–3. (http://www.thescientist.com)

Stone D., Patton B., and Heen S. 1999. *Difficult conversations: How to discuss what matters most*. Penguin Books, New York.

Stone F.M. 1999. *How to resolve conflicts at work: A take-charge assistant book*. AMACOM Books, New York.

Tannen D. 1990. *You just don't understand. Women and men in conversation*. Ballantine Books, New York.

Tannen D. 1994a. *Talking from 9 to 5. Men and women in the workplace: Language, sex and power*. Avon Books, New York.

Tannen D. 1994b. *Talking from 9 to 5: How women's and men's conversational styles affect who gets heard, who gets credit, and what gets done at work*. William Morrow. New York.

The New York Times. 1994. When mood affects safety: Communications in a cockpit means a lot a few miles up. The New York Times June 26.

Thiederman S. 1991a. *Profiting in America's multicultural marketplace*. Macmillan, New York.

Thiederman S. 1991b. *Bridging cultural barriers for corporate success: How to manage the multicultural work force.* Lexington Books, New York.

Thomas, Jr, R.R. and Woodruff W.M.I. 1999. *Building a house for diversity.* AMACOM Books, New York.

Thomas, Jr. R.R., Gray T.I., and Woodruff M. 1992. *Differences do make a difference.* The American Institute for Managing Diversity, Atlanta, Georgia.

Tingley J.C. 1994. *Genderflex. Men and women speaking each other's language at work.* AMACON Books, New York.

Toropov B. 1997. *The complete idiot's guide to getting along with difficult people.* Alpha Books, New York.

Umiker W.O. 1996. *The empowered laboratory team. A survival kit for supervisors, team leaders, and team professionals.* American Society of Clinical Pathologists Press, Chicago.

Walton S.J. 1994. *Cultural diversity in the workplace.* Mirror Press and Irwin Professional Publishing, New York.

Wheatley M.J. 1994. *Leadership and the new science. Learning about organization from an orderly universe.* Berrett-Koehler Publishers, San Francisco.

White K. 1995. *Why good girls don't get ahead but gutsy girls do.* Warner Books, New York.

Williams L. 2000. *It's the little things: The everyday interactions that get under the skin of blacks and whites.* New York: Harcourt, San Francisco.

Yandrick R.M. and Freeman M.A. 1996. *Behavioral risk management: How to avoid preventable losses from mental health problems at work.* Jossey-Bass Publishers, San Francisco.

Yentsch C. and Sinderman C.J. 1992. *The woman scientist: Meeting the challenges for a successful career.* Plenum Press, New York.

Zuckerman H., Cole J.R. and Bruer J.T., eds. 1991. *The outer circle: Women in the scientific community.* W.W. Norton, New York.

Dealing with a Group

Lab Morale

INFLUENCES ON LAB MORALE

All labs—even the largest and most successful—have times when morale is low, people do nothing but quibble, and no experiments seem to work. These dry intervals are seldom as much a part of lab lore as the high-flying times, when the publications and the talks and the individual successes have everyone in the lab on a euphoric cloud, but they do as much to shape the lab.

The lab culture must be maintained. If the lab culture is strong, it will sustain individuals through a personal crisis or lack of results and can even help the entire lab through a barren spell or a change in focus. Once the lab is big enough, the lab culture can usually buffer most assaults on the morale. Until then, the P.I. is the glue that must hold the lab together. It is up to you to remind everyone that ups and downs are normal and that each person must continue to work, do experiments, and read, and talk and think in order to move the cycle back to productivity.

During the good times, you must remind everyone that glory is ethereal and transient and that hard work and good science must be maintained. Celebrate the successes and keep the momentum going.

Lab morale will be influenced from within and without. The mood of the larger department or institution has an effect on the lab morale. A department filled with retirement-bound tenurees can cast a pall of pointlessness on all and make a struggling new lab feel that even their successes are for nothing. A very competitive institution, on the other hand, can act as if the papers and the grants the lab puts out are simply not enough.

In industry, the mood of the lab can be influenced by the finances of the entire company: when stock is up, and business looks good, everyone seems chipper. When stocks go down, the mood goes down. Within the lab, personal as well as work situations will affect the atmosphere.

It is harder to detect and deal with influences from within the lab. When results are spectacular and papers are coming out, everyone is happy. Success affirms everyone's choice. When a promising project fails, everyone—except those suffering from result jealousy—feels badly.

Motivation is obviously closely linked with morale: When morale is down, motivation is down. Motivation, the reason why people do what they do, influences both interpersonal relations and work. Peer pressure is a huge motivational force. But it will work best for a lab culture when used positively, not negatively. One lab member getting a paper published in *Nature* will show everyone else in the lab that such an accomplishment is possible: It is inspirational. However, if such a success is used as an implicit threat—if you do not get a *Nature* paper, you will be nobody in the lab and you will never achieve anything—peer pressure becomes negative. Lab members will start to compete unhealthily with each other, instead of working as a team.

ENCOURAGING SOCIAL INTERACTIONS TO IMPROVE THE LAB'S MOOD

Lab get-togethers

It is important that lab members get together in a relaxed forum. In some labs, this is routinely arranged by the lab members themselves and you just have to show up. However, especially in a smaller lab, which is not likely to have an unofficial social organizer, the P.I. should arrange lab get-togethers, as it shows the lab members that interacting with them is important to you. Through these gatherings, you can be interested in and appreciative of the members of your lab, without being intimate or intrusive. Perhaps on occasion, you might not be invited to the after-hours get-togethers. Do not be insulted—be happy and relieved to have a lab that is getting along so well.

> *I actively try to promote a good atmosphere in the lab. It is mainly a matter of attitude and expectations. More tangibly, by using positive reinforcement for good results and empathetic support for problems or failures; keeping a friendly social atmosphere—taking the lab out to lunch for special occasions, cakes for birthdays, food at lab meetings; supporting lab members through personal crises, e.g. death of family member.*

Creating rituals

Celebrating events and victories in research helps to promote the underlying reason for the lab. Establishing these as regular and predictable events forms and solidifies the spirit of the lab. The P.I. should regularly organize at least some of these events, for example, the celebrations of scientific successes, to make clear what is important.

It means a lot to lab members that you do more than ask a technician to order a cake for you. Make and bring in a family recipe, or commit to bringing platters of sushi for the holiday party. Below are some reasons to celebrate:

- **Scientific successes**
    Publication of a paper
    Completion of orals
    Thesis talks
    Promotions
    New jobs
    Awarding of a grant

- **Holidays and other celebrations**

  Birthdays

  Christmas/holiday parties

  Chinese New Year

- **Throughout the year**

  Dinners

  Barbeques

  Take-out in the lab

  Happy hour

  Sports, such as a departmental softball team

  Book club

  Exercise room, aerobics classes

Alcohol?

Before organizing any parties or celebrations in the lab itself, check on the institutional rules concerning alcohol: Many places prohibit the drinking of alcohol on site, and do not allow so much as a sip of champagne in the department.

Many labs have certainly appreciated the contribution alcohol makes toward lightening the mood. The stories from a night of excess might be told for years afterward. But as P.I., you must retain control and awareness of the problems that drinking might bring. Nondrinking lab members might feel excluded if all functions were fueled by alcohol. And it is your responsibility not to allow anyone to drink and drive.

Day-to-day socializing at work

A bit of social grease can help keep the lab running smoothly and encourage a friendly and supportive environment.

- *Greet people* in the halls, labs, and elevators. Ask about an experiment or a relative if there is time; use eye contact and a smile if there is no time.

- *Stop and listen* if someone speaks to you.

- *Try some small talk.* It suggests that you care for the person, beyond work.

- *Make the rounds of the lab* at a particular time of day. Stop by each lab bench and ask about the day's experiment.

- *Eat lunch with the lab members.*

Social activities help integrate people into the science. Not all scientists are comfortable and confident enough to discuss science with people they do not know well. Social functions help to relax people, to bring those who feel isolated into the group, and to help people identify with the others in the lab. They provide one more venue for communication that will help the lab function better.

WHEN LABS GO BAD

Great care is taken to create an us-versus-them mentality within innovation-driven cultures, a mentality that sustains paranoia about the competition while simultaneously inspiring employees to accept production deadlines that commonly seem impossible to meet. Sensing—or even fabricating—intense attacks from all competitors, innovation-driven companies remain on the edge of paranoia.

HARRIS AND BRANNICK (1999, P. 45)

It is worth noting that anything that produces strong feelings of fear tends to kill ideas. This includes fear of criticism, or ridicule or failure, of yelling bosses, of being fired. Over time, this fear undermines confidence and erodes allegiance, creating a climate of uncertainty, suspicion, and sabotage.

COOPER AND SAWAF (1997, P. 35)

A dysfunctional lab can occur when the lab culture turns negative, and only a change to a new culture can save it. How do P.I.s recognize that they have a dysfunctional lab? One of the problems with a lab that is falling apart is that the P.I. sees one symptom, individual lab members see other symptoms, but no one has all the data needed to recognize the overall problem. Some indications are:

- Constant or sudden loss of personnel.
- Rules, such as safety rules or laboratory-shared tasks, are ignored.
- Friendships among lab members are sparse.
- Signs of discrimination against a person or group: exclusion, condescension, sexual innuendo, hostility, tokenism, backlashing, and scapegoating.
- Deadlines are not kept.
- Attendance at lab meetings falls.

Lab members might also have opinions about a dysfunctional lab:

- The P.I. is never here, never talks, and never listens.
- People do not get credit for their work.
- No one is having any scientific success.
- People are not helpful.
- The research is not interesting.
- The boss plays favorites.
- People are secretive about their results.

Individuals might say:

• I don't have anything in common with anyone else.

• No one is interested in my project.

• I don't have any time for my family.

• I don't feel part of the group.

• No one respects me.

• My project is too hard.

Can a dysfunctional lab be fixed? Fixing a dysfunctional lab is not easy, but it can be done. It so often stems from yourself, yet your own possible failures are not so easy to self-diagnose.

• **Look first at yourself**

Are you unpredictable and often bad-tempered?

Do you have a rapport with the people in the lab?

Do you give credit where it is due?

Do you play favorites?

Are you pushing too hard or, the opposite, appearing uninterested in research?

• **Look at the lab dynamic**

Is everyone doing interesting experiments?

Are the experiments working?

Do the people in the lab get along with one another?

Is there some sort of power struggle going on?

Are there competing projects?

• **Look at the personalities**

Is there a chronically unhappy person in the lab?

Is there a person in the lab, with whom you have had a bad interaction, who might be spreading discord?

• **Solicit opinions**

Talk to colleagues. If not a mentor, someone else you can confide in discreetly.

Talk to *all* of the people in the lab, but be careful not to take sides in a simmering dispute until you have completely investigated any situation.

Take the time to reflect on the lab. Modify your behavior immediately and deal with any problem people immediately. You may not see the effects right away; most dysfunctional labs take time to deteriorate to crisis point, and it will take some time to repair the damage. A demoralized bunch of people need inspiration as well as repair, so let them know what went wrong, and where you want the lab to go.

One unhappy person *can* create a dysfunctional lab, but only if you allow it. This usually happens when the P.I. gets too out of touch with the lab and/or has a vested interest in not seeing clearly. For example, a P.I. may be unable to realize that the postdoc who produces several good papers a year is so manipulative and petty with all of the other lab members that most hate coming to work and are ready to abandon ship. Deal with this swiftly by talking to the person and getting rid of this lab member if talking does not help. It may amaze you to see how quickly the lab atmosphere and morale can improve if a troublemaker is removed.

A dysfunctional lab is not necessarily unsuccessful, at all—but certainly, one is more reluctant to fix a successful, dysfunctional lab for fear that tampering with it will stop the scientific success. A megalab can absorb a lot of unhappiness, and stories of sabotage and despair in scientifically successful but emotionally unhappy labs are legendary. But in a lab just a few years old, the building up of substantial group unhappiness can mean the end of your career.

Lab Romances

LAB MEMBER–LAB MEMBER ROMANCE

Relationships between lab members are common and fortunately, inevitable. The atmosphere in labs is intimate and passionate, and the lab is the most likely place to meet someone of like mind and interesting background. Romances can be wonderfully reviving in a lab! They charge the atmosphere, they give promise to the entire group. Good labs tend to be close places, with good friends, and a bit of excitement and voyeurism around the latest romance can really fuel the lab energy.

> After they broke up, she was so jealous that she would stop talking if he even showed someone how to work the spectrophotometer.

You have no control or say about a romance between members of your lab. Lab members will sometimes go to great lengths to keep a romance from the boss, fearing that it will make them look unprofessional to have a relationship where they work. They may also keep their association secret for the sake of privacy. Until the relationship is out in the open, avoid commenting about it not only to the people involved, but to the entire lab as well.

Be on the lookout for negative fallout, especially if there is a hostile breakup, and hope there is not a triangle, or your lab might never find peace! Be prepared to initiate damage control, and step in if repercussions are affecting the lab—collaborations, in particular, can be keenly affected. Everyone should still be professional to all lab members, and it is your job to maintain professionalism. As a P.I., taking sides in a breakup between members of the lab can cause bad feelings and must be avoided. If someone ends up weeping in your office, give comfort and advice as you see fit. But remember that you may have to live with both members for a while.

Lab romances in a dysfunctional lab can be very unpleasant. If there is already a problem with jealously, competition, or frustration, a romantic bonding even without a breakup can be like pouring gasoline on a fire. The positive way to look at this might be that such a romance can bring the bad relationships in the lab to a head and finish them.

P.I.–LAB MEMBER ROMANCE

Therefore, faculty are warned against the possible costs of even an apparently consenting relationship, in regard to the academic efforts of both faculty member and student. A faculty member who enters into a sexual relationship with a student (or a supervisor with an employee) where a professional power differential exists must realize that if a charge of sexual harassment is subsequently lodged, it will be exceedingly difficult to prove immunity on grounds of mutual consent.

From The Presidential Statement and Policy on Sexual Harassment, University of Minnesota, January 20, 1989.

HASSELMO (1989)

Everyone knows that it is completely inappropriate for P.I.s to have a relationship with someone in their own lab. The balance of power is too much in your own favor—you ultimately hold sway over the other person. It is not good for an equal relationship, and it usually is not good for the lab. P.I.s who are the least put off by the idea are those who run the lab as a gathering of equals, those who truly believe that among equals, a romance would be of no detriment to the lab. Here such a relationship would have the least impact.

But if you are working hard, the most likely place to find a romantic interest is in the lab. Coworkers in a lab are spending a great part of the day together and each might go weeks without meeting a person who is not a scientist. And another lab member can readily understand your particular problems and worries.

If it happens, change the working situation as soon as you can, if you can. Get off the person's thesis committee, put in a good recommendation for another lab, suggest a project with another advisor. Whoever you are involved with must leave the lab should you desire to carry on the relationship. Otherwise there is no way you can continue to maintain the idea of equality and fairness. This is not to say that you might not be fair. But you will always have the appearance of unfairness, of playing favorites. No matter how open you are, lab members will hesitate to dispute the word or actions of your romantic partner in the lab. And, sooner or later, it will bother them. You could also end the relationship.

If either you or the lab member is married, you are putting the other members of the lab, as well as the lab member, in an extremely awkward and dangerous position. For the lab member, there is the risk of being embroiled in a disruptive personal and public conflict. The lab members would be caught between loyalty and dishonesty, an extremely unfair position to inflict on them. No matter how sympathetic they are to your personal cause, the overall impression of your judgment and ethics would suffer. There is probably not a single other personal decision you could make that has the potential for causing havoc in the lab than the one to carry on with this kind of relationship.

You should not have to run your life according to what people say. But it is unfair to expect most people to trust that you have their best interests in mind when you get involved with a person in the lab. To minimize lab damage when you are involved with a lab member:

- Do not talk about other lab members.

- Do not talk about the relationship with lab members. It usually is not worth hiding it—usually *not possible* to hide it—but discussing one lab member with another always compromises someone.

- If there are decisions that you must make about the person, try to enlist someone in the department as a partner in the decisions, to avoid any whiff of favoritism. If the relationship falls apart badly, or if someone in the lab complains of biased treatment, you need to offer proof that decisions were made on an objective basis.

If the relationship goes well, i.e., it flourishes, and everyone in the lab is supportive, and you continue to spend as much time with lab members as before, and your partner is uncontestedly the best scientist in the lab, it may just be the grandest and happiest time of your life. But if there is one person unhappy with a project, or with you, favoritism rumors will fly.

If the relationship turns sour, but you are both exceedingly in control and remain friends, why try to involve anyone in the lab in your side of the story? Time will pass and you and your lab will be fine. But if there is the slightest tinge of hate or revenge or coldness on the part of either of you, trouble is likely to be merely a letter to the dean away.

SEXUAL HARASSMENT

Sexual harassment may be defined as unsolicited and unreciprocated behavior of a sexual nature to which the recipient objects or could not reasonably be expected to consent and may include:

- Unwanted physical contact.

- Lewd or suggestive behavior, whether verbal or physical.

- Sexually derogatory statements or sexually discriminatory remarks.

- The display of pornographic or sexually explicit material in the workplace.

Sexual harassment is a form of sex discrimination that violates Title VII of the Civil Rights Act of 1964 and Title IX of the 1972 Educational Amendment to that Act. It can occur among peers, or between boss and student, employee or client/patient (e.g., in a hospital). It is unwelcome sexual conduct and can occur between male and female, with either as the perpetrator, and it can occur between people of the same sex. The victim does not necessarily have to be the person harassed, but anyone affected by the offensive conduct.

> ## The Legal Basis of Sexual Discrimination
>
> The 1964 Civil Rights act included both Title VII and a provision that created the Equal Employment Opportunity Commission (EEOC). The EEOC requires that an employee file a complaint within 180 days of a discriminatory incident. The EEOC then has 180 days to investigate the matter, try to resolve it by settlement, or to file a lawsuit, which does not happen often. If the EEOC declines to sue, it will issue the employee a right-to-sue letter, and the employee has 90 days to file a federal lawsuit based on Title VII discrimination.
>
> Title VII applies to your business if it has 15 or more employees during at least 20 weeks of the year, and if your business affects commerce (which most can be proven to do). An employee who wins such a claim is entitled to receive back pay, reinstatement, and attorney's fees (Lynch 1995).
>
> The law is constantly evolving, and if you are involved in a sexual discrimination case, you should consult a lawyer, probably through your institution.

Most labs are places of such personal tolerance and friendliness that a discussion of sexual harassment seems to some out of place. But sexual harassment is pervasive, and labs are not exempt from its effects: In fact, the same casualness and intimacy of the lab that may encourage romance may also mask harassment. Many people resent the fact that casual flirting can be construed as sexual harassment. But this would be unlikely, and this expectation trivializes the reality of sexual harassment. The current atmosphere around sexual harassment seems uptight to some, but it is still possible to have an easy camaraderie among all lab members.

Responsibilities of the P.I. By your actions, and your statements on policy, it is up to you to make the lab a place in which sexual harassment will not be tolerated. It is not only your own actions for which you may be held responsible, but the actions of others in the lab if you have appeared to condone them.

Publicize both the lab and organizational policies of sexual discrimination. Look up your organization's policy on sexual harassment and include it in any lab talk on ethics. Post a copy of it in the hall and include it in the lab manual. If your organization does not have a written sexual harassment policy, you should make a written lab policy. One reason for this is to cover yourself in case of litigation. The other reason is that most workplaces benefit from having the policy stated up front.

The organization policy on sexual harassment will strongly influence the lab. The larger the place, the more likely that Human Resources may actually intervene in cases even of impropriety, such as the boss being involved with a lab member (Weiss 1998).

Part of the written institutional policy should contain the names and phone numbers of the people to contact in case of sexually harassment. There should be more than one person, and they will most likely be associated with an Affirmative Action Office, or with Human Resources. Grievance procedures are very different from institution to institution, but all involve the assignment of an impartial investigator to the complaint. If lab members come to you to complain of sexual harassment on the part of someone else in the lab or institution:

- Ask the individual whether you should take action or just provide advice. This will clarify for both of you what should be done.

- Listen, taking the complaint seriously.

- If you are being asked for advice, you must try very hard to give an unbiased answer. If the charge is against a colleague, this might make it impossible for you. If you feel you cannot give good advice, and that person would like advice before proceeding, suggest speaking to the designated person at Human Resources.

- Do not make any kind of judgmental remarks for or against any involved party; for example, remarks such as "It sounds as if he was only kidding" or "He has a reputation for doing this" should not be made.

- Acknowledge the emotions and feelings the person may have without labeling or discussing them. Saying "I would have been furious, too" implies an opinion about the guilt of the accused, whereas "This must be difficult for you" shows that you understand the pressures and feelings involved in such a case.

- Explain the institutional protocol for dealing with sexual harassment. Describe what you will do next, and what the time frame is for a sexual harassment case. If safety is an issue, notify the authorities immediately.

- Be ready to intervene if the institutional actions become stalled.

If a lab member asks you to stop the sexual harassment of someone in the lab, you will have to make quite a few judgment calls. Be guided by whether the person wants you to speak privately to the other individual or whether you should be there for a discussion/confrontation.

You will first have to get the other person's interpretation. This is not a court case, and you do not need to judge: However, you do need to make clear the fact that a particular behavior is wrong. For example, "Stan, Ann was really offended by the remarks you made to her about her shirt at the lab meeting. You know that such remarks can be sexual harassment, and you must be careful not to do that again."

A controlled confrontation can be useful if tactfully done, but you need to know your people to avoid any humiliation. If these conversations make you privy to personal details, you must never repeat or bring up those details again. Keep in mind that your conversations with a lab member may not be privileged communication and can be elicited in legal or administrative proceedings. Some institutions have voluntary and informal means for resolving sexual harassment complaints, and this is ideal for someone who does not want to get involved in legal action.

Your lab is your responsibility and abdicating any of this responsibility to administration may seem to you to be disloyal to your people and an indication that the lab is out of control. But it may be the only way to protect all the parties involved. Use all of the resources available to you.

If you are sexually harassed

Below is a list of steps to take if sexual harassment occurs.

- *Confront the person who is harassing you.* Make it clear that it is unwanted and that it should not happen again. If you are not able to confront the person, speak to the person designated to deal with sexual harassment at your institution.

- *Keep records of the incident or incidents.* Note the date, time, place, any conversations or actions, and your response.

- *Speak to an appropriate person* if the behavior does not stop (listed in the institutional policy).

- *Call the police immediately* if you have been physically hurt.

How to avoid charges of sexual harassment

Most people learn very early that where, when, and how they touch a member of the opposite sex can have serious implications. A person able to earn a Ph.D. is surely bright enough to insure that his intentions are clear, the circumstances proper, and his gestures appropriate when he touches a student.

DZIECH AND WEINER (1990, P. 180)

As the head of the lab, the P.I. is in a very vulnerable position and must be careful to avoid anything that might be construed as sexual harassment. This includes situations outside the lab. Even at Friday afternoon happy hour, you cannot permit yourself to indulge an attraction or make a sexual remark to lab members or to let anyone from your workplace do the same in front of you without stopping it.

Many lab members, mostly male, have first-hand experience of a sexual harassment accusation, against themselves or a lab member. Few of the accusations ended up with a formal charge, but it is not possible to overestimate the effect of an investigation for sexual harassment on the P.I. and the lab. No matter how innocent you are—everyone feels innocent, of course—huge blocks of time are taken up by the process that, once made, must run its bureaucratic course. A charge of sexual harassment can be made by an observer of the incident, so you must not only be careful with your own behavior, but caution other lab members as well to act without reproach.

A female in the lab accused a bunch of male postdocs of sexual harassment, which created enormous headaches...and this all sprung out of a few jokes and/or colorful language, which was probably mildly inappropriate (none directed at the student but said when she was in earshot), and it all got bottled up until she exploded and filed a formal complaint.

Many of the actions of a close or sexual relationship could be construed as sexual harassment after the fact. Quid pro quo harassment is when lab members believe they must submit to unwelcome sexual conduct in order to retain a job or obtain a recommendation. Hostile environment harassment occurs when the sexual conduct is severe and persistent and poses a physical or psychological threat to the lab member's work or position. Even hinting that a sexual relationship be entered into could create a situation in which it would be very hard to prove that the P.I. did not exert pressure on the lab member to agree. By refusing to enter into a sexually intimate relationship with a lab member, you can avoid the major risk of being charged with sexual harassment.

If you have been accused of sexual harassment, get a lawyer. No matter how innocent you feel, sexual harassment charges can be very serious, and you can lose your job. Guilty or innocent, you will need a lawyer's advice. The advice of the institutional lawyer may not be enough, as the institution's first priority is most likely to be to protect itself, not you.

A formal complaint against the P.I. or a lab member can be time consuming and enormously damaging. P.I.s have lost jobs over what they consider to have been permissible behavior, and which probably was considered permissible behavior 10 or 15 years ago.

Maintaining Personnel Equilibrium

WORKING WITHIN THE LAB CULTURE

Constant vigilance is needed to avoid personnel problems. This is especially true in the early days of a P.I.'s job, when a dependable system for hiring or dealing with people has not yet been developed. You cannot put people in the lab, disappear into the office, and assume that all will go well. It might, but it is terribly, terribly unlikely, especially as the lab gets bigger.

> *I did everything wrong at first! I spoke too directly. I talked too publicly. I talked about one person in front of another.*

Make clear what elements you think are important. If you think communication in the lab is important, communicate. If honesty is important to you, or kindness, or enthusiasm, demonstrate it. If you intend to work at preserving a productive culture in the lab, make that clear as well.

P.I.s have their own expectations about the kind of disputes they will get involved in. All assume they will be part of scientific disputes such as authorships and project priorities. Most believe they should have some role in territory or equipment problems. Some say they assume they will be involved in personal disagreements, and others will say it is none of their business at all, and expect the lab members to solve squabbles among themselves.

Very early on in the history of a lab, it will often be a luxury to *not* be involved in the lives of the people in the lab. You will be working side by side and will be witness to, if not a part of, most disputes. Your entire operation can be jeopardized by lab problems, and by your inability to fix them. Part of the lab culture that you must establish is that any disputes that disturb the lab will be handled by you.

WHEN DO YOU INTERFERE OR INTERVENE?

"I must spend sixty percent of my time trying to maintain a sense of harmony in the lab," he said. "I want people to get along, to cooperate. It's very difficult to do that, you know. It's hard enough to do that with your own family, but managing with twenty people is almost impossible. But really that's what my job is all about."
BOB WEINBERG TO ANGIER (ANGIER 1988, P. 46)

When, if ever, is the right time for the P.I. to take lab members aside and talk with them about their moods or attitudes? If a person will not discuss the problem with

> *I like dealing with people on scientific or research issues. I don't have much patience for dealing with other issues.*

you, should you persist? If you think the situation is serious enough that you must persist, how do you do it? If you know that a personal situation is what is weighing down the lab member, should you still try to help the situation? You should interfere:

- If you feel the mental or physical health of any person in the lab is at stake.

- If the dispute is affecting the lab member's ability to do research.

> *I try to arbitrate personality conflicts if things are getting very tense, but this is only if someone comes to me with complaints. I don't sniff around and pre-emptively try to head off problems.*

- When a power struggle puts your leadership into question or jeopardy.

- If cooperation, collaboration, and teamwork are compromised.

- When the social atmosphere becomes strained and the lab is an unpleasant place to be.

When a lab member comes to your office with a problem, your way of dealing with it will be partially determined by your role in the lab. If you have a highly personal, empathetic style, you may continually hear all kinds of problems and have to decide

> *I have certainly learned not to let things fester.*

which is important enough for you to do something about. If you have been personally standoffish, it is less likely that most people will come running to you for small matters.

Act swiftly. Do not let problems lie. Hoping that they will go away is another major new P.I. mistake. If you have perceived a situation that you know will continue unless you step in, it is time to act. Once you get into the habit of not getting involved in anything controversial, it gets harder and harder to step in. Have an idea, from early on, what you expect to make your business. Do not wait until damage control is your only option.

COMMON LAB DISPUTES

Equipment and maintenance problems

The person who was supposed to make the buffer did not. No one renewed the service contract on the ultracentrifuge. Someone is hoarding ice buckets. These may

> *Personality conflicts haven't really come up, and there haven't been any over work—everyone, including techs, has their own projects. But there have been some over physical space.*

seem trivial complaints, but they may reveal a lack of cooperation within the lab and are very troublesome to those working at the bench.

If you prefer to micromanage, deal with this swiftly and personally. If you have indicated that you do not want to be bothered with such details—well, you must, once it becomes a problem. For the most part, these problems can be dealt with in a lab meeting, with all members present, without even mentioning names. This affirms the lab approach to equipment and maintenance issues. Be prepared to follow up.

Territory problems

Territory problems are a subset of equipment and maintenance problems, but they involve a person's space and privacy. Examples are the use of a personal computer or reagents without permission. It helps to have a lab policy set up out front for this, as there are different philosophies, and it may not be clear to lab members what to do: Some labs are run with the idea that all reagents are for common use, whereas others have only very few common-use reagents.

> *I arbitrate personality problems probably more than I should. We did have authorship problems...and I fixed a big crisis by moving someone to another bench.*

These problems are best left to the individuals. Your premature involvement will be too much like babysitting. Repeat lab policy at a meeting; for example, without mentioning names, you could say "I just want to remind everyone that all reagents on the shelves are private and are not to be used without permission from the person who made it, every time." If the problems persist after the lab policy has been pointed out, it is time for you to step in.

Project problems

One person impinges on another's project, or "borrows" ideas. Someone is left off a list of authors on a paper. Someone will not share results. A natural progression has led to the convergence of two projects.

Call a meeting with the involved people, immediately. Listen, but here, *you* must make the decision. Without your trust and support, your lab will have continual problems, and the project and collaboration situation must be completely without gray areas (see the chapter on Setting the Course in this volume).

Personal problems

Dealing with personal problems—for example, a romance between two lab members has ended, and nasty comments are bouncing back and forth—is a very individual P.I. decision. Many P.I.s will deliberately not notice personal problems, and feel that it is not their domain. Some genuinely do not notice personal interactions. As much as possible, it is best to let the lab sort out their personal problems. You are the boss and it is, in a sense, unfair for you to be involved in judging personal issues. This is a decision many P.I.s have come to the hard way—they start off being very personally involved and back off as the lab grows.

But you must step in if the lab is being affected and as soon as possible. Talk to the individuals involved, alone or together, as soon as there is a bad problem. You may feel a very personal interest in the people in your lab, and they may look up to you tremendously. But, no matter how much older or more experienced you are, you cannot solve everyone's personal problems. And you cannot solve problems arising from relationships or alcohol or drug dependencies. You can make suggestions, refer people to agencies and counselors, and give what immediate support and aid might be needed, but you cannot be a parent or a partner.

PLAYING FAVORITES

Some P.I.s say they like everyone, yet most admit that they have a favorite, someone with whom the scientific conversation flows. Preferring the company of a particular

I have a favorite student, someone I like to talk with and bounce ideas off. I hope it doesn't show.

person sometimes cannot be helped, but you do have to ensure that scientific help and mentoring are given on a scientific basis. The P.I. can also be terribly taken advantage of by a favorite. You may want very badly to have an equal or colleague, someone you can always talk to, but you may turn that person into a prima donna.

If a relationship with a favorite turns sexual, there will undoubtedly be problems.

I do have an absolute favorite, but we yell at each other a lot. If I screamed at the others the way I do at him, they would be completely destroyed.

Lab members seem to accept favorites if the chosen is superior in scientific ability. What causes resentment is when one lab member is raised above the others for no reason that is apparent to the rest of the lab.

WHEN YOU DISLIKE A LAB WORKER

One of the major disillusionments new P.I.s may suffer is that they will often have to work with people they dislike, and some of these might be in their own lab. Most P.I.s do think it is important to hire people that they like. But this is not always possible, and anyway, like may be replaced by dislike over time.

If you find yourself sitting in your car in the parking lot, dreading to go into work, if you hide in your office, not wanting to go into the lab and see a particular person, if your heart soars when that person is not in, and you then get much more work done, then your dislike is a crisis and must be dealt with.

Figure out if the problem, for you, is personal and constant or situational. Does it happen when you have a discussion or confrontation? Does it happen when there is going to be a research lab meeting? Do you hate this person's politics, and the way this person handles private life situations?

This is not a topic for discussion in the lab. Do not let lab members know how you feel, and certainly avoid any temptation to tell the person. If you cannot get over it, you can wait until there is a natural break and it is time for the person to leave. Incompatibility issues are difficult, for if someone does not want to leave, you may not be able to make it happen.

WHEN A LAB WORKER IS DISLIKED BY EVERYONE

Try to hire people who get along with others. There are personalities that almost always cause trouble. Argumentative, abusive, disdainful, manipulative—most P.I.s look for disruptive qualities such as these during the interview to weed those people out. But, especially in the beginning, and if the person is scientifically adept, P.I.s may miss the clues or unconsciously ignore them, until the entire lab clamors, or at least murmurs, for the dismissal of that person.

A more benign problem that many P.I.s have encountered is the acceptance of a loner by the rest of the lab. Many people who gravitate toward science want to work alone and completely independently. But some people crave independence so desperately that they resent even mild questions from the P.I. or other lab members concerning their project, feeling that such questions imply a lack of confidence. They stay away from lab get-togethers and may not have many friends in the lab.

The group may not always be in the right. On the other hand, there can arise a situation in the lab where one person is shunned or left out by the others. New people who join the lab may always tend to side with the group, without knowing anything about the reason for the negative interaction. The problem could be one of jealousy. Some lab members might feel supplanted in the eyes of the P.I. or might resent the successful presentation or paper of another person. If the former has greater social power in the lab, they might be able to spread a bias against that person.

Sometimes race, gender, sexual preference, or another cultural difference is wrongly accepted as being a logical and valid objection by the rest of the lab. If lab members come to you as a group to talk about another lab member, however, it is very likely that there is a very serious problem. Listen very, very carefully and as objectively as possible.

The first step is to find the problem. The way that you find out about the alienation of a lab member might indicate the origin of the problem. If you have noticed that one lab member never eats lunch with the lab, that other lab members tend to roll their eyes and show other signs of ridicule during that member's seminar presentations, or that most complaints during gripe sessions are directed toward that lab member, you have clues about where to look for a problem.

"I Should Have Done It Sooner!"

EASING PEOPLE OUT

It is not easy to suggest that someone leave. Research is not for everyone. But most people go into research without any other career plan in mind. In fact, until rather recently, anyone who intended to do anything but bench research was considered not to be a serious scientist, and therefore not worthy of much time and attention. In some places, this philosophy persists (and you may agree with it). In such a place, it can be very difficult to suggest that someone leave, as it is perceived there is nowhere that person can go.

Other P.I.s report that few new students plan on a career in basic research. Many options now exist, and attitudes are more flexible, so that it is not necessarily an insult to be told that other occupations may be better than independent research.

Most P.I.s agree that it is much better to tell floundering students or postdocs that perhaps research is not for them and that they should not become boxed in a corner. But it is difficult to know when and how to suggest other options. Having a good rapport with a person will help considerably in letting you know what to do, and when to do it. Through conversations, you may learn about a person's insecurities and strengths and be better able to introduce the idea of options. Still, it is seldom easy. People who have invested years of effort in a lab are likely to have very fragile egos regarding the question of their competence. How to do this well and in keeping with the lab philosophy is completely dependent on the situation.

> *I have gently suggested that several people leave.... in each case, I asked "Are you really sure..."*

- You must first ensure that there is nothing that you or the lab can do to change the situation. Is there a personnel incompatibility that could be fixed? Could a change in hours help the person complete experiments? Would additional training compensate for a deficiency at the bench?

- Are your differences with the person in philosophy or style influencing your judgment of fitness? A suggestion that someone leave because of incompatibility with the lab is an issue very different from whether the person should think of another career.

Almost all P.I.s who have suggested to lab members that they leave worried incessantly about doing it, but felt satisfied and relieved that they had done so. In most cases, the P.I. is only saying what the lab member already knew and had not faced.

WRITING NEGATIVE RECOMMENDATIONS

Most P.I.s will not write an overtly negative letter of recommendation. Worry about lawsuits, hurting someone's feelings or being wrong, or wanting to be sure that the person gets another position and gets out of the lab preclude such a letter from the point of view of the P.I.

More common is a mediocre recommendation, with a tepid description of a few good qualities. Most P.I.s agree, though, that if asked in person or over the phone about a mediocre recommendee, they would be more explicit and honest, even if this means being negative.

All lab members should be clear about how you interpret their work performance, very much before it is time for a recommendation. Graduate students or postdocs may still request your recommendation, even if they suspect it will be tepid or even negative, because the lack of a letter from the advisor is extremely suspicious. If you feel you cannot write an expected recommendation or are not writing a good one, let the person know and give the reason you feel the person may not want your recommendation.

I know some people who say to the secretary, "send out the A letter, or the B+ letter"... I don't, I write pretty honest letters. I would say to the person "I can't write you a strong recommendation."

There are polite ways to attenuate a rejection for a recommendation request from a student from a class or a postdoc down the hall ("Actually, I don't feel I know you well enough to write a letter of recommendation..."). If you feel sufficiently committed to the person and feel the truth would be useful, you will probably be doing a thankless job and a very good deed ("I don't think you would be qualified for that position").

Confidential or open letter of recommendation? The recommender will sometimes be given a choice of whether the candidate can read the letter or not. Most P.I.s prefer to write a confidential letter, especially in the beginning of running a lab, as it seems so much safer. But never assume that anything you write will forever remain confidential. After a few years, many P.I.s would rather be more direct and skip the manufactured secrecy and have the confidence to stand behind what they say, positive or negative.

FIRING

Many P.I.s have, even in their very first years, wished that they had let a troublemaker go at the first sign of discord. For some, this was one of what they considered to be their very worse managerial mistake. Instead, they waited, hoping the situation would resolve in time. Or they thought that a new lab member, a different project—something!—would take away the problem. But it

As soon as I had done it, I felt a huge burden lift from me...It was clear from the beginning that things weren't going to turn around.

very seldom works. When you have honestly evaluated a personnel problem and have determined that the best decision would be to fire the person, it is quite unlikely that you are wrong.

When do you have to fire someone?

It is fairly unusual that people are overtly fired from labs, as there are ways many undesirable people can be eased out. Rotating students, for example, can be asked to not come back. But sometimes, there is someone who is so flagrantly not right for the position that there is no option but termination. The following are some reasons for getting individuals out of the lab:

- *Incompetence.* Cannot do the work.

- *Insubordination.* Will not do the work.

- *Troublemaking.* When you have tried to deal with the person and have had someone else talk to the person, to no avail.

- *Fraud.* Faking data, signing the P.I.'s name to timesheets or purchase orders without prior discussion.

- *Safety.* Compromises own safety and that of others in the lab.

If you have someone difficult, and you won't be able to resolve it, cut and run! It can only end badly, with time and money spent. Don't put off hard decisions, even if the person is your only person.

Document!

When you suspect you have a permanent problem, start documenting these problems. Documentation is needed not only for the officials at your institution, but also to convince yourself that termination is necessary. During this time, avoid conflicts: There is nothing to be gained through them, except a lot of anxiety. You would presumably already have given warnings or have tried to help the person change the behavior. In the case of incompetence, you must be sure that additional training has not been effective.

Speak with the institution's lawyer, and with Human Resources, to ensure that you will be protected and to work within your organization's guidelines. Do not let Human Resources fire the person, even if they offer to do so—it is your job. However, especially in a case in which you suspect a violent or hostile reaction to firing, a representative from Human Resources could be also present. Keep the firing secret from others in the lab so that there is not the smallest chance that someone in the lab might inform the person of the imminent firing. You owe the person the courtesy of privacy.

Even if you suspect sabotage, even if you know, you must be careful about how you look for confirming evidence. Legally, the privacy of the employee is well protected. You have no right to go into a lab member's purse, backpack, computer case, or any piece of luggage brought in and out of the lab. Unless they have been given notice that their desk drawers and files are subject to monitoring (and that would be quite an invasive announcement), you cannot open them. (Generally, bench drawers are public property.) Especially, but not exclusively, if the employees have been notified, e-mail records can be searched legally, and Web Sites that have been visited can be recorded: Voice mail records can also be used (Guernsey 1999).

The warning

There are very few terminations that should come out of the blue. Other than for overt fraud or violence, unsatisfactory employees should receive at least one warning about their job performance. Scientific incompetence is usually handled differently from personality problems, in that many offers of help are usually given to the incompetent lab member before a warning is even issued. When it is clear that termination is a possibility, benchmarks can be set, and a warning given if those benchmarks are not met ("Tony, you were hired to set up a particular series of experiments. Although we have extended the timeline, and provided you with an assistant, the assays are still not working. I'd like to give you another chance, to see if you can get those experiments going by the first of next month.").

Personality problems are more difficult to deal with. There are no clear benchmarks of behavior. Warnings about behavior tend to be nebulous, or to sound like threats, and thus are completely nonproductive. It may be uncomfortable for you, but someone who is in danger of losing a job because of social behavior certainly deserves a chance to change that behavior. Explain the problem, and give the person a chance to justify the problem, but make it clear that the behavior is not acceptable to you. ("Ann, if you are unable to hold your temper and again verbally abuse the technicians when an experiment doesn't work, I will have to let you go").

HOW TO FIRE SOMEONE

Firing someone in your lab will be very unpleasant, and you may find yourself awake through the night, dreading and planning the event. Although some P.I.s do not mind a confrontation, most will be very nervous at the thought of ruining someone's life or getting into an argument with the person. Do not take your nervousness as a sign that you should not go through with firing: It is normal and is best ignored.

There is no easy way to fire someone. However, the more you organize and plan it, the smoother it will go. This is a good time to speak with a mentor whose talent with people and strength of character you admire. It might even help you to run through a scenario with a friend, colleague, or someone in Human Resources.

> I tried to get an undergraduate to leave, and it was a disaster! By the end of the summer, we had not successfully managed to teach him the principles behind running a restriction digest, even that 10x could be diluted to 1x! I tried to let him go—I sat down with him and said "This isn't working out, in another year you may be ready... ." He wasn't going to hear it, and I didn't have the heart to come out and just say he was fired. I had every intention of firing him...I had him do plasmid preps the rest of the summer.

Do not fire anyone in anger. Only fire someone after much thought. So you should plan in detail what you will say, and when you will say it—leave nothing to chance.

- **When?** Do it when no one else is around in the lab. In companies, Friday is a traditional time to fire someone, as it gives the person a chance to have the weekend to recover. However, others would suggest that this gives the person time to stew and feel even more resentful. Weekends are not times off in most labs anyway, so just try to find a time when not many people are around.

- **Where?** In your office. This is an official act, so do not try to make it casual or informal.

- *How?* Make yourself a script.

  "Tom, we've talked about what the requirements for this kind of research are. Over the past few weeks, we've decided on a few goals, none of which have been met. I don't think this is the job for you, and I am letting you go.

  I'm really sorry to do this, but I believe you will find a place where you can be much happier. I've spoken with the personnel office, and I have here this week's check, the last one will be sent to you. You have 2 more weeks, officially, but we can discuss an earlier day, if you'd like..."

Do not leave room for the person to think that there may be a second chance (unless there is). Be kind, but firm. This is not the time to blame: Just make it clear that (in the current correct way to phrase such things) there is not a good fit between the employee and the lab.

The announcement may be met with tears, with coldness, with sarcasm, or with great hostility. Stay calm, and do not rise to any challenges. If the person is exceptionally angry, or if there has been a history of disruptive behavior, ask for the keys immediately: If you do this, you may want to have someone from security present.

Have a plan, something the person should do next, such as cleaning out personal belongings from the bench and/or desk, but do not expect the person to clean and prepare for the next person who will inhabit the area. Lab personnel should leave behind:

- Lab notebooks.
- Protocol book (unless it is a personal copy).
- List of clones, cells, experiments in progress.
- Keys and key cards.
- I.D.
- Equipment and supplies.

What to do when you cannot fire someone

It can be exceedingly difficult to fire someone in the lab and you will have to work with the administration or with Human Services to do so: It may be impossible otherwise. And it may be impossible anyway. Institutional rules may just about prohibit it or political correctness might dictate that you would be ensnared in red tape forever. One investigator at a large state university was informed that he could not fire an employee who admitted to fraud, even though this was the second time the employee was found changing the hours records: In fact, it was *because* it was the second time he was caught that he could not be fired! The first time, the lab member was temporarily suspended. When he was caught the second time, the university argued that firing him would show prejudice because of the prior event. Listed below are several approaches that P.I.s have taken to get rid of an unwanted employee.

> *I tried to get rid of my first postdoc, but I was told that I couldn't, that you can't fire postdocs. I just had to wait out the end of his fellowship.*

- Simply grit your teeth, and wait out the time. This is endurable only if employees have their own money.

- Make life difficult for the individuals—not be anything but coldly polite, to effectively shun them.

- Offer (usually, an unspoken offer) to write a good recommendation if the person will leave. This is the approach of choice at large institutions, where you often cannot get rid of an employee until that person has another job.

P.I.s are disgusted by the dishonest recommendations that accompany some candidates—and the same P.I. might in desperation write an even more glowing recommendation to get this person out. In general, only the newly crowned P.I. will not inquire deeply into a recommendation, and other P.I.s almost seem to believe that it is an initiation rite to hire a terrible lab worker with a good letter of recommendation. Thus, many propagate this unethical practice and feel they have no choice.

Violence in the Workplace

CAN VIOLENCE BE PREDICTED?

Scientists are not thought of as being a violent group: Most people would assume that scientists are one of the more peaceful bunches of people around. Scientists themselves assume a calmness and steadiness of character in their colleagues, despite the fact that very few scientists have not encountered violent or hostile behavior during their training and working days.

Given the emotional nature of the work, the wear and tear on the ego, the competition, and the sometimes ephemeral nature of results, it is perhaps remarkable that violent behavior is not more widespread. Added to the mix is the clash of cultures, with the various expectations that might never be understood or met. In addition, in a career in which the rational brain is considered to be ascendant, emotional release is sometimes looked down upon, and long pent up emotions can finally explode.

In retrospect, most cases of violence at the workplace were not unexpected. In reconstructing the events, people admit that they "had a feeling," or were scared, or felt they should back off: From further analysis, there were obvious indications that violence was likely.

Even the most obvious warnings are often ignored. This is usually because people fear that intervention will bring the violence to the surface, or because administrators fear the legalities of possibly invading the person's civil liberties.

SCREENING FOR VIOLENCE IN THE HIRING PROCESS

"One of the best predictors of someone becoming violent is if he or she had a history of violent behavior," says workplace violence consultant Larry Chavez (Dube 2001). Most Human Resources departments will do a criminal background check, but violence among scientists is not always overt. Only by asking former employers and fellow workers can violence such as threats and stalkings be found.

Nearly half of the 1085 employers polled by the American Management Association ask applicants to complete one or more psychological tests (Onion 2001). Some employers claim great success, believing that the most aggressive employees can be recognized with some of the tests. However, others claim that, as for all tests, some people can see what the questions are trying to determine and can answer appropriately.

Check with Human Resources to see if looking for potential violence is part of the screening process, and if not, ask for advice about questions that you might use. Human Resources may be concerned with a possible violation of employee rights and may step back from possibly invasive questions. This is because those who commit violence at the workplace are often mentally ill, and psychological problems are considered disabilities under the American Disabilities Act (ADA). Testing is certainly not fine-tuned enough to distinguish out-of-control aggression from other mental illnesses.

The P.I. may be able to ask questions in context without being obvious or offensive. For example, you might ask what a head of the lab should do if the head of another lab hears of a result through a student and publishes the result first. Suggesting that a letter to the editor might be written is an appropriate answer, but suggesting a physical confrontation is not. But most people will have the intelligence and sense to get through an interview without giving away a propensity to violence.

With or without screening, the P.I. still needs to be able to recognize signs of potential trouble.

DISCERNING POTENTIAL VIOLENCE

> . ...people don't just "snap." There is a process as observable, and often as predictable, as water coming to a boil.
>
> DE BECKER (1997, P. 143)

There is of course no truly accurate prediction of the perpetrator of violence at work. However, if a person has more than a few of the following characteristics, the P.I. should be especially cautious (De Becker 1997, pp. 151–152):

- *Inflexibility.* Resists change and will not discuss ideas contrary to own.

- *Weapons.* Recently obtained a weapon. May have a weapons collection, likes to discuss weapons, or has an obsession with weapons.

- *Chronic anger.* Sullenness or depression.

- *Feelings of hopelessness.*

- *Identifies with other perpetrators of workplace violence.*

- *Coworkers are afraid or apprehensive about the person.*

- *Threatened, tried to intimidate, or manipulate coworkers or bosses.*

- *Paranoia.*

- *Reacts adversely to criticism.*

- *Blames others.* Does not accept responsibility for own actions.

- *Undertaken crusades, or one-man wars for a cause.*

- *Unreasonable expectations.*

- *History of filing unreasonable grievances.*

- *History of assaultive behavior or has had recent police encounters.*

- *Monitored the behavior, activities, performance, or comings and goings of other employees.*

- *Instigated and maintained contact with current employees after being fired.* More focused on the job just lost than on finding a new one.

DEFUSING VOLATILE SITUATIONS

A recent case at the University of Washington Medical Center points up the consequences of not believing in the potential of violence (Kelleher and Sanders 2000; Sanders 2000). A scientist and pathology resident, unable to find another job when his present residency was going to be terminated, embarked on weeks of paranoia, complaints, and outbursts of anger and was seen searching for a gun on the Internet. Other members of the department were certain that there would be violence, and went to the administration. The police were contacted, but when the resident repeatedly refused counseling, stated his right to own a gun, and maintained that he was fine, the police and administration said there was nothing else that could be done. The resident shortly afterward shot his mentor, a pathologist in the department, and then himself, killing both.

It is hard to blame any particular person for what many felt was inevitable. University administrators were trying to buy time, hoping that he could be eased out of the university to another place before his anger spilled over.

But as one expert on violence in the workplace says, "When dealing with a difficult and violently inclined employee, it is important to understand that time is on his side unless you act quickly. Management may correctly intuit that he will not go quietly, but the sooner in the process he is fired, the easier it will be. If you believe it will be hard to fire him now, you can be certain it will be even harder later" (De Becker 1997, pp. 150–151).

What is clear is that you, as the P.I., cannot abdicate responsibility and depend entirely on Human Resources or the administration or even the police to help you deal with potential violence. If you feel that a violent explosion is likely to happen and not enough is being done about it, do not concur and do nothing. Do not ignore your instincts or conclusions or those of other lab members: Do not allow your lab members to remain in danger because someone is afraid of a lawsuit. Send your people home, change the locks, and look for someone who really does know how to help, perhaps at a hospital or through the police.

With suspicions of the potential for violence. If you suspect a potential for violence, but the person has not done anything overt:

- Speak gently, determine whether there is a problem. These individuals may be suffering from stress or depression, which share some markers with the potential for violence, such as hopelessness and isolation. If there does not seem to be the potential for violence by the criteria listed, help or suggest counseling, as appropriate.

- If you believe there is a potential for violence, again suggest counseling. This does not mean you should cut the person loose and not try for resolution, but make sure that you and the person will have all the help you might need.

- Try to address the person's problems in a straightforward way. People feel desperate when they have no control and when no one is listening, and suppressed violence can be one way to deal with extreme frustration.

- Document your conversations.

With probability of the potential for violence

- Enlist the help of Human Resources immediately if you have tried to remedy any grievance the person has with you, but the situation has not changed.

- Speak with Security if the Human Resources department at your institution does not seem to be acting quickly or decisively enough.

- Consider the safety of other lab members when talking to Human Resources or Security.

- Do not engage in an argument with the person.

- Never show fear, even at threats.

With violence imminent. If the person seems out of control, hostile, is making threats, or has a weapon:

- Get everyone out of the lab. Have someone call Human Resources or Security, depending on the threat: If the person has a weapon, call Security immediately.

- If you can leave the area without putting lab members in danger, do so.

- If you are with the person, try to defuse the situation with conversation.

  Stay calm, and show no fear or anxiety.

  Listen to the aggrieved party carefully and respectfully and allow the person to talk freely (Chavez 1999).

  Give the person your full attention. Find a private place to sit, look the person in the eye, and show the same respect that you would show a visitor.

  Do not interrupt, argue, minimize the persons concerns, or try to rationalize anyone's actions.

CAN VIOLENCE BE PREVENTED?

Yes and no. Some situations are out of your control, such as a family member or a partner who comes into the lab to settle a score with someone who happens to be a member of the lab. But there are certainly conditions under which violence is more likely to occur, and here, you do have control.

- *Know your lab.* The lab culture and your relationships with the people in the lab are the best way to recognize and defuse violence before it explodes. In an atmosphere in which discrimination and sexual harassment are discouraged, and there is communication between P.I. and lab members, as well as among the lab members, potential violent behavior will be more readily recognized.

- *Be cognizant of changes in personality* in the people in your lab. If you know the personalities of your lab members, you will be better able to recognize any changes in their behavior, changes that may signal potential problems. Also be aware of changes in the lab dynamics, particularly when one member is being isolated from the others.

- *Be sure that all lab members have someone who they can turn to.* Depending on how you manage the lab, be sure that you, or a mentor, or someone in Human Resources—someone who will listen—is available to or is known by all lab members. It is important that all lab members feel that they have options and do not feel trapped and without an outlet.

RESOURCES

Angier N. 1988. *Natural obsessions. The search for the oncogene.* Houghton Mifflin, Boston.

Baldrige L. 1993. *Letitia Baldrige's new complete guide to executive manners.* Rawson Associates/ Macmillan Publishing, New York.

Beatty R.H. 1994. *High performance models. Interviewing and selecting high performers,* pp. 51–86. John Wiley & Sons, New York.

Belker L.B. 1997. *The first-time manager,* 4th edition. AMACOM Books, New York.

Brown W.S. 1985. *13 Fatal errors managers make and how you can avoid them.* Berkley Books, New York.

Chavez L.J. 1999. Defuse impending violence! (http://members.aol.com/hrtrainer/defuse.html)

Cooper R.K. and Sawaf A. 1997. *Executive E.Q. Emotional intelligence in leadership and organizations.* Grosset/Putnam, New York.

De Becker G. 1997. *The gift of fear.* Little, Brown and Company, New York.

Drucker P.F. 1966. *The effective executive.* Harper & Row, New York.

Dube J. 2001. Office Wars. *ABC News,* July 29. (http://www.abcNEWS.com)

Dziech B.W. and Weiner L. 1990. *The lecherous professor: Sexual harassment on campus,* 2nd edition. University of Illinois Press, Urbana.

Goleman D. 1995. *Emotional intelligence: Why it can matter more than I.Q.* Bantam Books, New York.

Guernsey L. 1999. What employers can view at work. *The New York Times,* Dec. 16, p. D9.

Hamlin S. 1988. *How to talk so people listen. The real key to job success,* pp. 1–20. Harper and Row. New York.

Harris J. and Brannick J. 1999. *Finding and keeping great employees.* AMACOM Books, New York.

Hasselmo N. 1990. Presidential statement and policy on sexual harassment. In *The lecherous professor: Sexual harassment on campus,* 2nd edition (ed. B.W. Dziech and L. Weiner). pp. 203–212. University of Illinois Press, Urbana.

Kelleher S. and Sanders E. 2000. Troubled resident's case left UW with quandary. *The Seattle Times,* July 5, pp. 1, 10.

Kevles D.J. 1998. *The Baltimore case: A trial of politics, science, and character.* W.W. Norton, New York.

Lanthes A. 1998. Management and motivation issues for scientists in industry. *Science's Next Wave,* Jan. 28, pp. 1–4. (http://nextwave.sciencemag.org)

Lynch F. 1995. *Draw the line: A sexual harassment-free workplace.* The Oasis Press, Grants Pass, Oregon.

Marsh S.R. 2000. *Negotiation styles in mediation.* (http://adrr.com/adr1/essayb/htm)

Michal-Johnson P. 1985. *Saying goodbye: A manager's guide to employee dismissal.* Scott, Foresman, Glenview, Illinois.

Nierenberg J. and Ross I.S. 1985. *Women and the art of negotiating.* Barnes and Noble Books, New York.

Onion A. 2001. Pinpointing violence: Researchers looking for ways to weed out violent workers. *ABC News,* Jan. 3, pp. 1–3. (http://abcNEWS.com)

Pacetta F. and Gittines R. 2000. *Don't fire them, fire them up: A maverick's guide to motivating yourself and your team.* Simon & Schuster, New York.

Ratey J.J. and Johnson C. 1997. *Shadow syndromes.* Bantam Books, New York.

Russo E. 2000. Harmony in the lab. *The Scientist* **14:** 18–19. (http://www.thescientist.com)

Sanders E. 2000. UW couldn't stop troubled doctor from buying gun. *The Seattle Times,* June 30, pp. 1–20.

Sanders E. and Kelleher S. 2000. E-mail told of troubled UW doctor. *The Seattle Times,* Oct. 18, pp. B1–B5.

Schloff L. and Yudkin M. 1992. *Smart speaking.* Plume, New York.

Stone F.M. 1999. *How to resolve conflicts at work: A take-charge assistant book.* AMACOM Books, New York.

Toropov B. 1997. *The complete idiot's guide to getting along with difficult people.* Alpha Books, New York.

Umiker W.O. 1996. *The empowered laboratory team. A survival kit for supervisors, team leaders, and team professionals.* American Society of Clinical Pathologists Press, Chicago.

University of Wisconsin, Madison. 2000. Sexual harassment information and resources: Guidelines and advice. (http://wwww.wisc.edu/edrc/sexualharassment/guide.html)

Wacker W., Taylor J., and Means H.W. 2000. *The visionary's handbook: Nine paradoxes that will shape the future of your business.* HarperBusiness, New York.

Weiss P. 1998. Don't even think about it (the cupid cops are watching). *The New York Times Magazine,* May 3, pp. 43–47.

Wheatley M.J. 1994. *Leadership and the new science. Learning about organization from an orderly universe.* Berrett-Koehler Publishers, San Francisco.

For the Long Run

As Your Job Changes...

EVOLUTION OF THE LAB

The lab is a place for the young, and returning there you feel young again: with the same longing for adventure, discovery, and the unexpected that you have at seventeen.

PRIMO LEVI IN THE PERIODIC TABLE
LEVI (1984, P. 198)

Adjourning to a table in the garden, Kosterlitz sat beside a greenish-looking fountain and ordered tea and hot cross buns. "When you are forty," he said, "you have to make a decision. One can be enthusiastic until then, especially if your teacher was. But then you have to think about the future. Will I be so successful that I will be accepted by the scientific community? If not, what shall I do? You can teach or work in industry. Scientists who have gone a little mad—like me—will continue doing research. I can't stop, but then I have been successful."

GOLDBERG (1988, P. 211)

A few years after starting a lab, your job will start to change. The lab will probably become bigger, and you will spend less and less time at the bench. You may be on the road more and more, giving seminars at other institutions and promoting the lab's work at meetings. Or you may be spending more time promoting your lab's work within the institution. The talks you give may no longer be concerned with data as much as with concepts. You may still write grants, but hopefully fewer, and for more money.

Self-reflection and self-knowledge seem to come easier and easier as you grow experienced. Your problem-solving abilities might be sharper or you might be feeling left out and inadequate as the younger scientists rise around you. You may be peaceful, or frustrated. The setting is the same as when you started, but the situation is completely different. It might be time for readjustment. As the job changes, you might have to change. And as you change, the lab will change further. The lab you are running after 5 years will probably be almost unrecognizable as the lab you started with.

BIG LAB, SMALL LAB

The size of the lab should change to be appropriate for the kind of science you are doing at the time. Most P.I.s feel that a medium-sized lab consisting of 8–12 people is the ideal, whereas a lab with about 5 people would be considered a small lab, 15–20 people a large lab, and more than 20 people a megalab. With a medium-sized lab, the science can be competitive but the atmosphere intimate, since the P.I. can still be in touch with each lab member.

If I had a fantastic idea, a great thing to do, the lab could afford to be smaller. I have to have other people so they also can think of ideas..

A lab with one or two people is too small for innovation, and most P.I.s work hard to get out of the one or two people stage of the early years. The P.I. must usually remain at the bench with this size lab, which is, of course, often very beneficial to the lab members, as they will get to work side-by-side with the P.I. and can learn a great deal about everything in the lab. This is a also a good initial size, good for that time when you are organizing yourself and trying to keep your feet on the ground. Most people, however, would think a lab permanently this small might find survival and happiness difficult.

I think the small lab model is very difficult to maintain. I would like to have trained more intermediate-level co-investigators and expanded to a larger lab model with specific specialties and projects. A larger lab is more difficult to run administratively (and has more potential for personnel and personality problems) but is probably more productive in the long run.

With 10 to 12 max, the ups and downs are leveled out...In a small lab, too much depends on the talents of individual members of the lab and the luck of their projects, while if it is a little bigger, someone will always be on a roll even if a few are struggling at the same time.

A small lab with five or six people is fairly easy to control. You will know about every project and still control each experiment. If one of your priorities is getting to know people and working closely with them, this is the perfect size.

A medium-size lab has many benefits, as it has what most P.I.s consider to be of great importance—critical mass. Many ideas are generated, many projects can be carried out, and the lab seems to run itself. With at least ten people, and multiple projects, you can allow a lab member to explore a new area and not be so worried about small failures.

But there are some pitfalls to a lab of ten or so people. It is harder to stay in touch with every person and every project. If you have a lab this big before you have learned to delegate to your lab personnel and to trust and depend on them, you will be overtaxed and in constant turmoil. If your funding is shaky, you have the additional worry about the futures of the people in the lab.

Around 8 is an ideal size. You need a good number to pick up a project when somebody leaves, and to get good meetings and discussions going.

There are few starting P.I.s who actively plan to have a large lab, with more than 15 people. Perhaps it is just too difficult to imagine running, when three people in the beginning can take so much time. Perhaps it is a lack of confidence. But most P.I.s who are successfully running a large lab got there gradually, with bigger and bigger ideas requiring more

With a smaller lab, you can spend more time in the lab. You can watch and make sure nothing goes wrong.

and more people, over the course of years. With this many people, big science can be done. Success and funding allow a lab to grow this big. But it is not always good. A large lab in a small place may run out of resources or incur enormous resentment among other department members.

> *When you have a lab as small as mine, you have to keep moving, you have to keep finding new ideas and directions, you don't have the luxury to let things go...*

As you look at other labs around you for a model for your own lab, remember that small labs cannot do what the big, established labs can. You can use a big lab as a model to project where you would like your lab to be in 5 or 10 years, but you cannot expect to replicate the workings of a ten-person lab with just yourself and a technician.

> *I actually really like everyone in the lab now, which is good, but I wish there were more of them. I guess I do want to be an emperor, if only over 10 people or so. Or maybe, to be more honest, I would prefer to be in a place where a group of 5 or 6 is not a sign of shame.*

More experienced P.I.s caution not to let your lab grow too fast. Only in retrospect does a lab personnel growth rate seem too fast to the P.I. In the early days, most P.I.s have more ideas than people and are desperate to start moving. The rapid acquisition of people, however, can wreck havoc on a 5-year plan, adding a scale of work and a worry of fund-raising that interferes greatly with doing good science. More people do not necessarily make research easier.

> *The lab got too big, too fast. And it was stupid to get larger at the expense of quality.*

BENCHTIME

> *When I stopped doing experiments with my own hands—partly because other concerns had become too distracting to allow concentrated work at the bench, and partly because new techniques had made my own rather limited skills obsolete—teaching became even more important to me. Especially in microbiology, in which experiments tend to last for a few hours and be completed in a single day, the day's structure is provided by the routine of planning, setting up, and performing experiments, often one each day. Deprived of this routine I would have felt lost except for the alternative routine of class preparation, lectures, examinations, and grading.*
>
> LURIA (1984, P. 130)

Leaving the bench prematurely is one of the biggest mistakes a new P.I. can make. As a beginning P.I., it is difficult to resist the pressure of deskwork. But you are your own best investment, and taking the lab's strongest member away from the bench makes no sense.

After a few years, the need for you to do benchwork may no longer be pressing if you have enough qualified people. Your hands are not your most important commodity any longer. Over time, the techniques that you used have been modified or supplanted. The people in the lab probably know more than you do about the nitty gritty of doing an experiment: Instead of being the expert, you have hired expertise.

When I started out, I was much more inclined to be friendly and interactive at a personal level with people in the lab. The lab was small, and usually had 2 technicians who were very young, a student or two, a postdoc or two, and I was at the bench. I was in there as one of them, doing experiments, and physically working in the same way. I could more fundamentally understand what people were going through in working long hours and having experiments that don't work, and now I tend to forget that.

Accept that, as the lab grows, you will spend more time away from the bench. You might bitterly bemoan the fact that you have less time at the bench, and swear that all you really want is to do experiments. Unless you have, deliberately or reluctantly, maintained a very small lab, it is unlikely you will ever get back to the bench for any long-term work.

Many P.I.s, however, remain at the bench in an accessory role. Some like to initiate risky projects themselves and see if a project is feasible before turning it over to someone else. Some prepare reagents that have been requested by other labs. If you really work at the bench, this can be a fantastic morale booster for everyone. It will give you wonderful insights into the interaction among lab members. But if your lab bench is merely a reminder of your intention to do benchwork, it will soon be a lab joke. Worse is the sense of guilt the unused bench probably instills in you. Be honest about your role at the bench. If you are in the lab infrequently, turn your bench over to better use.

I sometimes still do benchwork for particular projects, and to help visiting scholars. As a role model, it lets people know that hard work is expected.

EVOLVING MANAGERIAL STYLE

The move into management brings with it a new set of companions who have not shared the experience of exploration and who speak a very different language. Moreover, as a boss, you experience subtle changes in your relationship with those around you. The usual hostility to authority remains largely hidden. Most of your associates seem to become increasingly agreeable; they say yes much more often. Conditioned to skepticism and argumentativeness in your colleagues, you may be pleased at this evidence that you have apparently become more consistently right about all sorts of things. But these early signs of the corrupting effects of power bring to the scientist turned administrator, in his more candid moments, a sense of lost innocence.

HOAGLAND (1990, P. 175)

The change in lab size alone will lead to changes in the way you deal with the people in your lab. But the experience you have garnered should change your style even more. After a few years, you know what works, what projects are likely to be funded, and which students will probably excel. Especially if your lab is bigger, many P.I.s find that adding another layer of management is the most effective way to run the lab. You have less time in the lab and may have more funds for salaries. Secretaries can become administrative assistants, taking on more of your administrative duties.

You may have a lab manager, someone who takes on the day-to-day technical and/or personnel issues of running the lab. Some P.I.s can create an independent position, elevating a postdoc to a researcher or assistant professor level.

If you are not happy with your style, consider hiring a personal coach. A personal coach can make suggestions about organizing the lab, dealing with difficult lab people, and finding the right software and can help you stay focused and motivated. Coaching can be done in person or over the phone, and you could use someone to help you get through a short-term crisis, such as having to fire someone or doing a thorough reorganization of the lab. The cost will be several hundred dollars a month for weekly 30- or 45-minute sessions. You can find a personal coach in the yellow pages or over the Internet by searching for "personal coach."

Personnel quality

In the late sixties and early seventies, (Seymour) Benzer gathered a remarkable group of graduate and postdoctoral students around him—Benzer's Raiders. His friend Francis Crick told me that without Benzer's enormous success in molecular biology he could never have drawn students into such a wildly improbably research program.

WEINER (2000, P. 37)

The more successful you are, the better-quality people you will be able to hire. In fact, people will come to you, and you will be in the fortunate position of being able to choose the best. Lab personnel will also be more capable because you are more experienced in selecting good people and in nurturing them once they are in your lab.

The loosening of control

Many new P.I.s would like to be more easygoing, but feel that they cannot afford a hands-off style in the beginning of their careers. Deadlines for tenure and promotion lie ahead, and there is a need to get papers out as soon as possible. Funds are limited, and the P.I. may not be able to allow people to tinker or dream without plans or to invest in innovative techniques and equipment. Success and experience are good teachers. Eventually, the P.I. realizes that good people can fly on their own.

I don't take things as personally as I did when I first started. With each publication, I feel a bit of weight removed from my shoulders, and can relax more. Of course, this is counterbalanced with the fact that I am more in tune with the field, and feel more competitive: Competitiveness is replacing the struggle for survival. Overall, though, I feel easier and can relax my vigilance.

Actually, as the lab gets bigger, it is not possible to spend the same amount of time on each person's results. Another reason that lab heads release some control of day-to-day life in the lab is that they often find lab personnel able to share responsibilities. Sometimes, it is an actual lab manager who takes over day-to-day problems and tedium. Sometimes, it is just the years of experience that make the students,

Now I am far less involved with people. I tend not to deal with personal problems at all. If someone does have a personal problem I refer them to the requisite agency that can help them. If someone has a psychological problem, there are counseling services available. If someone has a financial problem, there are other services.... I personally do not speak to them anymore about the personal problems. I do for acute problems, but I wouldn't touch a chronic problem.

postdocs, and technicians able to think through experiments, write papers, and share the worry about funding and the future.

Not all P.I.s will relax with time. For some, the increased demands of being on the road and away from the lab create an anxiety that can only be alleviated for them by increasing rules and regulations. But this can really go a long way to making a lab dysfunctional. People yearn to be independent and stopping this causes unhappiness.

WORKING WITH A LAB MANAGER

An amazing asset is a good lab manager who can be an administrator, a scientist, or both. Few starting P.I.s can find or fund a lab manager. Most lab managers come about through the passage of time in the lab, but they are not specifically hired as such. For example, a postdoc may find that running a lab is an enjoyable experience, without the pressure of always writing grants and will agree to stay with you as a lab manager. Sometimes a P.I. is fortunate enough to partner with a research assistant professor or another highly trained scientist, who is willing to share the responsibilities of the P.I. More commonly, a technician will take on more responsibility over time and become the most experienced person in the lab and the de facto manager of day-to-day life in the lab.

The people that I have now are more mature. The clinical fellows are older, at a different place in their lives, more serious, and that has made it easier. They themselves have had some experience in managing people, and they understand some of the problems and are more inclined to help me out.

Do not let the luxury of a good lab manager stop you from knowing what is going on in the lab, at least, in the early days. Unless you have a firm arrangement that you do not want to be involved in the personalities of the lab, do not automatically let the lab manager handle personnel problems.

Now I'm getting good people, but they were terrible for the first two years.

Mapping out your individual territories will most likely be a long-range project that requires a lot of tinkering. You must also be alert to the possibility that all of the tinkering in the world will not fix the differences in your personalities or working styles.

Not everyone welcomes the idea of a lab manager. Some P.I.s do not like the loss of control or the feeling that they are no longer the heartbeat of the lab. It is true that a lab manager gone bad can destroy a lab more quickly than any other person. It is also true that this person can bring back a joy of science that you thought you would never have again.

LETTING GO OF LAB MEMBERS

When the first person that worked in the lab decides to leave, P.I.s may have more trouble cutting the apron strings than they imagined. One day, your favorite student, your first student, will come to you and suggest that it is time to finish up and leave the lab. If, instead of feeling elation, you feel betrayed, know that you are not alone. You may feel panicked—the lab cannot possibly get along without this person! You may feel angry—here you have poured into this lab member all the training and time you could, and now this person is going to take everything away!

The departure of a good lab member *will* change the lab, and unless the departing person was a troublemaker, lab life might seem a bit low. There is cause for celebration, but it is a bittersweet celebration. But in an amazingly short amount of time, you and the rest of the lab members will readjust.

Keep in touch with the departed lab member, in the short term and long term. It is good for the lab, because seeing the result of effort in research is very inspiring to the other lab members, and keeping in touch builds the idea of a family. It is good for the person who is leaving to be able to touch base while venturing into a new life. It is wonderful for you to share in the success and to enjoy the lab member's growth into a colleague.

FOSTERING INDEPENDENCE

Over four years, Hughes had fought his way to a measure of independence while working under Kosterlitz's scrutiny; he was grateful, at least, that Kosterlitz did not tinker with his equipment or hover over his shoulder and nag, as he did with others in the Unit.

GOLDBERG (1988, P. 20)

Although one of the goals of most P.I.s is to produce independent scientists, the definition of independence may vary. For example, to some P.I.s, independence means that the lab worker conceives of an idea, does the experiments, and writes up the papers. To other P.I.s, independence may mean that the lab worker comes up with the plan to meet the P.I.'s research goals.

Promotions

Be careful not to promote people as a reward only: Promote on the basis of competence for the new responsibilities. Many a monster has been created by a P.I.'s desire for a colleague, for the inability to do a job seldom stops a person from expecting all the perks of a job and continued advancement. Perhaps no scenario causes more resentment in the lab than the undeserved elevation of a lab member to a more independent position. Not only are there issues of resentment among the other lab members, but the promotee tends to blame the P.I. for any problems with the job.

Allowing others to give your talks

During their training, postdocs and students will present talks at your institution, local get-togethers and hopefully, at national meetings. Their talks will usually be on their research alone, and will be very specific. At the same time, you will be giving talks on broader subjects, encompassing some or all of the projects of the lab. It may come about that a senior postdoc is working in collaboration with others or has taken over supervision of more junior members in the lab. The postdoc might also have the perspective and vision to put all of the lab's projects in context with each other and with the field. If so, that person is ready to represent you at meetings.

I have given him the opportunity to write an RO1—it is time for him to have his own lab. I have been sending other lab members in my stead to international meetings so they can get exposure...I tried to do it earlier. It was done for me. But people were very offended if I was invited and someone showed up instead. The better-known scientists are the draw cards. If you tell them you're not coming, they ask someone else instead. If you say you are sending someone for you, they get offended. What I've done recently is to ask that these people's names be put on the program. I say that I have a conflicting appointment and that this person could do the job better than me, anyway.

There are no rules concerning this passing of the mantle, and the P.I. must tread carefully to avoid insulting anyone. Some organizers of meetings may feel that you are not taking them seriously enough, and you must convince them of the quality of the person speaking. You must convince them that you are not sending the second best. At the same time, you must keep your own career afloat and keep yourself in the public eye to maintain interest and funding in your work.

Sending out manuscripts from your lab, without your name

Nusslein-Volhard published her Basel research alone, without Gehring's name on it. She was the only Gehring postdoc to do so. She wrote Holden that she had sent a small article about Drosophila *laboratory techniques without even telling him. As laboratory director, he was entitled to appear on all his postdocs' publications. She said Gehring didn't understand her major article about the fruit-fly mutant with a tail at each end. But she also said he was gracious enough to let her publish it on her own. He said the work was hers alone and didn't need his name.*

CHRISTIANE NUSSLEIN-VOLHARD
(MCGRAYNE 1998, P. 395)

With time, especially if you have a large lab, you may no longer conceive and keep in touch with every project in the lab. There may be senior lab members who have their own projects, and there may be independent lab members with their own funding. There will be projects you know very little of, and one day, a senior lab member will write up one of those projects and request that your name not be included as an author.

So here comes the dilemma: It is your lab, for you provide the place and the inspiration for the work. Perhaps you did not do any experiments or even edit the paper, but you discussed the results over many a lunch. Even if the lab member has funding, clearly, your own funding still provides the backbone of support. You have created the infrastructure for the research. You still need funding, and recognition, and continued results to maintain and better your own position. Yet you have a commitment to foster independence.

Of course, at institutions with an institutional hierarchy, you may not have the option to allow someone from your lab to publish a paper without you as author. It is also a situation that probably will not arise until you have been a P.I. of a large and successful lab for at least 10 years. You should have a game plan in effect before this happens, and you should never be so out of touch with the research in the lab that this could happen without your knowledge.

LETTING PROJECTS LEAVE THE LAB

My advisor had shown a great deal of interest in what I wanted to work on when I left the lab; I took this for mentoring (ah, sweet naiveté!). However, I realized that that this interest was based on retaining "my" project for future postdocs and graduate students in my advisor's laboratory!

CAVEMAN (2000, P. 26, IN
POLITICS IN SCIENCE, PP. 26–27)

Long before postdocs get ready to leave the lab, the question of what, if any, project they will take with them must be addressed. This kind of decision is usually an evolving one and is done on a case-by-case basis. There are P.I.s that make clear, always, that no one will take anything away, and some who let anyone take anything and everything. But most accept that in some situations, projects *will* be taken away. Below are some considerations about giving away projects or vital reagents:

- *Other lab members who are working on the same or related projects.* This is the most important consideration, for your primary responsibility is to the people still in the lab. If a present lab member may lose priority on a project, or might be scooped, then a working relationship must be negotiated with all participants, with your present lab member protected. Yes, this will be very difficult.

- *The future of the ex-lab member.* If a lab member leaves with part of a project, you may both agree to remain in collaboration. This, however, is much more difficult for the lab member than for you, for the lab member needs to establish an independent research project.

- *Competition.* Competition with a postdoc who has left is not necessarily an adversarial issue; it may just mean that you and the lab member agree to work within the same field. Few postdocs would engage in an adversarial competition, for they are the ones least likely to have the resources to be successful. Also, a declaration of war would most likely mean the end of letters of recommendation, as well as difficulties in getting grants from others in the field.

322 / As Your Job Changes...

Still, some postdocs feel very strongly that they developed the project and have the right to take the project away. As P.I., you have the power to make this decision, but you should be working on solving this problem before it occurs.

The decision to let a postdoc take reagents when leaving a lab depends on the collaboration/competition agreement you have made. Some lab workers will feel strongly entitled to take reagents that they have made. Your general philosophy should be known before such decisions must be made. These decisions are basically the same as project decisions, for the impact on you and the other lab members is the same.

KEEPING CONNECTIONS WITH DEPARTED LAB MEMBERS

Building a network of scientists who have left the lab is one of the greatest pleasures in running a lab. It is personally satisfying, and many P.I.s find that true friendship can flourish only after a favorite has left the lab. As collaborators and equals, you can find the kind of scientific relationship that you might have missed from your own postdoc days. Staying in touch is another way to enhance the productivity of your lab. Lab members have a role model and feel a connection not just to the lab, but to the network of science as well.

Maintaining Enthusiasm

SUCCESS IS NOT ALWAYS ENOUGH

I was pleased by my meteoric rise to fame but uneasy about how readily one could become an "expert." Indeed, it was this sense of having become superficially successful without much effort that impelled me to get more deeply involved in some solid biochemistry.

HOAGLAND (1990, P. 48)

Most faculty seeking tenure and promotion to associate professor, and later promotion to (full) professor, fail to realize that, despite the joy, relief, and sense of accomplishment that comes with these successes, there are difficulties. Faculty often feel initially directionless. Having achieved the goal they were so adamantly pursuing, they are also left feeling uncertain about what to pursue next.

MALONE (1999)

Many P.I.s find that their idea of success changes radically. In the first 5 years or so, success is measured in the number of scientific kudos—papers, grants, and promotions. P.I.s later tend to measure success by the success of present and alumni lab members: P.I.s take pleasure in the achievements of the extended "family," and the integration of their family members into the scientific world.

> I suspect that most scientists who seem successful by objective measures are subjectively disappointed in themselves—and hence driven to keep achieving. I've been moderately successful in terms of funding, promotion, productivity, etc., but often feel unsuccessful compared to those with larger lab operations, bigger reputations, National Academy membership, and so on up the ladder.

Later still, many P.I.s also incorporate personal happiness into their definition of success. It is very, very difficult for some people to do this, as altering their original and sometimes naive dreams may feel suspiciously like settling for second best, Yet most people can and do accommodate a merging of their new and old images of success. What is shocking for P.I.s is how empty success can feel, especially when defined by the external rewards of achievement.

TURNING DISAPPOINTMENT INTO OPPORTUNITY

There are, in general, no surprises in the outcome of promotions and tenure. Long before the official proclamation is made, the data are there for you to examine. And it is in your best interests to do so. Be prepared for the following:

- As soon as you arrive in a job, find out what the requirements are for promotion or tenure. Some P.I.s do not do this, trusting that hard work and scientific success will be enough to assure advancement. This is not true, for each department or institution has its own idea of what is important. Make no assumptions.

- Seek people out who have been through the process: Solicit their opinions, listen to their experience. There may be a committee whose job it is to keep people informed of their progress, but it is not enough to simply rely on the official view.

- Administrations come and go, so do not pin all your hopes on someone's assurance that the promotion is yours.

- Always have options in mind, even vague options. Know what you would do with your research and life both with a promotion and without a promotion. Thinking positively when going for a goal is vital, but it is also important to know that a particular success is only one in a range of possibilities for you.

Listed below are some ideas for dealing with a negative outcome:

- Not all refusals of a promotion are a vote of no confidence. There are many political reasons why someone might be denied a promotion. The most common is that it is "too early," and this often has more to do with the institutional culture and the egos of the decision makers than anything you have or have not done.

- Do not make a hasty decision in a huff. If you do not get a particular promotion, do not immediately decide to leave, no matter what. Accept offers of help or advice and seek further advice before you make a move.

- Do not let a negative decision affect your sense of self worth. You may have to work very hard at keeping your faith in yourself intact, but you must. Yes, you will have to look at yourself critically, but do not look at yourself too harshly.

- View this as a chance to find your ideal job.

When I didn't teach, I felt like my job was only to write papers and get grants: a discouraging image in the long run. When I started teaching I felt more like an academic and it was good for enhancing skills that I tend to overlook: long-term thinking, what is really the important question for non-specialists, what are the common mistakes that we all make in reading—which helps immensely in writing grants!

Keep the lab going even if you find out that you will not be getting tenure or an important promotion. You must prepare your lab as well as yourself for your next move. Your lab members' interpretation of the event will depend on you, as long as you are being realistic: If you act as if the loss of a promotion does not matter, you will lose credibility. In addition, everyone in the lab needs to know what this means for them.

Before you tell the lab members of your decision, have an idea of your own plans, and what you can do for each lab member. Have two plans for each person: One if they choose to stay with you and one if they want to leave. Do not be judgmental about a lab member's decision not to stay.

INSPIRATION

People often ask why I switched from a field as obscure as metallothionein research to one as controversial as homosexuality. The answer is the same that most scientists give for why they do what they do: a combination of curiosity, altruism, and ambition (especially curiosity, both personal and scientific), combined with one more factor—boredom. After twenty years of doing science, I had learned quite a bit about how genes work in individual cells, but I knew little about what makes people tick.

HAMER AND COPELAND (1994, P. 25)

Since science is what draws most P.I.s to the job in the first place, staying involved in research is the best thing you can do for yourself and your lab. Most P.I.s have found that it is exciting to venture into another field, rather than delving deeper into the work the lab already focuses on.

You could attend a meeting in another field but that can be alienating. Reading can leave you flat. It is through talking with people, and working with your hands, that you are most likely to rekindle that feeling that drew you to the lab in the first place.

A lot of the time, the more established faculty feel withdrawn, because they don't know some of the "new science." They can't get grants. They don't want to admit it to anyone, so they withdraw a bit from science, they feel worthless.

SABBATICALS

Academic and some industry jobs offer the chance to take time away from the institution with pay. This time is a resource that can be used in a number of ways:

- *Use this time to remain in the lab,* working at the bench, freed of administrative tasks and teaching. This can start out feeling like postdoc camp, but it often ends with the same frustrations that the "normal" job had.

- *Go to another lab to learn a new technique,* or to explore a new field, often with a collaborator. This option gives a great deal of satisfaction.

- *Take the time to embark on a personal project,* such as travel, volunteer work, building an addition on a house, anything that recharges the batteries. This option is more unusual, as it is hard for most scientists to stay away from the lab, altogether.

Set limited goals for any sabbatical. Plan a series of experiments, not the decimation of an entire field. Few sabbaticals turn out to be as wildly successful as the harassed investigator dreams it might be. If you failed to write the ten papers you planned or did not reorganize your files or learn and execute a new technique, be gentle with yourself. If you had a rest, and can charge in with fresh enthusiasm, consider the sabbatical to have been successful.

Good and bad effects of your absence on the lab. The effect on the lab will depend on how absent your absence really is, and how established the lab is. No matter how egalitarian the lab may be, some people will be delighted that the boss is gone, and some will feel lost. You want those members happy that you are gone to continue working from self-motivation and the insecure members to feel confident. The good effect is a growth in independence and confidence on the part of each person. The bad effect a P.I. might fear is that projects founder and lab members, especially junior ones, lose confidence.

Remain in contact with every member of the lab. Do not funnel all your communication through one person in the lab. You may choose to have more contact with a senior member of the lab, who has been left in charge, but it would be a mistake to let this completely substitute for your interaction with other lab members.

Keep on top of every project in the lab. Depending on money and time zones and personal inclination, you can choose between the phone or e-mail or even occasional visits, to keep up with the progress in the lab. Requesting a weekly e-mail update from each person is a good start: Reading and responding to each update are needed to make the updates effective. You must continue to lead, even at a distance.

Having a senior scientist who is on sabbatical in the lab can be the culmination of a wonderful collaboration. It can extend and strengthen a network between fields and revitalize your own interest in thinking about science. Although many of your lab members may be hesitant to intellectually challenge the boss, the scientist on sabbatical may have no intellectual or social reasons to hold back, and you may be stimulated anew. Other lab members may also be as stimulated by a more senior scientist. This is a chance to have another expert in the lab and another potential role model and mentor.

It is as important to assess the character and suitability of the potential sabbatical visitor as carefully as you would for any new person coming to the lab. In a way, it is more important to have someone who can get along well with the others for, although the position is a temporary one, the impact that such a potential role model can make on the lab is immense. It must be someone who sees being in your lab as a two-way street, who is as willing to share knowledge as much as to learn.

Picking a project may be the most difficult part of having a sabbatical scientist. Unless there for a specified project—which is a good idea—this person may be seen by the lab as someone coming to take techniques away. This is something that must be discussed before the sabbatical.

Before the person has been there very long, you should discuss arrangements about future collaborations, or reagents that are generated with the sabbatical visitor's help. Once the person is in your lab, treat this new person as you would any other. It might be harder to integrate a sabbatical visitor into the lab, as the differences in rank and age and experience might make the lab workers slow to relax. Treating the relationship as a collaboration and the person as a member of the team will help to set the standard of interaction.

YOUR STRESS AND TENSION

Nusslein-Volhard thinks she inherited mild tendencies toward manic-depression, a condition that involves swings between elevated and depressed moods. "Manic-depressive is probably what I am, not in a pathological (clinical) sense, but tendency-wise." Whatever the reason, as Anderson discovered, when Nusslein-Volhard was in a good mood, everyone else was too. "She could be the most charming person in the universe. When she was in a bad mood, she dragged everyone else down with her."

CHRISTIANE NUSSLEIN-VOLHARD
NOBEL PRIZE IN PHYSIOLOGY OR MEDICINE 1995
(MCGRAYNE 1998, P. 401–402)

Stress and tension are part and parcel of the P.I.'s job, as it is for everyone else in the lab. Of course, you will probably try to reduce the causes of stress and tension as much as you can. But it is not always possible, and you may find that you actually crave some tension, that stress pushes you to finish that last review, prepare that series of lectures. But only up to a point. Stress will have negative effects after a certain point and will probably prevent you from working effectively. If you have several of the negative reactions described below (National Mental Association 1999), you should take steps to reduce or control tension before it adversely affects you or your interactions with other lab members.

- Do minor problems and disappointments upset you excessively?

- Do the small pleasures of life fail to satisfy you?

- Are you unable to stop thinking about your worries?

- Do you feel inadequate or suffer from self-doubt?

- Are you constantly tired?

- Do you experience flashes of anger over situations that used to not bother you?

- Have you noticed a change in sleeping or eating patterns?

- Do you suffer from chronic pain, headaches, or backaches?

You must determine your personal tolerance level for stress and try to live within those limits.

- ***Be realistic about what you can do.*** If you feel overwhelmed, change your schedule.

- ***Do not expect perfection.*** Look at difficult situations as puzzles, but not necessarily as something you have to completely fix.

- *Visualize the end results of stressful situations.* Figure out how to manage them more successfully. The more exactly you can pin down what causes tension, the easier it is to solve that problem.

- *Triage!* Take one step at a time.

- *Do not be chronically critical* of colleagues or lab members.

- *Give in sometimes.* Choose your battles.

- *Take care of yourself physically.* Exercise, eat well, get enough sleep.

- *Know yourself psychologically.* Know whether it is home problems, financial worries, or work tensions that are making you tense.

Depression is a common response to chronic stress. In such cases, alleviating the source of stress can remove the depression. However, depression can also arise without an obvious cause. It can be a medical situation that cannot be ignored. It is often easier to recognize depression or other disorders in someone else than in yourself. Part of the disease is to deny that there is a problem. If someone suggests to you that you are acting depressed, do not just brush that person off. See someone. Some people are more comfortable doing this outside the work situation, worrying that the taint associated with mental illness might prejudice chances for promotion.

BURNOUT

Traditionally, companies have viewed personal life as competing with work life...many people equate long working hours with loyalty and productivity. Scientists, in particular, often measure dedication to their work by how single-minded they are, which may be gauged by what they sacrifice to their experimentation. They tend to view overworking as a badge of achievement.

EDWARDS (1999A)

Stress and burnout can be likened to fever and pneumonia. Similarly, the stress accompanying burnout is harmful and must be reduced, but focusing solely on stress does not negate the underlying causes of burnout.

POTTER (1998)

What does burnout feel like? Work you once thought was meaningful becomes boring or frustrating. Instead of enthusiasm, you feel depression and anxiety, perhaps even anger. When burnout occurs, it wreaks havoc on your ability to do a job. Your self-confidence is likely to suffer, as you feel that you cannot do the job well.

No matter how much you love the lab—and especially if you have loved it passionately—you may suffer burnout. Typically, this occurs somewhere between the ages of 35 and 50, when the fuss and clamor of establishing yourself are over and your career projectory is clear. It may happen more than once, and in bouts: It can happen whether you are male or female, successful or unsuccessful. It may happen gradually: You may realize that work is not as fulfilling as it once was, that you are not as happy as you were 5 years before, or that you are thinking more about your new kayak than about the great new results that your student just showed you. Or it can come with a sudden, sinking realization.

Reasons for burnout

One book has identified three dimensions of burnout: exhaustion, cynicism, and ineffectiveness (Maslach and Leiter 1997). Below are two of many reasons for burnout.

- *Misalignment with the laboratory culture.* Burnout is always more likely when there is a major mismatch between the nature of the job and the nature of the person who does the work. Misalignment with the culture may be on small or large issues. You may have a family, but the department expects long weekend hours: You may be eager to work nights and weekend, but find that you are the only one there. Other issues are those of teamwork versus independence, or secrecy versus openness.

- *Lack of control.* Scientists may especially feel the deleterious effects of powerlessness, for many enter science because it allows them to be in control. No matter what position they have, people in research are able to regulate their own time to some extent, and suppression of choices tends to be the ultimate insult. Feeling a lack of control is something that you must investigate immediately, and act on immediately. It usually comes from a situation that is not going to go away by itself, so you must remedy it yourself.

Preventing burnout

Anything you do to relieve stress will decrease the chance of burnout catching up with you. Therefore, managing your time and keeping track of your priorities can help prevent burnout. Another cause of burnout is having too much to do: Resetting this so that you are not always feeling that you will never catch up will help. To relieve stress and prevent burnout:

- *Make your peace with bureaucracy.* Go along with it or leave, but spending energy to fight it will leave you angry and drained.

- *Do not compromise your values.* Find a way to work in a way and for what you believe in.

- *Keep your skills updated.* Do not feel paralyzed because you feel left behind in a field.

- *Invest in your personal life.* Burnout is intensified when the job that is bothering you is all that you have.

> *When my daughter died, I said, this is it. I decided that science should be fun, and I would only work on things that were interesting...no more incremental science, no more doing things only to get grants and to please constituents to get more money to do what I don't want. Life is too short.*

Recovering from burnout

You do not necessarily need to switch jobs to reignite your work passion: Manipulating your time to give you a better chance to do what you want to do may be a satisfying enough change. For example, if you love discussing research with lab members and want more time to do this, find ways to cut your teaching load for a semester or hire more office help to deal with the paperwork that may flummox you daily.

Get out of your own patterns! You may have been writing a certain kind of paper and doing a set kind of research—now, take risks, make changes. Learn how to communicate better, try reading journals again, write a grant on a new topic. You have nothing to lose, nothing you would not lose anyway if you stop caring.

Do not let your cynicism affect the lab. You may feel "been there, done that," but do not allow your lack of enthusiasm to infect everyone. This can cause a self-perpetuating circle of doubt that can cripple everyone in the lab and worsen your own negative feelings.

Career Choices

CHANGING JOBS

In 1967, I was offered the position of Vice President in Charge of Research of Burroughs Wellcome Co. It was not a post I had sought, but my experience had suggested that a scientist was much better able to support the interests of working scientists than were administrators who got science second hand.

GEORGE H. HITCHINGS, JR.
(FRÄNGSMYR AND LINDSTEN 1993, P. 474)

There are gifted teachers who are inactive in research, as well as accomplished researchers who are dreadful teachers; but the best teachers are those for whom inquiry and communication are inextricably linked.

VERMEIJ (1997, P. 247)

It is not easy to determine whether you are happy or unhappy with your job. Even the best career and the best choice for you will feature times of frustration, depression, and longing for another existence.

- Distinguish between an acute and a chronic problem: Is there a temporary change that has occurred that has reduced your job satisfaction or are you unhappy with a situation that cannot be changed?

- Are you unhappy with a particular aspect of the laboratory or with the entire job?

- Are there parts of the day that you look forward to or do you dread the whole day?

- Are there particular people you do not want to be around? Or do you dislike the entire way in which you interact with people?

- Are the things about your job that appeal to you the most, the same things that are objectively the most important part of your job? If you have been hired for teaching, but find the research much, much more compelling, you should look around for a shift in responsibilities, and perhaps for a new job.

   Keep an open mind about changing or adapting your job. You may find that there are certain parts of your job that appeal to you more than others. It may be that you feel exhilarated teaching a class, or writing a grant, or helping students find

331

labs to work in—any one of the hundreds of components of your job as P.I. It may just be the thought of one particular aspect of your job that gets your blood boiling.

MOVING THE LAB

Most P.I.s move the lab at least once during their careers. If the first few years of running a lab have gone well, there will be perhaps more opportunities to pick and choose than there were for that first job. You will know more clearly what you want, and how to negotiate for it.

The first stage of a job hunt should not be obvious to anyone in your lab. First of all, because often the only way to get a raise or a promotion from your present institution is to show a bigger offer from another institution, P.I.s will go on job searches for jobs they do not intend to take. This institutionalized waste of time means that no one's radar will normally be alerted in the beginning of a job search.

For valid job searches, most initial explorations will appear to be routine seminars and come to nothing after preliminary negotiations. You will visit a company or university to give a talk and will return in a day or so. You will receive many phone calls and will make even more, trying to get as much information and advice as possible. But when you go for the first return trip to further investigate an offer or an opportunity, people in your lab will start to talk and unease will settle in.

Tell lab members before you tell the rest of your department. Job negotiations will probably take at least 1 year. After you deal with the place you are going to, you must then negotiate with your present employer about the transfer of equipment, money, and personnel. Lab heads do not want to tell lab members right away, as the air becomes thick with uncertainty, and people may decide that they do not even want to take the chance of moving to the new lab. But it is unethical to withhold knowledge that will impact on each lab member's life. It would also be unethical to take on new students or postdocs if you know you are leaving before they could finish their term with you. The logistics of timing for the move must be considered.

- *The best time for you.* The best time for some P.I.s centers around the best time for the family to make the move: This is usually during summer or winter break, a time that also works for students in the lab. Your timing may also be based on departmental tasks such as teaching.

- *The best time for lab personnel.* It will be extremely difficult to accommodate each person in the lab. You will probably only have a maximum of 6 months in which to be flexible, so the most you could do is to remain for the time it would take a finishing-up postdoc or student to complete a series of critical experiments. For those who will not be moving with you, but must stay at the institution, find a solid mentor and lab.

- *Taking people with you.* Any student or postdoc who moves with you is likely to lose months of work time while the lab is first getting up and running. So it is better to only move with people who intend to spend several years with you.

SWITCHING CAREERS

Many P.I.s have moved from industry or academia, or vice versa, once or several times in their careers. For many, the lifestyle associated with academia or industry is more compatible with their own lives at particular times, and they have moved to accommodate this.

Established programs can ease transitions. The Preparing Future Faculty program, for example, is a national program that gives aspiring academics the chance to experience faculty responsibilities at a variety of institutions and to be formally mentored by a member of another institution.

It is also very possible and potentially satisfying to move out of research altogether. There are jobs peripherally related to research, such as administrative or teaching positions at a research institution. There are jobs even more peripherally related, such as technical writing. And there are jobs such as investment banking or law whose only relationship to science is in the depth of analysis required by both.

The difficulty of switching careers cannot be minimized. It is stressful to start again at the bottom of the totem pole. A new career may result in an initial loss of income, and it may require a move to another geographical location. But the toll on individuals who are unhappy or uncomfortable with their present career can also not be minimized. Like all problems, unhappiness with your career is not likely to just evaporate, and the earlier you take action, the better.

Destiny vs. career choice

"If you feel that you don't have control of your life, see a therapist," advises Seymour E. Coopersmith, president of the training institute of New York-based National Psychological Association for Psychoanalysis. "If you feel you're in full control, see a career counselor. If you feel it's just a job situation, but you know that things will work out for you, then see a career counselor. And if it tends to repeat itself, see a therapist."

STEINBERG (2001, P. 4)

Scientists are often held captive by their degrees, instead of being empowered. "I have put so much time into this," many think, "that I can't throw it all away now." The passion most scientists bring to the job exaggerates the feeling that having a lab is sacred and that anything else will be a betrayal of science and of scientific training.

This feeling that science is destiny can be extremely motivating. The feeling of working for a higher cause, and not merely for money, is why it is easier to motivate scientists than salesmen. But it may not always be right for you. If you choose to leave research, you are not betraying science, or yourself.

Some of your colleagues may feel negative about another's decision to change careers because it suggest that their own careers are not as noble or all-encompassing or wonderful as they want to believe. Most people will get over it, and some never will. It should not be a consideration in your decision.

Knowing what work works for you

As you go through your days and years, there will be some parts of your routines that you dread and some that you anticipate with pleasure. If there are tasks that

These people are not my tribe—and I don't want to spend the next 20 years here.

you feel very satisfied doing, that you seem to learn almost effortlessly, that "click" for you, you are lucky, because you have a very clear indication of the work that most fulfills you. If you do not know what works for you, try to pinpoint what your ideal job *would* be:

- Are you in the job that is best for you?

- What would be your ultimate and perfect job? Can you picture it, roughly? Fill in the details? Imagine yourself there?

- Can you tailor your present job to fit the job of your dreams?

- Can you tailor yourself to be the person you want to be?

- Will your present job or another job offer the most satisfaction?

Seek help from a mentor. There may not be a time in your scientific career when you need a mentor more than you do when you are considering a major change. You need a fresh perspective, and you need as many perspectives and friends and mentors as possible. But P.I.s are sometimes reluctant to talk to others about a career change. It is hard to find the right mentor, for not everyone can be objective when someone is trying to leave the career the prospective mentor is in. Even if scientific colleagues are supportive, it can help your decision-making greatly to talk to a career counselor. Talk to head hunters—talk to everyone.

Having It All

FAMILIES AND LIFE BEYOND THE LAB

Wives, children, houses, regular hours are the bane of committed laboratory research, Watson made clear.

JUDSON (1996, P. 26)

So often men of genius were hellish to live with, but Bragg was a genial person whose creativity was sustained by a happy home life; typically one would find him tending his garden, with Lady Bragg, children, and grandchildren somewhere in the background, and before getting down to crystal structures, he would proudly demonstrate his latest roses.

PERUTZ, ON W.L. BRAGG (PERUTZ 1998, P. 294)

He told his young bride, pretentiously, that she had first claim on his love, but not on his time, made her buy her own wedding ring and often her own Christmas presents. So preoccupied was he with work that Jean had to be both father and mother to their four children. He had no patience with real people's emotional problems, but was spellbound when he heard them transformed into music in Wagner's operas. Wotan bidding Brunhilde goodbye in Die Walkure stirred him more that his own daughter leaving home for months.

ABOUT PETER MEDAWAR (PERUTZ 1998, P. 112)
PERUTZ, FROM JEAN MEDAWAR'S BIOGRAPHY OF PM

Hodgkin (Alan) comes across in this enjoyable book as a genial and humane scientist passionately devoted to his research for its own sake before and after being awarded his Nobel Prize. For 36 years he did most of his experiments with his own hands and yet found time to have a family life; to develop wide interests in literature, painting, and music; to watch birds; and to cultivate lasting friendships with a great variety of fascinating people.

PERUTZ (1998, P. 308)

A change in relationships, the purchase of a house or a move to another apartment, children, new hobbies and obsessions, local politics—as you grow older, your personal life is likely to evolve as well. It may at different times assume greater or less-

335

er importance than lab work: Either way, you will have to do some adjusting. Dealing with lab life and home life will take prioritizing and reprioritizing, in both the long term and the short term.

THE RIGHT TIME FOR KIDS

The hardest decision facing any young PI, whatever country they live in, is whether and when to have children. Although countries may vary in their maternity leave laws, in reality, young PIs cannot take time off or work part-time if they want to remain competitive.

ANNE RIDLEY, FROM FEATHERSTONE (1999, P. 19)

There is no right time to have children, and there is no wrong time. The general consensus among P.I.s is that, if you want to be a fully involved parent, the postdoc is the hardest time during which to have children. This is when you must produce enough to find a job, and, other than a second postdoc (entirely a viable possibility at times), there will not be another chance.

Of course, having kids has affected me. I haven't taken jobs I might have, because the kids don't want to move. If I had no kids, I would work more, I'd have more papers....but all in all, I don't think it has had that great an influence on my career.

Pretending that nothing will be changed by having children is unrealistic. Even if you have a spouse or partner at home, the impact not only on your time, but on your energy, priorities, and emotions as well is immense. Some people are affected more than others, and not everything is foreseeable: In a lifetime, many traumas besides children will occur. But plans for children should be considered when you look at your own career plans for 5 years down the road.

There is absolutely no doubt that a family will take time that could have been used in the lab. P.I.s who have chosen not to have families describe the joy of working until a problem is solved or of traveling to exotic locations after meetings. But it is not possible to say whether having a family or not affects the quality of the research. If a family makes you happier, could that not be as great a gift as an extra 3 or 4 hours a day? Everything depends on how you handle your life and lab, not how many hours you spend doing it.

Having children has impacted positively and negatively on my career. I'm happier, but there is just less time to do experiments when you have kids. Still, I'm not sure I would necessarily be doing better in research if I didn't have kids, as there is a law of diminishing returns as far as hours spent in the lab.

RESTRUCTURING THE WORKDAY

It was clear to me that in order to pull it off, I would have to change my work style. I was going to have to learn to make instant decisions, delegate like crazy, focus on the big picture rather than the details, and be adventurous in my thinking. And I was going to have to cease caring if people "liked" me.

WHITE (1995, P. 10)

With family responsibilities, the day that you may remember as being typical, filled with conversation, reading papers, experiments, and discussions about work over meals with lab members, is gone. It is very hard for most people in the lab to adjust to this loss of time to communicate while still keeping up with science. The following are some typical changes:

> *It would be impossible to do what I am doing without a supportive partner. Two days a week, I pick the kids up, two days a week, my husband does; we both go home on Friday, and take turns going into the lab on weekends. The kids have never seen us together in the same room, but it works!*

- Instead of reading papers, P.I.s rely on lab members to keep them up on current topics.

- Instead of attending as many meetings for the full time allotted, P.I.s either send junior people in their stead or only attend a few days of the meeting.

- Instead of having to know everything, P.I.s delegate more responsibilities to lab members.

Many of these changes are ones that come with time, anyway. The trick to survival is to not give up too much control, too soon.

ELIMINATING GUILT

> *Scientific research is a lifetime career for most who choose this vocation. There would be tremendously long-term benefits if mechanisms supporting these critical "family-building" years could be established, and if this support could be easy to obtain and sustain.*
>
> GORDON (1996, P. 2)

There is no other emotion as debilitating or as useless as festing guilt. Parent scientists are often plagued with guilt. Guilt that you are not home more, guilt that you are not in the lab at night, and guilt that you cannot keep up with the literature. These feelings come from not meeting your own expectations, and the fear that you are not measuring up in the eyes of others (project leaders, departmental heads, students).

Being committed to your family and work is not something to be ashamed of, but many people feel guilty when they must give priority to a family event or even to an emergency. Some workplaces foster this feeling, whereas others try to dispel it. Consider that you may be working in the wrong place if your workplace refuses to accommodate any flexibility for family responsibilities.

Do not allow yourself to feel guilty! There is no job that comes with the requirement that you should have no personal life. Of course, there is a line between responsibility and exercising your rights to personal time, and if your workplace does not support your ideas of time and work, you are likely to be uncomfortable. But feeling persistently guilty is a very big indication that something does not fit.

Subject that guilt to your best scientific analysis. Break the overall feeling into small pieces. If there is something that you have done wrong, and can fix, deal with it immediately. If you feel bad because you have not had a one-on-one conversation with your student for 6 weeks, set up a meeting, and arrange for weekly meetings thereafter. If you are writing a grant and have not seen your children before bedtime for a week, go home early, and go back to the lab when they are asleep.

The minute a guilty feeling reappears, reexamine it and see how altering your short-term priorities will fix it. If small fixes do not work, and are not likely to work for the long-term, you will have to reconsider all priorities.

WHO TO BLAME WHEN TIME RUNS SHORT

Women scientists married to other scientists publish on average 40% more than women who are married to nonscientists.

WEILER AND YANCY (1989)

The futility of some struggles leads women to give up and to readjust their expectations. Instead of comparing their husbands' contributions to their own, they shift to comparing their husbands' contributions to those of other men.

DEUTSCH (1999, CHAPTER 4)

It becomes easy to blame the system—science, the department, other lab members—when you are struggling to balance work and home. You may feel a constant sense of urgency and may so easily become furious when lab members or administration or anyone does not respond as quickly as you want them to, when it is actually the pressure from home that is troubling you.

Often the main source of trouble is actually your partner. Most people have a great resistance to admitting this. Each relationship has its own complicated set of rules and negotiations, and a child often changes the plan, frequently in unforeseen ways, leaving one person in a relationship with a life that was not as anticipated. Perhaps:

- One partner wanted the child more, and now assumes most of the burden of the childrearing.

- One partner's career seems to be more at a crossroads and expects to be "granted" more time at work.

- Both partner's agree to have a 50:50 split in home responsibilities, but one partner is reluctant to take on housework, childcare, or some previously agreed upon task.

- The split is 50:50, but one parent demands more appreciation than the other for the effort.

It is often the woman who loses more work time in the early days of child rearing. This is sometimes dictated by biology, for nursing mothers, or by inclination. She may meet resistance when trying to claim back equal time. Male P.I.s have pointed out the fact that many organizations will accept that a woman may take time off but are still wary of a man who does. As one prominent scientist said to a potential new recruit about a male P.I. at the institution, "He was one of our most promising lab heads until he had children."

Prioritizing and easing the time crunch at home. As at work, using time well at home is the key to achieving your goals. And as at work, you must know what you want before you prioritize. Most people see the need to manage time at work, but there are many who resent having to manage time at home, and do not. They associate time management with work, not realizing that it would buy them more time at home and at work. There are many books on the subject of managing time and tasks at home, and some of these are listed in Resources at the end of this section. The following are some points to consider which other P.I.s have found useful in organizing themselves at home:

- *Shorten the commute.* Many people love the psychological distance that physical distance puts between home and lab. But that distance might make it harder to go back to work in the evening and harder to leave children during the day.

- *Hiring help at home.* One possibility to make life more doable is to pay people to help you. Many people hire a once a week or twice a week housecleaner, and people with children hire a babysitter, and some even hire someone to run errands.

- *Simplifying home life.* Rather than hiring help, some people downsize, reducing purchases and furniture and cutting down on the amount of work there is at home.

- *Hands-on child care.* The actual physical care of a child is only one of the many tasks that must be done at home and it is not the issue usually struggled over. Buying clothes, arranging camps and babysitters, and picking up coats thrown carelessly on chairs cause much more agony, and these "details" should be part of any negotiation on who does what.

FITTING FAMILIES INTO THE CULTURE OF THE LAB

It is so important that you be a role model for the practice of balancing home and work priorities. By showing the lab members that you can embrace both personal life and research as priorities, you expand the options and choices for everyone else in the lab. The more comfortable lab members are with their individual choices, the better the work situation will be.

Whether or not you bring your family into the life of the lab is a very individual choice, for both you and your family. It is dictated by personality and lifestyle and distance and timing. If your partner is also a scientist, it is much more likely that your family and the lab members will be familiar with one another. But there are many reasons why P.I.s might want to keep the two worlds separate, the most common being that compartmentalization offers a chance to truly get away from work. When privacy turns to secrecy, however, the effect on the lab often turns negative.

Most P.I.s enjoy an easy familiarity about their families and the families of other lab members. Children come in and out of the lab and there are light-hearted discussions of schools and soccer games. P.I.s and lab members usually know enough of each other's families to be understanding when a time-consuming personal triumph or crisis occurs. There are lab get-togethers, to which all families are invited. An atmosphere in which the P.I. shows that home life is important, but maintains discretion about intimate details, works in most lab situations. There are labs that still run almost totally on the young-single-male culture, but those are growing scarce.

EXTENDING YOUR CIRCLE OF SCIENCE

Often, inspiration for the lab will come from work you may do outside the lab. With success and experience, you may feel a commitment to bring science to those who do not understand it or to be involved in science policy or local political, medical, or scientific issues. This kind of work can be very compelling and can help to motivate or enliven your entire lab. For example, some lab members may be interested in making a commitment to teaching high school students about molecular biology in a local high school or having students work at the bench. This can become part of the entire lab ethic, whether in an academic or industrial setting and remind you of why you came into science in the first place.

Never forget the joy you felt with your first experiment. If you accept less for your lab or yourself, it will be just another job. And that would be a shame.

RESOURCES

Adler N.J. 1997. *International dimensions of organizational behavior*, 3rd edition. South-Western College Publishing, Cincinnati.

The American Society for Cell Biology. 1999. Helping scientists and facilitating research: A federal job as a scientist administrator. *Am. Soc. Cell Biol. Newsletter* **22:** 16–19. (http://www.ascb.org)

Amero S. and Brandon M. 1998. The negative tenure decision. *Am. Soc. Cell Biol. Newsletter* **21:** 20–21. (http://www.ascb.org)

Boschelli F. 1999. Making the transition from academia to industry. *Am. Soc. Cell Biol. Newsletter* **22:** 12–13. (http://www.ascb.org)

Caveman. 2000. *Caveman*. The Company of Biologists Limited, Cambridge, England.

Clifton D.O. and Nelson P. 1992. Soar with your strengths, pp. 43–61. Delacorte, New York.

Cooper R.K. and Sawaf A. 1997. *Executive E.Q.: Emotional intelligence in leadership and organizations.* Grosset/Putnam, New York.

Deutsch F.M. 1999. *Halving it all: How equally shared parenting works.* Harvard University Press, Cambridge, Massachusetts.

Edwards C.G. 1999a. Get a life! New options for balancing work and home. *HMS Beagle* **54:** 1–5. (http://news.bmn.com/hmsbeagle)

Edwards C.G. 1999b. Surviving your first position. *HMS Beagle* **65:** 1–6. (http://news.bmn.com/hmsbeagle)

Emmett A. 1999. Merchant scientist. Deal structuring and pavement pounding are part of technology transfer. *The Scientist* **13:** 16. (http://www.thescientist.com)

Featherstone C. 1999. What a life! Five views from women cell biologists from across the pond. *Am. Soc. Cell Biol.* **22:** 15–19. (http://www.ascb.org)

Feibelman P.J. 1994. *A Ph.D. is not enough: A guide to survival in science.* Perseus Press, Reading Massachusetts.

Ferry G. 2000. Dorothy Hodgkin: A life. Cold Spring Harbor Laboratory Press, Cold Spring Harbor, New York.

Fiske P. 1996. *To boldly go. A practical career guide for scientists.* American Geophysical Union Special Publication. Washington, D.C.

Frängsmyr T. and Lindsten J., eds. 1993. Biography of George H. Hitchings, Jr. In *Nobel lectures: Physiology or medicine 1981–1990*, pp. 471–475. World Scientific, River Edge, New Jersey.

Goldberg J. 1988. *Anatomy of a scientific discovery.* Bantam Books, New York.

Goleman D. 1995. *Emotional intelligence: Why it can matter more than I.Q.* Bantam Books, New York.

Gordon K. 1996. Balancing career and family: A male perspective. *Science's Next Wave*, Oct. 18, pp. 1–3. (http://nextwave.sciencemag.org)

Hamer D. and Copeland P. 1994. *The science of desire.* Simon & Schuster, New York.

Hoagland M. 1990. *Toward the habit of truth: A life in science.* W.W. Norton, New York.

Hobfell S.E. and Hobfell I.H. 1994. *Work won't love you back: The dual career couple's survival guide.* W.H. Freeman, New York.

Janovy Jr., J. 1985. *On becoming a biologist.* Harper & Row, New York.

Judson H.F. 1996. *The eighth day of creation. The makers of the revolution in biology*, expanded edition. Cold Spring Harbor Laboratory Press, Cold Spring Harbor, New York.

Kreeger K.Y. 1999. Working in academia; preparing for changing roles. *The Scientist* **13:** 24–25. (http://www.thescientist.com)

Kreeger K.Y. 2000a. From classroom to boardroom. *The Scientist* **14:** 28–29. (http://www.thescientist.com)

Kreeger K.Y. 2000b. Research in the business world. *The Scientist* **14:** 25. (http://www.thescientist.com)

Kreeger K.Y. 2000c. Researchers in administration. *The Scientist* **14:** 28. (http://www.thescientist.com)

Lanthes A. 1998. Management and motivation issues for scientists in industry. *Science's Next Wave*, Jan. 28, pp. 1–4. (http://nextwave.sciencemag.org)

LOC Scientific. 2001. Laboratory Services. (http://www.locscientific.com)

Luria S.E. 1984. *A slot machine, a broken test tube.* Harper & Row, New York.

Malone R.J. 1999. Professional development and advancement. In T*he full-time faculty handbook* (ed. V. Bianco-Mathis and N. Chalofsky), pp. 155–164. Sage Publications, Thousand Oaks, California.

Manicone S. 2000. Laboratory renovation: The hidden cost. *Facilities Manager* **16**: 1–5.

Maslach C. and Leiter M.P. 1997. *The truth about burnout: How organizations cause personal stress and what to do about it.* Jossey-Bass Publishers, San Francisco.

McCabe E.R.B. 1999. *How to succeed in academics.* Academic Press, San Diego.

McGrayne S.H. 1998. Christiane Nüsslein-Volhard. In *Nobel prize women in science: Their lives, struggles and momentous discoveries,* pp. 380–408. Carol Publishing Group, Secaucus, New Jersey.

McKenna E.P. 1997. *When work doesn't work anymore.* Delacorte Press, New York.

National Mental Health Association. 1999. Stress: Coping with everyday problems. MHIC Factsheet, pp. 1–3. (http://www.nmha.org/infoctr/factsheets/41.cfm)

National Research Council. 1998. *Trends in the early causes of life scientists.* Committee on Dimensions. National Academy Press, Washington, D.C.

National Research Council. 2000. *Laboratory design, construction, and renovation: Participants, process, and product.* Commission on Chemical Sciences. National Academy Press. Washington, D.C.

Perutz M. 1998. *I wish I'd made you angrier earlier: Essays on science and scientists.* Cold Spring Harbor Laboratory Press, Cold Spring Harbor, New York.

Potter B. 1998. *Overcoming job burnout,* 2nd edition. Ronin Publishing, Berkeley, California.

Pycior H.M., Slack N.G., and Abir-Am P.G., eds. 1996. *Creative couples in the sciences.* Rutgers University Press, New Brunswick, New Jersey.

Reis R. 1999. Establishing your absence. *Chronicle of higher education,* Aug. 12, pp. 1–5. (http://www.chronicle.com)

Reis R. 2000. Top ten commandments of tenure success. *Tomorrow's Professor Listserve* No. 223. Stanford University Learning Library. (http://cis.stanford.edu/structure/tomprof/listserver.html)

Reis R.M. 1997. *Tomorrow's professor: Preparing for academic careers in science and engineering.* IEEE Press, New York.

Robbins-Roth C. 1998. Alternative careers in science. Academic Press, New York.

Rosen S. and Paul C. 1998. *Career renewal: Tools for scientists and technical professionals.* Academic Press, New York.

Sherman K.F. 2000. *A housekeeper is cheaper than a divorce: Why you CAN afford to hire help and how to get it.* Life Tools Press, Mountain View, California.

Sherwood N.T. 1997. Overview and comparison of family leave options in science. *Science's Next Wave,* Sept. 19, pp. 1–7. (http://nextwave.sciencemag.org)

Sinderman C.J. and Sawyer T.K. 1997. *The scientist as consultant: Building new career opportunities.* Plenum Trade, New York.

St. James E. 1994. *Simplify your life: 100 Ways to slow down and enjoy the things that really matter.* Hyperion, New York.

Steinberg D. 2001 Career guides for the perplexed: Counselors help scientists move from the lab to the office. *The Scientist* **15**: 26. (http://www.thescientist.com)

Swenson L. 1999. Awarding work/life leaders: Immunex programs garner top award. *Seattle's Child & Eastside Parent,* Aug, p. 60.

Theriot J. 1999. Crossing to the other side. *Am. Soc. Cell Biol. Newsletter* **22**: 21–22. (http://www.acsb.org)

University System of Georgia. 1998. *Design criteria for laboratory furniture and fume hoods.* Environmental Health & Safety and Right to Know, University System of Georgia, Interdisciplinary Task Force. (http://www.usg.edu)

Vermeij G. 1997. *Privileged hands: A scientific life.* W.H. Freeman, New York.

Weiler C.S. and Yancy P.H. 1989. Dual-career couples and science: opportunities, challenges and strategies. *Oceanography* **64**: 28–31.

Weiner J. 2000. Lord of the flies. In *The best American science writing 2000* (ed. J. Gleick), pp. 30–44. HarperCollins, New York.

Whicker M., Kornenfeld J., and Strickland R. 1993. *Getting tenure.* Sage Publications, Thousand Oaks, California.Inc.

White K. 1995. *Why good girls don't get ahead but gutsy girls do.* Warner Books, New York.

Yentsch C. and Sinderman C.J. 1992. *The woman scientist: Meeting the challenges for a successful career.* Plenum Press, New York.

Index

Anger. *See also* Conflict resolution
  self-control, 241–242
  violence in workplace. *See* Violence
Application, review, 82, 84
Authorship
  accountability, 172–173
  ethics, 175
  independence fostering, 320–321
  names on papers, 170–171
  persons writing, 168–169
  technicians, 171

Benchtime, principal investigator, 315–316
Benefits, industry versus academia, 12
Bibliographic software, overview, 223
Burnout
  features, 328–329
  prevention
    principal investigators, 329
    workers, 166
  reasons, 329
  recovery, 330

Career choices
  indications for job change, 331–332
  lab moving to another institution, 332
  promotion, negative outcome management, 324–325
  switching careers, 333–334
Collaboration
  departed lab members, 322
  good versus bad, 154
  policy setting, 154–155
Colleague, development in labs, 37
Communication
  cessation, 237
  criticisms, 236
  cultural differences, 248, 250
  emotion management, 240–242
  gender differences, 255–258
  guidelines, 234

language differences, 250–251
listening, 234–236
nonverbal, 237–238
orders and requests, 236–237
rapport building, 238–239
reticent lab members, 239–240
speaking effectively, 236
success importance, 233
Computers
  bibliographic software, 223
  care of computer, 225
  communication fostering, 220
  maintenance and repair, 226–227
  money tracking, 219
  needs assessment, 214
  presentation software, 224–225
  project management software, 223
  protocol management, 219–220
  reagent tracking, 215–219
  software, 214–215
  time management, 52
  word processors, 224
Conflict resolution
  backing-off, 262
  disputes
    equipment and maintenance, 292–293
    personal problems, 293–294
    project problems, 293
    territory, 293
  guidelines, 261–262
  intervention guidelines, 291–292
  volatile situation defusing, 305–306
Correspondence streamlining
  e-mail, 54–55
  letters, 54
  phone calls, 55
Coworkers
  conflict resolution. *See* Conflict resolution
  industry versus academia, 11
  romance. *See* Romance
Cultural differences
  authority figures, 249
  communication factors, 248

Cultural differences (*continued*)
    cultural I.Q. quiz, 246–247
    directness versus indirectness, 249–250
    emotion expression, 250
    fairness versus accommodation, 253–254
    family responsibilities, 252
    interview questions, 92
    intralab differences, 252–253
    language differences, 250–251
    mistake admission, 250
    money and salary, 251–252
    nonverbal communication, 250
    recognition, 243–245
    variables, 245
Culture, laboratory
    dysfunctional lab management, 280–282
    ethics. *See* Ethics
    expectation and consequences, 181–182
    family integration, 339–340
    five-year plan, 21–22, 181
    hiring considerations, 103–104
    money spending, 184
    morale, 277
    personnel equilibrium, 291
    roles for everyone, 184–185
    social interactions
        alcohol, 279
        day-to-day socializing, 279
        get-togethers, 278
        rituals, 278–279
    successful lab criteria, 4
    work ethic. *See* Work ethic

Daily to-do list
    free time utilization, 53
    importance, 52–53
    small pieces of time, 53
Depression
    guidelines for employee management,
        266–268
    stress response, 328
    suicide warning signs and prevention,
        268–269
    symptoms, 265
Dislikes
    management of lab worker disliked by
        everyone, 295
    principal investigator against lab worker,
        294
Diversity. *See* Cultural differences; Gender

e-mail, correspondence streamlining, 54–55
Emotion. *See also* Anger; Depression; Stress
    confrontation style, 261–262

cultural differences in expression, 250
    negotiation role, 260–261
    self-management in lab, 240–242
Enthusiasm maintenance
    burnout. *See* Burnout
    extracurricular science activities, 340
    importance in success, 323
    inspiration, 325
    negative outcome management, 324–325
    sabbaticals, 325–327
    stress management. *See* Stress
Equipment and supplies
    disputes, 292–293
    distribution and records, 217–218
    jobs in lab, 197
    negotiations, 15
    organizing and records, 215–217
    starting a lab, ordering
        departmental procedures, 26
        discounts, 26
        general lab use, 24–25
        office supplies, 26
        radioactivity, 25
        tissue culture, 25
Ethics
    authorships, 175
    competition, 175
    conflict of interest, 175
    data, 175
    duplication of material, 175
    establishment in lab
        role modeling, 182
        talks, 182–183
    fraud, 175–176
    policies
        institutional guidelines, 176
        lab, 175–176
    statistics, 175
Evolution, laboratory, 313

Family-work balance
    adjustments, 335–336
    blame, 338–339
    guilt elimination, 337–338
    home life time management, 339
    lab culture integration of families, 339–
        340
    planning for a family, 336
    workday restructuring, 336–337
Favorites
    lab workers, 294
    letting go, 319
Firing
    documentation, 299–300
    easing people out, 297

guidelines, 300–301
indications, 298–299
protected employee management, 301–302
warnings, 300
First impression, validity in hiring, 105–106
Five-year plan
  considerations
    career, 21
    core values, 22
    culture of lab, 21–22
    financial, 21
    project, 21
    social, 21
  importance in lab planning, 20
Foreign applicants
  cultural differences. *See* Cultural differences
  hiring, 88
  prejudice avoidance, 104–105
  seminar, 204–205
  visas. *See* Visas
Friendships, principal investigator and lab personnel, 36–37

Gender
  communication differences, 255–258
  stereotypes, 255
Glass washer, needs assessment, 75
Good lab, features, 5

Happiness, lab members, 3–4
Hiring
  accepting and declining candidates, 111
  checklist for new employees, 118–120
  culture of lab considerations, 103–104
  finding applicants
    graduate student, 79
    lead sources, 76
    physician, 79
    postdoc, 79, 109
    secretary, 78
    technician, 77–78
    undergraduate student, 78
  first day activity and importance, 117–118
  foreign applicants, 88
  human resources department, 57, 75, 81, 120
  immediate hiring limitations, 73–74, 109
  industry versus academia, 79–80
  interviewing. *See* Interview
  mistakes, 110
  needs assessment

glass washer, 75
postdoc, 75
student, 74–75
technician/lab assistant, 74
prejudice avoidance
  cultural differences, 104–105
  first impressions, 105–106
  liking of hirees, 106
recommendation
  interpretation, 84–86
  phone conversations with writers, 86–88
reference follow-up, 86–88
resume and application review, 82, 84
secretary, 57–59, 75
sequence of process, 82
structured protocol, 81–83
training partnerships, 120
traits to avoid in hiring, 110, 303–304
violence screening, 303–304
visas. *See* Visas
working relationship with first person, 121
Hours worked
  enforcement, 189–190
  flexibility, 189–190
  leave, 190–191
  vacation, 191–192
  work ethic example setting with hours worked, 183

Independence fostering
  authorship, 320–321
  promotion, 319
  seminars, 320
Industry
  coworkers, 11
  hiring practices versus academia, 79–80
  intellectual freedom, 8–9
  personal issues, 11–12
  working conditions, 10
Institution
  academic selection factors, 12–13
  geographic considerations, 13–14
  industry selection factors, 13
  selection for lab placement, 7–8
Intellectual freedom, industry versus academia, 8–9
Internet, lab management, 221–222
Interview
  conclusion, 101
  conducting, 93–94
  goals, 89–91
  illegal questions, 95–96

Interview (*continued*)
  interviewers in lab, 97
  pregnant applicants, 94–95
  questionnaire design, 91–93
  red flags
    anger, 97
    blaming, 96
    complaining, 96
    excessive demands, 96
    lying, 96–97
  selling the job
    importance, 97
    lab advantages, 100–101
    needs of workers, 98–100
  structured interview advantages, 90
  styles, 89–90
  time commitment of applicant, 97
  undirected interview, 89
Isolation avoidance
  lab members, 63–64
  principal investigator, 63

Jobs, assignment in laboratory, 197
Journal club
  benefits, 207
  presentation of papers, 207–208

Laboratory culture. *See* Culture, laboratory
Laboratory manager, management, 318
Laboratory manual
  contents, 199
  importance, 198
  rule limitation, 198
Laboratory meetings
  attendance, 202–203
  benefits, 201
  brainstorming, 209
  conducting, 201–202
  criticism guidelines, 205–206
  foreign language speakers, 204–205
  formal meetings, 205
  informal meetings, 205
  one-on-one meetings
    open-door policy, 210, 212
    rounds in lab, 211–212
    scheduled, 210
    unscheduled, 210–211
  organization and problem meetings, 209
  outside lab meetings, 206
  participation, 203
  retreats, 209
  speaking instruction, 203–204
  topic meetings within lab, 206

Laboratory notebook
  checking, 196
  kind of notebook, 193
  maintenance, 193–195
  ownership, 196
  requirements, 192–193
Leadership, 31–38. *See also* Management
Learning styles. *See* Training
Letters, correspondence streamlining, 54
Listening, guidelines, 234–236

Management
  authority types, 36
  communication. *See* Communication
  friendships with lab personnel, 36–37
  lab manager, 318
  lab size impact, 314–315
  list of skills, 34–35
  micromanaging versus hands-off
      approach, 36
  motivation. *See* Motivation
  perfectionism, 48–49
  personal interaction improvement, 37–38
  power perceptions, 35
  research skill overlap with management
      skills, 31–32
  style of management
    evolution
      experience impact, 316–317
      loosening of control, 317–318
      quality of personnel impact, 317
    examination of strengths, 33–34
    personality guidance, 32–33
  time management. *See* Time management
  training. *See* Training
Meetings. *See* Laboratory meetings
Mental illness
  guidelines for employee management,
      266–267
  privacy issues, 266–267
  resources, 267
Mentor
  functions, 134
  inside lab relationships, 136
  network building, 139
  nonresearch interest mentoring, 138–139
  outside lab relationships, 135–136, 139
  principal investigator mentor
    finding, 65–66
    importance, 64
    influence on mentoring style, 137–138
    multiple mentors, 65
    relationship
      goals, 66–67

personal comfort, 65
reevaluation, 67
termination, 67–68
requirements, 64–65
switching careers, 334
qualifications, 134–137
relationship types, 133
termination of relationship, 138
Mission statement, lab goals, 19–20
Money, spending and tracking, 184, 219
Morale
dysfunctional lab management, 280–282
influences, 277–278
social interactions
alcohol, 279
day-to-day socializing, 279
get-togethers, 278
rituals, 278–279
Motivation
burnout prevention, 166
decision to be in lab, 161–162
example setting, 165
problems
causes, 162–163
lack of ability, 165
physicians, 163–164
postdocs, 164
secretaries, 165
students, 164
technicians, 164–165

Negotiations
emotion, 260–261
equipment, 15
funding, 15
industry versus academia, 14–15
learning through conflict, 259–260
personal support, 15
positions, 15
salary, 15
teaching, 15
Notebook. *See* Laboratory notebook

Office, organization, 55–56
Ordering
money tracking, 219
responsibility, 218
starting a lab
departmental procedures, 26
discounts, 26
general lab use, 24–25
office supplies, 26
radioactivity, 25
tissue culture, 25

Organizing systems
computer systems
bibliographic software, 223
care of computer, 225
Internet resources, 221–222
maintenance and repair, 226–227
money tracking, 219
needs assessment, 214
presentation software, 224–225
protocol management, 219–220, 223
reagent tracking, 215–219
software, 214–215
time management, 52
word processors, 224
duplication avoidance, 51
items to be organized, 213
ordering, 218
paper, 51
personal information managers, 52, 220–221
supplies, 215–218

Paper. *See* Publication
Parental leave, 190–191
Party lab, avoidance, 184
Patent
laboratory notebook maintenance, 193–195
publication considerations, 174
Perfectionism, management, 48–49
Personality, laboratory, 4
Phone calls, correspondence streamlining, 55
Physician
finding applicants, 79
motivation problems, 163–164
needs in hiring, 99
training, 130–131
training partnerships, 120
P.I. *See* Principal investigator
Postdoc
finding applicants, 79, 109
motivation problems, 164
needs assessment
employee, 99–100
lab, 75
project-taking considerations when leaving lab, 321–322
training, 130
training partnerships, 120
Pregnancy
interview issues, 94–95
leave, 190
safety in lab, 188
Presentation software, overview, 224–225

Principal investigator (P.I.)
  responsibilities, 39–41, 151
  romance, 284–285
  success perception by lab members, 4
Procrastination
  avoidance, 45–47
  styles, 45–46
Project management
  overview, 219–220
  software, 223
Project selection. *See* Research
Promotion
  independence fostering, 319
  negative outcome management, 324–
    325
Publication
  authorship
    accountability, 172–173
    names on papers, 170–171
    persons writing, 168–169
    technicians, 171
  ethics
    authorships, 175
    competition, 175
    conflict of interest, 175
    data, 175
    duplication of material, 175
    fraud, 175–176
    policies
      institutional guidelines, 176
      lab, 175–176
    statistics, 175
  good versus bad paper features, 169
  patent considerations, 174
  prepublication analysis, 167–168
  promptness, 146
  unwritten paper management, 173–174
PubMed, access, 159

Recommendations
  confidential versus open, 298
  foreign applicants, 88
  interpretation
    applicants, 84–86
    employee performance, 298
  negative recommendation writing, 298
  phone conversations with writers, 86–88
References, follow-up in hiring, 86–88
Renovations, new laboratory, 16–17
Reports, written research reports from lab
    members, 160–161
Research
  benchtime of principal investigator, 315–
    316

  drifting, 150–151
  information sources
    Internet, 158
    journal club, 158
    lab members, 158
    meetings, 158–159
    networking, 159
    PubMed, 159
    reading, 158
    seminars, 159
    writing, 159
  keeping up with research field, 157–
    158
  people matching with projects
    good data generation, 148
    objective setting, 147
    risks, 148–149
  project performance and time invest-
    ment, 159–160
  project picking
    funding, 146
    independence from other labs, 146
    novel research areas, 147
    realistic goals, 145–146
  publication. *See* Publication
  team building, 149–150
  written research reports from lab mem-
    bers, 160–161
Resume, review, 82, 84
Romance
  lab member–lab member, 283
  principal investigator–lab member, 284–
    285

Sabbatical, management, 325–327
Safety
  emergencies, 189
  lab attitude, 187
  overreactors, 188–189
  protocols, 187–188
  safety department and officer, 188
Salary
  foreign applicants, 251–252
  negotiations, 15
Secretary
  finding applicants, 78
  functions in lab, 57–58
  hiring, human resources department, 57,
    75
  inclusion in lab activities, 62
  manners, 59
  motivation problems, 165
  needs in hiring, 98

part-time secretary, 61
principal investigator activities, 62
privacy issues, 60
reporting lines, 59–60
routines, 59
sharing, 61–62
skills, 58–59
Sexual harassment
avoidance of charges, 288–289
definition, 285
lawyer consultation, 289
legal basis, 286
management by victim, 288
policies, 286–287
principal investigator responsibilities, 286–287
Starting, laboratory
checklist, 23
guidelines, 22–23
hiring. *See* Hiring
problems, 23–24
supply and equipment ordering
departmental procedures, 26
discounts, 26
general lab use, 24–25
office supplies, 26
radioactivity, 25
tissue culture, 25
Stress
control in workers, 264
principal investigator
depression response, 328
limitations realization, 327–328
signs, 327
role modeling, 263–264
sources in science, 263–264
Student
finding applicants
graduate student, 79
undergraduate student, 78
motivation problems, 164
needs assessment
employee
graduate students, 99
undergraduate students, 98
lab hiring, 74–75
training, 130
Success, laboratory
criteria, 19
elements of success, 4
enthusiasm importance, 323
ideals, 323
Suicide, warning signs and prevention, 268–269
Supplies. *See* Equipment and supplies

Teaching
employees. *See* Training
negotiations, 15
Technician
authorship, 171
experience, 77
finding applicants, 77–78, 109
independent projects, 151
motivation problems, 164–165
needs assessment
employee, 98
lab, 74
training, 129–130
Time management
complaints, 41
correspondence streamlining
e-mail, 54–55
letters, 54
phone calls, 55
daily to-do list
free time utilization, 53
importance, 52–53
small pieces of time, 53
home life, 339
organizing systems
computer systems, 52
duplication avoidance, 51
paper, 51
personal information managers, 52
priority setting
Covey's Matrix
importance, 41
logs, 43–44
projects, 43
time, 43
procrastination avoidance, 45–47
rhythm setting, 44–45
saving time
delegation, 49
interruption avoidance, 50
speed-reading, 49
typing, 49–50
Training
bench training of new person
content of teaching, 124
importance, 123
learning styles, 124–127
partnerships, 120
physician, 130–131
postdoc, 130
students, 130
technician, 129–130
trainers, 120, 123
Typing, time-saving by learning, 49–50

Vacation, policy, 191–192
Violence
    discerning potential violence, 304–305
    hiring screening, 303–304
    prediction, 303
    prevention, 307
    volatile situation defusing, 305–306
Visas
    B1, 108
    concerns in hiring, 108–109
    E1, 108
    E2, 108
    F-1, 107–108
    H-1B, 107

H-2B, 107
H-3, 107
J-1, 106
J-2, 106–107
L-1, 108
TN, 108

Word processor, software, 224
Work ethic, establishment
    example setting with hours worked, 183
    goal-orientation, 183–184
    party lab avoidance, 184
Working conditions, industry versus academia, 10

Also from the author of *At the Helm:*

At the Bench: A Laboratory Navigator

By Kathy Barker, *Rockefeller University, New York*

A research laboratory filled with competent, busy people entirely familiar with its arcane customs and practices is a daunting place for newcomers. Kathy Barker knows this world. She was a technician, an undergraduate, then a graduate student at the University of Massachusetts, and as a postdoctoral fellow and assistant professor at Rockefeller University, she was a mentor to grad students, physicians in training, technicians, and research nurses. From this rich experience, she has written *At the Bench,* a unique handbook for living and working in the laboratory. Much more than a simple primer or lab manual, this book is an essential aid to understanding:

- how research groups work at a human level—and how to fit in
- what equipment is essential, and how to use it properly
- how to get started and get organized
- how to set up an experiment
- how to handle and use data and reference sources
- how to present yourself and your results—in print and in person

Wise, light-hearted, but thoroughly practical, Dr. Barker offers advice, moral support, social etiquette, and professional reassurance along with assume-nothing, step-by-step instructions for those basic but vital laboratory procedures that experienced investigators know—but may not realize novices don't.

If you are a graduate student, a physician with research intentions, or a laboratory technician, this book is indispensable. If you have to manage or mentor such people, giving a copy to each of them will greatly improve your life, and theirs.

1998, 460 pp., glossary, index
Concealed wire binding $49   ISBN 0-87969-523-4

What the reviewers have to say:
"Where was this book when 'I' started in the lab? Like the '(Computers, etc.). . . for Dummies' series in popular bookstores, this is an invaluable practical guide for working in a laboratory, and scientific life in general. It addresses questions the newcomer may not have thought of asking, and provides a 'safe' resource to find the answers to questions he or she may be reluctant to ask. For the established members of the lab, this manual relieves them of much of the basic training tasks for the newcomer, and provides a standardized body of knowledge everyone is expected to master; the latter also being important when establishing liability. Furthermore, this book provides a rare and insightful explanation of scientific culture, helping socialize the novice. Despite being written for beginners, this manual can serve as a timeless reference for the experienced scientist."
                                    —*ALAN R. SALTIEL, Ph.D., Parke-Davis Pharmaceuticals*

To order or request additional information:
Call: 1-800-843-4388 (Continental US and Canada)   516-422-4100 (All other locations)
FAX: 516-422-4097
Online ordering at http://www.cshlpress.com   E-mail: cshpress@cshl.edu
Write: Cold Spring Harbor Laboratory Press, 500 Sunnyside Blvd, Woodbury, NY 11797-2924